Anachronism and Antiquity

Also Available from Bloomsbury

Anticipation and Anachrony in Statius' Thebaid, Robert Simms
Antiquity and the Meanings of Time, Duncan F. Kennedy

Anachronism and Antiquity

Tim Rood, Carol Atack and Tom Phillips

BLOOMSBURY ACADEMIC
LONDON • NEW YORK • OXFORD • NEW DELHI • SYDNEY

BLOOMSBURY ACADEMIC
Bloomsbury Publishing Plc
50 Bedford Square, London, WC1B 3DP, UK
1385 Broadway, New York, NY 10018, USA

BLOOMSBURY, BLOOMSBURY ACADEMIC and the Diana logo are
trademarks of Bloomsbury Publishing Plc

First published in Great Britain 2020

Copyright © Tim Rood, Carol Atack and Tom Phillips, 2020

Tim Rood, Carol Atack and Tom Phillips have asserted their right under the Copyright,
Designs and Patents Act, 1988, to be identified as Authors of this work.

Cover design: Terry Woodley
Cover image © Giorgio de Chirico, *The Soothsayer's Recompense*, 1913.
Philadelphia Museum of Art, The Louise and Walter Arensberg Collection,
1950-134-38/© 2009 Artists Rights Society (ARS), New York / SIAE, Rome

All rights reserved. No part of this publication may be reproduced or transmitted
in any form or by any means, electronic or mechanical, including photocopying,
recording, or any information storage or retrieval system, without prior
permission in writing from the publishers.

Bloomsbury Publishing Plc does not have any control over, or responsibility for, any
third-party websites referred to or in this book. All internet addresses given in this
book were correct at the time of going to press. The author and publisher regret
any inconvenience caused if addresses have changed or sites have ceased
to exist, but can accept no responsibility for any such changes.

A catalogue record for this book is available from the British Library.

A catalog record for this book is available from the Library of Congress.

ISBN: HB: 978-1-3501-1519-4
PB: 978-1-3501-1520-0
ePDF: 978-1-3501-1522-4
eBook: 978-1-3501-1521-7

Typeset by RefineCatch Limited, Bungay, Suffolk

To find out more about our authors and books visit www.bloomsbury.com
and sign up for our newsletters.

Contents

List of Figures		vii
Preface		viii
List of Abbreviations		x
	Prelude: Look to the End	1
1	Inventing Anachronism	9
	Modern anachronisms	9
	The origins of anachronism	11
	From Byzantium to Italy and beyond	15
	Anachronism from literature to chronology	18
	Anachronism and related terms	22
	Anachronism and the idea of progress	24
	The historian's unforgivable sin	27
2	Anachronistic Histories	33
	Borges and Cervantes: A chivalrous pursuit	33
	Petrarch and Valla: Forging anachronism	39
	Altdorfer and Schlegel: Koselleck's pasts	45
	Anachronism and periodization	52
3	Anachronism and Philology	59
	Creative anachronism in antiquity	59
	Situating ancient criticism	62
	Anachronism and philological argument	65
	Anachronistic similes	69
	Anachronistic names	71
	Anachronism and the poet	76
	Anachronistic games: Orestes at the Pythia	80
	Historicizing literary anachronism	83
	Interlude: Dido versus Virgil	87

4	Anachronism and Chronology	93
	Scaliger and the birth of chronology	93
	Calendars out of joint	98
	Dating systems	103
	Prochronisms and metachronisms	110
5	Anachronistic Survivals	119
	Uneven development	119
	Anachronistic traces	125
	Anachronism in the city	129
	Anachronism on the periphery	135
	Anachronism incorporated	141
6	Anachronism and Exemplarity	145
	Exemplarity versus historicism	145
	Exemplarity in theory	150
	Exemplarity in action	157
	Exempla in their time	163
	Interlude: Ariadne on Naxos	169
7	Anachronism Now: Multitemporal Moments	175
	Theorizing multitemporality	175
	Seizing the moment	178
	Objects in time	182
	Epic mo(nu)ments	187
	Anachronic Ajax	190
	Coda: Ariadne at Cumae	193
	Interlude: Aeneas in the Underworld	195
8	Anachronistic Dialogues	199
	Anachronism and the *School of Athens*	199
	Philosophical dialogues across time	206
	Dialogues with the dead	212
	Reading communities	218
	Epilogue: Crowning the Victors	223
Notes		231
References		255
Index		271

Figures

1	Gaspar van den Hoecke, *Croesus showing his Treasures*	2
2	Letter of Aphrodite (papyrus)	14
3	Albrecht Altdorfer, *Alexanderschlacht*	46
4	Paris leading Helen away: red-figure skyphos attributed to the Makron painter	60
5	Page from manuscript of Jerome's version of Eusebius' *Chronicle*	96
6	The Parian Marble, detail	108
7	The Parian Marble, detail	109
8	Panathenaic Amphora, attributed to the Marsyas Painter	133
9	Togatus Barberini	151
10	Giorgio de Chirico, *The Soothsayer's Recompense*	170
11	Ajax preparing suicide: black-figure amphora attributed to Exekias	176
12	Hoplites riding on dolphins: red-figure psykter attributed to Oltos	183
13	Raphael, *School of Athens*	200
14	Raphael, *Parnassus*	203
15	James Barry, *Crowning the Victors at Olympia*, detail	224
16	James Barry, *Crowning the Victors at Olympia*, detail	224
17	James Barry, *Crowning the Victors at Olympia*, detail	225
18	James Barry, *Elysium*, detail	227

Preface

This book is a study both of anachronism in antiquity and of anachronism as a vehicle for understanding antiquity. We have tried to make it accessible to readers outside Classics with an interest in the history of temporality: we offer translations of all Greek and Latin (sometimes with small borrowings from published versions), and have offered guidance for further reading in the Notes rather than exhaustive documentation of secondary literature. Published translations of post-classical works have sometimes been adapted.

The writing of this book was supported by the Leverhulme Trust Research Project Grant 'Anachronism and Antiquity' (October 2016–September 2019: https://anachronismandantiquity.wordpress.com/), for which Tim Rood (TR) was Principal Investigator and Carol Atack (CA) and Tom Phillips (TP) Post-doctoral Research Associates; CA and TP are in addition preparing separate monographs for the project (on Plato and Apollonius respectively). Mathura Umachandran joined the project in September 2018 and provided intellectual energy and keen critical comments: the book owes a great deal to her involvement. John Marincola and Scarlett Kingsley were involved in preparing the Leverhulme application and supported the project throughout. Prior to the application, TR presented a collection of material on ancient anachronism and the history of anachronism at an exploratory workshop he organized in September 2015 with support from the Radcliffe Institute for Advanced Study at Harvard University; papers were also given at the workshop by Kate Gilhuly, Larry Kim, Scarlett Kingsley, Paul Kosmin, John Marincola, Francesca Schironi, Valeria Sergueenkova, Barnaby Taylor and Emma Teng, all of whom made it a very fertile occasion. John Marincola in addition secured funding for a stimulating conference on anachronism at Florida State University in March 2018, where CA, TP, Emily Greenwood, Constanze Güthenke, Brooke Holmes, Scarlett Kingsley, Ellen O'Gorman, Mark Payne and Barnaby Taylor gave papers (six of which form a special issue of *Classical Receptions Journal*). We must express gratitude, too, to the project's Steering Committee (Catherine Darbo-Peschanski, Emma Dench, Jaś Elsner, Constanze Güthenke, Nicholas Purcell and Kostas Vlassopoulos) and to the editorial team at Bloomsbury, Alice Wright and Lily Mac Mahon. The Musée Communale, Boulogne-sur-Mer, and the Bancroft Library, University of

California, Berkeley, kindly offered free use of images; the cost of other images was supported by the Jowett Copyright Trust.

All three authors share a connection with St Hugh's College, Oxford: TR as Fellow in Classics; CA first as Lecturer, then as Junior Research Fellow and Tutor for Equality; TP as alumnus. The college's staff (academic and non-academic), students, buildings, libraries, gardens and food make it a wonderful place to work and breathe: we would like to offer this book to all those whose dedication helps to make it so.

Abbreviations

DK   H. Diels and W. Kranz, eds, *Die Fragmente der Vorsokratiker*, 6th edn, Berlin, 1951.

FGrH   F. Jacoby, ed., *Die Fragmente der griechischen Historiker*, Berlin and Leiden, 1923–58.

FGrH Cont. G. Schepens and S. Schorn, eds, *Die Fragmente der griechischen Historiker continued*, Leiden, 1998–.

FRHist   T.J. Cornell, ed., *The Fragments of the Roman Historians*, Oxford, 2013.

OGIS   W. Dittenberger, ed., *Orientis Graecae inscriptiones selectae*, Leipzig, 1903–5.

SSR   G. Giannantoni, ed., *Socratis et Socraticorum reliquiae*, Naples, 1990.

TrGF   B. Snell, R. Kannicht and S. Radt, eds, *Tragicorum Graecorum fragmenta*, Göttingen, 1971–2004.

Prelude: Look to the End

Towards the start of his *Histories* (probably completed in the 420s BC), Herodotus of Halicarnassus tells of an encounter between the famously wealthy Lydian king Croesus and Solon, an Athenian poet and political leader (1.29–33). After taking Solon on a tour of the extensive treasuries in his capital Sardis, Croesus expectantly asks Solon who he regards as the most fortunate of mortals. Solon responds by praising an Athenian, Tellus, who had two adult sons, possessed enough wealth for a comfortable life, and finally died fighting for his city near Eleusis. When the incredulous Croesus proceeds to ask who was second most fortunate, Solon tells another story. Two strong youths, Cleobis and Biton, took up the yoke of their mother's cart and carried her to a festival of Hera. As all the other women admired the two young men, their mother prayed to the goddess to give them the best possible reward. They at once lay down in Hera's sanctuary and died in their sleep – the goddess showing, Solon explains, that it is better for humans to be dead than alive. Solon then explains to the now irate Croesus that any single day in the course of a human life may bring disaster and that before judging whether someone is blessed 'one must look to the end of every affair, to see how it turns out' (1.32.9) (Fig. 1).

Whether one views it as 'puerile' (Voltaire) or as 'clear and judicious' (Gibbon),[1] Solon's observation at first sight seems to fit a common characterization of the temporal consciousness of classical antiquity. It is often claimed that the Greeks and Romans had a timeless view of human nature and so were concerned to derive useful lessons from the past while remaining blind to the distinctive historical character of different periods. The exemplary character of ancient historical thought seems to be caught by the moral that Solon draws – and by its instantiation in the fate of Croesus, who thinks Solon foolish for ignoring present goods and telling him to look to the end, but whose own prosperity is soon to be upset by the death of his son and his subjection to the Persian king Cyrus. The ancients' lack of attention to historical detail seems to be shown, moreover, by the very existence of an anecdote which is hard to square with the chronology of

Fig. 1 Gaspar van den Hoecke, *Croesus showing his treasures* (1630). The meeting of Solon and Croesus was a popular topic in Dutch golden-age art – a confrontation between Solon's civic mindedness and the Croesus-like wealth acquired by Dutch merchants in the Orient. The pyre in the background points to the end that awaits Croesus; the juxtaposition of two time-periods underlines Solon's wisdom in not counting Croesus blessed until his end. M.Ob.577 MNW, National Museum of Warsaw.

its protagonists' lives (the general view is that Solon left Athens after his political reforms in the 590s BC, while Croesus' conquests belong in the 550s).[2]

A similar lack of temporal consciousness seems to be shown by the joint appearance of Solon and Croesus in the dialogue *Charon* composed by the prolific satirist Lucian (second century AD). In the spirit of the self-consciously nostalgic culture of his age (known as the Second Sophistic), Lucian's engagement with the past in *Charon* is mediated through its literary canon. He presents the god Hermes conversing with Charon, ferryman of the underworld, after Hades has given Charon permission to go up to the world above for a single day to see what humans make of their time while they are alive. Hermes and Charon pile mountain on mountain, imitating the action of the Giants in their attempt to overthrow the Olympian gods. But the concern of Hermes and Charon as they look down and eavesdrop on men in Asia and Europe is the futility of mortal aspirations. Hermes conveniently knows what lies in the future as they gaze at Cyrus preparing to attack Croesus, unaware that his expansionist dreams would lead to his death at the hands of the queen of a nomadic tribe; at Croesus himself talking to Solon;

at Polycrates, the tyrant of Samos, as he cuts open a fish only to find the gold ring he had thrown into the sea in his fruitless attempt to ward off misfortune; and finally at the Battle of the Champions, fought between 300 Spartans and 300 Argives hoping to gain possession of a plain in the Peloponnese, but destined to occupy in death a narrow patch of earth (26.9–10, 14, 24). Lucian draws all these scenes from Herodotus, but he plays fast and loose with history (it was Croesus who attacked Cyrus first) and in particular with chronology: on Herodotus' own showing, the story of Polycrates and the ring (3.40–3) belongs in the reign of Cambyses, successor of Cyrus on the Persian throne, while the Battle of the Champions (1.82) is synchronized with Cyrus' counter-attack on Croesus, which happens at least two years after his conversation with Solon. Lucian even changes the Herodotean version of the conversation between Solon and Croesus by making Solon rank Cleobis and Biton the most fortunate, with Tellus second. The historical sense missing in Herodotus' depiction of Solon seems just as absent in the use Lucian makes of the Athenian sage some six hundred years later.[3]

Many modern historians, as we shall see in Chapter 2, posit that the sort of historical sense apparently lacking in Herodotus and Lucian was central to the formation of the Renaissance. This sense of difference is generally illustrated by alleged contrasts between medieval and Renaissance art. While medieval artists are thought to have been happy to show figures from classical antiquity in the guise of chivalrous knights, Renaissance artists seem to show a much greater sense of temporal perspective (perhaps in keeping with their greater sense of spatial perspective). The unearthing of new pieces of Roman sculpture and of fragments of ancient buildings led to a stronger interest in both the artistic styles and the historical *realia* of antiquity, and artists began to pay greater attention to precise architectural details and to nuances of clothing and hair style, all of which were at the same time subject to antiquarian curiosity. Grouped with artists and antiquarians in the typical story of the discovery of historical difference are philologists such as Lorenzo Valla (1407–57), whose proof that the Donation of Constantine (a document supposedly of the fourth century AD which gave the Pope authority over the western part of the Roman empire) was a forgery is often hailed as a key intellectual advance.

This common narrative about the discovery of a 'proper' sense of history will be challenged throughout the course of this book. A preliminary sense of some of the complexities that are found in ancient texts can be gained by revisiting Herodotus' story of Solon and Croesus. That the ancients were in fact aware of the chronological difficulties in the story is shown by the re-telling of it by the biographer Plutarch (*c.* AD 50–120) in his *Solon*. Plutarch acknowledges the chronological arguments, but suggests that they are not decisive (a view still found in some modern scholars); he then justifies re-telling the story on the grounds that it is famous, true to the character of Solon, and ethically valuable in its own right (27.1).

Plutarch similarly allows the ethical claims of fiction priority over historical accuracy when he reports a tradition that Solon had been a lover of Pisistratus, later tyrant at Athens (*Solon* 1.4–5). Doubts had been cast on this relationship for chronological reasons in the *Constitution of the Athenians* (17.2), a work of the Aristotelian school written late in the fourth century BC. But, even though that Aristotelian work was certainly one of his sources, Plutarch ignores those doubts beyond prefixing the story with 'they say' – and even that phrase is more commonly a sign that a story is traditional rather than a strong indication of uncertainty. His concerns are again ethical: he notes that even though they became political opponents Solon and Pisistratus treated each other with consideration owing to the memory of their erotic relationship.

Whether Herodotus himself was aware of the difficulty of synchronizing Solon and Croesus is hard to say (though, as we shall see in Chapter 4, he was aware of the methodological problems of coordinating different time systems). The way he presents Solon and the stories he makes Solon tell do, however, imply a consciousness of historical difference. When Solon describes how the fortunate Athenian Tellus was buried at the site where he fell in battle (1.30.3–5), Herodotus' audience would have seen a contrast with the procedures of the Athenian democracy in their own day, when the cremated bodies of the war-dead were brought back to Athens and buried, tribe by tribe, in a great communal ceremony (Thucydides, *The Peloponnesian War* 2.34). When Solon labours to calculate the number of days in a human life, his calculation (1.32.2–4) – which involves allowing 360 days for a year and then intercalating thirty-day months every other year – is based on a calendrical system which, if it ever existed, was definitely outmoded at the time Herodotus was writing.[4] Plutarch similarly, despite his dominant ethical concerns, could portray Solon as 'simple and archaic' in his physical doctrines (*Solon* 3.6).

There is a further hint of historical difference in Herodotus' description of Solon as one of the 'sophists' who travelled to Croesus' court in Sardis when it was at the height of its wealth (1.29.1–2). Plutarch interpreted the term 'sophists' as a reference to the Seven Sages (*On the Malignity of Herodotus* 857f) – seven thinkers who were thought to have lived at the same time and were portrayed either in conversation with each other (as in Plutarch's own *Banquet of the Seven Sages*) or else communicating by other means, most famously when a prized object (a tripod or cup) that was to go to 'the wisest' was sent around from one sage to the next until finally it was dedicated to Apollo, either by Thales, who began the circulation, or by Solon, its final recipient.[5] What united these Seven Sages was a pungent wit, a competitive spirit, and a practical and political orientation. As expositors of traditional wisdom, they were even credited with what were clearly later sayings: thus Diogenes Laertius (third century AD) reports that an earlier biographer, Hermippus of Smyrna (third century BC), referred to Thales a saying generally attributed to Socrates, namely that he was glad to have been born a human, a man, and a Greek rather than an animal, a woman, and a barbarian (*Lives of the Philosophers* 1.33 (*FGrH Cont.* 1026 F13)). While the composition of and traditions about the Seven Sages varied, no one in antiquity seems to have questioned that, with the partial exception of Thales, they were a coherent synchronous group that practised a mode of wisdom distinct from what was later termed 'philosophy'. Diogenes Laertius underscores this difference by treating them in a book of their own at the start of his work.[6]

Even as Herodotus evokes the idea of an earlier group of sages at the court of Croesus, his use of the term 'sophist' seems to align these sages with the fee-charging intellectuals who were drawn to wealthy Athens in Herodotus' own day. There may be a danger that this argument is itself a back-projection from the use of 'sophist' by Plato, who was above all concerned to distinguish Socrates from these itinerant figures. But if the link with the sophists who flocked to Athens is justified, it is surely a deliberate allusion on Herodotus' part: it has often been suggested that Solon's warnings to Croesus about the dangers of trusting in his prosperity should be taken as a warning imparted by Herodotus himself to imperial Athens.[7]

Even the lessons that Solon gives Croesus show that it is far too restricted to see the ancient concern with exemplary wisdom as a matter of learning timeless truths from the past. The suggestion that it is better to be dead than alive may well be a timeless truth, but it is not one that provides much help with coping with the varied circumstances of life itself. There may be greater profit to be derived from Solon's other timeless truth – the injunction to 'look to the end'. But this maxim is itself grounded in an awareness of change over the course of a human lifetime. In Herodotus' account, Croesus, after taking Solon for a fool at first, comes to realize the wisdom of his utterance when he is himself conquered by Cyrus (1.86.3–5).

Both Solon and Herodotus can be read, then, as timeless treasuries of wisdom, with Tellus and Croesus on display as prize exempla. But the whole encounter between Solon and Croesus raises multiple questions about the interactions between different temporalities. As we shall see, these various questions all turn on a single concept: anachronism.

In current English the word 'anachronism' carries a range of meanings. We might call the meeting between Solon and Croesus an anachronism because it seems chronologically impossible. We might call Herodotus' use of the word 'sophist' an anachronism – if we assume that he is drawing on the resonances that the word was beginning to acquire in the Athens of his own day; and we might similarly suspect that the attribution of an opposition of 'Greek' and 'barbarian' to Thales is an anachronism, a retrojection of the ideological weight those terms gained in the years before and after the Greco-Persian wars of the early fifth century BC. We might see Solon's calendrical calculations as anachronistic, at least judged by the standards of Herodotus' day. We might regard Solon himself as an anachronism, a practitioner of a type of wisdom that seemed old-fashioned at the time Herodotus was writing. And we might even fancy that Solon's injunction to Croesus to 'look to the end' is an acknowledgement of the danger of anachronism inherent in historical judgements.

How does the English word 'anachronism' relate to the temporal conceptions of the Greeks themselves? The roots of 'anachronism' lie in a Greek word first attested at the turn of the second and third centuries AD. Like the various meanings the word has gained in the modern world, the Greek root turns on the notion of historical change. But rather different understandings of the mechanisms of change underlie the varied meanings the term has acquired since its adoption in vernacular languages. We shall trace in the next chapter the history of the term, exploring how it has acquired the conceptual richness it now enjoys as a marker of historical difference. This conceptual richness is explored in Chapter 2, but we will at the same time be alive to the methodological challenges of constructing and understanding a 'sense of anachronism'. The concept of anachronism can be identified before the appearance of the term, but there are many pitfalls in using this concept as the basis for a progressive narrative of increasing historical understanding.

The next two chapters will prepare the ground for the aim of the book as a whole – to explore the concept of anachronism in its full range of meanings across the whole of Greco-Roman antiquity. The book will look beyond the limited ancient uses of the root 'anachronism' and argue that, contrary to frequent assertions of the ancients' lack of complex historical consciousness, there are many indications that they did have a sense of anachronism that is not wholly different from modern notions. It will investigate anachronisms and the responses they generate in a broad range of textual and material evidence, tracking the history of the word 'anachronism' as it covers in successive chapters literary anachronisms and ancient scholarly discussions of them (Chapter 3); chronological writers (Chapter 4); ideas of historical survival in ethnographic settings (Chapter 5); and the ancient discourse of exemplarity (Chapter 6). It will then turn to the role of anachronism in the conceptualization of multitemporal texts and objects (Chapter 7) and of dialogues among communities of writers and readers, both living and dead (Chapter 8). Three Interludes (two of them devoted to Virgil) explore stories and images that have resonated with ancient and modern writers. The book as a whole will provide an overarching explanatory framework for understanding what earlier scholarship has at best treated as isolated instances of anachronism. Anachronism, it will emerge, is a powerful concept not just for capturing the varying modes of historical consciousness within antiquity but also for understanding the way we ourselves define antiquity – for to engage with the classical past at all is inescapably to become part of an anachronistic community.

1

Inventing Anachronism

Modern anachronisms

The title of this section might strike the reader as paradoxical. The grouping of anachronism with modernity jars with the type of perception encapsulated in the pronouncement of one of Oscar Wilde's characters in his dialogue 'The Critic as Artist': 'Whatever, in fact, is modern in our life we owe to the Greeks. Whatever is an anachronism is due to medievalism.' This claim owes much to a striving for epigrammatic wit: it follows the brazenly anachronistic claim that 'the Greeks chattered about painters just as much as people do nowadays … even the theatrical managers of travelling companies brought their dramatic critics with them … and paid them very handsome salaries for writing laudatory notices'.[1] Wilde's character, then, is enacting his professed Hellenic modernity even as he offers a fictionalized past as the basis of this enactment. But, for all that, his soundbite does capture a common perception that anachronism is opposed to modernity.

The sense in which Wilde was using 'anachronism' was quite recent at the time he wrote his essay. The word was applied in English first as a description of textual phenomena, typically allusions to institutions or places that were not yet in existence at the time of the events being described. It was subsequently used of errors in the fixing of dates. It was only in the early nineteenth century that the word started to be used of people or practices thought obsolete or out of date. Like all words, anachronism has a history, and this history has continued since Wilde's time. The word has continued to acquire new resonances – and in the process the division Wilde created between the medieval and the modern has been profoundly reconfigured.

'What does it feel like to be an anachronism?' is the question posed at the start of a discussion of medieval temporalities by Carolyn Dinshaw, a leading exponent of Queer Theory. One of the goals of Queer Theory is to disrupt the normative assumptions of 'straight' time, that is, a view of time as linear and oriented around transgenerational reproduction. To answer her question, Dinshaw turns to the mystic Margery Kempe (*c.* 1373–*c.* 1440). In her autobiographical writings, Kempe describes herself overcome with weeping before an image of Christ on the cross. At odds with her powerful sense of the immediacy of Christ's death is the detached figure of her priest, who tries to console her by saying that Jesus died long ago. On Dinshaw's reading, the priest, proud in the institutional power of the church, dismisses the emotional Kempe as a 'pathetic anachronism – a creature stuck in the past'. That is, he rejects Kempe's emotionalism with the same disdain with which Wilde rejects the medieval.[2]

As her essay progresses, Dinshaw starts to use 'anachronism' in a different sense. Rather than being applied to a sense of belonging to an earlier period, it becomes a sympathetic vehicle for expressing Kempe's spiritual and bodily absorption in the dying Christ. This broader use allows Dinshaw to connect her own subjective experience of time with the experiences of Kempe and of Kempe's twentieth-century editor, Hope Emily Allen. In effect, it is used as a synonym of 'asynchrony', to express the multitemporality of experienced life (and Dinshaw did indeed start a later version of her essay with the less snappy 'What does it feel like to be asynchronous?').[3]

Recuperation of anachronism as a sort of disturbed temporality that runs counter to the hegemony of straight time has also been a feature of postcolonial criticism (notably Dipesh Chakrabarty's *Provincializing Europe*). Anachronism or 'the recurrence of *being out of time*' is defined by one postcolonial critic as 'a condition produced by the British Empire's definition of time as a linear progression'. But this critic also attributes to 'anachronistic methods' the capacity to 'disrupt the way in which colonial history is written'.[4] Notions of anachronism are central, too, to some ecocritical attempts to think about human damage to the environment in what has been termed the Anthropocene period. An understanding of humanity's influence on the climate has led to an awareness that 'previous norms become uncertainly anachronistic'. Long-standing human practices such as wood-burning are now subject to a 'retrospective derangement of meaning',[5] and literature composed prior to knowledge of climate change has taken on hitherto unavailable meanings (as in J. Hillis Miller's 'anachronistic reading' of Wallace Stevens' 1942 poem 'The Man on the Dump'[6]).

The language of anachronism pervades many other modern discourses, notably memory studies, cognitive science and the history of art. In this last discipline, the historicizing iconological method of Erwin Panofsky has been challenged by Georges Didi-Huberman as well as by Alexander Nagel and

Christopher Wood in their 2010 book *Anachronic Renaissance*. While these scholars applaud Panofsky's erudition, they suggest that he uses his learning to shut down the meaning of images. In Didi-Huberman's reading, Panofsky (a German Jew forced into exile in the United States in the 1930s) reacted against the unreason of Nazism, but in the process 'exorcised the anachronisms and labilities specific to the world of images' by rejecting the approaches found in German Jewish writers such as Aby Warburg and Walter Benjamin.[7] While Didi-Huberman celebrates anachronism as 'the temporal way of expressing the exuberance, complexity, and overdetermination of images', Nagel and Wood prefer to speak of the 'anachronic' on the grounds that anachronism is 'a judgmental term that carries with it the historicist assumption that every event and every object has its proper location within objective and linear time'.[8] But the anachronic does similar work for them in resisting the notion that the circumstances of any artwork's production provide a sufficient explanation of its creation.[9]

The recuperation of the anachronic has been accompanied by a transformation in attitudes towards artistic and literary anachronisms. Features formerly ignored or regarded as flaws are now valued for challenging the constructedness of linear narrative. 'Creative'[10] or 'productive'[11] anachronisms are widely celebrated – while paradoxically the attempt to avoid anachronism in historical reconstruction is condemned as itself a pernicious anachronism.[12]

The origins of anachronism

The way 'anachronism' is generally used in the modern world would have meant nothing to the first exponents of the word in English. To understand its history, we need to probe into its roots in Ancient Greek and the transmission of those Greek roots (via Renaissance Latin) to vernacular languages.

Scholars outside the discipline of Classics have tended to approach the etymology of 'anachronism' rather adventurously. A monograph on *Modern Antiques* proposes the meaning 'against time'.[13] Joseph Luzzi, a scholar of comparative literature, suggests that the word derives from 'a fusion of the Greek compound meaning "late in time"', while Nagel and Wood split the Greek *anachronizein* into '*ana*-, "again", and the verb *chronizein*, "to be late or belated"' (they speak of artworks 'anachronizing' in the sense of being 'belated again').[14] These two explanations root the modern English word in an intransitive use of the Greek verb *anachronizein* that is attested, as we shall see, only once, in a short papyrus letter that was dug up in Egypt at the end of the nineteenth century – and even here the sense must be 'delay' rather than 'be late again' (the prefix *ana-*, like English *re-*, is used in this sense only with telic verbs, that is, with verbs expressing an accomplishment). But to criticize the etymology offered by Nagel and Wood may be to miss their point. They offer a creative redefinition to suit their view of the temporal dynamism of art: they explain that the anachronic artwork 'is late, first because it succeeds some reality that it re-presents, and then late again when that re-presentation is repeated for successive recipients'.[15]

The prominent French philosopher Jacques Rancière (to whose thought we will return) comes closer to the etymological truth in his important discussion of anachronism when he recognizes that the *ana-* prefix means 'up'. But, like Nagel and Wood, the way he develops his reflections on the word owes more to the work he wants it to do than to its linguistic history. He first claims that the prefix *ana-* refers to 'a movement from the rear toward the front'. While this is a possible sense of 'up' in Ancient Greek, he fails to explain why this should be seen as a movement 'from one time toward an earlier' (perhaps he associates the front line with an earlier time because it is first to advance). He complicates the picture further with a complex play on the literal meaning 'up': anachronism, he suggests, involves 'a vertical problem of the order of time in the hierarchy of beings'; that is, the concept serves to connect human time with 'what is above it' – namely eternity. As we shall see, Rancière thinks that anachronism has typically been cast out by historians as a sin because it is the dark side of correct historical time, a time that is itself a modern surrogate for divine immanence.[16]

From a philological perspective, a better interpretation of the prefix *ana-* is that 'up' implies 'back'. Among the Ancient Greeks, as in many cultures, the past could be conceived as lying *above*. The Greeks also at times used the image of time as a river flowing downwards.[17] The basic sense of *anachronizein*, then, is to date something back in time. Exactly the same idea of a backwards projection was sometimes expressed by the same prefix in the words *anagein* 'bring back' and *anapempein*, 'send back'.

The Greek verb *anachronizein* was typically used in scholarly exegesis of earlier literature. The word is found above all in the marginal comments known as scholia (sg. scholion) that are found in many manuscripts and that preserve material from older commentaries, perhaps in some cases dating back to Hellenistic Alexandria; another source is the voluminous commentary on Homer composed by Eustathius, Archbishop of Thessalonica in the twelfth century AD. Also used in similar contexts was the cognate noun *anachronismos*.[18] These various words are uncommon in extant Greek (there are no more than thirty occurrences of the root to the end of the Byzantine period). As we shall explore in Chapter 3, in keeping with their etymology, they were generally used of later practices imported into an earlier context: to give one example, a scholion on the first line of Sophocles' *Trachinian Women* identifies the maxim with which Heracles' wife Deianira starts the play (that a mortal's life cannot be judged until death) as an 'old saying' and 'anachronism' on the grounds that it is derived from Solon, who is earlier than Sophocles but later than the time of the play (the scholion goes on to provide a summary of Herodotus' account of his meeting with Croesus).[19]

The ancient history of the word is complicated by its appearance in documentary sources. Unlike the uses in ancient commentaries, this usage can be securely dated to the Roman imperial period. A new piece of evidence emerged late in the twentieth century with the discovery at Narmouthis in Egypt of a broken piece of pottery containing a petition to a local governor, Anubion. The governor's name dates the petition to AD 199. Part of the petition runs as follows: 'Soconopis son of Hormeinus, my brother by the same father, and Petermouthis and Horus pleaded with the *hēgēmōn* [prefect] together with Marcus' memorandum (which warned) that the petition has been anachronized (*anakechronisthai*) in the name of the *stratēgos* [governor] Marcus …'[20] The meaning of the word here is unfortunately unclear owing to the lack of context. Given that the perfect passive of the basic verb *chronizein* is frequently found on papyri in the sense 'dated', the plea may relate to a petition that has been wrongly dated. As petitions were dated by regnal years, there may have been an incorrect alignment of Marcus' year of office with a particular regnal year, resulting in a back-dating of the petition.

Harder to explain is the appearance of the verb *anachronizein* in a letter preserved on papyrus from Tebtunis, a city in the Fayoum in Egypt and dated to the second or third century AD (Fig. 2). The papyrus, which was found in mummy cartonnage during excavations at the turn of the nineteenth and twentieth centuries, was described by its first editors as 'badly written' and 'containing several curious words'. The letter was written by a woman (perhaps a slave) called Aphrodite and probably addressed to her mistress. Her letter includes an apology which starts 'we are anachronizing (*anachronizomen*) in sending you letters because we have no' – before her excuse is lost in a gap in the papyrus.[21] She is here, exceptionally, using the verb intransitively, with the meaning 'we are late', even though the plain verb *chronizein* was in use with the same sense. The new evidence provided by the ostracon perhaps suggests a misappropriation of bureaucratic terminology.

Fig. 2 A letter on papyrus from a slave, Aphrodite, to her mistress, with an early example (five lines up) of the Greek verb *anachronizein*. P. Tebt. 2.413, AD c. 175-299, Bancroft Library, University of California, Berkeley.

A few passages in the scholia do not fit the interpretation 'date back'. In Euripides' *Phoenician Women* (written c. 409 BC), the seer Tiresias reports that he has travelled to Thebes from Athens, where he has made the Athenians victorious in their battle against Eumolpus, leader of neighbouring Eleusis (852–7). The scholia on line 854 use the verb *anachronizein* to draw attention to a chronological inconsistency: the war between Eumolpus and Erechtheus took place four generations prior to the conflict at Thebes between Eteocles and Polyneices which the *Phoenician Women* recounts. But they describe the earlier war as pushed *forward* to the time of the main action of the play rather than the play's action as pushed back, as the etymology appears to demand.

The apparent etymological sense of the Greek root also fails to catch some uses of the noun *anachronismos* in the scholia to the *Prometheus Bound* (a play attributed in antiquity to Aeschylus but now dated by most scholars after his lifetime). These scholia label as 'anachronisms' a number of prophecies made by the eponymous hero – for instance, his statements that the monster Typhon will be imprisoned under Etna and cause volcanic eruptions (362) and that the Amazons 'will one day settle at Themiscyra' (723). This usage might seem to be making the slightly pedantic point that accurate prophecies necessarily involve a sort of chronological casting back of later events; on this reading, the prophesied events, like almost all the other 'anachronisms' picked up in the scholia, are in some sense placed too early. But in the case of the Amazon prophecy the scholia offer an overt justification of the label 'anachronism' that points to a more complex configuration of time: 'He refers to something that occurred a long time ago as if it were about to happen.' That is, the prophecy is deemed anachronistic on the basis that events that were in the past for the audience are referred to as being in the future for the characters. It is out of time because the temporal orientations of the characters within the play clash with those of the audience.

These ancient uses already show, then, some of the variety that 'anachronism' was to achieve in later settings. But they give little hint of the appeal the word would gain beyond antiquity. To understand that, we have to follow the word's spread to Renaissance scholarship and its emergence in the vernacular.

From Byzantium to Italy and beyond

The accounts modern scholars have given about *when* the word 'anachronism' was formed are as fragile as their explanations of its etymology. There are evident clashes in the claims made in the most recent accounts. Joseph Luzzi dates the word's appearance in English to 1669 and in Italian a century earlier.[22] The intellectual historian Peter Burke, author of several treatments of the Renaissance sense of anachronism, suggests that it was 'around 1650' that the term 'began to come into use in Latin, Italian, French and English'.[23] The Shakespearean scholar Margreta de Grazia similarly claims, in a much-cited 2010 treatment of anachronism, that the word emerged in English in the mid-seventeenth century, while adding that it surfaced at the beginning of the seventeenth century, but 'only in its Greek form and in an esoteric treatise'. And she complicates the picture further by stating that the word, though without ancient lineage, was 'coined from the Middle Greek' (the beginnings of which are variously dated to between AD 300 and 700).[24]

These various treatments of the origins of anachronism are concerned to place the concept within a broader history of temporal consciousness. De Grazia acknowledges that 'a grasp of the concept has been identified much earlier', but proceeds to cast doubt on the familiar story of the Renaissance discovery of anachronism – suggesting that a true understanding of cognitive distance in fact comes later.[25] Burke and Luzzi are similarly interested in the paradoxes apparently thrown up by the linguistic development of the word: Burke concludes that 'to speak of the sense of anachronism of Mantegna or Erasmus is ... literally speaking, anachronistic', while Luzzi, noting the word's origins in 'the oldest of Western high-cultural idioms', claims that it appeared in English 'millennia after that culture had disappeared' – and hence that 'the term's etymology stands both as an ironic gloss on its semantic connotations and an allegory for its thematic claims'.[26]

Implicit in these claims about the history of anachronism is an ideological construction of space and time. The irony Luzzi sees in the surprisingly late appearance of a classically derived word for belatedness is gained only at the expense of a misunderstanding of the Greek word, which most commonly describes something that appears too early rather than too late. And the seventeenth century is scarcely 'millennia' after the disappearance of Ancient Greek culture. His allegorical reading of the etymology can be seen as a way of separating off antiquity from its aftermath. A compelling counter-claim would be that the Greek culture whose disappearance Luzzi misdates has never disappeared at all.

A similar spatial ideology is conveyed by de Grazia's statement that anachronism surfaced in its Greek form early in the seventeenth century and by Burke's *bon mot* about the anachronism of speaking of anachronism. These should be understood as claims about *where* the word was used as much as about *when* or *how*. And they do not make much sense even if their scope is restricted to Western Europe.

The Greek word *anachronismos* had been known in Italy at least since the arrival of Byzantine manuscripts in the fifteenth century. It is found, for instance, in the margins of the famous manuscript of Aeschylus now known as the

Mediceus, which was one of more than 200 manuscripts brought to Italy in 1423 by Giovanni Aurispa, a Sicilian sent as translator on a papal mission to the Byzantine court.[27] The diffusion of the word can be traced further through the publication of the manuscripts that contained the word. 'Anachronism' appears in the scholia on Sophocles published by Janus Lascaris in 1518 (scholion on *Trachinian Women* 1) and in those on Aeschylus published by Francisco Robortello in 1552 (scholion on *Eumenides* 723), and again in an edition of Eustathius' commentary on the *Iliad* published in Rome between 1542 and 1550. The word 'anachronism' had been in existence, then, for more than a millennium when Mantegna and Erasmus were alive, and was available in Italy in manuscripts during Mantegna's lifetime (c. 1431–1506) and in print during Erasmus' (1466–1536).

The invention of 'anachronism' in Western Europe was one consequence of the dispersal of Greek learning with the weakening and eventual collapse of Byzantium. From Greek *anachronismos* appeared the Latin *anachronismus*. This transliteration into the common language of European scholarship is attested in a collection of notes on classical authors and topics published in 1542 by Lodovico Ricchieri (also known as Caelius Rhodiginus). Ricchieri uses the term in relation to one of the passages designated an anachronism in the scholia, the start of Sophocles' *Trachinian Women*: 'this figure of speech is called *anachronismus*'; the gloss suggests a consciousness of neologism.[28] Indicative of the conceptual reach of the term is the fact that Ricchieri includes in his discussion some passages where the term anachronism was not expressly used in the scholia: a speech in Virgil's *Aeneid* in which a character refers to the 'Veline harbour' even though the eponymous town Velia (Greek Elea) had not been founded, and a messenger speech in Sophocles' *Electra* which recounts Orestes' supposed death in the chariot race in the Pythian games, though these games were founded 'about 600 years after Orestes'.[29]

'Anachronism' was soon used in the sophisticated literary criticism written in Italian in the second half of the sixteenth century. Lodovico Castelvetro uses it in his voluminous commentary on the *Poetics* of Aristotle, precisely with reference to the passage from Sophocles' *Electra* mentioned by Ricchieri ('I also believe that the offence is not to be excused by an appeal to the figure known as *anachronismos*' – as in Ricchieri, the formulation betrays a sense of novelty); not content with rejecting *anachronismos* as an excuse, he coined the Greek words *anatopismos*, *anaprosōpismos* and *anatropismos* for the (equally unacceptable) practices of changing the place, character or events of a story.[30] *Anachronismo* was subsequently the subject of a chapter in Jacopo Mazzoni's *On the Defence of*

Dante's Comedy, an important work of literary criticism published in 1587. Starting with an allusion to Castelvetro's commentary, Mazzoni includes an extensive collection of ancient passages that pertain to anachronism, largely inspired by ancient critics but including many not covered by the Greek term and some apparently independent examples (such as the naming of Cape Pelorias in Polybius).[31]

A formidable array of arguments about anachronism as a literary phenomenon emerged in Latin and Italian well before the term's appearance in English. Inspired by his knowledge of ancient criticism, Mazzoni was thoroughly alive to justifications for literary anachronism, notably the distinctions between history and poetry and between the voices of the character and narrator – much the same arguments that would continue to be used over the following centuries. In due course, moreover, 'anachronism' seeped into the language of creative artists: Giulio Strozzi gave his 1620 play *The Birth of Love* the sub-title *Anachronism* because it brought together characters from different mythical eras, and justified the practice by allusion to Plato's dialogues and Virgil.[32] He would be followed in this overt apology for anachronism in recreations of the classical world by writers such as Henry Fielding in Britain (in a dialogue between the cynic Diogenes and Alexander of Macedon) and Barthélemy in France (in his widely read *Travels of the Younger Anacharsis*).[33] The birth of anachronism, then, was an event in literary studies rather than chronology. And this literary usage was still prominent when the word appeared first in English.

Anachronism from literature to chronology

The common statement that 'anachronism' entered English in the middle of the seventeenth century is based on the earliest instance cited in the *Oxford English Dictionary* (*OED*) under 'anachronism'. This entry is from a chronological work by John Gregory (1609–46), a chaplain of Christ Church in Oxford. Dating the birth of Christ 'Anno Mundi 3949, Anno Period. Jul. 4713, Olympiad 197, and 748 of Nabonassar', Gregory explained that 'this Connexion of things is called Synchronism', while 'an error committed herein is called Anachronism'. This passage is cited from Gregory's 1649 *Posthuma*, and so dated 'a[nte] 1646', the year of his death.[34]

The problem with the common view of the origin of 'anachronism' in English is that the *OED* itself commits an anachronism. Its entry for 'hysterosis' contains an earlier appearance of the word, from William Lisle's 1623 edition with translation of *A Saxon Treatise concerning the Old and New Testament*, written by a monk called Aelfricus. Lisle took a phrase used by Aelfricus, 'Lingua Britannica', to be a reference to Old English, 'by Hysterosis or Anachronisme (a figure much used in Historie, yea even in the Bible)'.[35] As the *OED* advances alphabetically, the entry for 'metachronism' ('the placing of an event later than its real date') reveals a still earlier usage of 'anachronism' in a sermon delivered at St Mary's Church in Oxford in Easter week, 1617, by John Hales, Regius Professor of Greek. Addressing the biblical text 'Which the vnlearned and vnstable wrest, as they doe the other Scriptures, vnto their owne destruction' (2 Peter 3.16), Hales warned against unwarranted projections of Calvinist doctrines such as predestination on to obscure biblical passages: 'there are in Scripture of things that are *hustera protera* [later earlier], *seemingly confus'd, enantiophanē* [opposite-seeming], *carrying semblance of contrarietie, anachronismes, metachronismes*, and the like, which bring infinite obscuritie to the text: there are I say in Scripture more of them, then in any writing that I knowe secular or divine'.[36] Here 'anachronism' is one in a powerful list of forces that disrupt Calvinist attempts to find meaning in texts that, for Hales, could only be clarified through divine revelation.

Why the mistake in the *OED* entry for 'anachronism'? The misleading date it gives for the first appearance of the word could, at a pinch, be taken as a subtle in-joke, the entry for 'metachronism' metachronically revealing an anachronism in the entry for 'anachronism'. But it is easy enough to understand why the editors of the original *OED* (or rather: *A New English Dictionary on Historical Principles*) failed to pick up these earlier usages: the dictionary itself appeared in fascicles over the course of forty-four years, with the entries for 'anachronism', 'hysterosis' and 'metachronism' first appearing in 1884, 1899 and 1906. Those editors are rather to be admired for their coverage: digital resources such as *Early English Books Online* reveal no earlier instance of the word in English.

The lexical history summarized above is made more complicated by the existence of an almost identical form, 'anachronicism'. The only occurrence of this word cited in the *OED* is taken from Thomas Blount's 1656 *Glossographia*, where 'an error in Chronology, or an undue connexion of time, a false Chronicling, a repeating of time' is offered as a joint definition for both 'Anachronicism' and 'Anachronism'.[37] The source for Blount himself was probably Sir Walter Ralegh's *History of the World*, which was written in the Tower of London and published in November 1614 (two and a half years before the earliest attested occurrence of 'anachronism'). The word appears in an address to the reader placed at the end of the narrative part of the history immediately before an extensive 'chronologicall table': Ralegh explains that this table 'may serue to free the Booke, and likewise the Reader (if but of meane iudgement) from anie notorious Anachronicisme' – and that the secure chronological frame provided by the appendix was needed 'not onely for some errors of the Presse, in the numbring of yeares, but for some hastie mis-reckonings of mine owne'.[38]

The importance of dating the first appearance of anachronism correctly lies not in the insight it offers into the workings of the *OED* but in the correction the earliest usages offer to a restricted focus on the word's chronological sense. The *OED* definition ('An error in computing time, or fixing dates; the erroneous reference of an event, circumstance, or custom to a wrong date') puts the chronological ahead of the literary without allowing for the possibility that the reference of an event to a wrong date may be deliberate rather than erroneous. In lexicographical works, this chronological focus can be traced all the way back to Blount's *Glossographia*. But while Ralegh's coinage 'anachronicisme' does appear in a chronological context, the earliest English usages of 'anachronism' itself emerge in the realm of rhetoric and biblical exegesis: John Hales' sermon was concerned with the difficulty of understanding the Bible, while William Lisle's identification of 'Lingua Britannica' as an anachronistic allusion to Old English is an example of the sort of literary exegesis practised in the Greek scholia.

That the term 'anachronism' did spread from literature to chronology is no surprise. As it was taken up in Renaissance scholarship, it could easily be transferred to one of the new questions that scholars applied to the literary remains of antiquity: how to make sense of the competing temporal systems and the conflicting temporal signals found in classical and biblical texts. In this scholarly setting, 'anachronism' was now used to mean not a literary technique, as in the Greek commentary tradition, but an error in the calculation of time.

The chronological usage of anachronism has been particularly associated with the French scholar Joseph Scaliger (1540–1609), author of *De emendatione temporum* (*On the Improvement of Times*). In published writings, Scaliger used the word first in the 'Prolegomena' and appended notes on select fragments in the 1598 edition of this work, where he applies it (in its Greek form) both to erroneous datings transmitted in annalistic works and to errors resulting from a poor judgement of sources.[39] His influence can also be seen in Ralegh, who throughout his chronological table uses the dating system known as the Julian Period as 'deuised by that honorable and excellently learned IOSEPH SCALIGER'.[40] But while Scaliger was undoubtedly important in the development of the chronological use,[41] that use antedates him: a 1578 diatribe on the legendary figure of Pope Joan refers to the identification by some writers of a historical figure (John Scotus Eriugena, 815–77) as a pupil of Bede (672–735) as 'no trivial anachronism' (*non levi anachronismo*). What marks this usage out from any use of the word in the Greek commentary tradition is that the establishment of a fact is at stake.[42]

'Anachronism' retained some fluidity even after it was adopted in serious chronological scholarship. Scaliger's pupil Daniel Heinsius could use *anachronismus* in a work of biblical exegesis to convict Bede of chronological error. But in his 1623 *Praise of the Ass*, a work inspired by the ancient tradition of paradoxical panegyric, he applies it to a story reported by Tacitus in his brief ethnographic account of the Jews (*Histories* 5.3). The story in Tacitus was that the Jews, expelled from Egypt, were wandering thirsty in the desert when Moses saved them by inferring a source of water from the sight of a flock of wild asses making for a rock shaded by trees. Heinsius drew on the language of anachronism to dismiss this challenge to the biblical version: 'I do no way dout but that this error sprang from *Anachronisme*, and confusion of Histories: which I suppose might have its rise, from what they had heard touching the Asses cheek, wherewith *Samson* slew a thousand men; and from when by *Samsons* prayers there sprang a fountain' (the allusion is to Judges 15:14–19).[43] The confusion supposed by Heinsius has nothing to do with time. It is simply the transfer of two motifs (asses and thirst) from one story to another.

Linking anachronism closely with chronological calculation nonetheless fundamentally altered perceptions of the concept. Its impact can be strongly felt in the changing tone of literary discussions, as wittily evoked by Margreta de Grazia's description of 'the routine tasks of eighteenth-century critics': 'applying chronology to poetry about the past in order to expose anachronisms ... becomes one of the many ways in which the Whiggish Augustan age asserts its literary superiority over its less refined predecessor'.[44] An example of what de Grazia has in mind is the exegesis of 'one of Shakespeare's most remarkable *anachronisms*' (Lear's 'Nero is an angler in the lake of darkness') offered by Zachary Grey in 1754: 'King Lear succeeded his father Bladud anno mundi 3105; and Nero, anno mundi 4017, was sixteen years old, when he married Octavia, Caesar's daughter. See Funccii Chronologia p. 94.'[45] Such anachronisms could be simply noted, as here, or explained as poetic license, or again emended away or deleted as editorial interpolations.[46] On the other hand, leading lights in the Augustan age could equally assert themselves by dismissing a hyper-consciousness of anachronism as pedantry. In the 1730s, for instance, the philosopher and politician Bolingbroke wrote in his *Letters on the Study and Use of History* that he would 'rather take the DARIUS whom ALEXANDER conquered [i.e. Darius III, who reigned 336–330 BC] for the son of HYSTASPES [i.e. Darius I, who reigned 519–486 BC], and make as many anachronisms as a Jewish chronologer', than sacrifice half his life 'to collect all the learned lumber that fills the head of an antiquary'.[47] Bolingbroke here dismisses as irrelevant the identity of the king whose defeat had structured many historical narratives based on the ancient idea of a succession of empires.

We have traced some of the shifting fortunes of 'anachronism' in its journey from the margins of Greek manuscripts to a settled part in learned literary and chronological scholarship. To gain a better understanding of its temporal domains, however, we must attend to some of the related words that accompanied it through that journey – before succumbing to the radical transformation of the concept in the course of the nineteenth century.

Anachronism and related terms

'Anachronism' has from the start existed in English and other vernacular languages alongside a number of terms that have not endured or adapted as well. We have already seen it used alongside 'metachronism' and 'hysterosis' – the former probably coined by analogy with 'anachronism' from the Greek adjective *metachronos* 'after the time' (one instance of the noun *metachronismos* does survive[48]), the latter apparently derived from medieval Latin (though ultimately from a Greek root meaning 'later'). Another word that fell within the range of 'anachronism' was 'prochronism' (again derived by analogy with 'anachronism' from a Greek adjective *prochronos*, 'before the time'[49]). This neologism appears alongside 'metachronism' in the typology of anachronisms produced by John Gregory. Explaining, as we have seen, that an anachronism is an error committed in synchronism, he distinguished between an error that 'saith too much, and that is a Prochronism; or too little, and that is a Metachronism'.[50] As we shall see in Chapter 4, Gregory carelessly reverses the definitions found in Scaliger's 1606 *Thesaurus temporum* (*Treasury of Times*).

Other terms used with much the same sense as 'anachronism' were 'antichronism' and 'parachronism'. Greek *antichronismos* was occasionally used in ancient philology, albeit with the meaning 'exchange of one tense for another'. The anglicized form appears in the Preface written by the legal scholar John Selden to the prose 'illustrations' that he wrote to accompany Michael Drayton's 1612 topographical poem *Poly-olbion*: he opposed the 'Intollerable Antichronismes' found in some of the traditions on which Drayton drew to 'Synchronisme, the best Touch-stone'.[51] The noun 'parachronism', by contrast, had no ancient precedent: it was formed from the Greek phrase *para tous chronous*, 'against the times', which was used by a number of literary scholars in antiquity.[52] It too was an invention of the first half of the seventeenth century, appearing, for instance, in the writings of the church historian Richard Montagu, who resorted to textual emendation to defend Justin Martyr against the charge of 'Parachronisme' for making the 'ancient Sibyl' (a prophetess who is mentioned in Plato's *Phaedrus*) a daughter of the third-century BC Babylonian historian Berossus.[53]

The arrival of 'anachronism' in Western Europe after the fall of Byzantium and the subsequent invention of other -chronisms might seem to point to a heightened consciousness of temporal dislocation in the course of the sixteenth and seventeenth centuries. But such a claim would be to inflate the significance of the lexical realm – and to ignore, in any case, a range of other words that could be used to express the idea of anachronism. Most important of these is 'prolepsis'. Greek *prolēpsis* was used in the criticism of rhetoric as a term for the 'anticipation' of later arguments, but it was applied only rarely to criticism of narratives. It is found in Latin, however, notably in discussions of Cicero by Asconius in the first century AD and of Virgil by Aulus Gellius in the second century and by the commentator Servius in the fourth, to denote an 'anticipation' of something that has not yet happened, typically with reference to the use of a personal name bestowed subsequently to the events in the narrative. Owing, no doubt, to the popularity throughout late antiquity and the Middle Ages of Servius' commentary on the *Aeneid*, the word was picked up in biblical criticism, for instance in commentaries on Genesis by Stephen Langton, Archbishop of Canterbury, in the thirteenth century and the reformer John Calvin in the sixteenth. It then entered English in translations of Calvin, before being used by Philemon Holland in the notes to his 1606 translation of Suetonius' *Lives of the Caesars*.[54]

The French versions of anachronism's cognates were dismissed by Jacques Rancière as inventions of nineteenth-century dictionaries – logical complements of 'anachronism'.[55] Rancière's observation may charitably be taken as a joke which captures well the fate of these various words. They had in fact remained popular well into the eighteenth century. Spotting 'prolepsis' was one of the weapons used by the classical scholar Richard Bentley in his renowned demolition of the authenticity of a series of letters attributed to the sixth-century BC Sicilian tyrant Phalaris.[56] When Joseph Robertson tried in 1788 to prove that the Parian Marble, a Greek chronological inscription that had been brought to England in the seventeenth century, was a fake, one of the arguments he used against the Marble's authenticity was the presence of 'parachronisms' and 'prochronisms' – chronological mistakes in the placement of particular people and events.[57] Revealing of the limited range of 'anachronism' at this date is that he failed to use the term in advancing some of his other arguments, notably his claims that the letter forms did not have the proper antiquity and that some of the factual data was derived from authors later than the supposed date of the Marble. But 'anachronism' was soon to eclipse its rival forms still further, and these rivals are now largely the preserve of the pretentious.

Anachronism and the idea of progress

The continuing hold of the chronological usage of anachronism is demonstrated by a typology produced by the Neapolitan philosopher Giambattista Vico (1668–1744) in the third edition of his *New Science*. Vico's view of anachronism was informed by the recursive patterns he saw in history as human society moved from barbarism through stages of social development and back to barbarism. He identified four kinds of chronological error that might be committed by historians who did not take account of the patterns of history:

> The first error regards as *uneventful* periods which were actually full of events. For example, Varro regards as a dark age that age of the gods in which we have found nearly all the origins of civilized institutions. Conversely, a second error regards as *eventful* those periods which were actually uneventful. The age of heroes only lasted some 200 years, but people filled it with events from the age of the gods, because they mistakenly believed that myths were invented all at once by the heroic poets, and especially by Homer. (In fact, these events should be pushed back to the earlier age.) A third error *unites* periods which should be separated. During the lifetime of Orpheus, the people of Greece were supposed to have passed from a bestial existence to the illustrious deeds of the Trojan War.... Conversely, a fourth error *divides* periods which should be united. Greek colonies were supposed to arrive in Sicily and Italy over 300 years after the wanderings of the heroes of Troy, when in fact they arrived there with the heroes' wanderings.[58]

Vico's identification of anachronism is based on his *a priori* perception of the shape of the historical process rather than on breaches of synchronism: while ancient traditions are united in the relative placement of Orpheus and the Trojan War, it is Vico's judgement that none of them allows sufficient time for the passage from savagery to a more civilized state.

The perception of patterns and process in history was to be fundamental to the decisive shift in conceptions of anachronism in the first half of the nineteenth century. It was at this time that the term began to be applied, in what remains its dominant modern usage, to attitudes and practices that were deemed obsolete; with time the label spread to the people who upheld them. The earliest example of this new usage cited by the *OED* is in a 'lay sermon' on education composed by Samuel Taylor Coleridge in 1816. Coleridge calls for a return to 'a more manly discipline of the intellect on the part of the learned themselves': without the dawning of 'the light of an idea', 'experience itself is but a Cyclops walking backwards under the fascination of the past', liable to 'seduce its worshipper into practical anachronisms'.[59] Coleridge's 'practical anachronisms' could equally be re-framed as 'anachronistic practices': the term refers not to chronological errors in the world of book-learning but to outmoded pursuits in the realm of action.

Coleridge's term was picked up by many other writers in the course of the nineteenth century. Of particular note are the glosses on the term provided by Thomas de Quincey in one of a series of essays on 'The Caesars' written in the 1830s. Discussing a short-lived attempt by Decius (emperor at Rome from AD 249 to 251) to revive the republican institution of the censorship, de Quincey suggested that this proposal 'must be viewed as the very grossest practical anachronism that has ever been committed' – equivalent to 'an attempt, in 1833, to revive the ancient office of *Fool*, as it existed down to the reign of Henry VIII in England'. After explaining what he meant by an anachronism ('in common usage, that sort of blunder when a man ascribes to one age the habits, customs, or the inalienable characteristics of another'), de Quincey separated trivial anachronisms of a few years from the 'far worse kind of anachronism ... where a writer ascribes sentiments and modes of thought incapable of co-existing with the sort or the degree of civilisation then attained, or otherwise incompatible with the structure of society in the age or the country assigned'.[60]

Underlying the new use of anachronism are ideas of societal development elaborated in the Scottish Enlightenment by thinkers such as John Millar and the historian William Robertson as well as notions of history as process derived from German Idealist philosophers. Coleridge himself was certainly well-versed in the writings of the German philosophers, and de Quincey's discussion of anachronism strongly resembles the content of the lectures on Aesthetics that Hegel delivered at Berlin in the 1820s (though it is not known whether he was aware of their contents). Like de Quincey, Hegel contrasts unimportant anachronisms (relating merely to externals) with anachronisms that cross divisions between different cultures or periods (for instance, those that involve a confusion of Christian and ancient Greek concepts). While insisting that the 'essential kernel of a period and a people must be within the poet's ken', Hegel also suggested that the gap between the time of the represented action and the time of the representation inevitably leads to transgressions of naturalness, or what he termed 'necessary anachronisms': 'the inner substance of what is represented remains the same, but the development of culture makes necessary a metamorphosis in its expression and form'.[61] Hegel's slightly older contemporary Goethe expressed a similar vision, albeit with less of a fixation on the mechanisms of the historical process, in an essay on a historical drama by Manzoni: 'The *Iliad* and the *Odyssey*, all the tragedians, and all true poetry that remains for us, lives and breathes only in anachronisms ("lebt und athmet nur in Anachronismen"); the modern is lent to all situations so they can be contemplated, or even endured.'[62] Evidently Goethe is here thinking of anachronism not as literary trope or chronological error, but as a sensitivity to historical change. Anachronism in this sense is for Goethe the precondition of literary creativity: modern habits of thought must be applied by poets, dramatists, and novelists who engage with historical material if they are to make their representations of the past bearable for a contemporary audience.

Even before Hegel the term 'anachronism' had been applied with an eye to period detail. In 1710, for instance, Alexander Pope's correspondent Henry Cromwell explicitly classed as an 'anachronism' the use of 'knightly' in a translation of the first-century AD poet Lucan: using the same spatial metaphor found in Greek *ana-*, he questioned whether chivalry could be traced 'up higher than *Pharamond*' (a legendary king of France).[63] Towards the end of the eighteenth century, moreover, a finely printed series of volumes of *Sepulchral Monuments in Great Britain* spoke of 'the romantic anachronism of honest Lydgate, who represents *Hector* buried in a *Gothic cathedral* in a chapel and tomb of the 12th century' – referring probably both to Lydgate's poem *Troy Book* and to the illustrations that accompanied it in the manuscripts.[64] These assessments of anachronism drew on the contrast between the classical and the gothic or chivalrous.

The impetus for the new use of anachronism (as we shall see in Chapter 2) was a view of history as a process and the growing belief in the possibility of progress in the future. With differences within and between societies now more strongly seen in temporal terms, anachronisms could be identified in the present and across a range of domains: just to draw on some of the usages tracked in the *OED*, phrases and words could be 'linguistic anachronisms' (1864); the masters of the Inns of Court in London could be 'living anachronisms in this age of progress' (1871); and a woman in a novel could be 'a smoldering anachronism, a throwback to one of ... Turgenev's heroines' (1952).

In whatever domains it is applied, the idea of anachronism as obsolescence implies a judgement on the direction of history. As a political judgement, moreover, any claim of anachronism is itself subject to revision over the course of successive generations or even within a single lifetime. A wry acknowledgement of this capacity of judgements about anachronism to become themselves anachronisms was made by Evelyn Waugh in the Preface to the 1962 re-issue of his novel *Black Mischief*: 'Thirty years ago it seemed an anachronism that any part of Africa should be independent of European administration. History has not followed what then seemed its natural course.'[65] (Half a century on and the very title of Waugh's work appears an offensive anachronism to many.) A more accelerated sense of change was expressed by an American feminist on a visit to Britain in 1926 to whom 'it seemed an anachronism to be going to a suffrage meeting' – even though female suffrage had been introduced in the US only six years earlier (two years after women over the age of thirty were allowed to vote in the UK).[66] Whatever the perceived speed of change, the refrain 'it seemed an anachronism' acknowledges the subjectivity involved in claims about the direction taken by history.

The politics of anachronism are laid bare in the writings of James Harvey Robinson, a leading exponent of the self-styled 'New History' in the United States in the first half of the twentieth century. Dismissing the study of the distant past, the 'New History' aimed to draw lessons not from the exemplary actions of individuals but from the historical process itself. For Robinson, 'the long-disputed sin against the Holy Ghost' was 'the refusal to cooperate with the vital principle of betterment': 'History would seem, in short, to condemn the principle of conservatism as a hopeless and wicked anachronism.'[67] Conservatives would presumably beg to differ – and even progressives might now be more inclined to ask who it is that claims to judge on behalf of History.

The historian's unforgivable sin

The nineteenth century saw a range of developments in the practice of historiography in which the concept of anachronism played a part. The professionalization of the discipline was accompanied by the collection and exploitation of many new sources. At the same time, there was a heightened attention to the importance of the historian's perspective and to the problems involved in drawing connections between past and present, especially in the wake of the enthusiastic use of classical paradigms in early stages of the French Revolution. The failure of the revolutionary attempt to revive ancient republican virtue was targeted by the French historian N. D. Fustel de Coulanges both in his inaugural lecture in 1862 and in the preface to *The Ancient City*, his groundbreaking 1864 study of religious and civic institutions: in the former he blamed an inadequate understanding of historical difference for the 'inept imitation of antiquity' that led to the Reign of Terror, and in the latter he insisted that the civilizations of Greece and Rome must be studied 'as if they were entirely foreign to us'.[68]

The problem that Fustel highlighted came to be seen over the course of the century as a problem of 'anachronism' – and inflected with the same religious language used by James Harvey Robinson to denounce the opponents of progress. The year after Fustel's death, the historian Albert Sorel suggested that for Fustel 'the anachronism of ideas' had been for him 'the sin without mercy' ('le péché sans miséricorde').[69] By the 'anachronism of ideas', Sorel evidently meant any projection of conceptions distinctive to historians' own times back to the times of their subjects.

The religious tone of the debate over historical method was continued in the twentieth century in the Annales school (known for its focus on the long-term history of societal development). In a study of the religious views of François Rabelais, Lucien Febvre (along with Marc Bloch the leading early representative of the Annales methodology) took issue with the claim that Rabelais could be classified as an atheist. The prevailing mentality of sixteenth-century France was one of largely unthinking participation in the rituals of the Catholic Church. Could Rabelais live in this world and be an atheist? For Febvre, to present him as such was 'like giving Diogenes an umbrella and Mars a machine gun' and an example of what he termed 'the worst of all sins, the sin that cannot be forgiven – anachronism'.[70]

The problems of anachronism were debated in British writing on historiography too. Here the debate particularly focused on what Herbert Butterfield castigated in a 1931 polemic as *The Whig Interpretation of History* – an evolutionary interpretation of British history that saw a seamless development from early Anglo-Saxon liberty towards the parliamentary democracy that arose in the aftermath of the Glorious Revolution of 1688. This interpretation of British history came under particular fire from legal historians such as F. W. Maitland, who decried anachronism as an offence against 'taste'.[71] Developing the lessons of this revisionary legal scholarship, Butterfield himself concluded that 'the study of the past with one eye, so to speak, upon the present' is 'the source of all sins and sophistries in history, starting with the simplest of them, the anachronism'.[72]

In recent decades anachronism has become a catch-all term for the problem of historical hindsight. Typical is its role in methodological debates within the history of political thought: Quentin Skinner, the leading figure in the contextualist 'Cambridge school', argued in a 1969 article 'Meaning and Understanding in the History of Ideas' that 'knowledge of the social context' of a text helps to avoid the 'anachronistic mythologies' that arise when the text itself is the sole focus of study.[73] By 'mythologies' Skinner means the 'historical absurdities' that he believes arise from studying what a writer says without reference to its historical context or any awareness of the risk of retrojecting later conceptual developments. The history of political thought is not one of timeless wisdom, but of writers responding to highly specific circumstances using and developing the ideas available to them.

Condemnation of anachronism has been accompanied by a growing readiness to acknowledge that the sin is unavoidable. This shift of perspective is reflected by a variation in the religious imagery applied to anachronism. In an essay published in 1926, the constitutional historian A. F. Pollard spoke of anachronism as 'the historian's evil spirit': 'he cannot help its dogging his steps, because he is seeking to tell the truth about earlier times, when he can only think in the terms of the present and write in a language clogged with later accretions.'[74] The persistence of the religious imagery points to an underlying anxiety about the lack of temporal co-ordination between words and the things they describe. Whether explored under the heading of anachronism or of related terms such as hindsight or historical distance, the problems of representing the past in all its difference remain intensively discussed by both philosophers and historians.

A provocative critique of denigrations of anachronism is advanced by Jacques Rancière. Rancière directs his attack on Febvre's work on Rabelais as well as on the *longue durée* approach of the Annales school. Developing a *reductio ad absurdum* in which Annales methodology renders historical change, the object of its inquiries, impossible, Rancière argues that Febvre's repudiation of the possibility that Rabelais could have been an atheist goes beyond claiming that something did not happen to claiming that it could not have happened. Rancière constructs instead a complex model in which anachronism as a concept is misappropriated to provide support for a theory of time that guarantees historical truth (it is in this context that he claims that the *ana-* prefix provides a bridge from the transience of mortal time to eternity, now viewed not as the realm of divine immanence but in terms of discrete historical periods freed from anachronistic disruptions). Thinking that which is unthinkable within existing cultural frameworks creates an 'anachrony', a moment when an individual's ideas cannot be explained by the prevailing mentality.[75]

Rancière's thought emerged from a seminar on anachronism held at the École des Hautes Études en Sciences Sociales in 1991–2 as part of its research programme 'Usages modernes de l'Antiquité'. Another contributor to the series was ancient historian Nicole Loraux, who developed her contribution into paradoxical praise for the practice of anachronism by historians. Loraux emphasized that any attempt to work on history as distant as that of Ancient Greece necessitated some anachronism in the construction of analogies between past and present. Her critique was in part aimed at the anthropological method of ancient cultural and intellectual historians such as Jean-Pierre Vernant and Pierre Vidal-Naquet. She argued that their approach emphasized the difference between ancient and modern at the expense of connections that might make the past comprehensible. The practice of leaving conceptual terms untranslated, for example, avoided the anachronism of importing later meanings into Greek-derived terms that had accreted meaning through centuries of political change, but laid itself open to the counter-charge of denying the possibility of connection across time. While the practices of anthropological historians asserted a separation of past from present, Loraux embraced the use of anachronistic analogies as a means of enabling understanding.[76] In support of her position, she cited the Athenian amnesty in which the re-united Athenians agreed to forget the crimes committed during the oligarchy of 404–403 BC so as not to hinder the reconstruction of their democracy.[77] For Loraux this event held specific lessons which might help the French to overcome the Vichy regime's legacy of distrust and division.[78]

This chapter has traced the development of the word 'anachronism' since its first secure attestation in Greek AD c. 200. Greek *anachronismos* was used chiefly in scholarly exegesis of classical texts. The word then entered Latin with the dispersal of Greek learning after the fall of Constantinople, before emerging in French, Italian and English in the late sixteenth and early seventeenth centuries. In keeping with the Greek usage, the term was first employed in literary contexts, typically of allusions to institutions or toponyms that were not yet in existence at the time of the events described in the text. It next came to be applied to mistakes in the fixing of dates. In the wake of an increasing attention to historical periodization, anachronism began in the nineteenth century to be used of anything thought obsolete.[79] And since then it has been used variously to denote the adoption of a presentist or teleological perspective; in relation to a general sense of the past as different; and, most recently, to convey the multitemporality of the human experience of life.

What does the history of the word 'anachronism' tell us? We have already seen some reason to be cautious in mapping its development against changing perceptions of time: *prolepsis* did in the Latin commentary tradition much the same work that *anachronismos* did in the Greek. We should exercise a similar caution before assuming too readily that changes in the term over the last two centuries support the many scholars of the history of temporality who have posited a rupture in historical consciousness at around the time of the French Revolution.

If we look beyond the lexical level, many passages from classical authors speak to the historicizing usage (Coleridge's 'practical anachronisms') as well as to the other meanings anachronism has acquired. This book as a whole will explore the relevance of the different connotations of anachronism to classical antiquity, with succeeding chapters following the changing uses of the word. We will be applying the term in ways that go beyond the use of anachronism (or related words such as prolepsis) in antiquity, but we hope to show that the anachronism involved in this enquiry is a productive one. As a first step before this chronological journey starts, however, we need to consider the various ways in which the concept of a 'sense of anachronism' (understood as an awareness of the distinctiveness of different historical periods) has been used to structure modern histories of historical understanding. It is to the use of this concept as a way of policing the borders of modernity that we turn in the next chapter.

2

Anachronistic Histories

Borges and Cervantes: A chivalrous pursuit

Jorge Luis Borges' famous tale 'Pierre Menard, Author of the *Quixote*' tells of an imaginary contemporary writer who sets out to write *Don Quixote* – not by crudely transcribing the classic text written by Miguel de Cervantes in the early years of the seventeenth century, but by composing himself, after many crossings out, after all the frustrations of literary creation, pages that coincide word for word with Cervantes' version. Borges' conceit turns on the fact that the sections Menard manages to complete demand to be interpreted differently from Cervantes' originals. Menard's writing of a chapter where Don Quixote tussles between the relative merits of war and literature before concluding he prefers the former is a richer and more ambiguous text, Borges' narrator claims, than the original – given that Menard was writing in the age of Bertrand Russell, an age with different attitudes to militarism. The story then picks out Menard's (re-)crafting of the following phrase for particular analysis: 'truth, whose mother is history, rival of time, depository of deeds, witness of the past, exemplar and adviser to the present, and the future's counsellor'. In the original version, these words are 'a mere rhetorical praise of history'. But as written by Menard, the view of truth and history is 'astounding' and 'brazenly pragmatic'. Menard's work is also celebrated for its use of language. While Cervantes 'handles with ease the current Spanish of this time', Menard's 'archaic' style is a jarring affectation. He has succeeded, Borges' narrator concludes, in enriching the 'rudimentary art of reading' with a new technique, 'deliberate anachronism'.[1]

Borges' sensitivity to the cultural and chronological gap between Cervantes and Pierre Menard chimes with the view of developments in historical consciousness posited by many influential modern philosophers of history. A strong break in conceptions of time is often thought to occur in the second half of the eighteenth century. The notion of history as 'exemplar and adviser to the present, and the future's counsellor' presupposes, it is claimed, a view of an unchanging human landscape – a view that came under fire from the historicizing trends in eighteenth-century German thought and from the political disruption of the French Revolution. Modern philosophers of history tend to see the human experience of time as context-specific rather than universal. Different understandings of time hold sway in different periods, and these understandings determine the other intellectual modes available to the culture in question.

An influential exponent of this position is the French historian François Hartog, whose *Regimes of Historicity* (2003) offers a model of changing perspectives on the past, charting the ways in which the past and future are viewed from the present. For Hartog, a conception of the past as providing examples for future action was prevalent in historiography from antiquity until the start of the revolutionary period in France. The French Revolution marks the beginning of an acceleration of history (the regime of modernity), and this temporal acceleration sets in motion the forces creating Hartog's third regime, the 'presentist' regime of memory and heritage that has held sway since the end of the Cold War.

Hartog's model is informed by the writings of the German philosopher of history Reinhart Koselleck (1923–2006). Koselleck suggests that European historical thought in the medieval and early modern periods was given its orientation by Christian eschatology. Particular historical events, such as the conflict between the Holy Roman Empire and the Turks, were seen as iterations of the conflict between Christ and Antichrist, and were interpreted in relation to the Final Judgement as prophesied in the Book of Revelation. In this mode of temporal understanding (similar to Hartog's regime of exemplarity), past, present and future exist on a 'common historical plane', an experiential continuum in which the future can be predicted owing to the expectations derived from knowledge of the past. This historical orientation was gradually undermined as a result of the Reformation, the wars of religion during the sixteenth and seventeenth centuries, and the Enlightenment. What occurs as a result of these interlocking historical and intellectual upheavals is a 'temporalization (*Verzeitlichung*) of history'. As a teleological conception of the future based on the certainties of Christian theology is replaced by that of a domain determined by human concerns and projects, planning and rational calculation replace eschatology and prophecy as the dominant modes through which futurity is conceived. A philosophy of historical process detaches humanity from its past, opening up the progressive future that is distinctive to modernity, characterized for Koselleck by the 'increasing speed with which it approaches us' and its 'unknown qualities': a gap developed over the second half of the eighteenth and the first half of the nineteenth centuries between the 'space of experience' (perceptions generated by the past) and the 'horizon of expectation' (anticipation of the future).[2]

While the language used by Koselleck is rooted in German philosophy, especially the hermeneutic thought of Hans-Georg Gadamer, Anglo-American scholars have tended to formulate changes in historical consciousness in terms of the development of a 'sense of anachronism'. They have also focused much more on the humanist philology of Renaissance Italy than on the German Reformation as the motor of historical change. A new awareness of historical difference is seen as spreading north from Italy: one classic study of historical thought in Tudor England proposes that 'the importation of Italian humanism introduced first, and most important, the concept of anachronism'; with the introduction of this concept (glossed as the perception that 'the past was different from the present'), historians are said to have sought after 'those things which made for uniqueness rather than for similarity'.[3]

The history of art has played a prominent part in these debates over shifting understandings of time. One of that discipline's most renowned figures, the German Jewish scholar Erwin Panofsky, did not himself use the language of 'anachronism' as a shorthand for the discovery that the past was different from the present, preferring instead to speak of an awareness of historical 'distance' (that is, a consciousness that humans contemplating past events were removed in time from the objects of their observation).[4] He illustrated this awareness in a study of a sketchbook that belonged to Giorgio Vasari, whose *Lives of the Artists* is often hailed as a foundational text in the discipline of art history. Vasari's decision to enclose a drawing attributed to the thirteenth-century artist Cimabue within an architectural frame from what he saw as a parallel period of development marks for Panofsky a self-consciousness of historical distance.[5] In his monograph *Renaissance and Renascences in Western Art*, Panofsky groups this self-consciousness with the discovery of spatial perspective as two distinctive features of the Italian Renaissance (by contrast with earlier periods when a sense of renewal was felt). While a British historian speaks of Panofsky's analysis of Vasari's sketch as offering the best account of the creation of a 'sense of anachronism',[6] Panofsky himself uses 'anachronism' only of specific stylistic breaches: in his essay on Vasari's sketchbooks, he applies the term to some unavoidable lapses in the artist's historicism, while in *Renaissance and Renascences* he uses a shift from unconscious anachronism (figures from antiquity depicted in knightly guise) to deliberate anachronism (Raphael giving Apollo a modern lyre) to illustrate the new self-consciousness of the Renaissance.[7]

Despite the stress on the Italian Renaissance as an inaugural moment, narratives focused around the idea of anachronism have allowed for a gradual development over the course of the centuries in which Koselleck plots the temporalization of history. Panofsky himself thought that artistic anachronism persisted in Northern Europe until the eighteenth century. Similarly, the idea of a timeless human nature is seen as lingering in some areas. The survey of the concept of anachronism in Ritter's *Dictionary of Concepts in History* concludes that 'although the growth of anachronist consciousness is clearly displayed in painting, sculpture, and philology from the fifteenth century onwards, the new sensibility was ironically slow to emerge in the writing of history itself ... Only in the late 18th and early 19th centuries did the awareness of anachronism finally triumph in historiography.'[8]

How does classical antiquity fit into these narratives? Categories such as historical process and progress have played much the same role in accounts of ancient Greece and Rome as they do in Koselleck's analysis of pre-modern Europe. J. B. Bury, one of the most notable intellectual historians of the early twentieth century, suggested in lectures on the ancient Greek historians delivered at Harvard in 1908 that the cyclical theories prominent in antiquity were dropped in the Christian era, when 'the historical process was for the first time definitely conceived as including past and future in a totality which must have a meaning'; they were then resumed in the Renaissance before being 'abandoned once more' in the eighteenth century 'for the idea of indefinite progress'.[9] Bury's terms were echoed half a century later by Moses Finley in a shorter and more damning introduction to the Greek historians: 'there was no idea of progress ... and therefore there was no reason to look to the past for a process of continuing growth'.[10] A more complex picture was presented at about the same time by the historian of political thought J. G. A. Pocock (then based, like Finley, in Cambridge) at the start of a now classic book on the ancestral constitution in English legal thought. Pocock suggested that the Greeks and Romans 'did not quite reach the point of postulating that there existed, in the past of their own civilization, tracts of time in which the thoughts and actions of men had been so remote in character from those of the present as to be intelligible only if the entire world in which they had occurred were resurrected, described in detail and used to interpret them'; a strong recognition of difference, Pocock continued, was precluded by the lack of a 'sense of organized dependence on the past' and of 'the means of studying and interpreting this dependence', especially in circumstances when tradition came under attack.[11] While Pocock is focusing on historical approaches to English common law rather than the Enlightenment sense of progress, he is just as prone as Bury and Finley to the use of later concepts as an exclusionary mechanism.

The concept of anachronism has been exploited for this same rhetoric of exclusion. One introduction to historical thought begins by speaking of 'the awareness of anachronism' as 'lacking in ancient and medieval historians'.[12] Peter Burke's chapter on 'The Sense of Anachronism' in his 1969 classic *The Renaissance Sense of the Past* does at least allow some sense of historical perspective to the Romans – though it denies any such perspective to both the Greeks and the Middle Ages: following Bury and the philosopher R. G. Collingwood, he thinks that the Greeks' historical imagination was thwarted by a restriction of the bounds of knowledge to the realm of the permanent, thereby excluding changing historical circumstances.[13] As with the once popular but now discarded opposition between the cyclical thought of the Greeks and the linear conceptions of time in the Judaeo-Christian tradition,[14] a partial reading of a single Greek philosopher, Plato, is made to stand for the perceptions of the Greeks *tout court*.

A different development is plotted by the American historian Zachary Sayre Schiffman in his 2011 book *The Birth of the Past*. While Schiffman regards the narrative ambition of ancient historians as unsurpassed, he argues that the ancients lacked a conception of 'the past' and so did not have 'an idea of anachronism'. They conceived what we name history as 'things that had passed', in a way which did not 'entail a sense of difference between past and present', and consequently did not 'constitute the past as an intellectual construct'; instead, they 'conceived of multiple "pasts" characterized by different time frames, each disassociated from the next', and 'could not subsume these pasts under a single entity – "the" past – because they could not integrate these time frames'. Schiffman does allow that the ancients 'perceived "local" distinctions between past and present', but dismisses these distinctions as 'sporadic and naïve'.[15] Schiffman shares with the philosophers of history mentioned above a perception that what is distinctive about modern temporality must be placed in contradistinction to antiquity's under-negotiated temporal consciousness. By charting the development of concepts such as 'anachronism' and 'the past' in the Renaissance, and their maturity in the eighteenth century, he relegates classical authors to achieving only localized anachronism.

The goal of this chapter is to explore and criticize the way anachronism has been used to structure narratives of historical consciousness. By analysing some notable examples of classical reception at the historical turning points that typically provide support to these accounts, it will probe both the accounts themselves and the methodological assumptions underlying them. As a first step, we may return to Borges' story of Pierre Menard and his anachronistic re-writing of *Don Quixote*.

Borges' story, as we have observed, is supported by the assumption that the age of Cervantes is separated from the present by a wide cultural gap. As a fable about reading, it suggests that to engage with a classic work such as *Don Quixote* is to be involved in an anachronistic encounter; it could even be interpreted as a story about the anachronism of all acts of reading and interpretation – no matter how far removed they are from the worlds of the original. But a closer reading suggests that the rich ambiguity with which Borges' creation, Pierre Menard, is endowed is partly the result of a deliberately obtuse reading of Cervantes.

Don Quixote is the great forebear of Borges' metafictional play. The sentence that Borges' narrator ruthlessly historicizes – the description of history as 'witness of the past, exemplar and adviser to the present, and the future's counsellor' – is a deliberate cliché. In context, it is a critique of the faithlessness of the invented Arab historian Cid Hamet Ben Engeli, on whose account of Quixote Cervantes' narrator conveniently stumbles after his first source breaks off at a climactic moment in a duel (Cid Hamet, despite his supposed propensity for lies, then becomes the main source of the story).[16] The whole story of Quixote, moreover, is an affectionate parody of the exemplary ideal as expressed in chivalric romance. Quixote himself invokes the exemplary model when he hears of the accounts of his exploits that have appeared (including Cid Hamet's): he cites famous men of times past who were calumniated by malicious contemporaries, including Alexander, who 'is said to have had a little smack of the drunkard'.[17] The accusation of malice is a response of sorts to the challenge to traditional models of exemplarity posed by conflicting accounts about supposedly virtuous heroes, but is scarcely a serious defence of exemplarity itself.

Quixote's own attachment to exemplarity is revealed to be an anachronism. The only other passage to which Borges alludes directly, the disquisition on the relative merits of war and literature, is a parody of what was a commonplace topic at the time Cervantes was writing. The normal solution was to view arms and letters as complementary rather than opposed; Quixote's choice of arms over letters is a throwback to (his own perception of) the values of the age of chivalry. Quixote himself, moreover, recognizes that his own idealization of warfare is an anachronism: he laments the changes in warfare produced by 'powder and lead' which now make the valiant hero vulnerable to a chance shot from a coward.[18]

The treatment of anachronism in 'Pierre Menard' turns out to be more complicated than the narrator's glosses initially lead us to expect. Borges' story asks to be read not just as a fable about the anachronism of reading but also as a warning against reducing the history of historical consciousness to a series of binary contrasts between past and present. As we shall see, it is a warning that retains its value amidst the proliferating explorations of ideas of the past in modern scholarship.

Petrarch and Valla: Forging anachronism

'In the history of the sense of history, it is difficult not to start with him.' Thus Peter Burke half a century ago on the poet and scholar Francesco Petrarca (Petrarch, 1304–74) – though he acknowledged at the same time that descriptions of Petrarch as 'the first modern man' had fallen out of fashion.[19] The division between the (pre-modern) Middle Ages and the (early modern) Renaissance has been even more forcefully questioned in the decades since Burke wrote,[20] but Petrarch continues to play a leading role in debates about developments in ideas of the past.

The distinctive historical sensitivity attributed to Petrarch tends to be located in his attitude to classical antiquity. Petrarch, it is often noted, applied imagery of darkness not to pagan antiquity, as many earlier Christian writers had done, but to the period since the decline of Roman civilization. Overcome with malaise at this sense of cultural decline, he tried to recover as much of classical antiquity as he could, whether by searching for unknown manuscripts, by emending the corrupt text of Livy, or by commissioning (with Boccaccio) a Latin translation of Homer. In addition, he tried to bridge the chasm separating himself from the peaks of Roman literary achievement by writing letters to classical authors, including not just staples of school curricula such as Cicero but also writers whose works were almost entirely lost (the polymath Varro, the orator and historian Asinius Pollio). In these letters, he at the same time gauges his distance from the pagan past by the precision with which he marks the time and place of their composition: the subscription of his letter to Livy (*Letters to Friends* 24.8), for instance, starts 'from the world above, in the part of Italy and the city in which you were born and buried', and then zooms in to a specific Christian site ('in the vestibule of the Virgin Justina and before the actual monument of your tomb') and date ('on February 22nd in the year 1351 since the birth of the One whom you would have to have lived a little longer to know or hear of').[21] But while Petrarch's letters bask in a sense of loss, they are also exercises in spiritual communion: he expresses the wish that Livy could have lived in his own day or he himself in Livy's, so that they could have conversed about the great heroes of Republican Rome. Petrarch expresses here a sense of temporal displacement that has led a modern Renaissance scholar to call him 'a living anachronism'.[22]

Petrarch has at the same time been credited with a pivotal role in the discovery of a sense of anachronism.[23] His awareness of anachronism is most commonly illustrated by a letter (*Letters of Old Age* 16.5) he wrote in 1361 to Holy Roman Emperor Charles IV, who had consulted him about some privileges supposedly granted to Austria (at that time a Duchy within the empire) by his eleventh-century predecessor Henry IV.[24] Those privileges were themselves based on earlier grants supposedly made by Julius Caesar and Nero, but both Henry's grant and the Roman precedents had in fact been forged at the instigation of Rudolf IV, the Hapsburg Duke of Austria. After receiving the text of these grants from Charles IV, Petrarch replied with a scornful dismissal of their authenticity. He pointed to usages that were at odds with conventions during the time of Caesar (notably the dating formula, which included a regnal year rather than the names of the consuls) and with the character of Nero (who was notoriously scornful of religion, yet here styled himself *amicus deorum*, 'friend of the gods'). He also pointed to some linguistic features that he claimed were later than the age of Caesar – features that we could classify as anachronisms: thus Caesar used the plural 'we' for himself, a form that in Caesar's time, Petrarch claims, was starting to be used by flatterers, but that was not employed by Caesar himself; and Caesar also includes the title 'Augustus', which was first adopted by his successor – an error that could be spotted by everyone except 'this jackass now braying so rudely'. More broadly, Petrarch objected to what he described as the 'rough and recent' style of the Latin. The forgers, one modern scholar concludes, 'were living in the Middle Ages' and 'wholly without the historical perspective to notice that Julius Caesar was not likely to employ "Augustus" as an honorific' – whereas 'Petrarch naturally had that perspective'.[25]

The sense of anachronism that is thought to underlie Petrarch's exposure of the inauthenticity of the ancient grants is rooted in philology. He supports his comments on Caesar's avoidance of the first-person plural by citing letters written by Caesar himself – thereby flaunting his own greatest scholarly discovery, the Verona manuscript of Cicero's correspondence with Atticus in which Caesar's letters were quoted. Less spectacularly, he cites a range of other authorities in his letter, among them Suetonius, Florus and Orosius.

The modern scholar can nonetheless point without much trouble to elements of Petrarch's argument that seem to betray some philological naivety. Does the use of the first-person singular in three private letters justify the assumption that

Caesar could not have adopted the plural form in a public decree?[26] And why should the impious Nero not have adopted hypocritically the title 'friend of the gods'? Petrarch also seems rash when he uses the poet Lucan's account of the civil war between Pompey and Caesar as evidence of historical developments in flattery at Rome, or again when he takes a speech denouncing kingship attributed to Scipio in Livy's account of the Second Punic War as evidence for attitudes more than a century and a half later.

The shaky philological argumentation in Petrarch's unmasking of the forgery is matched by some anachronistic slips he makes in his correspondence with the ancients. Unaware that two separate authors, father and son, were covered by the name 'Seneca', he thinks that a remark about a certain Quintilian in (the elder) Seneca's *Controversiae* alludes to the famous educational writer, who was born at about the time this Seneca died (*Letters to Friends* 24.7). And in a long letter to Homer (24.12) Petrarch refers to a story that the poet was treated as a madman at Athens, even though there is an anachronistic reference to coinage (the poet was fined 'fifty drachmas') in his likely source, Diogenes Laertius, *Lives of the Philosophers* 2.43, which he knew in a Latin translation; he then adds an anachronism of his own by calling Athens 'the most scholarly city', a retrojection of the intellectual position acquired by Athens in the fifth century BC.[27]

A further problem with attributing to Petrarch a new conception of anachronism is that he betrays no consciousness of any such novelty himself. On the contrary, he attributes to the forger himself a theoretical consciousness of historical difference, however inept his practice. Petrarch comments, for instance, that the forger's style as a whole is 'far from what it wishes to appear – namely from antiquity and the style of Caesar', but that 'a notion of antiquity, striven for childishly' does stand out 'in individual words'.[28] Petrarch's judgement can be supported by Nero's description of himself as 'a friend of the gods', a phrase which evidently places him in an age of polytheism as insistently as Petrarch's use of Christian dating formulae separates him from his beloved classical correspondents. What Petrarch parades, then, is not a new sense of anachronism, but an improved use of philology in the tackling of forgery.[29]

Accounts of the role of anachronism in the development of historical criticism often suggest that the potential unlocked by Petrarch was fully realized by Lorenzo Valla (1407–57).[30] Valla wrote a variety of philosophical and philological treatises, including important studies of the Latin language and of the text of the New Testament. He was also commissioned to produce the first Latin translation of Thucydides. The work for which he has been more celebrated in histories of historical thought, however, is his declamation *On the Forged and Mendacious Donation of Constantine*.³¹ The Donation was a document supposedly composed by Constantine, the first Roman emperor to convert to Christianity, which gave the Pope control over the western lands of the empire. Valla's treatise (written in 1440 when he was secretary to Alfonso, King of Naples and Sicily, a political opponent of the papacy) used in expanded form the same sort of arguments, and the same rhetoric of abuse, that Petrarch had deployed against the exemptions supposedly granted to Austria.³²

Valla's polemic paid attention to what he claimed were egregious factual and stylistic errors. At one point he notes that the text of the Donation referred to 'Constantinople', and yet at the time it was meant to have been composed 'the city was still Byzantium, not Constantinople' (45). Elsewhere, drawing on the attention to the historicity of Latin that he employed in his philological writings, he claims that the 'barbarous way of talking' in the Donation attests that 'this nonsense was not concocted in the age of Constantine' (57). And he took particular delight in contrasting its style with the classicizing idiom of Constantine's adviser, Lactantius: 'Come back to life, Lactantius, just for a moment, and shut up the gross and monstrous braying of this ass.... Did imperial scribes in your time talk like that?' (43).

The weight traditionally given to Valla's treatise in the story of anachronism has come under attack in recent scholarship. For one thing, it has been noted that Valla did not apply his philological skills to the Donation itself: some of his polemic is directed at errors in the copy of the text he was using. Valla has also been criticized for not taking account of the variations in fourth-century Latin: he relied on the Ciceronian Latin of Lactantius as his standard rather than the diplomatic Latin attested by inscriptions.³³ Far from exposing the Donation as a forgery, moreover, Valla is seen by recent scholars as initiating a change in the conception of documents. Others both before and during Valla's lifetime were sceptical that the text of the Donation derived from the time of Constantine, but they had seen it as apocryphal rather than forged. But though Valla initially (4) speaks of the Donation in the same terms in which Cicero (*On Duties* 3.39) alludes to Plato's self-consciously 'fabricated and fictitious' tale of Gyges' ring of invisibility,³⁴ he goes on (38) to berate its author as a 'falsifier' (*falsarius*) who is guilty of a 'most shameless lie' (*imprudentissimum ... mendacium*). He also pays attention to the materiality of the text, asking why it was written on papyrus rather than inscribed on stone or bronze (39) and how its author could claim in the text itself that he had left it on the body of St Peter (66). That is, Valla turns into a deliberate forgery a text whose aim may have been to supply through an obvious historical fiction an aetiology for the expansion of the church's concerns beyond the spiritual.[35]

Questions have been raised, too, about the extent to which Valla's philology was specifically concerned with categories of time. One scholar has stressed that Valla (like Petrarch before him) lacks a single concept such as anachronism to denote temporal errors.[36] And Margreta de Grazia goes even further by arguing that 'the treatise's philological analyses' are not concerned with 'temporal discrepancies' at all: 'It is not the forger's anachronisms that incense Valla, but his barbarisms. He denies Constantine's authorship of the document not because it refers to phenomena that postdate Constantine but because he never would have written such bad Latin.' Valla's text should be seen, she suggests, more as a rhetorical display-piece than as evidence of increasing chronological sophistication.[37]

The rhetorical style of Valla's attack on the Donation of Constantine seems to tell against a strong concern for historical difference. Towards the start of the thesis, he presents himself addressing an imagined gathering of kings and princes, asking them whether they, had they been in Constantine's place, would have considered ceding so much power; his transhistorical argument for powerful rulers' tendency to expansionism is capped by the example of Alexander of Macedon (7). Valla subsequently presents three imaginary attempts to dissuade Constantine from his proposed course of action: first his sons deliver a speech, then a spokesman for the Roman senate and people, and finally Pope Sylvester; with some rhetorical aplomb, he makes the Romans invoke the spirit of Brutus avenging the rape of Lucretia (17) while Pope Sylvester uses exclusively biblical and Christian examples of the spiritual dangers of worldly power (21–6).

While Valla's treatise owes much to his formal training in rhetoric, the temporal dimension in his arguments should not be underestimated. His rhetorical exercises are based on an idealization both of Republican Rome and of the purity of the early Church similar to that which is found in Petrarch's writings. This idealization is based on a rather uncritical acceptance of a myth of simplicity corrupted, but it nonetheless implies a sensitivity to the difference of the past.[38] As for Valla's linguistic arguments, it is true that he makes no attempt to discover *when* the document was written. But his opposition between pure and barbaric Latin is likewise grounded in a sense of before and after: the language of 'barbarism' had been used before the fourth century for impure Latin, but Valla makes it clear that the barbarisms he notes are a sign that 'whoever composed the text of this grant lived long after the time of Constantine' (45).

The notion that Valla did not have at his disposal terminology for dealing with temporal error is also misguided. We noted in the last chapter that the term *prolepsis* was regularly employed in exegetical commentaries throughout late antiquity and the Middle Ages. That term is also used in a commentary on Sallust's *Catilinarian War* that was published in Valla's name in 1491.[39] While the attribution of the commentary to Valla is uncertain, there is no reason to doubt that he could have used the term *prolepsis* had he wanted, at least in relation to anachronisms such as the use of 'Constantinople' for 'Byzantium'. That he did not use it in his treatise on the Donation is probably because it was used of textual anticipations of toponyms that were in use at the time of the author. It was not a suitable weapon with which to disprove the authenticity of a text that purported to have been written earlier than it actually was.

Like Petrarch, Valla was more concerned to expose the crassness of the forger than the novelty of his own historical perspective. And again the explanation for this silence may lie in the fact that the Donation itself, like Rudolf's forged grants, shares something of that sense of historical difference. Like those grants, the Donation evokes the pagan religion of ancient Rome: it starts with a miraculous account of how Constantine, suffering from leprosy, was initially advised by 'the priests of the Capitol' to sacrifice infants and bathe in their blood (6), before he (or *nostra serenitas*, 'our serenity' – a formula adopted from genuine imperial texts) was moved by the sight of their mothers' tears and visited in a dream by the apostles Peter and Paul. Besides this, the Donation uses a more convincing dating formula than the regnal year that prompted Petrarch's scorn: 'given at Rome on the third day before the Kalends of April, when the distinguished consuls were our lord Flavius Constantine Augustus for the fourth time and Gallicanus'.[40] As it happens, that dating is impossible: Constantine was never consul in the same year as Gallicanus, who was consul just once, in AD 330, the year after the fourth consulship of Constantine's son, the future Constantine II.[41] Valla himself was not aware of that objection to the formula: evidently basing his polemic on a corrupt text, he mocked the implausible coincidence that it was the fourth consulship for both consuls.

Our discussion of Petrarch and Valla suggests that the much-vaunted 'sense of anachronism' has been made to do too much work in accounts of the development of Italian humanism. Suggestions that it was their sense of anachronism that enabled Petrarch or Valla to dispute the authenticity of documents gloss over the part played by their philological acumen (even if we have seen reason to question some of their arguments). It may be the case that their fine-grained knowledge of Latin enabled a distinctive sort of appreciation of historical difference – that is, that it led to a qualitative and quantitative shift in the conception of change. But it was nonetheless that acumen, not a discovery of historical difference itself, that enabled them to dismiss the documents.[42]

The ease with which Petrarch uncovered the incompetent forgery of the Austrian grants has been taken to illustrate 'the abyss between north and south' in his time.[43] That philological rift was carried over into the next century, at the time of Valla's dismissal of the Donation of Constantine. But a century later Valla's anti-clerical treatise was to be widely disseminated in print by supporters of the Protestant Reformation. It is to this northern intellectual revolution, and its distant repercussions, that we turn for our final case study.

Altdorfer and Schlegel: Koselleck's pasts

Among the many visitors to Paris in 1804 drawn by the artworks from Germany and Italy looted by Napoleon was the German philosopher and philologist Friedrich von Schlegel. At one time a committed Hellenophile, Schlegel had become increasingly interested in the poetry of ancient India and in the European Middle Ages. Among the works of art he saw in the Louvre was the *Alexanderschlacht*, a panel painting by the German artist Albrecht Altdorfer depicting the victory of Alexander of Macedon over the Persians at the battle of Issus in 333 BC (Fig. 3). One of a series of biblical and historical paintings commissioned by Duke William IV of Bavaria, Altdorfer's work (completed in 1529) sets a highly detailed rendition of the battle in its lower half against a dramatic backdrop of mountains and sea stretching into the distance. Schlegel's response to the work (first published in 1805 in his journal *Europa*) brought to both the painting and its artist the recognition that they continue to enjoy to this day.[44] In recent decades, however, the painting and Schlegel's response have also come to be frequently invoked in debates about shifting understandings of time – debates in which an important role has been played by anachronism.

The inspiration for these uses of Altdorfer and Schlegel is the opening essay in Reinhardt Koselleck's collection *Futures Past* (originally his inaugural lecture at the University of Heidelberg). Koselleck's essay focuses on what he sees as the 'temporalization of history' in the centuries between Altdorfer's painting and Schlegel's visit to Paris. He begins by noting that there is 'a conscious anachronism' in the painting: it shows the battle in progress, but includes details about the result of the battle such as casualty figures on a tablet in the sky as well as on

Fig. 3 Albrecht Altdorfer, *The Battle of Alexander at Issus* (*Alexanderschlacht*) (1529). Altes Pinakothek, Munich.

banners held by soldiers. Koselleck then notes 'another anachronism' that he claims is 'much more obvious to us today' – the style of armour worn by the two armies: 'we believe we see before us the last knight Maximilian [Holy Roman Emperor from 1508 to 1519 and an important promoter of Hapsburg power] or the crowds of *Landsknechts* [mercenaries] at the battle of Pavia [a decisive Hapsburg victory over the French in 1525]'; in addition, 'most of the Persians' are wearing turbans, and so modelled on the Turks, who were laying siege to Vienna at the time Altdorfer was painting. Koselleck concludes that 'the historical event which Altdorfer recorded was for him as if contemporary. Alexander and Maximilian ... move together in an exemplary way; the historical space of experience drew life from the depth of generational unity.'[45]

Koselleck's argument for the timelessness of Altdorfer's painting is reinforced by Christian eschatology. Alexander's conquest of the Persian empire was widely seen in the sixteenth century as the transition from the second to the third of the four empires prophesied in the Book of Daniel; though their interpretation had varied considerably over time, the four animals in the prophecy were generally at this time taken as signifying the Assyrians (or Babylonians), Persians, Greeks and Romans. At the time of Altdorfer's painting, this prophecy was acquiring an acute contemporary relevance. Thanks to the principle of *translatio imperii* enunciated by thinkers such as Otto of Freising, the Roman Empire itself was thought to endure in the Holy Roman Empire founded by Charlemagne. While this idea of continuity was used to validate the authority of the Germanic emperors, it fed apocalyptic fears during the Reformation when it was linked with biblical prophecies such as those of Daniel or the Book of Revelation, which seemed to point to a climactic battle of good against evil (identified by Lutherans with the papacy itself).[46] These eschatological ideas feed into Koselleck's interpretation of Altdorfer's painting: though it celebrates the status of the Hapsburgs within the Empire, the battle waged between Alexander and Darius beneath the cosmic pairing of sun and moon could have been viewed by contemporaries as a figure of the final battle between Christ and Antichrist.

The timeless fusion of past and present that Koselleck detects in the *Alexanderschlacht* contrasts with Schlegel's 'astonishment' at the sight of the painting:

> In long cascades sparkling with thoughts, Schlegel celebrated the work, in which he recognized 'the highest adventure of old knighthood'. He thus gained a historical-critical distance with respect to Altdorfer's masterpiece. Schlegel knew how to distinguish the painting not only from his own time but also from the ancient time which it pretends to represent. For him, history had thereby gained a specifically temporal dimension which is clearly lacking in Altdorfer.[47]

Koselleck here sees the difference between Altdorfer and Schlegel in the development of a sense of period detail.

Koselleck's historical trajectory can easily be questioned. He distinguishes between two types of anachronism: a conscious anachronism relating to narrative arrangement (the anticipation of casualty figures on the banners) and an unconscious anachronism in the depiction of costume (the style of armour and the turbans). That the second sort of anachronism would have been less obvious to Altdorfer's contemporaries, however, is hard to believe. The anachronisms stand out in part because the painting is not uniformly anachronistic. One contrast with current-day modes of fighting is the absence of any weapons fired by gunpowder, such as the cannons that can be found in fifteenth-century illustrations of the *Alexander Romance* or again in a painting of the siege of Alesia, a climactic moment in Julius Caesar's campaigns against the Gauls, in the series of historical paintings commissioned by Wilhelm IV (and also seen by Schlegel in Paris).[48] Altdorfer's painting, by contrast, shows signs of detailed engagement with ancient accounts of Alexander's campaigns.[49] It is true that details from the battles of Issus (the topography and the presence of royal Persian women) and Gaugamela (notably Darius' wounded charioteer) have been merged, but these mergings can themselves be read as a pointed display of the painting's historical consciousness, especially when viewed alongside its attention to antiquarian detail. Especially notable is the scythed chariot in which Darius rides – a type of vehicle described in ancient historical writings and military manuals.[50] In attempting to reproduce this exotic vehicle, Altdorfer was following in a tradition that includes the illustrated manuscripts of the Roman military writer Vegetius and the drawings of Leonardo da Vinci. The selectivity of Altdorfer's anachronism is seen, too, in his portrayal of the Persians. Darius wears an elaborate diadem possibly modelled on ancient accounts of Persian headwear.[51] Some of the Persians, especially those close to the fleeing figure of Darius, are, it is true, wearing head-dresses that resemble turbans, but even these could claim support from accounts of ancient Persian clothing. But in the cavalry clash forcefully depicted in the bottom tier of the painting, the Persians are wearing exactly the same style of full-metal armour with elaborate crests as Alexander's troops. Altdorfer, then, makes the distant battle comprehensible to his audience while also evoking the specificity of the encounter. He deliberately portrays the battle as both familiar and unfamiliar.

The suggestion that Altdorfer's chivalrous depiction of the battle represents a deliberate choice is supported by comparison with contemporary practice. Some of the other historical paintings produced for Wilhelm IV's cycle do portray the past in a stereotypically ancient manner: Burgkmair's painting of Cannae, for instance, presents the confusion of battle from a low vantage point with armour *all' antica*, while, in the parallel series devoted to pagan and Christian heroines, depictions of the suicide of Lucretia and of the Empress Helena receiving the cross (by Breu and Beham respectively) have backgrounds of classical architecture.[52] A sense of period style can be seen, moreover, in some of Altdorfer's other works, for instance a *Crucifixion* painted c. 1520.[53]

The context of Altdorfer's commission further calls into question Koselleck's distinction between two types of anachronism. Clearly depicted on one of the banners on Alexander's side is a Hapsburg eagle – the heraldic emblem of Altdorfer's patron Wilhelm IV and of Wilhelm's uncle, the Emperor Maximilian, before him. That emblem is a clear sign of the painting's propagandistic intent. The point of the propaganda is not, as Koselleck suggests, to merge Alexander with Maximilian, who had been dead for almost ten years when it was commissioned. Rather, it asserts the continuity of the empire against the threat of the Reformation while holding out the hope that Wilhelm IV might become a new Alexander.

That the use of anachronism in Altdorfer's painting was propagandistic is also suggested by the writings of Wilhelm's court historian Johannes Turmaier, generally known as Aventinus.[54] Aventinus is known above all for his *Bavarian Chronicle*, which traces the distant ancestry of the Bavarians but also covers much non-Bavarian history, including a relatively full account of Alexander's campaigns, which are explicitly interpreted in terms of Daniel's prophecies. Among his other writings were works on military strategy and on the Turkish war, and in these he cites Alexander's victory at Issus as an example of how a small force could defeat a larger one, while also pointing to the Turkish incursions into Europe along with Scipio's invasion of Africa as illustrations of the effectiveness of sending troops into enemy territory.[55] The significance of Aventinus for understanding the *Alexanderschlacht* is that it is likely that he both orchestrated Wilhelm's gallery of historical paintings and provided Altdorfer with specific details of Alexander's campaigns. Altdorfer's painting stands in a similar relation to earlier illustrations of Alexander, which often showed fantastic episodes taken from the *Alexander Romance*, as Aventinus' account of Alexander in the *Chronicle* does to popular earlier re-tellings of the *Alexander Romance* which it explicitly sought to surpass.[56] Both painting and chronicle are composed in a style felt to be appropriate for their propagandistic goal, and the anachronisms in the painting can themselves be seen as enacting Aventinus' view that the past offers lessons for the present.

The exemplary quality of Altdorfer's painting should not be equated with a sense of timelessness. It is not just that the painting contains clear hints of historical distance. It is also that the very attempt to establish continuity with the past can itself be a response to a sense of historical rupture – in this case the threat posed by the Turks in Europe which carried with it the prospect of the fulfilment of biblical prophecies. Nor need the idea of the succession of four empires be interpreted as timeless: each empire can be seen as superseding its predecessor in the Christian narrative. It provides a model of periodization that is effaced by Koselleck's exclusive focus on the shift to a modern understanding of historical process.

Koselleck's presentation of Schlegel's response to Altdorfer is as misleading as his reading of Altdorfer's anachronisms. Koselleck, as we have noted, quotes Schlegel's comment that he recognized in the painting 'the highest adventure of old knighthood' and infers from this that Schlegel was conscious of historical difference both between his own day and Altdorfer's and between Altdorfer's and antiquity. Properly understood, Schlegel's discussion points to a more complicated sense of temporality. Key to grasping Schlegel's point are two phrases in the same sentence that Koselleck omits: Schlegel was suggesting that Altdorfer, in portraying the battle as a chivalric adventure, was presenting it 'not in mere imitation of the antique manner', but 'as in medieval poetry'.[57]

Schlegel's chivalrous reading of Altdorfer's painting exemplifies the transformation of attitudes to medieval art and literature during the German Romantic period. Rejecting the universal tenets of French Neoclassicism for reasons of both religion (the anti-Christian tenor of the French Revolution) and patriotism (Napoleon's invasion of the Holy Roman Empire), Schlegel turned to Gothic art and architecture and to chivalric literature. He developed his thoughts on the literature of the Middle Ages in lectures he delivered some years later in which he discussed how chivalric poetry emerged at the time of the Crusades and peaked by the end of the thirteenth century. He saw this period as the youth of the European nations, marked by a spirit of creativity comparable with the spirit which produced the Homeric poems; and one area where this creativity was displayed was in the chivalric re-fashioning of the past, no matter whether poets were dealing with non-classical subjects (the Germanic migrations, the deeds of Arthur) or re-working classical themes such as the Trojan War or the exploits of Alexander, whose deeds 'bear the greatest resemblance to heroic traditions'.[58]

By comparing Altdorfer with the poets of the Middle Ages, Schlegel was endowing him with the sort of temporal consciousness denied him by Koselleck. While conscious of Altdorfer's anachronism (he called the costumes 'throughout Germanic and chivalric'[59]), he was suggesting that it was Altdorfer's choice to depict the battle in a chivalric manner – a more compelling picture than the historically naive figure posited by Koselleck. Altdorfer, after all, was not responding to the Battle of Issus in a vacuum, but following in the wake of numerous chivalric re-imaginings of Alexander: his adviser Aventinus suggested in his *Bavarian Chronicle* that Alexander was better known 'to our people, including the unlearned, than our own kings and emperors, whose names they hardly know'.[60]

The choice that Altdorfer made was for Schlegel one that was available to artists in his own time. Far from using the idea of chivalry to set the painting in an unbridgeable past, as Koselleck suggests, Schlegel was proposing Altdorfer as a possible inspiration for a chivalric revival. He concluded his discussion of the painting by addressing 'the thinking painter who strives after new and grandiose subjects, who wishes to abandon at once the sacred sphere of Catholic symbology and seeks to create a truly romantic painting', and suggesting that 'this little *Iliad* in colours could teach what the spirit of chivalry was and meant'.[61] The comparison with the *Iliad* suggests the sort of comparative approach to the development of chivalry that Schlegel would later offer in his lectures and that had already been articulated by eighteenth-century writers such as Richard Hurd. But the lesson that Schlegel wants to draw from Altdorfer shows that he views the spirit of chivalry as a transhistorical ideal: he concluded the article in which he discussed the *Alexanderschlacht* by urging painters to 'adopt the well-considered creed of the old Dürer, who said: "No, I don't want to paint in the antique manner, or the Italian manner, what I want is to paint in the German manner."'[62] Historical distance is here collapsed further by the brazenly anachronistic words that Schlegel puts in Dürer's mouth: Dürer himself is made to take on the role of national German icon that was thrust on him at the turn of the eighteenth and nineteenth centuries.[63]

The sense of history shown in Schlegel's reading of Altdorfer is much richer than Koselleck allows. Koselleck posits that Alexander and Altdorfer both stood on a common historical plane, but that this plane had been ruptured by the time of Schlegel. But we have seen that there is good reason to allow not only that Altdorfer had a more nuanced conception of historical change, but also that Schlegel was suppressing as much as accentuating the difference between himself and Altdorfer. It is true that Schlegel sees Altdorfer as 'early' in terms of style: he speaks of the painting having 'the stiffness of the old style' and of its workmanship being typical of 'the high style of the old German school'.[64] But these stylistic features were central to Schlegel's exercise in patriotic recuperation. The anachronistically 'German' character of the painting made it an appropriate model for current-day artists (Schlegel notably avoids any comment on the slight *Turquerie* of the turbans).

Anachronism and periodization

We have examined so far in this chapter three case studies where the concept of anachronism has been used as a vehicle for historical periodization: two relating to forgery (Petrarch's exposure of grants supposedly made by Julius Caesar and Nero; Valla's disquisition on the Donation of Constantine) and one centred on an image (Schlegel's reading of Altdorfer's *Alexanderschlacht*). The aim of these case studies has not been to deny that there have been changes in the ways in which historical difference has been configured: in the centuries that divide Altdorfer from Schlegel, the collapse of the model of the four empires and the increasing hold of the idea of progress are just two of the notable changes on which Koselleck's account of the 'temporalization of history' rightly focuses. The problems we have observed should rather be seen as the product of a polarizing use of anachronism. A more nuanced view of change over time can be gained from the metaphor of multiple co-existing temporal layers (*Zeitschichten*) that Koselleck himself elaborates in his trademark conceptual histories (*Begriffsgeschichte*). Koselleck developed this metaphor partly as a way round the opposition between 'linear' and 'cyclical' time: he sees the historical process as structured by patterns of singularity and recurrence, themselves subject to varying processes of change.[65]

The case studies we have presented raise a number of general points about how narratives of historical change are constructed. One feature of many histories of temporal consciousness is their refusal to address adequately the question of what it is at stake in writing a history of time. Whose ideas of the past are we talking about? This question can be asked at a national level: French and German historians such as Hartog and Koselleck have focused on a sense of rupture in the late eighteenth and early nineteenth centuries in part because of the experiences of the French and German peoples at those times (the French Revolution, Napoleon's dissolution of the Holy Roman Empire, incipient German nationalism); historians with a British focus, by contrast, have tended to stress continuities, while post-colonial critics have been particularly concerned to criticize the way in which the static time of the colonized has been opposed to the linear progress embodied in the colonial powers.

The question of identity is relevant at the personal level too. As we have seen, scholars have often structured their stories around a progression of heroic figures who both represent their own moment in history but also stand ahead of it, prefiguring the future course of temporal consciousness (the forgers Petrarch unmasks belong in the Middle Ages while Petrarch himself does not). The problem with this exclusive focus on great names is that at any given historical moment there are multiple different conceptions of the past both across different societies and within one society. Even a single individual may have many different ideas of the past at any one time, and these ideas will change over the course of her or his life.

The need to look beyond a restricted intellectual elite has been seen in our discussion of forgery. Both the faked grants awarded by Caesar and Nero and the text of the Donation of Constantine show some sense of historical perspective, even if they are in other ways vulnerable to the charge of anachronism. In the case of Rudolf IV of Austria, moreover, the very effort to base a claim to authority on grants made by Roman emperors implies a sense of distance not so different from Petrarch's own use of the Roman past for self-validation.[66] The importance of taking a more expansive approach to the history of a sense of anachronism can be illustrated even by cases where forgeries are not spotted: a manuscript history of the monastery of St Augustine of Canterbury which was produced in 1413 displayed a historicizing sensibility towards handwriting by including facsimiles of some forged old documents alongside transcriptions in the style of documents of the copyist's own day.[67]

Another problem in many scholarly approaches to historical representations is their failure to allow for the significance of genre. Accounts of developing historical consciousness have repeatedly made use of paintings and histories. While it is certainly reasonable to try to extrapolate an idea of the past from a painting or an historical account, the idea of the past extrapolated in this way necessarily relates to a representation of the past in a form that can be communicated to others. It does not correspond straightforwardly with the manifold impressions of the past that the creators of those artistic or literary works carry with them over the course of their lives.

The problems that arise from the neglect of genre are particularly clear in the account of the birth of the past offered by Zachary Sayre Schiffman. Schiffman, as we noted earlier, detects only 'local' anachronisms in classical historians such as Thucydides. He proceeds to chart the development of new forms of temporal consciousness first in the Christian era, when there was 'a vision of history as a self-contained entity with a beginning and an end', but 'the immediate connections it fostered between past, present and future ... precluded any sustained idea of anachronism by which to distinguish past from present'; and then in the Renaissance, when there was a sense of a 'living past', 'a synchronous space that preserves temporal differences while annihilating time', involving an increased but still limited consciousness of anachronism. The climax comes with the 'birth of the past' in the French philosopher Montesquieu's *Considerations on the Causes of the Greatness of the Romans and their Decline* (1734). Montesquieu introduces a cross-historical perspective by comparing early Rome with a village in the Crimea in his own day, and again by aligning the clash of ancient Gauls and Romans with the wars of the Mexicans and the Spanish. What distinguishes Montesquieu, in Schiffman's reading, is a 'relational view' that allows him properly to contextualize entities within a unified conception of 'the past'.[68]

Schiffman's bold analysis of the birth of the past fails to address the generic differences between the evidence he deploys for antiquity and for later periods. For antiquity, Schiffman relies on historical narratives. Beyond antiquity, he draws on the analytical genres used by select authors from Montaigne to Montesquieu. As a result of this restricted evidence, Schiffman is able to claim that the ancients looked at the past as a series of separate narratives. But the same claim could equally be made of modern conceptions of the past on the basis of the narratives that modern historians actually produce. It is true that both Greek and Roman writers tend to adopt phrases such as 'the things that have happened' (*ta gegenēmena* in Greek, *res gestae* in Latin), but both cultures offer ample evidence for a view of the past as a linear sequence, and the recurrence of similar patterns (of decline or development or both) in a wide variety of ancient evidence makes it appropriate to speak of a global rather than just a localized sense of anachronism. The evidence discussed in this book will show that many of the tropes which Schiffman sees as post-antique stages on the way towards the birth of the past can be found in antiquity.

The failure in many accounts of historical thought to take account of modes of representation is closely tied to their teleology. That is to say, the discovery of a 'proper' sense of historical difference in a particular era necessarily springs from a reluctance to engage sympathetically with earlier forms of historical representation. The problem of teleology is especially seen in the policing of the division between the modern and the medieval: in the words of two scholars of medieval France, 'by rendering history as a teleological unfolding that leads inexorably to a moment of intellectual awakening (whether in Dante, Petrarch, or Valla) at which time and history are finally grasped for what they truly are, modern historians repeat the gestures of a Whig history they otherwise repudiate'.[69] According to this teleological pattern of thought, medieval illustrations of ancient warriors in knightly garb are dismissed as unconscious anachronisms rather than appreciated as deliberate attempts to familiarize the unknown. But this patronizing view of medieval art is liable to the objection that earlier images *seem* anachronistic only once artists have started to reproduce period styles of clothing.

The related problems of genre and teleology are both illuminated in the French historian Paul Veyne's reflections on the writing of history. For Veyne, *any* historical account implies an understanding of difference: 'An event stands out against a background of uniformity; it is a difference, a thing we could not know *a priori*'.[70] This observation can be illustrated by the beginning of Herodotus' *Histories*. When Herodotus expresses the view that wrong-doing between Greeks and barbarians started (to the best of his knowledge) with the Lydian king Croesus' subjection of the Ionian Greeks (1.5–6), he stresses a cardinal moment of difference in marked opposition to the alleged Persian claim that wrong-doing started with the Phoenicians' seizure of the Argive princess Io (1.1). But equally when Herodotus writes a bit later that 'all the other sophists from Greece arrived at Sardis . . . among them Solon an Athenian' (1.29.1), he is still offering information that is not available to the audience at the level at which they ordinarily engage with the world. In Veyne's words, 'the historian does not exhaustively describe a civilization or a period . . . he will tell his reader only what is necessary so that the latter can picture that civilization starting from what is always taken to be true'.[71] History is difference – even when, to return to our Herodotean example, Solon's arrival is picked out because it makes a difference to Croesus' (and to our) general conceptions of the world.

Veyne's discussion of historical concepts sheds further light on the problems involved in writing histories of anachronism. He suggests that historians tell their selective stories about the past with the help of concepts (such as 'revolution', 'nationalism' or 'capitalism') which facilitate understanding even though their breadth necessarily makes them hard to define. The problem with these concepts, according to Veyne, is not just that they are ill-defined, but also that they do not keep up with the new ways of understanding the world that have emerged since they were formulated. Outmoded though they may be, these concepts are nonetheless used by historians to impose boundaries on the unlimited domain of the historical. The history of historiography, he concludes, is 'partly the history of anachronisms caused by ready-made ideas', and the history book 'is to be seen as a battle-ground between an ever-changing truth and concepts that are always anachronistic', with historians 'in the position of designers of historical monuments'.[72] Veyne's provocative view that all attempts to write the past are transient monuments to its ever-changing difference receives support from the histories of anachronism we have discussed in this chapter. In these histories, the anachronistic concept is precisely the notion of historical difference – and the definitions of both 'historical' and 'difference' are at stake in these anachronisms.

It may be helpful to close these methodological reflections by going beyond the limits of the written and visual evidence with which we have so far been concerned. There is a strong case for claiming that a sense of difference is inherent not just in genres such as historiography and historical painting but also in the processes of human consciousness. The varying conceptions that individuals have of the past will be expressed with different degrees of explicitness and self-reflection, but to be conscious of living in the present is to be aware that the past is different.

Taking account of cognitive processes suggests, too, that observing many forms of textual or visual anachronism is not among the most complex operations carried out by the human brain. When a scholar suggests that Petrarch's 'conception of anachronism' was what 'underlay his understanding of the fact that no knowledge of Christianity could be attributed to Livy',[73] the abstraction of the language glosses over the relative simplicity of the mental operation. The birth of Christ marked the transition from the fifth to the sixth of the ages formulated by Augustine in his *City of God*, and by Petrarch's time it was firmly embedded in the sort of dating formula he used in the subscriptions to his letters to classical authors. To return to an example from our discussion in Chapter 1 of ancient uses of the word 'anachronism', the conceptual grasp shown by a petitioner in Egypt objecting that a document has been dated in the name of the wrong official matches Petrarch's understanding that Livy died before the birth of Christ.

Our concern in this book will not be the anachronism inherent in all historical writing and in all human consciousness but the workings of anachronism in explicit formulations of historical difference across a wide variety of Greek and Roman genres. Applying later conceptions of anachronism to antiquity is, as we have noted, necessarily anachronistic. But, for all that, it is a story worth telling both because it is relatively unfamiliar and because it makes a difference to how we conceive the barriers that separate antiquity and modernity. The need to reconfigure those barriers is suggested by the fact that the structures of the anachronistic histories that have been discussed in this chapter themselves replicate common patterns in accounts of the past in antiquity.

The structural resemblances between ancient and modern patterning of the past will be a theme throughout this book. It will be helpful nonetheless to pick out at this point some of the most notable resemblances. The binary division that we have noted in some modern accounts between simple and complex conceptions of time adopts an opposition found in ancient evolutionary narratives, which often made simplicity the hallmark of 'old' or 'heroic' times. A particularly close link lies in the move that Schiffman sketches from a 'sporadic' to a global sense of anachronism; this move echoes numerous Greek developmental narratives which use the adverb *sporadēn* or cognate words for the 'sporadic' settlement of humans prior to the foundation of towns.[74] Equally significant is patterning in terms of decline rather than development. The two figures who, as we have seen, commonly play a foundational role in the development of historical perspective, Petrarch and Valla, both operate with a notion of decline from the virtues of the Roman republic that is directly inherited from the poets and historians of Augustan Rome; the reason why Petrarch wanted to commune with Livy was not because he saw the Augustan age as a peak of human achievement, but because so much of Livy's account of the nobler republican past had been lost. This conception of decline that Petrarch inherited from Livy can itself, moreover, be seen as a re-working of a notion of a decline from a heroic past that is strongly expressed in the earliest surviving Greek poetry.

It is time now to begin to explore in more detail the different conceptions of anachronism that can be found in antiquity. Following the plot outlined in the previous chapter, we turn first to the origins of anachronism in the literary discourses of late antiquity, to an educational setting where teachers and students sought to understand remote texts that themselves looked back to an even more remote and heroic past.

3

Anachronism and Philology

Creative anachronism in antiquity

Understood in its original sense as the retrojection of later practices, people or objects into earlier periods, anachronism was a persistent feature of all the ancient literary genres (including drama, fiction, biography and historical narrative) that sought to recreate the past. There is much evidence, too, for what might be taken as anachronism in the visual arts in antiquity, including extant vase paintings (Fig. 4) and a range of written sources describing art and artists. Among the latter are two striking stories in Plutarch's *Lives*. The first appears in his life of Cimon (one of the military heroes of fifth-century Athens), where he reports that the painter Polygnotus, while he was painting the sack of Troy for a famous monument (the Stoa Poikile) in the Athenian agora, had an extra-marital affair with Cimon's sister, Elpinice, and painted the Trojan princess Laodice with her features (*Cimon* 4.6). The second story concerns the Athenian statesman Pericles: Plutarch tells how Phidias, the greatest sculptor of the day, decorated the shield of a divine statue with an image of the battle between Theseus and the Amazons that included likenesses both of himself as 'an old bald man lifting a rock on high' and of Pericles fighting with an Amazon, with his face partly covered by a hand holding a spear but easily visible from the sides (*Pericles* 31.3).

These two stories from Plutarch appear to suggest strong disapproval for the intrusion of a contemporary face into an artwork depicting the heroic age. Plutarch expressly states that Phidias' enemies latched on to his self-display, and the fact that the Elpinice story was transmitted at all suggests that Polygnotus' use of her as a model was seen as scandalous – both a product and a reflection of sexual transgression (Elpinice was also accused of an incestuous relationship with her brother). But were these artworks specifically regarded as breaches of *temporal* decorum? The appearance of Pericles' face in an important public monument may have offended because it seemed to celebrate an individual citizen rather than the democratic collective. Similarly, including a living woman's features may have been

Fig. 4 Red-figure skyphos attributed to the Makron painter, Athens, *c.* 490 BC. Paris holds Helen by the wrist as he leads her away; his gesture reproduces one that would have been familiar from Athenian marriage rites. 13.186, Boston, Museum of Fine Arts.

felt as an infringement of societal values. The open display of a high-status citizen woman ran counter to Athenian norms, hinting at sexual deviancy.

Slightly different questions may be raised about the presence of anachronism in literary re-workings of the past. Anachronism can seem little more than a casual feature of the writings of antiquity, as in one version (G 32) of the *Life of Aesop* (a popular work in the Roman imperial period), where Aesop's ability as a speaker is compared with that of the Athenian orator Demosthenes, renowned for his futile resistance to the growing power of Macedon some 200 years after Aesop is supposed to have lived. In other works, anachronism is a much more persistent element, but its very prevalence may raise doubts as to how strongly it was felt. Virgil included in the *Aeneid* (the events of which are set in the aftermath of the sack of Troy) numerous objects that were widely thought to have been invented after the heroic age, including biremes (ships with two banks of rowers), hooked metal anchors, bronze columns, and battering rams for use in sieges (1.182, 1.169, 1.448, 12.706); in one critic's words, the material culture of his poem is marked by a 'pervading modernity'.[1] The appearance of post-heroic elements is frequent, too, in another genre set in the heroic period, Greek tragedy. In the Homeric poems, grooms pay a bride-price, but in a famous speech outlining the sufferings endured by women, the eponymous heroine of Euripides' *Medea* complains that 'we must buy a husband at an exorbitant price' (232–3) – an allusion to the fifth-century BC practice of dowry, and viewed by a modern commentator as 'a normal "anachronism" of tragedy'.[2]

This type of literary anachronism has caused a good deal of controversy in modern scholarship, particularly in discussions of Greek tragedy. Rather than seeing anachronism as 'normal', many scholars of Greek tragedy have dismissed the notion that tragedies could contain anachronistic references as misconceived. In a famous reading of Sophocles' *Oedipus the King* as a meditation on the possibilities and fallibilities of democratic Athens, Bernard Knox offered the strong claim that 'the contemporary reference in all Attic tragedy is so obvious and insistent that the term "anachronism", often applied to details of the tragic presentation of the mythical material, is completely misleading', since 'anachronism is not the exception but the rule'.[3] Approaching the topic through a comparison of Attic tragedy and comedy, Oliver Taplin stressed instead 'the mutual exclusivity of the world of the tragedy and the world of the auditorium', and concluded that 'it is doubtful whether there are any anachronisms in Greek tragedy to be noticed *as such*'. Taplin did acknowledge that 'the best candidates are probably philosophically avant-garde notions', such as a prayer offered by Hecuba in Euripides' *Trojan Women* ('Zeus, whether you are the necessity of nature or the mind of mortal men', 886), which evokes the cosmological speculations of fifth-century thinkers such as Anaxagoras. The Spartan king Menelaus' baffled response ('How newfangled (*ekainisas*) your prayers to the gods are!', 889) seems to contradict Taplin's claim, but he counters that we moderns are 'particularly obsessed with the temporal history of ideas', whereas fifth-century Athenians might have taken Menelaus to be 'commenting on her unconventional phrasing rather than her anachronistic metaphysics'.[4]

Superficially the readings of Knox and Taplin might seem at odds with one another: Knox dismisses anachronisms because they are so common, Taplin because he reads tragedies as thematic and affective unities. But in fact they agree on the cultural contingency of anachronism: Attic tragedy, it is implied, constructs an order of time that cannot properly be understood as either heroic or contemporary. They offer a more nuanced variation on the sense of history revealed in some nineteenth-century dissertations on tragic anachronism: J. A. Stricker, for instance, contrasted ancient audiences' laissez-faire attitude to anachronism with the historical consciousness of their modern counterparts; Rudolf Schwenk similarly opposed the dramatic poets of his own day, who took pains to be historically accurate, with Shakespeare and the Greek tragedians, who 'were not ashamed to imbue events on the stage with the colour of their own times'.⁵ Anachronism is here (as in Koselleck's analysis of Altdorfer and Schlegel (pp. 45–52)) a tool for historical periodization, separating the historically alert citizens of modernity from the naive and credulous inhabitants of the pre-modern world.

A slightly different view is suggested by Pat Easterling in a classic 1985 article. She emphasizes the tragedians' aim of constructing a consistent and recognizably heroic world, and so of avoiding customs or practices that were obviously the products of later ages: hence tragedians' references to writing (which was attested in some representations of the heroic age), but not to books (which would have seemed too modern). While generally suggesting that anachronisms were masked by this sort of 'heroic vagueness', Easterling does nonetheless suggest that they could produce 'startling and ironic effects' to which audiences needed to be receptive.⁶

One of the strengths of Easterling's article is that she pays attention to the treatment of anachronism in ancient scholarship. Temporal breaches were often picked up by commentators, as we can tell from the marginal comments (scholia) in extant manuscripts: the scholia on the *Medea*, for instance, call her reference to dowries 'an anachronism' derived 'from the custom in his own time' and at odds both with the practice in the *Iliad* and with Euripides' other works (scholia on lines 232, 233). For Easterling, this language of anachronism was a sign of disapproval – the implication being that the scholiasts, in seeking to highlight their own more acute sense of temporality, proved themselves less sensitive than the original Athenian audience.⁷

In this chapter we will build on Easterling's approach, but we will look at a broader range of ancient genres and critical traditions. This larger corpus will offer some evidence that supports Easterling's view that anachronisms were disparaged, but also good reason to doubt that bare references to anachronism were necessarily negative. Commentators from antiquity to Byzantium pointing out anachronisms were often putting a finger on literary effects of considerable sophistication. Sensitivity to anachronism was not simply scholarly nit-picking, but symptomatic of an awareness that literature often configures time in counter-intuitive, unsettling ways. We start by sketching the contexts in which these debates over literary temporality took place.

Situating ancient criticism

We saw in Chapter 1 that Greek *anachronismos* and related forms are found almost exclusively in scholia, while Latin equivalents such as *prolepsis* are found in commentaries (such as Servius' on the *Aeneid*) that had a continuous manuscript tradition. On both sides, studying the history of the commentary traditions is difficult. In the case of the *Aeneid*, analysis of manuscripts has led scholars to differentiate the original Servius commentary (early fifth century AD) from a seventh- or eighth-century expansion (known as Servius Auctus) which drew on a more extensive fourth-century commentary by Donatus that was itself one of the sources of the original Servius. For the Greek scholia, by contrast, it is often impossible to ascertain the date or authorship of particular comments. Their origin lies in the numerous commentaries (*hupomnēmata*) produced in the Hellenistic and Roman imperial periods. These commentaries offered in varying proportions historical, allegorical and moral readings of canonical literature as well as glosses on difficult words; over time, and perhaps particularly as a result of the change in reading medium from papyrus roll to codex (similar in form to modern books), scribes extracted notes from these commentaries and included them in copies of texts.

Despite the uncertain history of the scholia, we can be certain that the historical approach revealed by their critical engagement with anachronism took root in the great library founded at Alexandria under the Ptolemies in the third century BC. It was fostered in particular by the most famous scholar of the Hellenistic age, Aristarchus, head librarian in the first half of the second century BC:[8] explicit citations of his Homeric commentaries as well as comments attached to a set of marginal signs that he invented show that he distinguished the temporal perspective of participants in the Trojan War from the eras of Homer, of later poets, and finally of the critic himself. While he saw room for debate about some features,[9] Aristarchus assumed that Homer offered a coherent picture of the cultural practices of the heroic age, a key feature being the simplicity and self-sufficiency of ancient manners. This Homeric picture in turn provided the template for assessing later poetic re-workings of heroic material.

The commentaries were complemented by detailed monographs on particular topics of antiquarian and literary interest. While most of these are lost, they were exploited in the Roman imperial period and beyond by commentators as well as by the writers of extant encyclopedic and miscellaneous works such as Athenaeus' *Deipnosophists* and Aulus Gellius' *Attic Nights* (second century AD).[10] Besides this tradition of textual exegesis, works such as Pliny the Elder's *Natural History* and Pausanias' *Description of Greece* (first and second century AD respectively) offer important evidence for a similar philological approach to material remains. Pausanias' account of Athens, for instance, includes a description (1.3.3) of a painting by Euphranor (mid-fourth century BC) in the Stoa of Zeus that showed

Theseus together with allegorical images of Democracy and Demos (representing the Athenian constitution and people respectively). Understanding the picture to be representing Theseus 'as the one who gave the Athenians political equality', Pausanias objected that Athens continued to be a monarchy under Theseus and his immediate successors, and sought the origins of the anachronism in people's naive belief in 'whatever they have heard from childhood in choruses and tragedies'. For Pausanias, then, these artistic and literary anachronisms were interlinked: together they illustrated the Athenians' politically charged manipulation of the heroic past.[11]

The historicizing approach of the earliest commentaries drew on still earlier critical approaches to literature. A tradition of Homeric exegesis had developed by the second half of the fifth century BC; in part it took the form of glosses on obscure words, but, as we shall see in the next section, lexical research showed a nuanced sense of historical change. This same intellectual milieu also provides the earliest evidence for critical engagement with anachronism as retrojection. The comic playwright Aristophanes presents in *Frogs* (405 BC) Dionysus, god of the theatrical festival at Athens, staging a contest in the underworld between Aeschylus and Euripides to determine which tragedian he should restore to the upper world. At the start of the contest, Euripides readily assents when Dionysus asks him if he has his own gods to pray to, 'a newfangled (*kainon*) coinage' (890) – using the same root for novelty found in Menelaus' response to Hecuba's strange prayer in the *Trojan Women*. In the contest itself, Euripides boasts of 'staging household (*oikeia*) scenes, things we're used to, things that we live with, things about which I could be refuted because these spectators knew about them too' (959–61). While Euripides is here making a point as much about social as about temporal distinctions (he boasts too of his 'democratic' introduction of slaves and women, both young and old, as speakers (952)), he is repeatedly aligned with the 'new' as opposed to the 'old' in Aristophanes' plays, and this contrast must be associated not just with formal aspects of tragedy such as his adherence to a new style of music that became popular in the late fifth century, but also with the self-consciousness of his introduction of 'newfangled' speculation into plays set in the heroic age.

One of the reasons for approaching literary anachronism through ancient philology is their interconnectedness. Perhaps already latent in the example of Euripides and Aristophanes, the links between anachronism and criticism are clear by the time of Virgil. Servius Auctus picked up on the anachronism of Virgil's mention of biremes (*Aeneid* 1.182) by citing Varro, a learned late Republican author whose writings were known to Virgil, as evidence that they were introduced after the Trojan War. Other anachronisms in Virgil, as we shall see, engage with the existing debates on anachronisms in commentaries on earlier epic authors.

In the rest of this chapter we will be exploring some of the central concerns of ancient philological discussions of anachronism, in particular the distinction between the perspectives of literary characters and their creators as it is theorized in discussions of anachronistic similes and names and of the persona of the poet. As well as being an important part of the history of anachronism as a literary concept, the material we will discuss will enable us to tease out some of anachronism's creative possibilities in antiquity. We turn first to the varied ways in which literary scholars in antiquity, ever alert to the possibility of change over time, used anachronism as a tool in clarifying the philological issues with which they were concerned, including questions of grammatical interpretation, chronology and authorship.

Anachronism and philological argument

A common use of anachronism in ancient scholarship was as a way of eliminating solutions to interpretative problems. In the third book of the *Aeneid*, Virgil describes how Aeneas on his journey to Italy finds to his surprise the Trojan seer Helenus settled in Epirus. Helenus then warns Aeneas that Italy is teeming with formerly hostile Greeks, mentioning among other new Greek foundations 'that small Petelia, supported by a wall, of Philoctetes the Meliboean leader' (*Aeneid* 3.401–2: *ducis Meliboei / parva Philoctetae subnixa Petelia muro*). In his commentary on these lines, Servius discusses whether the genitive *Philoctetae*, 'of Philoctetes', should be taken with the toponym *Ptelia* or with *muro*, the wall that surrounds the town. To solve the grammatical ambiguity, he turns to historical analysis, citing the historian Cato, who claimed that wall was built by Philoctetes at some point after the city's foundation (*FRHist* 5 F64). 'Of Philoctetes', then, is to be joined with 'the wall', not with 'Petelia'; to read it otherwise would produce an anachronism.

An interest in detecting anachronisms was promoted, too, by scholarly interest in the history of particular words.[12] Scholia on Aeschylus' *Seven against Thebes* (line 277) and Sophocles' *Oedipus the King* (line 391) observe that the words *tropaia* (trophies) and *rhapsōdos* (rhapsode) did not yet exist at the time of the events described; similarly Servius Auctus describes the word *legio* (legion) as an instance of *prolepsis* (note on Virgil *Aeneid* 10.120). This sort of lexical interest is attested already in the intellectual culture of the fifth century BC:

Hippias of Elis, a writer with wide-ranging philosophical and historical interests, noted that the word *turannos* (tyrant) 'spread among the Greeks only late, in Archilochus' time' (*FGrH* 6 F6; DK 86 B9). This observation survives in a *hypothesis* (introduction) to *Oedipus the King*, where it supports the argument, which may or may not go back to Hippias himself, that 'there is something peculiar (*idion*) about the post-Homeric poets who address the kings ruling before the Trojan War as "tyrants"'. The use of *turannos* breaches an apparent expectation of fidelity to the lexical usages of a particular period.[13]

The concept of anachronism was enlisted in lexical disputes in other ways too. Aulus Gellius in his *Attic Nights* describes a conversation in which a young man rejects the common view that *spartum*, Spanish brushwood, was unknown to the Greeks at the time of the Trojan War (17.3). Some 'ill-educated' men then mock the young man, suggesting that his edition of the *Iliad* cannot contain the one Homeric line (2.135) where the word *sparta* was used. Provoked, the young man has resort, like many a Roman in a philological crisis, to Varro, who had argued that *sparta* in Homer referred to a different type of plant – 'a type of broom which is said to grow in Theban land' and specified that 'in Greece a supply of *spartum* began only recently to be available from Spain'. Thanks to Varro, Gellius reports, the young man was able to skewer his adversaries.

Anachronism could also provide fertile ground for evaluating the attribution of lines. Pausanias cites the Doric dialect of a cult hymn in the Peloponnese as a reason why it could not have been composed by Philammon, a famous musical performer from the Argonautic era, a time when not all of the Hellenes had even heard of the Dorians (2.37.3, citing a contemporary scholar, Arriphon of Triconium). A similar argument from the geopolitical landscape of the heroic age relates to the definition of Hellas itself. At much the same time that Hippias noted the absence of the word *turannos* in Homer, Thucydides observed that Homer did not speak of 'the Hellenes' as a single unit nor, by extension, use the term 'barbarians' to describe all non-Hellenes *en masse* (1.3.3). *Hellas* in Homer, on this view, denoted the region of Thessaly rather than a more expansive area of Greek settlement. In line with Thucydides' observation, Aristarchus proposed that a line in the *Iliad* which referred to 'the Panhellenes' (scholion D on *Iliad* 9.395; cf. scholion D on *Iliad* 16.595) was an interpolation, reflecting a later, broader conception of 'the Hellenes'.

Interpolations were uncovered, too, through an awareness of other sorts of cultural and political change. Aristarchus claimed that two lines in the seventh book of the *Iliad* should be rejected because they referred to the practice of cremating fallen warriors in order to bring their bones back to their homeland;

in the heroic age, by contrast, warriors were cremated where they died 'not to enable their bones to be conveyed home, but as a matter of custom' (scholion A on *Iliad* 7.334–5). Modern scholars have often agreed with Aristarchus' judgement, suggesting that the lines were created in response to the Athenian practice instituted in the first half of the fifth century BC.[14] As with the delineation of *Hellas*, the identification of anachronistic practice here turns on a key aspect of communal self-definition.

A different sort of pressure was identified by some critics as lying behind the addition of a single line to the Catalogue of Ships in the *Iliad*, in which Ajax stationed his fleet from Salamis next to the Athenians (2.558). An allusion in Aristotle's *Rhetoric* (1375b29–30) suggests that this interpolation was suspected already in the fourth century BC, but fuller accounts survive from the Augustan and imperial periods, in Strabo's *Geography* (9.1.10), Plutarch's *Life of Solon* (10.2–3) and Diogenes Laertius (1.48). The fullest version (Plutarch's) is that the Athenians and Megarians were continually at war over the island of Salamis until they called in the Spartans to adjudicate; Solon at this point cited the Homeric Catalogue in support of the Athenian claim, adding after 'Ajax from Salamis brought twelve ships' an extra verse: 'And bringing, stationed them near the Athenian hosts' (*Iliad* 2.557–8). The anecdote provides an explanation for the origin of a line that could be taken to presuppose Athenian control over Salamis at the time of the Trojan War; Strabo adds that some attributed the insertion to the Athenian tyrant Pisistratus and that critics showed from evidence elsewhere in the *Iliad* that Ajax was not in fact stationed next to the Athenians. Whoever was responsible for the ploy, the verbal display of anachronistic ingenuity highlights the political motivations behind the policing of heroic time.[15]

Literary chronology was another area where arguments from anachronism played a role. They were used, for instance, in solutions to one of the most popular scholarly conundrums in antiquity, the relative dating of Homer and Hesiod (scholion T on *Iliad* 23.683), as well as in a discussion of funeral orations by the first-century BC historian Dionysius of Halicarnassus (*Roman Antiquities* 5.17.4). Dionysius there complains that Euripides included in *Suppliant Women* a eulogy delivered by the Argive king Adrastus, sole survivor of the Seven against Thebes, in honour of his fallen comrades, whose burial had been secured by Theseus' intervention (Pausanias, we noted earlier, similarly took offence at this play's presentation of Theseus as a democrat). Though normally keen to assert that Romans used Greek customs, Dionysius argues that the first funeral oration was in fact delivered for Lucius Junius Brutus, who led the revolt that drove out the last king at Rome, at least sixteen years prior to the earliest possible use of such speeches in Greece (after the battle of Marathon). None of the old poets or reputable historians mentions funeral orations in Greece, he notes, 'except the tragedians at Athens, who toadying to their city told this fanciful tale too about those who were buried by Theseus, for the Athenians were late in adding the funeral oration to their custom'. Dionysius' reasoning here is unclear. Given that the eulogies in Euripides' play were delivered in honour of Argives, not Athenians, he may be suggesting that the mere inclusion of the speeches magnified the glory the Athenians won by securing the heroes' burial. Equally, he may himself be making the anachronistic assumption that Euripides was trying to assert Greek priority over the Romans. In either case, he was, like Pausanias, using anachronism as a way of critiquing a patriotic Athenian myth on historical grounds.

The use of anachronism to solve exegetical problems continued in Byzantine scholarship. In his *Works and Days* Hesiod repeatedly insists that his addressee, his brother Perses, must toil for his livelihood. The necessity of work is explained by a story from the early days of human existence: but for Prometheus' theft of fire, the poet claims, the gods would have made life so easy that a day's labour would have produced food for a year (43–4) and 'you would have immediately hung your rudder in the smoke' (45–6, referring to how rudders were stored when not in use). The scholia on this passage reveal that critics were troubled by Hesiod's mention of the rudder. While the fifth-century AD Neoplatonist commentator Proclus had suggested that Hesiod meant that humans living the easy life would take to the sea one day a year, the prolific twelfth-century grammarian John Tzetzes objected that the event being recorded (Prometheus' theft of fire) predates the invention of sailing. He suggested that Hesiod was either speaking 'allegorically', employing the figure of the mind as a 'steersman' of a ship, or employing a deliberate anachronism: he 'understands accurately' that sailing did not exist at the time he writes about, but 'he anachronizes the account and attaches the things that happen in its time to times of old'. On this interpretation, anachronism is a legitimate part of the poet's toolkit. By mixing temporal domains, Hesiod allows Perses and his listeners to imagine the events of the primordial past through the tools they use in their own lives.

This section has sketched the varied uses to which anachronism was used in philological arguments. Throughout, we have seen that ancient scholars and their Byzantine successors, whether debating literary chronology or authenticity, were alert to chronological irregularities, in line with their broader sensitivity to the possibility of historical change. Similar uses of anachronism as a trump-card can be found in philological disputes about the post-heroic period,[16] as well as beyond scholarship in the cut-and-thrust of contemporary politics.[17] We now turn, however, to explore attitudes to the literary use of the sort of anachronism made possible by the necessary gap between action and narration.

Anachronistic similes

Athena appearing with a gleam 'As when Bikini flashlit the Pacific'. Isos and Antiphos 'as proud as astronauts' before they ride out to their deaths. Hector coming home in full armour 'Like a man rushing in leaving his motorbike running'.[18] The vocabulary and ideas dexterously used in two of the most vivid contemporary re-imaginings of the *Iliad*, Christopher Logue's *War Music* and Alice Oswald's *Memorial*, seem obviously anachronistic, in the sense of not belonging to Homer's world. The nuclear explosion, the astronauts and the running motorbike show the poet's workings, tracing imaginative equivalences through which the *Iliad* becomes freshly meaningful. Hovering between the modern and the ancient, lines like these lay bare the untimeliness of our engagement with Homer: Oswald herself speaks of *War Music* unleashing a 'theatrical energy' that has 'nothing to do with backdate or update' but shows that 'like any good poem' it is 'contemporary with all other good poems'.[19]

The type of untimely simile used by Logue and Oswald had numerous antecedents in ancient epic. Ennius in his *Annals* (second century BC) aligns the anxious audience of herdsmen watching the augural contest of Romulus and Remus with a crowd waiting for the consul to give the signal for a chariot race to start (79–81 Skutsch). Among a number of anachronistic similes in the *Aeneid* is one where Virgil likens the crash of a huge body on the battlefield to the stone foundations of a new seaside villa being allowed to fall down into the sea (9.710–16). The technique was picked up by his successors: in his Theban War epic, set a generation before the Trojan War, Statius introduces the Parthians, Rome's great enemy in the East from the first century BC onwards, when he compares a character chosen to take over the position of seer to a young prince 'in Achaemenes' line' on the death of his father (*Thebaid* 8.286–93).[20]

The capacity of similes to produce temporal juxtaposition is reflected in the way they were studied in antiquity. Ancient commentators on Homer recognized that elements of similes often reflected the practices of the poet's own time, and thus allowed listeners and readers to imagine the heroic age with reference to phenomena with which they were familiar. To give three examples: when Achilles' battle cry is compared with a trumpet that 'cries out' in 'a city surrounded by murderous enemies', the scholiasts note that 'the poet names the trumpet from his own times, because it had not yet been invented in ancient times' (scholion A on *Iliad* 18.219);[21] when Hephaestus burning the river Scamander is likened to a cauldron coming to the boil and melting 'the lard of a fatted hog', they comment that the poet 'knows about the boiling of meat, but he does not introduce the heroes as using it' (scholion A on *Iliad* 21.362); finally, when Ajax leaping from ship to ship in battle against the Trojans is compared with 'a man skilled in riding horses' who yokes four horses together and drives them across a plain, they claim that horse-riding was practised in the poet's time but not at the time of the Trojan War (scholion AT on *Iliad* 15.679).[22] In all these cases, the scholia draw attention to the juxtaposition of separate temporal domains in similes. The discordance created by employing later practices such as trumpet blasts to describe events in the heroic age highlights the challenges listeners face in developing an adequate imaginative grasp of the poem's extraordinary events. The comment in scholion b that the loud noise of trumpets 'summons and stirs up the masses in war' hints that Achilles' voice inaugurates a new phase of war while pointing by contrast to his isolation on the battlefield.

Should these similes be called anachronistic? This term is commonly applied to such similes in modern scholarship. A precedent for this usage can be found in the Iliadic scholia, including one on the Ajax riding simile (scholion bT on *Iliad* 15.679): 'it is an anachronism, because the Greeks do not use riding-horses' (the present tense here refers to the events of the poem as present to us as we read it).[23] This usage was, however, criticized by Eustathius, Bishop of Thessalonica in the twelfth century, in his commentary on this passage (3.785 van der Valk):

> Those of old (*hoi palaioi*, i.e. the old scholiasts) say that the poet here uses the figure of anachronism. For there were not riding-horses among the heroes, but the discovery is later in origin. And yet perhaps this sort of thing is not necessarily anachronism. For the poet does not say that the event happened in the time of the Achaeans, but he makes the comparison himself knowing that it happens in his own time, and speaking to people who know about it.

For much the same reasons, Oliver Taplin has suggested that 'time-tension' would be a better term than anachronism.[24]

That Eustathius took the trouble to criticize the older scholia suggests that he found the label 'anachronism' disturbing. As we noted above, Pat Easterling writes in similar terms of the tragic scholia, suggesting that they employ the language of anachronism as a mark of disapproval.[25] Perhaps, however, the scholiasts' bare references to anachronism were originally merely factual claims. That is, their comments could have been showing an awareness of changing practices without implying any criticism of the authors in question; in the case of Homeric similes, they could even be expressing appreciation of the dexterity with which the poet played on the distinction between the heroic world and the present.[26] At any rate, Homeric practice and its ancient reception both show what we might call a sense of historical perspective: some features of the poet's world, even if they did not belong in the Trojan War itself, could still be deployed to good effect and in a way that underlined for the careful reader the consistency of the poems' construction of the heroic world.

As we shall see in our next section, a similar sense of historical perspective – but with stronger normative assumptions – can be found in critical discussions of changes in place names.

Anachronistic names

Aulus Gellius (14.6.4) reports that a friend approached him with a collection of 'curiosities' (*miracula*) that he thought might be useful for Gellius' engaging miscellany, the *Attic Nights*. Among the incidental information he had gathered was a list of regions and cities that had changed their names: 'Boeotia was previously called *Aonia*, Egypt *Aeria*, Crete too by the same name *Aeria*, Attica *Acte*, Corinth *Ephyre*, Macedonia *Emathia*, Thessaly *Haemonia*, Tyre *Sarra*, Thrace *Sithonia*, Paestum *Poseidonia*.' It is easy enough to see how the friend had gathered this information. Poets, historians and geographical writers often introduced seemingly irrelevant notes on earlier or later names held by particular places: so prevalent was the practice that an allusion in Virgil to 'a lofty mountain' (*monte . . . aerio*) beneath which one of Aeneas' companions was buried, 'which now from him is called Misenus' (*Aeneid* 6.234–5), was taken by some commentators, according to Servius, to be a toponym, Mount Aerius.

Far from being frivolous, this enterprise involves a serious political issue. Given that names change in response to migration and conquest, what name should be used at a given moment to refer to a place with a history of toponymic change? This political dimension is not expressly discussed by ancient critics. They focus instead on the question of narrative norms. Thus Pausanias at one point offers a historical interpretation of a verse inscription by adducing 'the custom for Greeks to introduce into their poetry older names instead of later ones' (7.17.7); later he offers a specific example of this practice when he claims that Homer (*Iliad* 2.519) deliberately called by its older name Cyparissus a city that already at the time of the Trojan War was called Anticyra (10.36.5, citing as evidence the fact that the eponym Anticyreus was a contemporary of Heracles). Taking historical change for granted, Pausanias focuses on the poet's licence to shape the past.

Implicit reflections on anachronistic names can be found in poetry. In his version of Aeneas' arrival in Italy in the *Metamorphoses*, Ovid recounts how Aeneas 'approaches the shore which did not yet bear the nurse's name' (14.156–7). He alludes here to the end of the sixth book of the *Aeneid*, where Virgil says that Aeneas and the Trojans came 'to the harbour of Caieta'[27] – Caieta being the nurse to whom Ovid refers. As Servius points out in his commentary on the line (6.900), the name 'Caieta' is spoken in the voice of the poet, the name not yet having been given to the place at the time when Aeneas arrived there. The chronological breach occurs at the mid-point of the *Aeneid*, soon after the parade of future Roman heroes whom Aeneas sees in the underworld. In the opening lines of the following book, Virgil flaunts his technique by addressing Caieta directly: 'when you died you gave eternal fame to our shores' (7.1–2). Ovid in turn advertises his understanding of Virgil's technique, making it unmissable for the reader.[28]

A fuller picture of attitudes to onomastic anachronism emerges from a passage where Aulus Gellius (10.16) records criticisms of Virgil made by Hyginus, a freedman who was in charge of the Palatine Library at Rome and was reputedly a friend of Ovid's. Hyginus wrote a work on the *Aeneid* in which he 'blamed' Virgil for making the dead but unburied Trojan helmsman Palinurus ask Aeneas to return to the 'Veline harbour' to complete the necessary rites (*Aeneid* 6.366). It made no sense, Hyginus argued, for Palinurus to refer to a town founded several hundred years later, 'unless anyone believes that in the Lower World he had the power of divination' – and even then Aeneas could not have understood which harbour he meant.[29] Hyginus castigated this lapse as 'extremely stupid' (*inscitissime*) by contrast with passages where the poet himself mentions 'by anticipation [the Greek phrase *kata prolēpsin*] in his own person some later facts which he himself could have known' (he cites two toponyms, the 'Lavinian shores' and the 'Chalcidian citadel' (*Aeneid* 1.2–3, 6.17)). A similar language of blame was applied in Servius' commentary to this and a comparable breach (3.703, 6.359).[30] We see here a firm conception of the relationship that should obtain between poets and their material: speeches within narratives should reflect the perspectives of the speakers, but poets may use their own situation as a lens through which we view the narrative.

The clear distinction between the times of the poet and the characters is derived from earlier Greek scholarship. Aristarchus noted that Corinth, a famous city in antiquity, is mentioned only twice in the *Iliad*, while there are several mentions of an obscure city called Ephyre (e.g. *Iliad* 6.152); he explained that a single city was at stake, called Corinth by the poet and Ephyre by the characters (scholion Ab on *Iliad* 2.570).[31] He saw Homer, that is, as achieving consistency between his designations and the knowledge of the speakers responsible for them. That poets' toponymic practices were still open to debate is shown by the scholia on a passage where Apollonius of Rhodes calls Italy 'Ausonia' (*Argonautica* 4.555). This usage was censured by some critics because that name 'was given in times after the Argonauts, and came from Auson the son of Odysseus and Calypso', but defended by others 'because the poet himself uses this name, even if it did not exist in their [sc. the Argonauts'] times'. Again the debate turns on the perspectives of character and poet.

Critics were aware that judgements on anachronistic names depended on generic differences. The first-century AD Roman historian Velleius Paterculus, in a brief sketch of early Greece, expresses irritation at tragedians having their characters refer to 'Thessaly' at a dramatic date that preceded this name; using the Ephyre/Corinth example, he suggests that it is acceptable when poets such as Homer employ such references in their own voice (*Roman History* 1.3.2–3). That commentators on tragedy were alert to possible breaches is shown by the designation of the phrase 'Cadmus, leaving the Phoenician land' in Euripides' *Phoenician Women* (line 6) as 'proleptic'. That judgement is supported by a citation from a now lost play by Euripides, the (second) *Phrixus*, where it was stated that Phoenix, in many accounts one of Cadmus' brothers, was the eponym of Phoenicia.[32] What is left open is how the prolepsis was viewed: on Velleius' terms, it could be defended on the grounds that the prologue is spoken by Jocasta, Cadmus' great-granddaughter, in other words at a time when the name Phoenicia could already have taken hold.

Comments on anachronistic names show the same sense of historical perspective found in treatments of similes. The difference is that they are normative rather than simply descriptive. They openly use the language of praise and blame to mark out the temporal positioning that the poet should adopt.

The fullest normative assessment of anachronism in the Greek scholarly tradition is a difficult passage in Eustathius' commentary on the *Iliad*. As in his discussion of similes, Eustathius again approaches anachronism through the scholia. The reason for discussing this passage here is that Easterling has suggested that naming is Eustathius' criterion in assessing anachronism;[33] the complexity of his argument requires a detailed analysis.

Eustathius' discussion relates to a line in the catalogue of Trojan allies which mentions Paphlagonians 'from Eneti, from where the race of wild she-mules comes' (*Iliad* 2.852). After explaining the reference to 'Eneti' with citations from two standard works (the *Ethnica* of Stephanus of Byzantium and Strabo's *Geography*), he turns to Euripides' mention of Enetian mares at *Hippolytus* 231, which earlier critics understood as coming from the Enetians who lived at the northern end of the Adriatic, and this discussion leads into a small digression where Sophocles' use of anachronism is praised (1.567–8 van der Valk):

> People of old blame there [sc. in the *Hippolytus*] the bad style of anachronism (*ouk euzēlon anachronismon*) involved in the mention of such horses, given that at that time there were not yet Enetian horses among the Greeks, but they came into use later, when Leon, a Spartan, first won at the eighty-fifth Olympiad with Enetian mares, as is indicated by an inscription; Euripides has anachronized this type of horse to heroic affairs. Artful tropes of anachronism (*tropoi ... anachronismou eumethodoi*) are found in Sophocles, too, when he mentions the lot 'that was bound to leap first out of the crested helmet', as it was not 'a lump of wet earth' like the useless method of the Athenian[34] Cresphontes, who was born later [*Ajax* 1286–7]. Also in the proem of *Trachinian Women* [1–3], where the aged Deianeira uses a gnomic phrase that belongs to Solon, who was later in time (*husterou tōi chronōi*). And again in 'they would not have voted such a decision' [*Ajax* 448–9]. For heroes did not yet know voting, but the invention of votes happened later in time (*metachronion*).

Why the contrasting judgements on Euripides and Sophocles? Easterling has noted that the artful Sophoclean anachronisms do not contain specific allusions to later practices: the first example at most hints at Cresphontes' attempt to fix a lottery (he threw a clod of earth as his token into an urn full of water); the second consists of a proverb; the third example, voting, seems more concrete, but was perhaps (like Hesiod's rudder) more easily tolerated in a counterfactual.[35] Easterling suggests, then, that it was Euripides' naming of the Enetians that upset Eustathius. Rather as ancient commentators objected to characters using toponyms they could not have known, Eustathius would be complaining about a name that was historically impossible.[36]

Eustathius' distinction between good and bad anachronisms is not found in the extant scholia on the passages which he cites. The Enetian horses in the *Hippolytus* and the Solonian maxim in the *Trachinian Women* are both marked as anachronisms, but without any explicit approval or disapproval; Cresphontes' clod is merely said to have been 'brought back in time' (scholion on *Ajax* 1285); while the word 'voted' receives the simple gloss 'judged' (scholion on *Ajax* 449).

If Easterling is right, the concern with names is presumably due to Eustathius himself rather than to commentaries now lost.

Attractive though Easterling's argument is, Eustathius' discussion can be read as taking issue with the older commentators rather than with Euripides. The extant *Hippolytus* scholia add that the Enetians originally lived in Paphlagonia (the Iliadic tradition) and 'later' (after the Trojan War) crossed to the Adriatic – a migration known to Eustathius, too, as is shown by a cross-reference to his discussion of the Enetians in his commentary on the geographical writer Dionysius the Periegete (line 378). Given this pattern of movement, it is not clear why the commentators detected an anachronism at all: an audience with some knowledge of the *Iliad* could interpret Euripides' Enetian horses as coming from Paphlagonian 'Eneti' (Paphlagonia was known for horses as well as mules), or else from Thrace, where the Enetians were said to have stopped *en route* for the Adriatic.[37]

Interpreting Eustathius is made more difficult by the uneasy transition from criticism of Euripides to praise of Sophocles. The connecting phrase 'artful tropes of anachronism are found in Sophocles, too (*kai*)' implies a positive view of the previous Euripidean examples (an alternative translation 'even in Sophocles' is equally hard to square with what precedes). It seems that Eustathius moved abruptly from direct use of the Euripidean scholia to his own observations on Sophocles.[38]

The difficulties may be solved by the suggestion that Eustathius (as in his discussion of anachronistic similes) was rejecting the charge of blameworthy anachronism. On this reading, he starts by noting that Euripides was using a Homeric designation, and the shift to the criticisms made by the 'old' scholiasts is implicitly adversative. His mini-digression then makes the claim that Sophocles uses anachronism to good effect – implying that the old critics would be wrong to blame Euripides even if the Enetian horses were an anachronism. As for the reason for mentioning Sophocles at all, that perhaps lies in a perception that this sort of anachronism was typical of Euripides but avoided by the more correct Sophocles.

If this reconstruction is right, then (Eustathius assumed that) the old scholia criticized Euripides for a chronological error in naming Enetian horses, and Eustathius in turn criticized them for missing the clear Iliadic reference. This difficult example confirms, at any rate, that anachronistic names were as much a matter for debate and negotiation as the 'time-tension' common in epic similes, and that with them too proper poetic interpretation required a well-calibrated sense of historical perspective. We turn now to explore how retrojections of later practices and beliefs into the heroic world could be linked with the construction of a distinctive poetic persona.

Anachronism and the poet

We noted in the first section above that Virgil's inclusion of anchors in the *Aeneid* runs counter to the Homeric portrayal of the heroic world. A precedent for this anachronism is found in the fifth-century lyric poet Pindar. In a long narrative of the Argonautic expedition in his fourth Pythian Ode, Pindar relates how the heroes as they depart to fetch the Golden Fleece 'hung anchors over the prow' (191–2). This short phrase attracted two comments by eagle-eyed commentators. The 'prow' was glossed as a wooden structure 'on which the anchor was tied up', but it was noted that 'this did not exist in the time of the heroes': 'So we say that Pindar has composed this in a peculiar way (*idiōs*). For it is very common for men who are about to set sail to draw up the anchor and bind it around the ship.' The second comment noted (with the same word, *idiōs*) the oddness of Pindar's mention of an anchor, given that the heroes 'did not use anchors, but stones, as Apollonius too says'. Here the commentators cite an epic poem (Apollonius of Rhodes' *Argonautica*) that was written two centuries later than Pindar's poem as evidence for the practices during the Argonautic expedition. While, as with most scholia, it is uncertain when the content of these brief notices was first formulated, they probably antedate Virgil, and so can be seen as the scholarly background to the transgressive inclusion of anchors in the *Aeneid*.

What is the meaning of the scholiast's gloss *idiōs*? This adverb and the root adjective *idios* are frequently used in ancient commentaries as well as in miscellaneous works such as collections of marvels;[39] in the Pindaric scholia, they are typically used of the poet's distinctive lexical and mythographic choices (e.g. scholia on *Olympian* 6.106a and *Pythian* 11.26 respectively).[40] In relation to the Argonauts' anchor, the commentators highlight the distinctiveness of the poet's portrayal of the heroic age without offering any evaluation as to whether Pindar was simply inattentive to the details of history or deliberately conflating the practices of his time with those of the past. This silence leaves open the possibility of seeing anachronism as a tool for the poet's creative autonomy.

The notion that anachronism could reflect a distinctive poetic vision emerges in comments on other domains too. A particular target of this approach was the tragedian Euripides. We have already seen that his anachronisms provoked controversy in his own time as well as in later writers such as Dionysius and Pausanias. One of the striking features in the notes on alleged anachronisms in the Euripidean scholia is a tendency to generalize and relate them to broader questions of poetics.

This perspective emerges clearly in a comment on a speech in Euripides' *Hecuba*, in which Hecuba is criticizing Odysseus for not taking account of her having spared his life when he visited Troy as a spy. Decrying his lack of gratitude, she says 'you are an ungrateful breed, you men who seek after the honour of leading the people' (254–5). A scholion on line 254 sees Hecuba as an authorial mouthpiece, claiming that Euripides 'addresses the orators in his time who curried favour with the people'. Another scholion expands the point: 'he directs these remarks at political affairs in his own time. And Euripides is this sort of poet, attaching things of his own time to the heroes and mixing up (*sugcheōn*: literally 'pouring together') times.' The reference to 'mixing up' times might carry a pejorative sense, as the verb employed here is often used of activities that generate confusion.

A similarly negative judgement on Euripides' poetic persona seems to be implied by responses to supposed allusions to Athens' external affairs. Critical presentation of the Spartan king Menelaus in the *Andromache* (probably produced in the 420s BC) and the *Orestes* (408 BC) was thought to reflect antagonism to Athens' main political opponent in the Peloponnesian War; in keeping with Taplin's model of generic convention, these temporal breaches were seen as an intrusion of comic lampooning (scholia on *Andromache* 150, *Orestes* 371) – that is, as a breach of the tragedian's proper persona.

Anachronistic allusions to contemporary political situations could be recuperated through a different vision of poetics. In one scene in the *Andromache*, Menelaus explains his wish to return to Sparta by saying that 'a city' near Sparta which 'was once friendly is now hostile' (734–5). A scholion on these lines claims that 'some say the poet is hinting, contrary to the times, at the Peloponnesian War. And it is not necessary to criticize Euripides captiously, but to say that he uses fiction.' The scholion refers to a tradition in which the shifting allegiance of that nameless city reflects current political events (modern scholars who follow this line have suggested that Argos or Mantinea may be intended). The appeal to fiction (*plasma*) in Euripides' defence implies that he was exercising his creative agency.[41]

Another image of Euripidean dramaturgy that found ready acceptance in antiquity was the idea that he typically used characters as vehicles for expressing his own metaphysical opinions. An epitome of a work *On the Opinions of*

Philosophers by the philosopher Aetius (first or second century AD) quotes a speech from a play that he attributes to Euripides (a different source names the politician Critias as author) in which Sisyphus argues that the gods were fabricated by a 'clever man' who wished to devise a means of ordering people's social conduct. Sisyphus' propositions clearly mimic those of fifth-century thinkers such as Prodicus. According to Aetius, these were beliefs shared by Euripides himself, but he 'did not wish to disclose' that he did not believe in the gods because he feared being punished by the Areopagus (a court at Athens); he therefore 'introduced Sisyphus as a champion of this opinion, and acted as advocate of his position' (Ps.-Plutarch, *Moralia* 880e). We cannot, needless to say, know whether there is any truth in this assertion. What is important here is that ancient writers felt that such motivations and devices could plausibly be ascribed to Euripides. The playwright was similarly said to have evaded an Athenian ban on mentioning the death of Socrates by hinting at it in his *Palamedes* (*hypothesis* to Isocrates *Busiris*). The obvious anachronism of that anecdote (Euripides died several years before Socrates) was pointed out by the third-century BC Athenian historian Philochorus (*FGrH* 328 F221). But, like the Sisyphus story, it derived from a broader perception that Euripides provocatively introduced contemporary philosophical speculation into his plays.

That this practice was explicitly conceived in temporal terms is shown by a scholion on some lines in the *Hippolytus* in which Theseus, driven to rage by his belief that his son Hippolytus has attempted to seduce his stepmother Phaedra, attacks his son's habits. Vegetarianism, mystic rites and adherence to obscure, vacuous texts coalesce in an attack on Hippolytus' modishness: 'Continue to boast, and adopt your meatless diet and show off with your food. Take Orpheus as your king and revel away, honouring the vapours of many writings' (952–4). Ancient commentators, discussing the phrase 'show off with your food', saw a reference to Pythagorean philosophical beliefs:

> like the philosophers, eating nothing from the living creatures that are eaten or from others, but only grain, and taking Orpheus as king because he is sensible. For when Pythagoras was in high repute, many people held off from animate beings. Euripides retrojects (*anagei*, literally 'brings up/back') the times, for he wants to speak about himself through hints. He is like this, always introducing heroic characters as philosophers.

While there is evidence that Pythagoras was connected with Orpheus in the fifth century BC, it is by no means clear that vegetarianism was seen as a distinctive Pythagorean tenet at that time.[42] The scholiast's shaky doxography underscores the appeal of this image of Euripides. It was reinforced by his presentation in the biographical tradition as an eccentric loner. His plays were mined for biographical hints, and supposed biographical details were read back into the plays.[43]

Euripides was not the only tragedian suspected of retrojecting his own idiosyncrasies into the heroic world. Aeschylus' dramatic practice, too, was thought to reflect an aspect of his own character – a fondness for wine: a speaker in Athenaeus' *Deipnosophists* claims the 'the tragedian conferred on the heroes the same deeds he did himself; at least, he would write tragedies drunk, which is why Sophocles said in reproach: "Aeschylus, even if you create the right sort of works, you do so unknowingly"' (10.428f). This claim (which is supported by a reference to the appearance of Argonauts onstage drunk in the *Cabiri*) is advanced as part of a scholarly debate about who was the first tragedian to present drunks onstage (others, it seems, held Euripides responsible, though the biographical tradition did not present him as much of a party animal[44]). Such disputes were the stock-in-trade of ancient scholarship, but in this case the question had a strong ethical aspect. Earlier in his fictional banquet Athenaeus devotes several chapters to discussing Homer's ethics, advancing the argument that Homer generally represents his heroes behaving modestly with regard to food and drink, by contrast with other poets who 'retrojected (*anepempon*, literally "sent up/back") the extravagance and laziness of their own times as if they existed during the Trojan Wars too': 'Aeschylus at any rate rather inappropriately brings on the Greeks drunk enough to break pisspots on each other's heads' (1.17c). He then quotes a fragment of Aeschylus, and follows it with a similar quotation from Sophocles' *Fellow-Diners*.

Ethics and temporality are closely connected in these debates over literary portrayal of drunkenness. Aeschylus' and Sophocles' construals of the heroic age are conceptualized as a disruption by the worst contemporary practices of the ethically well-regulated realm as represented by Homer. Strikingly absent from Athenaeus' account is any attempt to justify the playwrights' decisions with reference to the genres in which they were writing: the instances Athenaeus cites are largely from satyr plays, in which humorous subject-matter was *de rigueur*. Athenaeus' speaker focuses not on the scenes' effect as pieces of drama but on the breakdown of social order that they represent: 'Not even when he introduces suitors drunk did Homer introduce as much disorder as Sophocles' and Aeschylus' (1.17f), the worst Homeric excess being the moment at which the suitors throw a cow's foot at Odysseus (*Odyssey* 20.299–300). The detail which the speaker lavishes on the misbehaviour suggests a little tongue-in-cheek humour: the suitors were after all a negative paradigm in philosophical readings of the *Odyssey* (Horace, *Epistles* 1.2.28; Bion of Borysthenes fr. 3 Kindstrand; Diogenes Laertius 2.79).

Anachronistic projections into the heroic era were of concern, then, not so much as threats to the norms of narrative but because of their potential to disturb the social order. Though there was, as we see with the suitors, differentiation within the heroic period, anachronism was a disruptive force when the idealized simplicity of the past clashed with the polyphony and excess of later, and more luxurious, epochs. This disruptive potential was particularly great with biographical readings: rather than functioning as educators of morality (in keeping with a common didactic view of the function of poetry), poets emerge from these accounts as agents of corruption.

Anachronistic games: Orestes at the Pythia

To illustrate more fully the dramatic potential of anachronism, we turn now to a famous instance from Sophocles' *Electra*. The play, which dramatizes Orestes' return to Mycenae to avenge his dead father, Agamemnon, departs in numerous ways from previous treatments of the story, especially that of Aeschylus' *Libation-bearers*. One of the most obviously innovative elements in Sophocles' treatment is the play's account of Orestes competing at the Pythian games. As part of their plot to trick Clytemnestra, Orestes and his Tutor concoct a story that Orestes has been killed during a chariot race at the games. The fabrication is announced in the play's opening scene (47–50), and given full realization in one of its most powerful episodes, in which the Tutor gives an extended account of the events which led to Orestes' death, before presenting Clytemnestra and Electra with an urn which supposedly contains his ashes. Electra, not knowing the truth, is shattered by unappeasable grief. These events prepare the way for Orestes' recognition by Electra, their joyful reunion, and the matricide with which the play reaches its climax.

Sophocles' use of a messenger to report events at the Pythia was criticized in Aristotle's *Poetics* (1460a28–32): 'Stories should not be composed out of irrational parts (*merōn alogōn*); it is best if they have no irrationality (*alogon*) or, failing that, if it is outside the plot, as with Oedipus' not knowing how Laius died; it should not be inside the drama, like in *Electra* those who report on the Pythian games.' The rationale of Aristotle's critique has been much debated since the Renaissance. The sixteenth-century commentators Robortello and Castelvestro both thought that he found it implausible that Argives had not brought news of Orestes' death first.

A further objection added by Castelvestro (though he did not think that this was what Aristotle had in mind) was that the chariot contest did not exist during Orestes' lifetime.⁴⁵

The chronological objection to Sophocles' treatment of the Pythian games was (as we noted briefly in Chapter 1) discussed by ancient scholars. A scholion on the first mention of the chariot race comments that 'it has been brought back in time: for at the time of the Trojan War he says there was a Pythian contest, 600 years before' (scholion on *Electra* 47). A similar gloss is offered for the beginning of the Tutor's speech: 'the Pythian contest did not yet exist in the time of Orestes' (scholion on *Electra* 682).⁴⁶ These comments draw on a tradition that the Pythian games originally consisted of contests in music, with athletic competitions being added in 586 BC (Strabo 9.3.10; Pausanias 10.7.5). While the interval of 600 years corresponds closely to the date for the sack of Troy established by the second-century BC chronographer Eratosthenes, the tradition about the Pythian games may have been based on research by Aristotle and his nephew Callisthenes, who are credited with composing a list of victors at the games in the mid-330s BC. If the 'irrational' element in the *Electra* to which Aristotle objects in the *Poetics* is the anachronism,⁴⁷ it is tempting (even though the date of the *Poetics* is uncertain) to connect his objection with his systematic chronological enquiries.

Modern scholars have tended to downplay the significance of chronology to Sophocles' treatment of the chariot race. The idea of Orestes competing at the Pythian games could have been rendered plausible by a different tradition, namely that those games were founded by Apollo after his establishment of the Delphic oracle. A *hypothesis* to the scholia on Pindar's *Pythian Odes* reports that the earliest victors in the games were Castor (running), Polydeuces (boxing), Calais (long-distance running), Zetes (race in armour), Peleus (discus), Telamon (wrestling) and Heracles (pancratium) – heroes all connected with the Argonautic expedition, and so from the generation of Orestes' grandparents. According to this tradition, which some modern scholars think is derived from Aristotle, there would be nothing chronologically incongruous about Orestes competing at the Pythian games;⁴⁸ and even if this tradition is discarded, the chariot race at the funeral games for Patroclus in the *Iliad* (23.262–652) gives credence to the idea that such practices were known to the heroic age.

Sophocles' audience could still have been alive to the possibility that his account was doing something chronologically inventive. An interest in the early history of athletic festivals is attested in Thucydides' history. Discussing the Athenians' revival in 426 BC of the Delia, a festival of Apollo on the island of Delos, Thucydides first uses the *Homeric Hymn to Apollo* as evidence for the musical components of an earlier festival there, then specifies that the revived festival included an additional contest – a chariot race (3.104). Modern scholars argue that the Athenians revived the Delia to rival the Pythia in response to Delphi's support for Sparta at the start of the Peloponnesian War.[49] The chariot race appears as an addition in the traditions about the Pythian games too: it is not included in the list of contests at the Argonautic-era games in the Pindaric scholia, and ancient accounts of the later development of the games at Delphi specified that it was added at the second iteration of the reorganized games, in 582 BC (Pausanias 10.7.6).

The presentation of the chariot race in the *Electra* strongly suggests that Sophocles' inventiveness would have been noted by ancient audiences. Two features of the opening lines of the Tutor's speech repay attention. The first is that the speech makes no mention of the tradition that the games were founded by Apollo. The second, stronger hint lies in the framing of the first day's events. The speech moves from an account of Orestes' success in the running race, which is the 'first contest' (684), and then 'all the other contests' (692), before moving on to give the story of the chariot race, which took place on another day (698–9). But before embarking on the chariot race, the Tutor describes Orestes' name being announced as victor in the running race (693–5), and makes a gnomic statement about men's vulnerability to the will of the gods (695–7), which has the effect of framing the first day's events as a self-contained story in its own right. This narrative framing correlates with one of tone: while the account of the first day's events is celebratory, the register of the chariot race narrative is tragic. The marked break between the two days hints at a version of athletic history in which the Pythian games did not initially include chariot competitions.

However the original audiences responded, the stress on chronological incongruity in the ancient scholia would have framed the way generations of readers understood the speech, whether they were guided through the play by a teacher at school or read it with a commentary in a library or at home. Indeed, the fact that the scholia do not record any attempts to rebut the anachronistic reading suggests that it might well have been the accepted way of interpreting the speech. For such readers, the invitation to read the chariot race as an anachronism might well have led to admiration for the descriptive power of the Tutor's fictional narrative.

Aristotle's objections to the messenger scene, by contrast, presuppose that the Tutor's narrative of Orestes' death is unsettling. Spectators and readers know that it is false, but insofar as they allow themselves to be carried away by the vivid description, they are acceding to the Tutor's (and the playwright's) control over events. Aristotle's criticism of irrationality expresses an anxiety about the power of plays to generate orders of coherence which are particular to them and not dependent on intuitive modes of time-reckoning and plausibility.

Historicizing literary anachronism

This chapter has suggested something of the variety and sophistication with which anachronism was handled both by creative artists and by the philologists who commented on their works. Poets could advertise or disguise anachronisms, critics could censure or celebrate them. Anachronisms could produce glancing incongruities between distinct temporal periods. Equally, they could be criticized in the service of linear chronology and narrative coherence. However they were treated, the philological scrutiny they received itself reinforced a sense of historical difference: the literary canon was approached through mediating interpretative voices that spoke to (even as they tried to mitigate) its lack of ready accessibility. With seeds in the writings of Thucydides and Hippias at the end of the fifth century BC, this interest blossomed in the Hellenistic era under the auspices of scholars such as Aristarchus and remained an important component in approaches to literature right up to the Byzantine period.

Can a story of change over time within antiquity be constructed? In his dissertation on tragic anachronism, Stricker mapped a progression from one ancient tragedian to the next: Aeschylus wrote plays steeped in the heroic spirit; Sophocles for the most part kept the dignity of the heroes, but in more trivial matters he expressed the manners of his own era; Euripides, by contrast, offered an image of a more recent mode of life, thereby bringing tragedy closer to comedy.[50] The development Stricker outlines can easily be criticized as schematic. The reason for rehearsing it here is that its roots lie in equally schematic ancient views of tragedy. Already in the fifth century BC, as we have noted, Aristophanes exploited the opposition of Aeschylus and Euripides in order to bring out the daring of Euripides' exploration of the differences and similarities between the present and the mores of the heroic world. Writing at a time of Athenian political decline, Aristophanes had his own reason for making a simplified image of Aeschylean grandeur stand for the glory days of Athens.

There are good reasons for rejecting this schematic account of fifth-century literary history. Aeschylus can in fact be seen as an innovative playwright, as bold as Euripides in his handling of anachronism. There are hints, to be sure, of this more daring Aeschylus in the ancient condemnation of his portrayal of drunkenness. But much of our vision is skewed by the accidents of survival. If fuller scholia survived for Aeschylus' *Eumenides*, we might find comments on the contemporary resonances of Athena's foundation of the Areopagus, the court that tries Orestes and a cause of recent political strife in Athens when the play was written. Again, ancient scholarship might present a more nuanced view if Aeschylus' *Myrmidons* – which portrayed Achilles as senior partner in a pederastic relationship with Patroclus – had become one of the canonical school-texts in antiquity; as it is, we find a speaker in Plato complaining about Aeschylus' reversing the relative ages of Achilles and Patroclus (*Symposium* 180a) but no objections to what seems to have been the retrojection of Athenian-style pederasty to the heroic era (Aeschines 1.142–50 suggests rather that Homer offers hints of an erotic relationship to a learned audience).[51]

Whatever the stories told about the surviving tragedians, it is clear that what was at stake in fifth-century tragedy was not the invention of historical difference itself, but a new way of articulating it, one that gave rise to the Hellenistic tradition of critical exegesis that we have explored in this chapter. The idea of the heroic was as culturally fertile from the Hellenistic period onwards as the idea of the antique has proved since the fifteenth century, and for some of the same political reasons.

The uses of anachronism varied with new political configurations. Virgil was creating the *Aeneid* at a time when Augustus was seeking to reverse Rome's supposed moral decline. His constant inclusion of post-heroic technology is in keeping with the continuities he creates between past and present by means of persistent aetiologies of elements of Roman culture. The anachronisms become more intensive, moreover, the closer the poem comes to home. Aeneas' band of Trojans become more Roman as soon as they land in Italy. This Roman re-writing of the past is the flipside of the future Jupiter projects for the Romans, 'empire without end': 'for them I do not set times' (*Aeneid* 1.278–9). Virgil's use of anachronism is inseparable from his nuanced sense of history as national story.[52]

The continuity of certain techniques suggests that anachronisms came to be relished for the creative challenges they offered. Particularly important is the interconnection between the commentary tradition and new creative re-workings. As we have seen, the connectivity of these two approaches can be seen in the responses to Virgil's anachronism of two friends, the librarian-critic Hyginus and the poet Ovid, and in Virgil himself. The critical tradition on earlier poets, not just in the scholia but also in genres such as rationalizing mythography, informed the handling of anachronism by their successors.

Critical interest in the relation between the persona of the poet and the personae of the poet's characters owed much to rhetorical theories of narrative and to the practices instilled by an education in rhetoric. Critics at least from the time of Plato categorized narratives in terms of whether or not they included direct speech by characters. Though there was a strong countervailing tendency in ancient citations and anecdotes to attribute to authors statements made by characters, the attention to the role of speakers within texts fostered an awareness of temporal perspective. This sense of perspective was fostered in turn by practices such as literary *imitatio* (seen, for instance, in two pseudo-letters to Julius Caesar composed in the archaizing style of Sallust, probably in the imperial period); traces of it can even be traced in declamatory genres that strove for wit more than historical accuracy (a declaimer who made a Spartan at Thermopylae anticipate Caesar's 'veni vidi vici' presumably thought he was being clever[53]).

All histories are anachronistic, the product of hindsight. Our goal in this chapter has not been to construct a strong(ly anachronistic) history of the intersections of anachronism and philology in antiquity, but to offer a survey of the dominant themes of scholarship on anachronism in antiquity and the Byzantine period. Suggestions that an awareness of anachronism in Renaissance criticism reflects a new sense of historical consciousness ignore at their peril the strong influence exercised by the ancient critical tradition on writing in Western Europe from the sixteenth century onwards.

The varied deployments of arguments from anachronism that we have encountered confirm the argument of our last chapter. There was nothing cognitively unusual about the sense of historical difference seen in the way philologists engaged with the heroic world. The ability to spot anachronisms depends on access to knowledge. What was distinctive about scholarly approaches to anachronism in antiquity was their fine-grained awareness of the distinctive features of the heroic world. The Homeric poems were subjected to intense textual and historical study from the fifth century BC onwards, and the results of this scholarship are paraded in the showmanship that pervades the pages of writers such as Athenaeus. As we shall see, a similar systematization of knowledge lay behind the interest in anachronism that developed in the study of chronology in antiquity..

Interlude: Dido versus Virgil

Walter Scott's novel *Peveril of the Peak* (1823) is prefaced by an epistle written by Scott's fictional antiquarian Dr Jonas Dryasdust to Captain Clutterbuck, the equally fictional editor of some of Scott's novels. Dryasdust has a strange story to tell. He had received from the author of *Waverley* a manuscript of a new historical fiction, *Peveril of the Peak*, and applied himself to reading it with his usual pedantic zeal: '"Here are figments enough", said I to myself, "to confuse the march of a whole history – anachronisms enough to overset all chronology!"' Dryasdust then relates how he had his usual afternoon doze, only to be interrupted by an unexpected visitor – the author of *Waverley* himself (at this stage not openly acknowledged as Scott). There ensued a discussion of the merits of historical fiction in which 'the Author' appealed to the precedent of Shakespeare's history plays, but Dryasdust remained unconvinced:

> Dryasdust: I doubt if all you have said will reconcile the public to the anachronisms of your present volumes. Here you have a Countess of Derby fetched out of her cold grave, and saddled with a set of adventures twenty years after her death, besides being given up as a Catholic, when she was in fact a zealous Huguenot.
> Author: She may sue me for damages, as in the case Dido *versus* Virgil.
> Dryasdust: A worse fault is, that your manners are even more incorrect than usual.

When the Author departs, Dryasdust notes that his decanter is empty – and his manservant denies that he even received a visitor.[1]

Dryasdust's account of his tipsy afternoon typifies the self-conscious engagement with anachronism in Scott's fiction. A propensity to anachronism is frequently acknowledged, and sometimes excused, in his prefaces and notes. He added to later editions of *Waverley* and *Ivanhoe* footnotes responding to critics: in the former, he admitted that his account of Scottish agriculture 'Sixty Years Since' had rightly been 'censured as an anachronism', while in the latter he defended his inclusion of 'negro slaves' in the entourage of a Templar knight.[2] In some works, as in *Peveril of the Peak*, he used the preface to pre-empt criticism: thus in *Rob Roy* 'the Author', after explaining that the work is based on a parcel of papers delivered to his publisher with a request to edit them, confesses that 'several anachronisms have probably crept in'.[3] In *Peveril of the Peak*, however, he went beyond merely acknowledging anachronism and offered instead a defence of historical fiction by appealing to Shakespeare's history plays and to Virgil's epic.

Dido's complaint against Virgil is based on the temporal gulf that was conventionally thought to separate the Trojan War from the foundation of Carthage. The *Aeneid* reports that Aeneas' fleet is driven by a storm from Sicily to North Africa in the seventh summer of his journey from Troy. There he finds Dido, a princess from Tyre who has fled from her brother Pygmalion and is now founding a new city, Carthage. Aeneas and Dido proceed to have a love affair, culminating in Dido's suicide when Aeneas leaves for Italy. The chronological problem with this story lies in the date of Carthage's foundation. Some ancient sources (Philistus *FGrH* 556 F47; Appian, *Punic Wars* 1) place this earlier than the sack of Troy (a key date in ancient chronology) and exclude Dido from any involvement in it. The majority (including Timaeus *FGrH* 566 F60, Velleius Paterculus 1.12.6, Justin 18.6.9 and Solinus 1.27) date it either some decades before or at the same time as the foundation of Rome – which in the world of the *Aeneid* lay 333 years after Aeneas' arrival in Italy. In either scenario the meeting could not have taken place as described in the poem. Virgil (or whoever was responsible for the story) seems to have adapted an earlier version in which Dido was a chaste princess who committed suicide to avoid the advances of a barbaric neighbour.[4]

By the time Scott penned the preface to *Peveril of the Peak*, Virgil's account of the love affair between Dido and Aeneas was long established as *the* anachronism above all others. It is, for instance, the only example offered in definitions of anachronism in treatises of universal history such as Thomas Hearne's *Ductor Historicus* and Edward Button's *Rudiments of Ancient History*.[5] It is similarly the only citation in entries on 'anachronism' in classic reference works of the eighteenth century such as Diderot's *Encyclopédie* and Samuel Johnson's English dictionary (where the preface to Dryden's translation of the *Aeneid* is cited).[6]

The canonical position of the Dido episode in definitions of anachronism was derived from its role in discussions of the licence poets should be permitted in dealing with historical events. It established itself in this role soon after the word 'anachronism' was adopted in Italy. In 1587 the critic Jacopo Mazzoni (p. 18) acknowledged that Virgil 'altered the truth of history with this anachronism', but defended his version as 'poetically credible to the populace'.[7] The anachronism was also discussed by Torquato Tasso, author of a partly fictionalized epic on the First Crusade, in his 1594 *Discourses on Heroic Poetry*. Drawing on Aristotle, Tasso distinguished between the false (the meeting of Dido and Aeneas), the fabulous (Aeneas' descent into the underworld in the sixth book of the *Aeneid*) and the unhistorical (the war between Aeneas and the Latins, which was based on fact but included wrong details). False though the story was, it could be defended, Tasso argued, by the example of ancient practice and theory as well as on aesthetic and political grounds (the erotic theme mitigated the poem's seriousness and the episode assigned 'an ancient and hereditary motive' to the conflict between Rome and Carthage).[8]

The terms of these Italian debates were echoed in the seventeenth century in both France and England. Jean Regnault de Segrais devoted a section of the preface to his translation of the *Aeneid* to a defence of Virgil's anachronism. He started by citing Tasso on the poet's patriotic goals. He further suggested that it would not be permissible to make Scipio and Hannibal contemporaries of Alexander,[9] but that the meeting of Dido and Aeneas was justified by virtue of temporal distance and (with appeal to Aristotle) the poet's concern with probability rather than truth.[10] In England, an anonymous 1697 treatise on Homer and Virgil (which Walter Scott was involved in re-publishing[11]) took the opposite view, berating Virgil for his 'achronism and slander' – 'a base and unpardonable fault' that involved 'ruining the good name of a woman' for the glory of Rome.[12] The same year saw the publication of John Dryden's strong defence of Virgil. Dryden drew extensively on Segrais' arguments, but added a contemporary political spin, praising Virgil for not making himself a 'Slave' to 'the Laws of Poetry': 'he might make this Anachronism, by superseding the mechanick Rules of Poetry, for the same Reason, that a Monarch may dispense with, or suspend his own Laws, when he finds it necessary so to do'.[13] Dryden, who had served as Historiographer Royal under James II, here alludes daringly to James' suspension of legal restrictions on Catholics – the perceived abuses that led to his deposition in 1688.[14]

Dryden's political terms were picked up in a literary dispute between the Catholic Alexander Pope, a Jacobite sympathizer, and the Whig critic John Dennis. In his *Essay on Criticism* (published in 1711) Pope came out in favour of obedience to the traditional rules of poetry: 'And tho' the *Ancients* thus their *Rules* invade, / (As *Kings* dispense with Laws themselves have made) / *Moderns*, beware!'[15] In a response in the same year, Dennis initially conceded that in poetry the periods of time should not be 'transpos'd or confounded', but then noted that Virgil broke this rule in the Dido episode 'by a bold and a judicious Anachronism, in order to make his Poem more admirable, and the more to exalt the Glory of the *Roman* Name': 'Whatever the Ancients justly did, the Moderns may justly do.'[16] Dennis was here taking his stand in the contemporary 'quarrel of ancients and moderns' – and helping his cause by cutting Pope's poem short (it continues: 'Or if you must offend / Against the *Precept*, ne'er transgress its *End*').

While critics from Tasso to Dennis discussed Virgil's anachronism with an eye to the precepts of ancient criticism, the French aristocrat and royalist François-René de Chateaubriand (1768–1848) approached it with typical self-absorption in describing his thoughts at the ruins of Carthage. Chateaubriand visited the site on the return leg of a journey in 1806 from Paris to Jerusalem, and this visit closes his later account of the journey. He lingers on the varied historical associations of Carthage – brave women such as Sophonisba and Hasdrubal's wife who killed themselves to avoid captivity; the legions of Hannibal and Scipio that fought nearby; and not least St Louis (Louis IX of France), who died at Carthage on his way to the Holy Land. As he reflects, too, on 'the happy anachronism of the *Aeneid*', he concludes that the imaginative freedom of poetry enables fiction to be as weighty as truth:

> Such is the privilege of genius that the poetic misfortunes of Dido have become a part of the glory of Carthage. At the sight of the ruins of this city, one searches for the flames of the funeral pyre; one believes one hears the imprecations of a woman abandoned; one admires these powerful falsehoods that can occupy the imagination in places filled with the grandest memories of history.[17]

The obsession with ruins that Chateaubriand parades throughout his Eastern journey comes to a head at Carthage as he cuts away at historical distance, bringing the past in all its multiplicity into the present of his own imagination.

Walter Scott, then, was drawing on a long critical tradition when he summoned up the case of Dido versus Virgil to justify the occasional anachronism in his historical fictions. But the greater weight he attached in his prefaces to the depiction of manners points to the transformation by which 'anachronism' came to be applied to practices felt to be outdated. By contrast with the typology of the *Aeneid*, where Dido's eventual hostility to Aeneas stands as precursor of the wars of Rome and Carthage, Scott's anachronisms are linked to a more complex national-historical trajectory (see p. 124).

The reception history of Virgil's Dido narrative tracks not just shifts in poetics from the Renaissance to Romanticism but also earlier shifts in the word 'anachronism'. Attention had been paid to Virgil's anachronism in Western Europe long before the adoption of the term itself. In late antiquity Augustine (*Confessions* 1.13) suggested that learned readers viewed the story as 'untrue'; Servius (on *Aeneid* 1.267) called the story 'invented' (*ficta*) on the grounds that Carthage was founded seventy years before the city of Rome; and Macrobius (*Saturnalia* 5.17.5) argued that readers connived in the fiction because of Virgil's poetic power.[18] These comments were in turn cited by Petrarch in a letter (*Letters of Old Age* 4.5) in which he argued that 'Aeneas and Dido were not contemporaries nor could they have seen each other, since she was born about 300 years after his death'.[19] The chronological problem was linked for Petrarch with the question of Dido's character: like many others in his time, he favoured the image of a chaste Dido found in the non-Virgilian tradition.[20] For him, as for the ancient writers he cites, Virgil's story was a falsehood rather than an anachronism.

It was, as we have seen, in the second half of the sixteenth century that the meeting of Dido and Aeneas came to be called an anachronism. But from the start it was generally seen as a temporal breach different in kind from the retrojection of later practices that was typically covered by the term *anachronismos*. Mazzoni recognized that it was impossible to say whether Dido had been retrojected to the time of Aeneas or Aeneas projected forward to the time of Dido,[21] while Tasso pointed both to the term's novelty with his gloss 'the figure that the Greeks called *anachronismos*' and to the shift in usage with the qualification 'or rather . . . the licence that Plato and the Greek poets first took in introducing men conversing together who lived centuries apart'.[22] This usage prepares for the shift of anachronism from the realm of literary exegesis to that of chronology.[23]

Chronological concerns went hand in hand with poetics in discussions of Virgil. Mazzoni, for instance, noted the variations in the evidence for the foundation of Carthage, while Segrais (drawing on a letter from the biblical scholar Samuel Bochart) thought that the anachronism could be securely established only with the help of the Bible and some 'Tyrian annals' preserved by the historian Josephus (*Against Apion* 1.106–11). The notion that Dido's encounter with Aeneas was an anachronism even met resistance. The translator Michel de Marolles offered a generation count for Dido that made her coeval with Aeneas; he suggested that Dido had founded the acropolis of Carthage, Bursa, rather than the city.[24] The anachronism was rejected, too, by Isaac Newton, who downdated the Greek chronology of the heroic age by hypothesizing that reign- and generation-lengths had been confused; on Newton's reckoning, Troy was sacked in 904 BC, twenty-one years before Carthage's foundation.[25] Newton's reconfiguration of chronology found some support at first with the youthful Edward Gibbon and with critics who found Virgil's 'monstrous anachronism' inexcusable, but soon fell from favour.[26] More commonly, authors gave a rough figure of 200 or 300 years for the anachronism. But there were attempts to measure its extent more precisely. Joseph Scaliger calculated the interval between the sack of Troy and the foundation of Carthage as 299 years; Walter Ralegh made it ten years less; the timeline in Helvicus' *Theatrum historicum* separates the two events by 291 years; while Thomas Hearne went one higher.[27] Behind all these calculations loomed the presence of Virgil: 'By so many years did Aeneas antecede Dido' was the pithy conclusion to Scaliger's discussion of the Near Eastern evidence.

Modern scholars continue to debate Virgil's anachronism. Whatever their explanations, they are concerned with the ideology and artistry of Virgil's temporal breach rather than with its extent; the early modern scholarly enquiry into the order of time has come to seem an anachronism. Virgil is seen rather as offering a self-conscious comment on the anachronism through the allegorical figure of *Fama*, 'Rumour' or 'Renown', that haunts the fourth book of the *Aeneid*,[28] or else through chronological inconsistencies internal to the poem: it is still, oddly, the seventh summer of his wanderings when Aeneas finds himself back in Sicily, despite spending a winter in Carthage – an 'annihilation' of time and space that marks his stay in Carthage as nothing but a fictional interlude.[29]

4

Anachronism and Chronology

Scaliger and the birth of chronology

On the crowded mantelpiece of contributors to the debate on the anachronism of Dido and Aeneas explored in our first Interlude, the scholar who stands out in the history of chronology is Joseph Scaliger (1540–1609), a French Protestant based in Leiden in the later stages of his career. Scaliger has been called 'the founder of modern chronological science',[1] and even (in the words of the Victorian scholar Mark Pattison) 'perhaps the most extraordinary man who has ever devoted his life to letters'.[2] In this chapter we will use Scaliger's scholarship as a means of exploring both ancient attitudes to anachronism as chronological error – the sense that the word acquired in Scaliger's lifetime – and the place of chronology in the history of temporalities ancient and modern. The upshot of these discussions is that ancient chronological method was informed by a strong sense of historical process. Far from being an isolated, purely technical discipline, ancient chronography parallels its modern successors in its reflection of ideological concerns.

We start with ancient calendars and their irregularities, the topic to which Scaliger devoted the first books of his first major chronological work, *De emendatione temporum* (*On the Improvement of Times*, 1583). We then analyse the concern with anachronism revealed by the dating systems used to record the past as well as the ancient interest in detecting isolated chronological mistakes. We will close by exploring how a sensitivity to anachronism was fostered by the conflicting temporalities – and the divergent religious practices – found in different cultures. First, however, we discuss in more detail a topic at which we glanced in Chapter 1 – Scaliger's own place in the history of chronology and anachronism.

The myth of Scaliger has been unsettled by Anthony Grafton's remarkable intellectual biography and by other scholars following in Grafton's steps. The claims in Scaliger's favour made by admirers such as Pattison were that he opened up the chronology of the ancient world to critical study by comparing classical and Near Eastern sources (some previously unknown) and by using astronomy to provide secure dates for eclipses, and that he secularized time by treating years as mere numbers rather than as clues to the patterns of history. Grafton and others have shown that the comparative approach to chronology was widespread, that the use of astronomy for dating can be traced back to the thirteenth century, and that Scaliger's arguments about the date of the Passion were entangled in contemporary religious disputes as well as strongly typological (that is, an Old Testament event – in this case Abraham's sacrifice of a lamb – prefigures one in the New Testament – here Christ's death). The immensely learned but fallible Scaliger who emerges from recent accounts is not quite a modern, but nonetheless still a pivotal figure in the history of chronology.[3]

A topic not treated by Grafton is Scaliger's contribution to the language of anachronism. As we saw in Chapter 1, Scaliger has often been credited with the spread of the Greek word to Western Europe. In fact the adoption of the term in Latin and Italian pre-dates him by some decades, and his own earliest uses show no consciousness that the word is a new coinage: he did not gloss it in a letter he wrote in French in 1591 in which he argued that 'anachronismes' in the Old Testament book of Judith show that it is a Jewish fiction,[4] nor when he first used it in print (in its Greek form) in the second edition of *De emendatione* (1598). While not a neologism, *anachronismos* did lend powerful support to his advocacy of the value of Near Eastern chronological traditions. Responding to a Catholic historian, Cesare Baronio, who had criticized him for rejecting the date for the destruction of the temple in Jerusalem offered by the Christian chronicler Eusebius of Caesarea (*c.* 260–339), Scaliger suggested that Eusebius had been led by his contempt for the Jewish historian Josephus into 'those *anachronismoi* by which his whole interweaving of the times is disturbed'. Again, in his notes on a fragment of the Babylonian historian Berossus he suggested that 'portentous *anachronismoi*' were born of chronologers' 'barbaric contempt' for local chronological traditions.[5]

The idea of Scaliger as innovator in the study of anachronism does nonetheless have some justification. He elaborated in his 1606 *Thesaurus temporum* (*Treasury of Times*) a distinction between *anachronismus*, defined as 'perversion of a heading of time, or dislocation of an epoch', and two specific types of error: *prochronismus* ('displacement of an epoch through removal, when less is said') and *metachronismus* ('displacement of an epoch through addition, when more is said').[6] These definitions were the prop for the long commentary on Eusebius that Scaliger included in *Thesaurus temporum*. Eusebius' *Chronicle* consisted of two parts, a *Chronography* (a collection of king-lists and other chronological data which survives in excerpts and in an Armenian translation that was unknown in the sixteenth century) and *Chronikoi Kanōnes* (*Temporal Tables*); the second part, which was widely known through Jerome's translation into Latin, arranged the information from the *Chronography* in parallel columns with a summary of events alongside a continuous numbering of years from the birth of Abraham (2016 BC in our terms) as well as other dating systems (regnal years, Olympiads) where appropriate (Fig. 5).[7] In his commentary, Scaliger scrutinized Eusebius for internal chronological inconsistencies as well as for contradictions with other evidence. He was able, for instance, to detect a 'prochronism of six years' in the entry for the year of Abraham 1598, 'the disaster which happened to the Athenians in Sicily', because of 'the lunar eclipse which intervened in that disaster' and because historians such as Thucydides and Diodorus preserved a year-date relative to the start of the Peloponnesian War which could be aligned with Olympiad years.[8] The originality of the commentary lay, however, in scope rather than in method. The eclipse in Sicily had been used to disprove Eusebius' date in Petrus Apianus' 1540 *Astronomicum Caesareum*,[9] and even the language of 'removal' and 'addition' in Scaliger's definitions of prochronism and metachronism was drawn from the third-century Christian chronographer Julius Africanus (F34 Wallraff).[10] But no one before Scaliger had devoted so much time and learning to elucidating the chronological errors in a single work.

Scaliger's keen eye for anachronism contrasts with the lax attitude to chronology that is often attributed to antiquity. As we noted in Chapter 2, some modern scholars attribute to the Greeks and Romans a sense of time as episodic, relative and multiple, with no conception of the past as an entity in itself and 'no cognitive awareness of absolute chronology'.[11] Such views might be supported by the approach to chronological exactitude that we noted in our Prelude. Plutarch, we saw, was prepared to retell the meeting of Solon and Croesus even though its historicity was strongly questioned by 'the so-called temporal tables (*chronikoi kanōnes*) which countless people are to this day correcting without being able to bring the contradictions into any general agreement' (*Solon* 27.1). And he took an even stronger stand in his biography of the Roman king Numa, berating as childish those writers who prided themselves on solving intractable problems such as the tradition that Numa was educated by the Greek philosopher Pythagoras (*Numa* 8.21).[12] But Plutarch also notes that part of the problem lay in the 'late' date at which the Greeks turned to chronology (*Numa* 1.6, alluding to the Olympiad list constructed by Hippias of Elis at the end of the fifth century BC). And his polemic reveals at the same time that many people in antiquity did take such questions seriously. One of Horace's poems is set at a

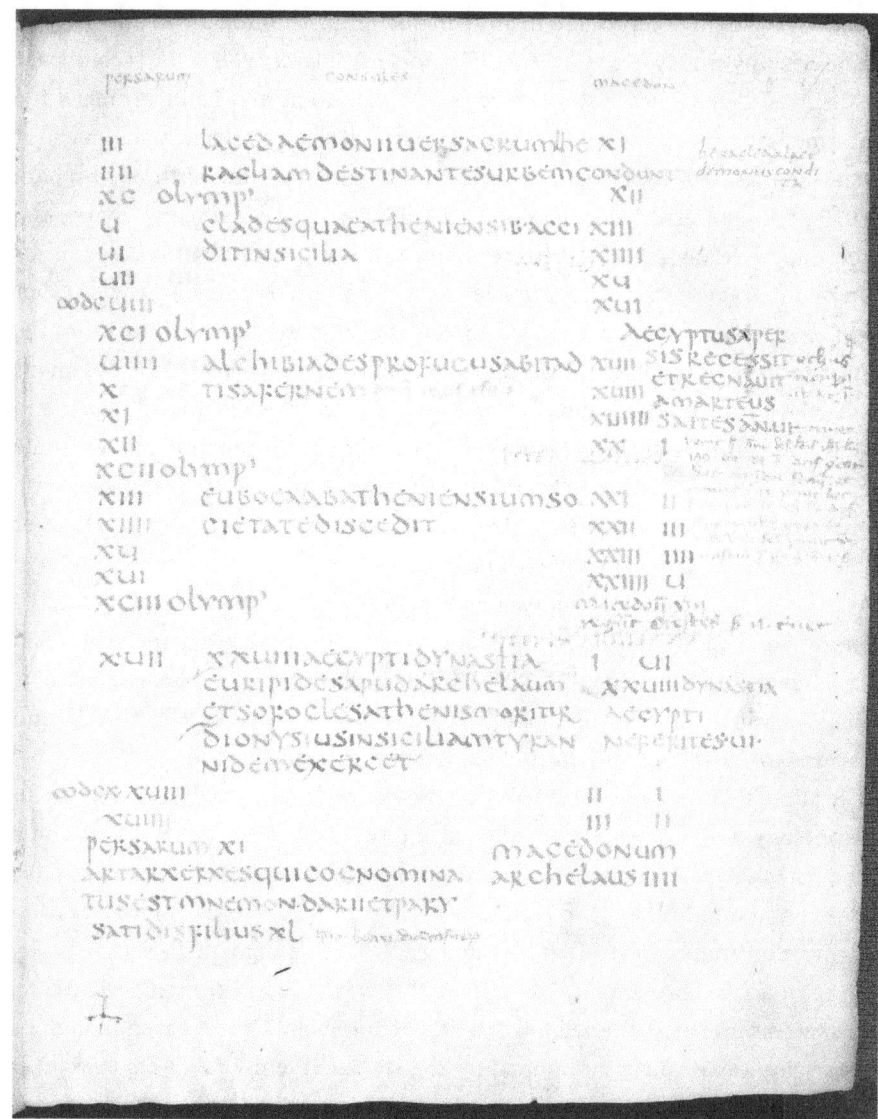

Fig. 5 A page from a manuscript of Jerome's version of Eusebius' *Chronicle*, showing the date for the Athenian defeat in Sicily during the 90th Olympiad. Bodleian Library, Oxford. MS. Auct. T. 2. 26, fol. 87r. Photo Bodleian Libraries.

party where a guest keeps going on about the number of years that separated Inachus, first king of Argos, from the Athenian king Codrus; Horace would rather he got on with the drinking (*Odes* 3.19.1–3). Dry-as-dust pedantry inspired such dislike partly because it had so many adherents.

Scaliger saw himself as heir to the scholarly strand of classical chronography.[13] At the start of *De emendatione*, while admitting (like Plutarch) that the Greeks and Romans were 'later than they should have been' in applying themselves to the reckoning of times, he laments that much of what they wrote has been lost; in particular, of the Greek writings 'which concerned chronology', 'nothing is left us except a longing for them'.[14] He then singles Eusebius' *Chronicle* out from those works that do survive (in some form at least), but he does so critically, as one of those books which 'today in the lack of better ones are valuable to us' – but which would be ignored 'if the tables (*canones*) of Thallus, Castor, Phlegon, and Eratosthenes were extant'.[15] Looking beyond Christian chronography, Scaliger here traces out a pagan chronological tradition that started in Hellenistic Alexandria, where Eratosthenes was based, and continued under the Roman empire with writers such as Castor of Rhodes (first century BC) and Phlegon of Tralles (second century AD). Scaliger knew from their scanty remains that these authors had specified the intervals in years between epochs such as the sack of Troy and the military expeditions of Xerxes and Alexander – the same task that he would himself undertake, in much amplified form, in Books Five and Six of *De emendatione*.

Scaliger linked the task of the chronologer with another Renaissance science, archaeology. What chronologers attempt is, in his words, 'to pull back fugitive antiquity' and 'each day with heroic courage to dig up (*eruere*) chronology from the darkness and silence of oblivion, dead and buried as it is through the neglect of earlier generations'.[16] Among his own contributions to this scholarly pursuit was the editing of 'fragments' – a term that itself evokes a sense of the past as broken like the pots and statues dug from the ground. He also edited and commented on many previously unpublished chronological works. More than that, he himself included in *Thesaurus temporum* an Olympiad chronography, *Anagraphē Olympiadōn*, that he had worked over time into a form that seemed so authentic that careless readers mistook it for an ancient text – and that even in the nineteenth century received the tribute of a commentary of its own that corrected its occasional mistakes with the help of the Scaligerian panoply of metachronisms and prochronisms.[17]

'Chronology' was itself a recent coinage in Latin when Scaliger defined its remit. First attested in Greek in the Byzantine chronographer George Syncellus, the word entered Latin in 1531 in an edition of Livy with a chronological appendix as well as a dedicatory letter by Erasmus which praises *chronologia* as the 'thread' without which 'inextricable error envelops even the erudite reader in the labyrinths of historical events'.[18] Scaliger now becomes our thread as we

Calendars out of joint

One of the pieces of evidence about the Greek calendar with which Scaliger grappled was the episode we discussed in our Prelude: Herodotus' account of Solon's lecture to Croesus on the fragility of human life. Solon there calculates that the normal human life of seventy years has 26,250 days – on any of which misfortune may occur. His calculation is based on a year of twelve thirty-day months with another thirty-day month added every other year so that 'the seasons tally as necessary' (1.32.3). Solon's inclusion of this intercalary month boosts his rhetoric (an extra 1,050 days for disaster to strike). But his method would signally fail to keep the seasons in sync: as the Greeks were aware (by the sixth or fifth century BC), a 360-day year would need to add twenty-one days every four years rather than thirty every two to do that.

Scaliger's response to this puzzle was to include a section 'On Herodotus' false year' at the end of the first book of *De emendatione*. As the title suggests, he put the blame for Solon's ridiculous system firmly on Herodotus. The problem was not so much the 360-day year in itself. Scaliger in fact argued for a new interpretation of the Athenian calendar based on twelve thirty-day months, thereby abandoning the consensus that Athenian months were lunar; elsewhere in *De emendatione*, moreover, he allows that a 360-day year was widely used 'in ancient times, especially in Egypt', as 'the most ancient and simple form of the year – and the one most appropriate to popular time-keeping ... because it divides up so evenly'. But he assumes that Herodotus did not understand the principles of intercalation: by Herodotus' time, in Scaliger's view, the Athenians were using a complex system based on a seventy-six year period comprising nineteen four-year cycles.[19]

In the second edition of *De emendatione*, Scaliger again devoted a section to Herodotus' 'false year'. He had in the meantime developed a radically different view of the fifth-century Athenian calendar. He now posited a year of 354 days formed of six 'hollow' (twenty-nine-day) and six 'full' (thirty-day) months, with three thirty-day months intercalated every eight years. Herodotus' mistake, he suggested accordingly, was based on a misinterpretation of the hollow/full alternation (days were numbered up to thirty even in hollow months, with a day earlier in the month being subtracted). Besides adjusting his view of how

Herodotus slipped up, Scaliger attempted to cast new light on Herodotus with the help of a Greek text that first appeared in print in 1590: *Introduction to the Phenomena* by Geminus, a first-century BC astronomer and mathematician. Included in Geminus' treatise was a discussion of the history of the months (8.26): 'The ancients had thirty-day months, with intercalary months every other year, but, the truth being swiftly tested in the phenomena, because the days and months were not in harmony with the moon and the years were not aligned with the sun, they sought a period that would be in harmony with the Sun in respect of the years and with the moon in respect of the months and days.' According to Scaliger, this new evidence from a 'most accurate writer' confirmed that the system of intercalation applied by Herodotus' Solon had been used 'in ancient times'.[20] He did not consider that Herodotus himself might have been Geminus' source and that Geminus' goal might be pedagogical rather than historical: modern editors suggest that 'he means to show his reader how one might begin to solve the problem of finding a good lunisolar cycle with a simple first step'.[21]

Scaliger's approach to the ancient Greek calendar is throughout marked by a strong sense of anachronism. By equating the 'most ancient' and the 'most simple', he points both to his own cognitive distance from antiquity and to historical changes within antiquity itself. In positing that the ancient calendar had gradually diverged from an ancient simplicity, he was adopting a model of uneven development that was commonly found in ancient accounts of the evolution of human society (as we shall see in Chapter 5) and had been applied to the determination of months and years by many earlier writers from antiquity to the Byzantine period.

An intermediate source for the developmental model was a work *On Months* by Theodore Gaza, a fifteenth-century scholar from Thessalonica who played an important part in introducing the study of Greek in Italy.[22] Gaza's work presents the classical order of the months as developing from disorder: the 'most ancient' peoples determined the months 'without calculation or order' (*On Months* 7 (*Patrologia Graeca* 19.1188): *alogistōs kai ataktōs*). Gaza here follows the common ancient pattern of defining early human existence in terms of the absence of features that emerged later.[23] His inspiration for applying this model to the calendar was Plutarch, who spoke in the same terms of the Roman calendar under Romulus (*Numa* 18.1: *alogōs . . . kai ataktōs*); both Gaza and Plutarch were drawing in turn on the famous cosmogony of Plato's *Timaeus* (43b1–2 *ataktōs . . . kai alogōs*; cf. *alogōs* at 43e3, 53a8 and *ataktōs* at 30a5, 69b3). A similar image of early calendrical disorder is found in a sixth-century AD treatise *On Months* by John the Lydian, where the Sicyonians and Arcadians, the first inhabitants of

Greece after the flood, are said to have been called *proselēnoi* (pre-moons) 'because they are said to have arisen before the delineation of the months' (3.1).[24]

The accounts of the calendar that survive from antiquity offered Scaliger schematic outlines of the process by which order had been achieved. Geminus, following his initial account of the 'two-year' cycle, describes the successive creation of cycles of eight, nineteen and seventy years, each one offering a superior fit between the rhythms of the moon and the sun (8.26–59). A more detailed but equally schematic account is offered by the Roman grammarian Censorinus in *On the Birthday*, an unusual work offered as a present to his patron in AD 238 which includes chapters on numerous different aspects of time. The 'great year' (a term for the cycles Geminus describes) was in the 'ancient states of Greece' two years, with one intercalated month (the system Herodotus' Solon uses, but without specification of days[25]); Censorinus adds the explanation that twelve or thirteen new moons were observed in each solar year. Then, when 'error was recognized', the 'great year' was doubled to four years, and then again to eight; and in due course more complicated cycles of nineteen, fifty-nine and seventy-six years were created (18). Similarly, in relation to months Censorinus writes that the Egyptians initially had one, then four, then thirteen (emended by Scaliger to twelve) with an extra five days (19). This pattern of steady numerical increase is found in the histories of many other domains, including ship design (Pliny, *Natural History* 7.207–8), the colours used in painting (Philostratus, *Life of Apollonius* 2.22.4), actors in tragedy (Aristotle, *Poetics* 1449a15–18) and holes or strings on musical instruments (Horace, *Art of Poetry* 202–19; Athenaeus 4.183c). Scaliger followed this evolutionary model in criticizing Censorinus' suggestion that the eight-year cycle might have been devised by the fourth-century BC mathematician Eudoxus of Cnidus, even though the Athenian Meton (active in the fifth century) had already created a nineteen-year cycle.[26]

Scaliger's approach to the Roman calendar was shaped by similar assumptions – and again he was following a pattern established in antiquity. According to a common tradition, picked up in the third-century AD miscellany-writer Solinus (1.35–9), the year set up by the founder of Rome, Romulus, had 304 days divided into ten months (starting with March);[27] the second king, Numa, raised the number of days to 355 by adding two extra months, January and February. Scaliger ridiculed the assumption that a 'shepherd' such as Romulus could have set up a calendar system, and attributed the first (inept) reforms to 'Numa or some other bumpkin or rustic'.[28] Similarly the fifth-century writer Macrobius (*Saturnalia* 1.13.1) describes the initial Roman calendar as the product of an 'uncouth and still unpolished age' (*saeculo rudi et adhuc impolito*), while Ovid in his *Fasti* (a month-by-month account of the Roman year) attributes Romulus' 'error' to the fact that he 'knew arms better than stars' (1.29). Ovid further suggests that Romulus named March after the god of war and made it the first month in part as tribute to the Romans' warlike character (3.79–80).[29]

Scaliger also followed ancient sources in his approach to the calendar introduced by Julius Caesar (a year of 365 days with one day inserted every four years). Ovid writes that 'the times were wandering even now (*errabant etiam nunc tempora*)' – until Caesar took control (*Fasti* 3.155–6); the phrase 'even now' (often used to express the surprising survival of a practice (p. 126)) here suggests that the Romans were surprisingly late to introduce changes. A similar account is found in Censorinus: Caesar 'corrected' the calendar after observing that 'the months did not correspond as they should to the moon, nor the year to the sun' (22.8). Other writers add that the leap-year rules were misapplied after Caesar's death until the error was corrected by Augustus (Suetonius, *Augustus* 31.2; Solinus 1.45–7; Macrobius, *Saturnalia* 1.14.13–15).[30] Heir to these developmental assumptions, Scaliger was even more vigorous in his language: all of Caesar's military triumphs, he wrote, are 'mere trifles set against this arrangement of the year'.[31]

The idea of progress paraded by ancient accounts of calendar reform gave rise to the possibility that different temporal strata could be conceived as co-existing.[32] Plutarch was one of a number of ancient authors to note that the last six months of the Roman year were named after the ordinals 'fifth' to 'tenth' (or the last four after Quintilis and Sextilis had been renamed after Julius Caesar and Augustus). The names of these months supported reconstructions according to which the original Roman year, whether formed of ten or twelve months, started in March; on either view, the months kept their names when the calendar was reformed even though they had lost their etymological significance (Plutarch, *Roman Questions* 268a–b). A similar conservatism was observed in the festival calendar: a speaker in Macrobius notes that with Caesar's calendar (which added two days to December) the Saturnalia were now celebrated on the sixteenth rather than the fourteenth day before the Kalends of January, but that some of the common people kept up their celebrations 'according to the old custom' (*vetere more*); the result of this confusion was that the festival expanded from one day to three (*Saturnalia* 1.10.2).

The progressivist understanding of ancient calendar reform has been criticized by some recent scholars. In his important study *Caesar's Calendar*, Denis Feeney suggests that the sort of attitude reflected in Scaliger's celebration of Caesar's triumph is anachronistic: 'as inhabitants of Caesar's grid we take it for granted that a calendar is there precisely to measure time, to create an ideal synthesis of natural and socially or humanly organized time and in the process to capture a "time" that is out there, waiting to be measured'.[33] That is, prior to Caesar's reforms calendars were geared towards the civic time of festivals and other human institutions. It was the creation of a system with identical years (or at least years differing by one day every four years) that gave rise to the idea of a regular succession of measurable time independent of political manipulation. Feeney's argument is supported by the fact that many cities kept their traditional systems of intercalation even when more precise systems were available; in addition, the standardization of calendars in the first millennium BC can be seen as part of the administrative centralization carried out by large imperial powers such as the Seleucids and Romans – even if the Romans also tolerated local exceptions such as the prestigious Athenian calendar.[34]

Feeney offers a brilliant picture of the changes wrought by Caesar's calendar. He points, for instance, to changes in accounts of the festival and agricultural year before and after the reforms as well as to the new importance of anniversaries as pathetic markers of transience.[35] Nonetheless, the notion that a calendar captures a time that is there to be measured should not be dismissed as the product of the post-Caesarian mindset. A strong awareness of the continuity of 'time' as a separate entity is caught in images of *chronos* as 'best saviour for just men' (Pindar fr. 159), 'ancient father of days' (Euripides, *Suppliant Women* 787–8) and 'unwearying' and 'begetting itself in its ever-flowing stream' (Critias, DK 88 B18).[36] The calendar year, moreover, was used for measurement not just in rhetorical demonstrations such as Solon's diatribe on the fragility of human existence, but also in the realms of politics and diplomacy: when the Athenians ostracized politicians for ten years (from 487 BC), or made a treaty with the Spartans for thirty, the years were defined by the magistrate associated with each calendar year (archons at Athens, ephors at Sparta); at Athens, decrees began to be inscribed with the archon's name from the 430s BC, and a list of annual archons was inscribed in the 420s.

The practice of intercalation in ancient calendars is itself a further reason for thinking that progressivist approaches are not totally anachronistic. The practice implies that cities were keen to keep some form of correspondence between months and the solar year – even if pre-Caesarian Rome tolerated calendars that were at times two or three months out of joint with the seasons. A desire for close correspondence is, moreover, at times made explicit in justifications of intercalation: Herodotus, as we have noted, speaks of ensuring that the seasons 'tally (*sumbainōsi*) as necessary' (1.32.3; cf. 2.4.1), and a reform to the 365-day

Egyptian calendar proposed in the third-century BC (though only applied by Augustus) aimed to ensure that winter and summer festivals were held in the proper season (*OGIS* 56.40–6: the Canopus Decree, 238 BC). Something of the Scaligerian mind set likewise underlies the Moon's complaints (as reported by the chorus of Aristophanes' *Clouds* (607–26)) that the festival calendar has gone awry.

We have seen, then, that ancient accounts of calendars show a sense of anachronism in the developments they posit from simple to complex, and that calendrical systems reveal a desire to match the different rhythms of the moon and the sun. As we shall see in the rest of this chapter, detection of historical anachronisms is founded on a similar concern to match different temporal cycles.

Dating systems

One of Scaliger's contributions to chronology was the invention of the Julian Period, a period of 7,980 years based on a 28-year solar cycle, a 19-year lunar cycle and a 15-year indiction cycle (a system used for administrative purposes from late antiquity to the early modern period), with a starting date equivalent to 4713 BC (year 1 in each of the three cycles). The advantage of the Julian Period was that it provided a continuous timeline well adapted for astronomical calculations (it is still used for this purpose). Scaliger also, however, displayed his historicizing instincts by looking at the evidence for other dating systems and even, as we have noted, creating his own Olympiad-based chronology of ancient Greek history.

What seems to be an odd slip appears in Scaliger's chronography in the entry for the second year of the eighty-seventh Olympiad. He offers the name of the Athenian archon, Euthydemus, and then a single historical notice: 'Beginning of the Peloponnesian War, which Thucydides son of Olorus wrote up.'[37] As the nineteenth-century German scholar Ewald Scheibel noted in his commentary on the chronography, Scaliger was following a view found in Diodorus (12.38) and implied in Aulus Gellius' dating of the start of the war to the 323rd year from Rome's foundation (17.21.16).[38] Thucydides, on the other hand, offers a different and, in Scheibel's view, more accurate date at the start of his second book. After announcing that he will give an account of the war by successive summers and winters, he fixes the war's start with the Theban invasion of Plataea in 'the fifteenth year' of 'the Thirty-Year Treaty made after the capture of Euboea', 'when

Chrysis had been priestess at Argos for forty-eight years, when Aenesias was ephor at Sparta and Pythodorus [Euthydemus' predecessor] still had two months to serve as archon at Athens, in the sixth month after the battle at Potidaea and at the start of spring' (2.2.1). If this date is accepted, Scaliger seems to have committed a metachronism of one year.

Scaliger's decision not to follow Thucydides was not due to a lack of knowledge. In *De emendatione* he uses this passage as evidence for the start of the Athenian year, and he alludes to it again, albeit sloppily, in his commentary on Eusebius' *Chronicle*, which was published alongside *Anagraphē Olympiadōn*, to explain why the start of the war is there placed the year before Euthydemus' archonship: 'It is true the Archidamian or Peloponnesian War began when there were still a few days left of Pythodorus' magistracy.'[39] But he at once adds that 'writers of this war take its beginning from the following magistrate Euthydemus'. That is, Scaliger consciously overrides Thucydides even though by his usual principles he would have favoured him as contemporary with the events he describes.[40]

The anachronism committed by Diodorus and other 'writers of this war' results from a clash of different dating systems. Diodorus dates each year by Athenian archons and Roman consuls while noting Olympiads every four years. Since each of these systems had a different starting point within the calendar year, it was possible to date an event correctly in one system but incorrectly in the others: thus in our example Diodorus dates the start of the Peloponnesian War correctly in Roman terms but to the wrong archon and Olympiad year. Scaliger himself had no such excuse since his chronography included only Olympiad and archon years. He may have felt that his dating was justified instead on historicist grounds: he was producing what a (reasonably accurate) Olympiad list might have looked like.

Thucydides' own dating system reflects his concern to avoid precisely the sort of anachronism found (four centuries later) in Diodorus. His synchronism of different systems at the start of Book 2 implicitly underlines their disjunction both with each other and with the seasons which control the rhythm of military campaigns by land and sea; the passage is a concealed polemic against his near-contemporary Hellanicus of Lesbos, who composed a Panhellenic chronicle entitled, after its dating system, *Priestesses of Hera at Argos* as well as an *Atthis* (history of Athens) which used archon years. The polemic becomes explicit later in the work when Thucydides defends his claim that the first part of the war lasted for almost exactly ten years: only dating by seasons, he suggests, can bring out its length with the required accuracy (5.20).[41]

Further light is shed on Thucydides' hostility to local dating systems by his account of the closing years of the first part of the war. In the ninth year, a year-long armistice was agreed between Athens and Sparta; two years later, a short-lived fifty-year peace was formalized. Thucydides cites the terms of both treaties, including their start dates in each city's calendar: for the armistice, 14 Elaphebolion at Athens, 12 Geraestius at Sparta (4.118.12); for the peace, 25 Elaphebolion and 27 Artemesius (5.19.1). The difference in the days of the month in itself points to the lack of alignment between the calendars;[42] the second set of dates shows, moreover, that in two years the alignment of both months and days in the two cities' calendars has changed. This variability of local calendars is one reason why Thucydides was unwilling to use them for dating events within his war seasons; other, equally deep (and related) reasons are their parochialism and their absence from his main literary model, Homer.

The example of the armistice does nonetheless reveal the role that local calendars could play in detecting chronological errors. Thucydides reports how news of the armistice reached the Spartan general Brasidas as he was in the process of welcoming Scione, a city defecting from Athenian control. A dispute then arose as to whether this revolt happened before the truce, as Brasidas claimed, or afterwards, as the Athenian envoy asserted 'by reckoning up the days' (4.122.3). It is only at the end of his account of the episode that Thucydides reveals that the Scionians revolted 'two days too late' (4.122.6) – evidently on 16 Elaphebolion in the Athenian calendar. Rather than revealing that date at the outset, Thucydides leaves it to be inferred at the end. He thereby preserves narrative tension while showing how the meaning of events was controlled by the perceptions of participants.

The propensity of annalistic dating to give rise to anachronism was discussed by other historians too. Both Polybius in his history of Rome's rise to power and Tacitus in his account of the Roman emperors offer year-by-year narratives, but they note on occasion that they have grouped together in a single year events that took place in more than one year, either because the events would seem insignificant if narrated separately or (in Tacitus' case) to offer some respite from a relentless narrative of internal discord (Polybius, *Histories* 14.12.4–5, 32.11.2–7; Tacitus, *Annals* 6.38.1, 12.40.4). Polybius further explains that one consequence of his geographical arrangement within each year's narrative (outlined at 5.30.8–33) is that later events in one area are narrated before earlier events in another area even when they are causally connected (15.24a, 28.16.5–11).

Another problem in annalistic dating was alleged by the late antique historian Eunapius in his continuation of the *Historical Chronicle* composed by the third-century AD Athenian Dexippus. Dexippus' work evidently used Athenian archons and Roman consuls as its chronological frame, presumably with a king-list for earlier periods. Eunapius (F1 Blockley) in his proem suggests that he has learnt from his predecessor that writers of annalistic history are forced to admit that their narratives are chronologically imprecise: Dexippus himself, he claims, described his chronicle as 'wandering and full of contradictions, like an unchaired assembly'. Eunapius proceeds to dismiss excessive precision about hours and days as fitting only for accountants and astrologers: 'What contribution do dates make to Socrates' wisdom?' He even appeals in support of his position to Thucydides' account of the dispute over Scione, which he distorts entirely by claiming that the disagreement was unsolvable. While this sort of distortion of historiographical predecessors was not uncommon, Eunapius was probably unusual in his willingness to profess his neglect of chronological accuracy for the relatively recent past. The problematic dates to which Dexippus himself alluded presumably sprang from the large scope of his work: as Livy too noted (*From the Foundation of the City* 2.21.4), it could be hard when treating distant times to know to which year events belonged.[43]

Besides facilitating anachronism as chronological error, ancient dating systems could reflect a sense of anachronism as historical difference. Part of the difference of the distant past for ancient historians was the difficulty of discovering reliable information about it: many ancient writers evoked this with the imagery of darkness,[44] while Plutarch compared undertaking his *Theseus* with travel to the uncertain spaces on the edges of maps (1.1). The point at which knowledge became more secure did, however, vary from author to author and region to region. Some historians (Thucydides among them) were prepared to offer year-dates after the Trojan War; others (for instance Diodorus) started from the return of the Heraclids (placed by Thucydides eighty years after the Sack of Troy); others again rejected reliable records before the first Olympiad (e.g. Julius Africanus F34 Wallraff). Castor of Rhodes, by contrast, provided year-dates before the Trojan War using the king-list of Sicyon; his method was developed by Christian chronographers such as Eusebius, who synchronized regnal years at Sicyon, Argos, Mycenae and Athens prior to the Trojan War. Similar variety can be found in Roman historians: Livy, for instance, offers for the regal period reign-lengths without much internal precision; it is only with the start of the Republic that he adopts an annalistic structure. A sense of when reliable chronology becomes possible can also be revealed by patterns of incidental dates within works that lack a strong chronological frame: Phlegon of Tralles, for instance, author of a book of marvels in addition to a chronology, offers a narrative of sex changes in which he presents no dates for Tiresias and Caeneus, whose bodily transformations resulted from divine intervention, while offering archon- and consul-dates for some more recent sex changes accomplished without divine help (evidently cases where intersex children were re-classified at puberty) (*FGrH* 257 F4.6–10).

The difficulty of dating by years in early periods is reflected in the continuing use of generations as chronological signposts. Dating by generations, found to a limited extent in the Homeric poems, structured the heroic age in the Hesiodic *Catalogue of Women* and again in the more systematic chronologies found in early prose works such as Hecataeus' *Genealogies* (early fifth century BC); it also played an important role in Herodotus' structuring of the more recent past. Generations continued to be useful chronological tools, moreover, even after some chronologers had offered year-dates for the heroic age: thus Pausanias (10.17.4) rejects as 'nonsense' a story that Daedalus took part in a colonizing expedition with Aristaeus since Daedalus lived 'at the time of Oedipus' while Aristaeus married the daughter of Cadmus (the unstated part of the argument being that Cadmus was Oedipus' great-great-grandfather);[45] similarly he rejects a local Laconian tradition that Achilles was one of the suitors of Helen (3.24.11) by appealing to explicit indications of generations in the Homeric poems.

The changing nature of the historical record was itself a basis for periodization. Particularly notable is a passage in Censorinus (*On the Birthday* 21) to which Scaliger was repeatedly drawn. Censorinus records three 'distinctions of times' (*discrimina temporum*) defined by Varro, who was himself probably drawing on a Hellenistic chronographer such as Eratosthenes: the first interval, 'from the beginning of humans to the earlier flood', was 'called "unclear" (*adēlon*) because of our ignorance', and was of uncertain length (perhaps even infinite); the second, 'from the earlier flood to the first Olympiad', was 'called "mythical" (*muthikon*) because many fabulous things are reported in it', and was believed to be around 1,600 years; the third, 'from the first Olympiad to us', was 'called "historical" (*historikon*), because the events done in it are contained in true histories'. The interest of this passage for Scaliger lay initially in the fact that the first Olympiad was the basis for the reckoning of times;[46] subsequently he suggested that 'heroic' was a better label than 'mythical' for Varro's middle period (a small tweak, as Varro equally allowed for a substantial non-fabulous element in this period) and, more daringly, equated the first two periods with the new concept of 'proleptic' time that he developed in response to Babylonian and Egyptian king-lists that stretched beyond the Biblical creation date.[47]

Variations in dating systems expressed a sense of political development as well as the changing contours of historical knowledge. Eusebius tracks political change at Athens by successively dating years through kings, life-archons and ten-year archons; this schematic and probably unhistorical progression culminates in the establishment of the annual archonship, at which point he drops Athenian dating from his parallel columns. The Athenian annual archonship nonetheless retained its use for historians such as Diodorus and Dionysius of Halicarnassus, partly because it was used by the Athenian Apollodorus (second century BC) in his very influential verse chronology, partly as homage to Athens' past cultural superiority; it remained so familiar that the geographer Pausanias felt the need to explain the changes in the archon system when he synchronized an early Olympiad dating with the *fifth* year of a (ten-year) Athenian archon's office (4.5.10).

The potential of chronology itself to mark difference is well illustrated by the Parian Marble (*FGrH* 239) (Figs. 6 and 7), a chronological list inscribed on stone on the island of Paros in the third century BC. This inscription uses two different systems: it dates events back by years from the archonship of Diognetus in Athens and his equivalent in Paros (264/3 BC), using a system of acrophonic

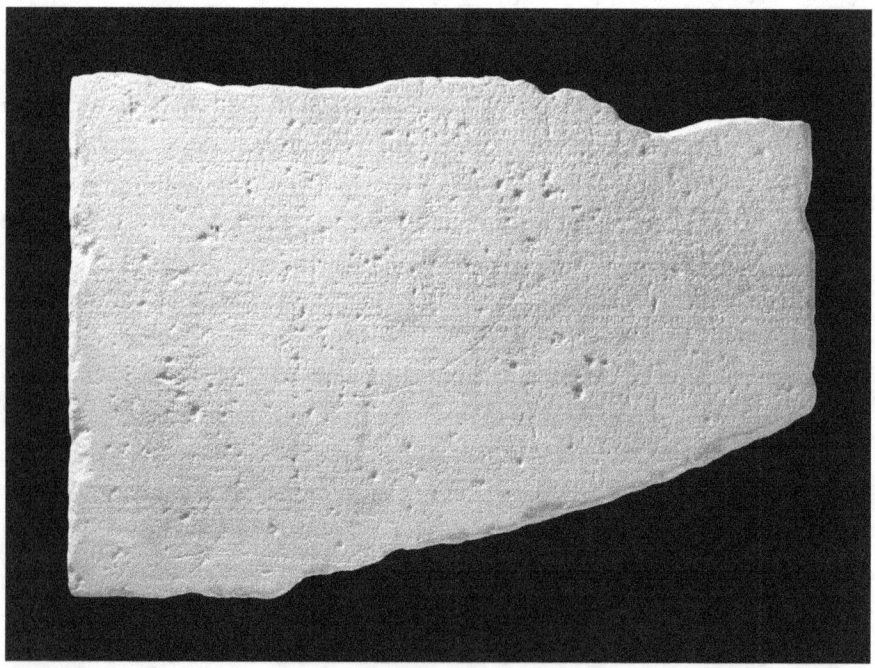

Fig. 6 Middle section of chronographic inscription from Paros, known as the Parian Marble, *c.* 266/5 BC. ANC Chandler.2.23. © Ashmolean Museum, University of Oxford.

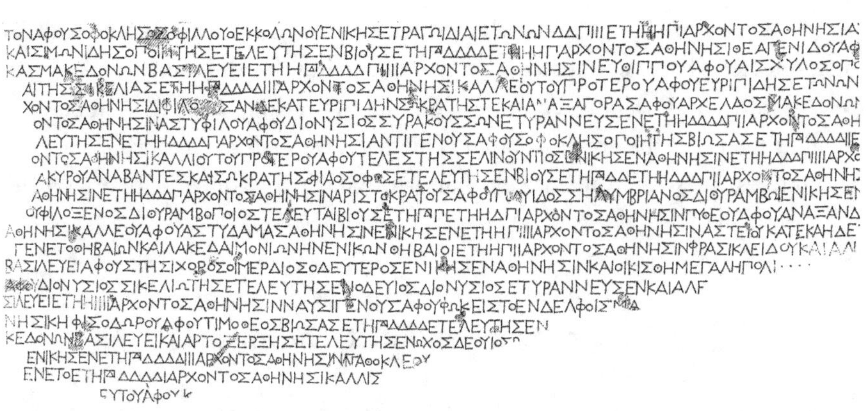

Fig. 7 Detail of text from the Parian Marble, showing the use of both acrophonic numerals (e.g. Δ = 10, H = 100) and archon names for dates. © Ashmolean Museum, University of Oxford.

numerals (i.e. with thousands, hundreds, fifties, tens, fives and ones marked by the first letter of the Greek word for the number);[48] and it names the Athenian king or archon in that year (using the term 'king' for life-archons too, while omitting the ten-year archons and marking the start of annual archons as an event in itself). Only three times does it mark the regnal year: for the start and end of the Trojan War and the foundation of Syracuse (the final event listed before the annual archonship). The status of the Trojan War as a chronological marker is further highlighted by the unique inclusion of a calendar date (with Athenian months) for its fall and possibly by an empty space on the inscription (the relevant part has been lost since its transcription in the seventeenth century).[49]

External political change, too, could be reflected in changes of dating systems. Eusebius' synchronistic tables tracked the rise and fall of kingdoms: the parallel columns become fewer and fewer until the Roman conquest of Judaea, at which point only Rome is left.[50] The rise of Rome similarly underlies a change in the system used by Polybius. For most of his work he adopts an annalistic method, dating by Olympiad year, but at the very start of his main narrative he treats in single units events in different regions in the four years of the 140th Olympiad. This variation is linked to his key thesis that the rise of Rome led to an unprecedented 'interconnection' (*sumplokē*) of events throughout the inhabited world in the third year of the 140th Olympiad; previously, he explains, he introduced synchronisms purely to clarify the chronological link between events (4.28).[51]

Accuracy in synchronism is a key concern of the various dating systems we have explored in this section: Thucydides synchronizes local dates for the start of the Peloponnesian War; Polybius offers explicit synchronisms of (initially unconnected, later connected) events occurring in different parts of the Mediterranean; Eusebius combines dating by various regnal systems with continuing use of the era of Abraham's birth. As we shall see in our next section, this interest in synchronism went hand-in-hand with concern for its flipside, anachronism.

Prochronisms and metachronisms

In the preface to the posthumous edition of *De emendatione*, Joseph Scaliger wrote of his ambition to save chronology from the 'ravings of the ignorant and the tyranny of sophists' by preparing the ground for the completion of a 'perfect Chronicle' (*Chronicon absolutissimum*). A key step towards that goal was the commentary on Eusebius' *Chronicle* that he provided in *Thesaurus temporum* – a series of detailed notes on those entries (and there were many of them) where he detected chronological problems. The commentary was throughout embellished with his new typology of anachronism. At times, as we have seen with Athens' Sicilian disaster, he identifies prochronisms (entries placed too early). Entries placed too late include those for years of Abraham 1701, where Plato's nephew Speusippus is listed as a distinguished philosopher, and 1859, where Terence's death is announced (metachronisms of twenty-four years and one year respectively).[52] At times, too, Scaliger uses 'anachronism' without any indication of years: the report 'Theseus seized Helen', placed by Eusebius in the thirteenth year of Theseus' reign, is a 'ridiculous anachronism', since 'Theseus seized Helen during the reign of his father Aegeus'.[53] Often, too, he departs from his typology by indicating chronological mistakes through periphrastic expressions: the time allotted to Phoenix and Cadmus 'is not congruent' with that assigned to Busiris; 'the epoch of Capua's foundation . . . is thirty-four years before the time assigned by Eusebius or rather by Diodorus'.[54] Again, there are entries, such as that for Hannibal's death, where he simply notes the existence of conflicting sources.[55] And occasionally he even explains that Eusebius got the date (more or less) right, as with the placing of the poet Terpander twenty-nine years after his victory at the Spartan Carneia.[56]

Scaliger's commentary on Eusebius offers a snapshot of the scholarly laboratory in which the chronology of the ancient world was distilled from a vast range of famous and obscure authorities. It is not that he was the first to attempt the task of chronological reconstruction in early modern times: the correct BC date of one key epoch, the first Olympiad, had been established slightly earlier in the sixteenth century by Paul Crusius.[57] In many cases, indeed, Scaliger was picking up ancient controversies over dates – while also, as we shall see, suppressing in the cause of chronological precision some of the distinctive ideological disputes that lay behind those controversies.

Let us start with the date of Hannibal's death. Scaliger notes that three possible consul-years are preserved for this date; for two of these he names sources (the late antique historians Eutropius and Orosius). He omits to mention that the first-century BC biographer and chronologer Cornelius Nepos (*Hannibal* 13.1) had offered the same three consul-years, with a source for each possibility: the *Annals* of Cicero's friend Atticus (*FRHist* 33 F8), Polybius (23.13) and Sulpicius Blitho (*FRHist* 55 F1), a writer known only from this citation. For a sense of what was at stake in the dispute, however, we need to turn to Polybius (the one author named by Nepos whose account survives independently) and Livy (who wrote after Nepos). Polybius places Hannibal's death in the same year as the deaths of Scipio, Hannibal's great adversary in the Second Punic War, and of his own political hero Philopoemen, who had attempted to defend Greek independence in the face of Roman expansion; he further stresses the synchronism by writing parallel obituaries for the three men (23.12–14). While Polybius was evidently trying to boost the standing of his fellow Achaean Philopoemen, Livy rejects the synchronism with detailed arguments for the date of Scipio's death (directed against Polybius and the historian Valerius Antias (*FRHist* 25 F56)) based on the dates of his replacement as *princeps senatus* and of a court case in which he was involved.[58] Livy then offers a different basis for comparison: 'the deaths of these three men, each the most famous among his own people, seem comparable not so much because of the coincidence of their times, as because no one of them met an end worthy of the brilliance of his life' (39.52.1–3). At stake in the debate over Hannibal's death, then, was the use of synchronism as a means both of pattern-finding in history and of ethnic self-definition.

Disputes over Helen's dates, by contrast, reveal normative assumptions about gender. One important chronological problem was addressed by Eusebius himself in an entry where he places the Argonautic expedition under the year 756. Noting that Castor and Pollux were included among the Argonauts, Eusebius queries how Helen could be their sister, 'as she was seized as a virgin by Theseus many years later' (he puts her rapes by Theseus and Paris in years 795 and 826). The obvious solution (which Scaliger adopted[59]) was to place the Argonautic expedition much closer to the Trojan War. But even with that chronology, fixing the date of Theseus' rape of Helen posed difficulties: while Scaliger, as we have seen, placed this event before Theseus became king, many ancient writers followed the version of Hellanicus (*FGrH* 4 F168a, from Plutarch, *Theseus* 31.1), according to which Theseus was fifty years old at the time of the rape – and all the more reprehensible on that account: thus Plutarch (*Syncrisis of Theseus and Romulus* 6.1) blames Theseus for seizing Helen when 'she was an unripe child, while he was already of an age too great for even lawful wedlock'.

The chronology that Eusebius questioned could also be put to moralizing ends. Lucian's dialogue *Cock* starts with a poor man who dreams of wealth complaining of being woken up by a cock. The cock, it turns out, is none other than the latest incarnation of Pythagoras – who had famously claimed to be the Trojan warrior Euphorbus in a still earlier incarnation. As part of a typically Cynic diatribe against wealth, the cock rejects the version of the Trojan War told by Homer (who was a camel in Bactria at the time) – including the reputed beauty of Helen: 'she was very old, almost the same age as Hecuba, inasmuch as Theseus, who lived in Heracles' time, seized her first and held her at Aphidnae, and Heracles captured Troy on the former occasion in our fathers' time, our then fathers that is' (22.17). Lucian's engagement with chronology here is strictly *ad cock*: elsewhere he plays on the contrast between her beauty at the time of the Trojan War and her sorry state in the Underworld, exposing the futile sacrifice of so many lives for her sake (77.5).

Different issues are involved in ancient debates on the foundation of the Campanian capital Capua. Scaliger's view that Eusebius dated the foundation of this city thirty-four years late applies to a notice for the year 1580 that refers more generally to the unification of the Campanians.[60] The date Scaliger calculates is based on evidence from Cato the Elder (*FRHist* 5 F52) that is preserved by the first-century AD historian Velleius Paterculus. Applying his usual method of dating back from the consulship of Marcus Vinicius (AD 30), Velleius counts 240 years to the sack of Capua by the Romans while also citing Cato's claim that the city's sack happened 260 years after its foundation. What Scaliger fails to note is that Velleius alludes to the foundation as an event 'in which there has been much error and in which the views of the authorities show great discrepancy'. Velleius himself agrees with the 'vastly different' view that Capua was founded 830 (rather than 500) years before his own time: 'I can hardly believe that such a great city grew, flourished, fell, and rose again so quickly' (1.7.2-4). Velleius' reasoning here is based on an *a priori* assumption about the rhythms of history that is close to the model of anachronism developed by Vico in the eighteenth century (p. 24): just as Vico detected an anachronism in putting events from the 'age of gods' in the 200 years of the 'age of heroes', so Velleius suggests that Cato's date for Capua's foundation puts too many events into 500 years. Vico himself listed the Capuans as one of three peoples conquered by Rome who had resisted the natural course of human civil institutions – in their case because they 'developed too rapidly because of their mild climate and the abundance of fertile Campania'.[61]

Scaliger's notes on Eusebius frequently reflect one of the key areas of chronological interest in antiquity, literary history. From the fifth century BC onwards, there was a persistent interest in the dates of Homer and Hesiod;[62] from the Hellenistic period onwards there were biographies of them, as of early Greek poets, generally with little firm evidence to go on. Divergent views on Homer's dates were grist to the mill of Christian apologists such as Tatian (*To the Greeks* 31) and Clement (*Miscellanies* 1.117), while their near-contemporary Pausanias was so alarmed by the 'censoriousness' of present-day professors of poetry that he refused to publish his own research on the issue (9.30.3). One place where Scaliger pays attention to this Homeric question is an entry for the historian Herodotus (prochronistically placed in year 1548, i.e. 468 BC). Scaliger digresses to note that Herodotus claimed in his *Histories* that Homer and Hesiod lived 'not more than 400 years' before his own time (2.53), but that his biography of Homer gave an interval of 622 years between his life and Xerxes' crossing from Asia to Europe (in 480 BC). While modern scholars reject the attribution of the biography to Herodotus, Scaliger's solution was to emend the text to 422.[63]

The complexity of literary chronology can be seen equally well in the case of the poet Terpander. As we noted, Scaliger accepted Eusebius' dating for Terpander as approximately correct owing to its proximity to the first Carneia. A passage in Athenaeus – a small diversion in a long discussion of the disputed chronology of certain musical instruments – reveals how comparison of different scholarly sources on the history of poetry could throw up very different datings (14.635e–f):

> Terpander was the first victor at the Carneia, as Hellanicus reports in both his metrical and prose *Carneian Victors* (*FGrH* 4 F85a). The Carneia was established in the twenty-sixth Olympiad, as Sosibius states in his *On Dates* (*FGrH* 595 F3). But Hieronymus in *On Citharodes* – the fifth part of *On Poets* – says that Terpander lived at the time of Lycurgus the lawgiver, who is reported by all without disagreement to have organized the first numbered Olympics together with Iphitus of Elis (fr. 33 Wehrli).

Athenaeus' discussion shows that Terpander's link with the Carneia clashed with a different synchronism, with the lawgiver Lycurgus, who flourished over a hundred years earlier. Other sources muddy the picture further by showing that Lycurgus' date was much more contested than Athenaeus implies (Plutarch begins his *Lycurgus* by stating that 'there is nothing to say that is undisputed ... least of all the dates when the man lived').[64]

Even though biographical traditions about early Latin poets were recorded much sooner after their deaths, they too gave rise to chronological disputes. Cicero's dialogue on the history of Roman oratory, *Brutus*, attests early and late chronologies (by Varro and Accius respectively) for one of the first figures of Latin literature, Livius Andronicus (72–3); accepting the former, Scaliger blames a metachronism of fifty-four years in Jerome's entry on his 'haste, the mother of hallucination'.[65] For the death of Terence, on the other hand, Scaliger notes that Jerome follows Suetonius' *Lives of the Poets*, albeit with a metachronism of one year. But he omits to note three scandalous stories which Suetonius mentions – but rejects on chronological grounds. One of these stories was that Terence was born a slave at Carthage and came to Rome as a prisoner of war; Suetonius dismisses this story on the grounds that Terence was born before the Second and died before the Third Punic War, and that the Romans did not at that time trade with Carthage's other enemies (*Terence* 1). Terence's date of birth was also cited against claims that he had been the younger lover of the Roman aristocrats Scipio Africanus and Laelius and that he had received help from them in writing his plays (*Terence* 1, 4, citing the historian Fenestella and grammarian Santra); the basis for these rumours seems to have been in the one case a scurrilous poem cited by Suetonius and in the other some oblique lines in the preface of one of Terence's own plays (*Brothers* 15–21). These anachronisms follow a common pattern whereby famous figures are attached to other significant figures or events: there were similarly stories that the comic playwright Eupolis died at sea during the Sicilian expedition and that the Sicilian philosopher Empedocles fought in that war – stories rejected on the grounds that Eupolis had written plays dated later (Eratosthenes *FGrH* 241 F19) and that Empedocles was either dead or too old to fight at that time (Apollodorus *FGrH* 244 F32).[66] At the same time, the disputes over Livius Andronicus and Terence reflect a pervasive Roman interest in mapping the (belated) development of their own culture against Greek literary history.

The propensity for anachronism in the biographical tradition about philosophers was equally strong. Scaliger notes that Speusippus, who succeeded Plato as head of the Academy, is mentioned as having died twenty-four years prior to his appearance in Eusebius as a 'distinguished' philosopher in year 1701; indeed, he is mentioned as 'distinguished' already in year 1622. Scaliger thought that such doublets resulted from Eusebius' use of different sources; the variation among the sources may itself have reflected either attempts to attach dates to free-floating anecdotes or the influence of deliberate comic fictions. The particular interest in the chronology of philosophers lay in the importance of teacher–pupil relationships in ancient biographical traditions (as reflected, for instance, in Diogenes Laertius' *Lives of the Philosophers*, which is structured by the various philosophical schools that claimed descent from Socrates). The attempt to map chains of pedagogical influence gave rise to many suspect ties: claims that Themistocles and Thucydides were taught by the philosopher Anaxagoras were rejected on chronological grounds by Plutarch (*Themistocles* 2.5) and the Byzantine scholar John Tzetzes (scholia on Thucydides 8.109, responding to Marcellinus, *Life of Thucydides* 22) respectively.[67]

The ideological implications of pedagogical anachronism are highlighted by a short treatise by Isocrates, *Busiris*. The work is in the form of a letter to a sophist Polycrates criticizing his paradoxical *Defence of Busiris*, a king of Egypt who was said to have sacrificed foreigners until, in one version, he was killed by Heracles. Isocrates says that Polycrates made the Egyptian even worse than traditional accounts; he counters by presenting Busiris as the founder of a political order that bears some resemblance to the imaginary city Callipolis described in Plato's *Republic*. The charge of anachronism is raised against Polycrates twice. First Isocrates rejects Polycrates' claim that Busiris emulated Aeolus and Orpheus, whose deeds were the opposite of his and whose fathers were not yet born in Busiris' time (7–8). Later he argues that the claims made about Busiris' misdeeds fail on chronological grounds because they are linked with the story that he was killed by Heracles, 'but it is agreed by all writers that Heracles was four generations younger than Perseus, son of Zeus and Danae, and that Busiris was older by more than 200 years' (36–7). While, as often, claims about the universal agreement of chronographers deserve some scepticism (Eusebius offered up, to Scaliger's bafflement, a 'first Hercules' even earlier than Busiris[68]), Isocrates' rejection of the claim that Busiris was influenced by non-Egyptian figures and his dismissal of the Heracles story together prepare for the hints that Busiris' own political measures have been copied by others.[69]

The stakes become higher still when chronologies have to deal with different cultures' perceptions of the divine. Herodotus tells how the historian Hecataeus, during a visit to a temple in Egyptian Thebes, boasted of being descended from a god in the sixteenth generation; the priests responded by showing statues of the holders of a priesthood that had been handed down from father to son for more than 300 generations, with no gods in sight (2.143). Herodotus in addition dismisses as far too late the dates assigned by the Greeks to Dionysus and Pan (1,000 and 800 years before his own time), suggesting instead that those were the dates when they first received knowledge of these gods from Egypt (2.145). And when he hears of a Heracles who was deified some 17,000 years earlier, he infers that this Heracles is separate from 'the other Heracles, whom the Greeks know', that is, the son of Amphitryon whom they worship as a hero (2.43).[70] Herodotus, that is, undermines Greek pretensions by exposing the anachronisms in their views of the gods and their relative belatedness by comparison with the Egyptians: it was, he writes, 'yesterday or the day before (*prōēn te kai chthes*), so to speak,' that they learnt about the gods from Homer and Hesiod (2.53).[71]

With these Herodotean musings on the chronologies of the gods we return once more to concerns central to Scaliger's chronological researches. On the title-page of the first edition of *De emendatione*, Scaliger quoted a dictum of the second-century Christian theologian Tatian on the impossibility of historical truth when 'the recording of dates is incoherent' (*To the Greeks* 31). In context, that dictum was directed against the contradictory chronological records of the Greeks by contrast with the secure antiquity of Moses and Jewish law – a common refrain of the early Christian chronographers. While Scaliger himself avoided the polemical anti-paganism of writers such as Tertullian, who gave the earlier Hebrew prophets credit for Solon's exhortation to Croesus to look to the end (*Apologeticus* 19), he did in his later commentary on Eusebius praise Eusebius' success in proving the priority of Jewish traditions even while he showed up anachronisms within Christian chronography. Enemies of Christianity, he noted, used the age of their own gods as a weapon against Christians, suggesting that 'Christianity appeared yesterday and the day before (*chthes kai prōēn*)'[72] – a pointed echo of Herodotus' comment on the recentness of Greek knowledge of the gods. In response, Christian writers such as Tatian and Clement dated Moses to the time of Inachus, first king of Argos, but (and now Scaliger shifts to first-person possessive adjectives) Eusebius had not thought it enough that 'gentiles be overwhelmed by their own testimonies, unless they could be refuted by ours too' (that is, by the 'sacred page'). Eusebius' achievement, Scaliger concluded, had been to draw on a wider range of evidence in placing Moses 400 years later – but still to show the greater antiquity of the Jewish traditions.[73]

Our analysis in this chapter has suggested that a sense of historical process was at stake in many of the pre-Christian tussles over time-reckoning. We have encountered many authors in both the Greek and Roman worlds who presented calendrical systems as developing from simple to complex or whose approach to chronology modelled their understanding of political change. Even seemingly pedantic disputes over isolated chronological difficulties often had ideological and ethical sub-texts, not least when they involved clashes between different religious and cultural systems. In particular, Egypt was in some respects for Greece what Greece was later to be for both pagan and Christian chronologers under the Roman empire – a site of chronological comparison that exposed the uneven rhythms of historical development.[74] As we shall see in our next chapter, this perception of uneven rhythms was accompanied by a heightened awareness of the possibility of cultural outdatedness and obsolescence – concepts that over the past 200 years have come to be seen as the definitive characteristics of anachronism itself.

5

Anachronistic Survivals

Uneven development

How would a group of Hopi Indian children living in New Mexico in 1896 draw lightning? The humanist scholar Aby Warburg (1866–1929) wanted to find out whether they would depict it realistically, as a zig zag, or symbolically, as a snake-headed figure, in accordance with Hopi tradition. After travelling from Hamburg to New York in 1895, he had crossed the continent, following a series of chance meetings and moved (in his own words) by a 'will to the Romantic',[1] in order to see at first hand the cultures of the indigenous peoples.[2] Though he was aware that his encounter with these cultures had been short and hindered by the lack of a shared language, the result of the lightning experiment (US Zig-zags 12, Hopi Snakes 2) was just one of the experiences in the course of this journey on which Warburg drew as he developed his theories about the *Nachleben* (Survival) of pagan antiquity and *Pathosformeln* (Pathos-formulas), the emotional gestures in artworks that transmit the traumatic energy of past cultures – theories that culminated in his projected *Mnemosyne Atlas*, an assembly of images that drew unexpected connections across different times and cultures.

Warburg returned to his trip to the American West in 1923 in a lecture on 'Images from the Region of the Pueblo Indians of North America' that he delivered while recovering from mental illness in a sanatorium. In this lecture, Warburg related the depiction of lightning as snakes to the dry climate of New Mexico: the storm that brought rain was fused with the snake, a creature associated both with the earth and with renewal (through the sloughing of its skin). In addition, though he had not seen the Hopi 'serpent ritual' himself, he drew points of comparison and contrast with Dionysiac snake-rituals in classical Greece, 'the very cradle of our own European culture', where 'cultic habits were in vogue which in crudeness and perversity far surpass what we have seen among the Indians'; he saw the role of snakes in ritual as a development away from blood sacrifice, as part, that is, of the process of 'religious sublimation' that was central to 'the history of religious evolution from east to west'.[3] Still more broadly, Warburg placed the Hopi in an evolutionary schema determined by the human use of symbols:

> The togetherness (*Nebeneinander*) of logical civilization and fantastic, magical causation shows the Pueblo Indians' peculiar condition of hybridity and transition. They are clearly no longer primitives dependent on their senses, for whom no action directed toward the future can exist; but neither are they technologically secure Europeans, for whom future events are expected to be organically or mechanically determined. They stand on middle ground between magic and logos, and their instrument of orientation is the symbol. Between a culture of touch and a culture of thought is the culture of symbolic connection.[4]

Despite these comments, Warburg did elsewhere claim that Hopi rituals were survivals of a 'primitive' paganism and that his exposure to their world shaped his understanding of the development of Europe from the Middle Ages to the Renaissance. He did not, however, equate this evolution with progress: he closed his lecture by regretting the imminent loss of the symbolic culture whose traces he had seen and by blaming that loss on 'Uncle Sam' and the age of electricity.[5]

The temporal assumptions in Warburg's cultural model have been both praised and condemned in modern scholarship. On the one hand, as we noted in Chapter 1, critics such as Didi-Huberman suggest that Warburg's concepts offer a means of capturing the temporal instability of images. On the other hand, he is seen as instantiating the epistemological problems of ethnographic research, in particular its embeddedness in unequal (typically colonial) power dynamics. Claire Farago argues that Warburg's writings and photographs place him in a long history of reactions against modern civilization through engagement with the 'Other'. Warburg reflects thereby 'a major problem inherent in every center/periphery model of art history': 'the structure itself unavoidably reiterates the historical relations of power that its critical reemployments attempt to dismantle'.[6] Farago questions, too, the ethical propriety of Warburg's dealings with the Hopi as well as the subsequent commercial use of his photographs of rituals; as she notes, the modern Hopi council has appealed to divergent models of temporality in arguing against the re-publication of these images.[7] Farago's critique of Warburg builds on a self-reflexive turn in anthropology which has identified a problematic 'denial of coevalness' or 'allochronism' between privileged observer and marginalized object.[8] That is, the category of time is used to define ethnographic objects as primitive, through evolutionary models, or else as bound in static cultural systems that lack any sense of linear progress. The same structural imbalance, as we noted in Chapter 2, has often been applied to temporally distant periods as a way of 'othering' classical antiquity or the Middle Ages.

As we shall see, Warburg's idea of the Hopi as pagan survivals has deep roots in earlier European anthropological and sociological thought. One important influence was the tradition of comparative ethnology that arose out of the first encounters with the inhabitants of the American continent. American Indians were from the start compared with peoples of the ancient world, notably the heroic warriors presented by Homer and Tacitus' Germans. These comparisons fed into debates on origins: similarities between the customs observed or reported in the New World and ancient ethnographic writings were used to support arguments about patterns of migration. Already present in Spanish writers such as José de Acosta (1540–1600), this debate was continued with a wealth of comparative material by the Jesuit Joseph-François Lafitau in his *Customs of American Savages compared with Customs of the First Times* (1724).[9] Nor was this comparative model confined to European colonial contexts: mainland Chinese visiting Taiwan in the seventeenth century spoke of the inhabitants' 'savage customs' as 'remnants from remote antiquity'.[10]

The empirical data gathered during the European colonization of the Americas shaped the approach to social development adopted by Scottish Enlightenment thinkers. Writers such as Adam Ferguson, author of *Essay on the History of Civil Society* (1767), traced the uneven progression in human societies from a uniform state of savagery through stages of barbarism and pastoralism to the 'polite' manners of mercantile civilization.[11] In Ferguson's stadial model, the study of peoples still living in a state of 'barbarism' opens a window into the distant past of European peoples: 'the inhabitants of Britain, at the time of the first Roman invasions, resembled, in many things, the present natives of North America', those 'many things' including ignorance of agriculture and the use of animal-skins for clothing.[12] He even imagined a time-traveller reporting back from classical Greece as if from a contemporary primitive culture: the traveller visits two cities which are not named but are evidently to be taken as Sparta and Athens, and contrasts Sparta, with its notorious broths and its lack of coinage, with the more civil customs at Athens, where wearing a sword was 'the mark of a barbarian'.[13]

A particular inspiration for Warburg's explorations of Hopi culture lay in the emerging discipline of anthropology.[14] The idea of survivals was developed by E. B. Tylor in his 1871 study *Primitive Culture*. Like Ferguson, Tylor looked for surviving traces of early human development in contemporary 'barbarous' peoples such as Greenlanders and Maoris. In addition, he found in his own culture the continuation of customs which 'have been carried on by force of habit into a new state of society different from that in which they had their original home'[15] – for instance, a rural woman weaving with an unmechanized handloom (rather than a flying shuttle) and the use of bows and arrows in games rather than in war (the military use being retained only by 'a few savage tribes').[16] Like Warburg, Tylor was not committed to a uniform belief in progress. But he was convinced that that he was living in an era when rational advancement was possible, and he concluded *Primitive Culture* with the reflection that it was 'a harsher, and at times even painful, office' of ethnography to 'expose the remains of crude old culture' and 'mark these out for destruction'.[17]

A further influence on Warburg's model of the evolution from symbolic to rational thought lay in the writings of Hegel. Hegel saw the human spirit as developing through a series of stages, each represented by a model society in which its primary characteristics are most evident. In his Berlin lectures on the philosophy of world history (1822–31) Hegel set out a model in which development of the state is seen to occur across time and space, following the direction of the rising sun from east to west. The first stage, the Oriental, is marked by patriarchy and despotism, and equates to the childhood of the state; the second, the Greek, offers an 'adolescence' of 'beautiful freedom', in which the unstable beginnings of the state occur; this stage is followed by the adulthood of the Roman Empire (by which Hegel means both the classical and the later Holy Roman Empire) and the maturity of the German state in which subjective freedom can be realized.[18]

The strands we have explored thus far – comparative ethnography, Scottish stadialism and Hegel – were important influences on Marxist theories of uneven development. Marx identified a phenomenon similar to the survival in the idea that different classes occupy distinct temporalities, appropriate to their relationship to economic forces. He noted the standardization of time under industrialization – the advent of railway timetables and factory clocks – but also that that process was incomplete in some industrializing countries, such as Germany. In the Preface to *Das Kapital* (1867), he identified the 'passive survival of antiquated modes of production' with 'their inevitable train of social and political anachronisms' as a source of social discord.[19] In later writings, seeking to understand how non-industrialized societies such as Russia might be reconstructed without going through all the stages, Marx developed the image of 'layers' of temporal and social experience that co-existed within a society but were full of revolutionary potential.[20]

Marx's views were developed further by social theorists seeking the causes of the difficulties some societies experienced in modernization and industrialization. The idea of the 'contemporaneity of the non-contemporaneous' (*Gleichzeitigkeit des Ungleichzeitigen*) – in other words, that 'not all people exist in the same Now' – was formulated by Ernst Bloch as he attempted to make sense of the breakdown of German society and the rise of Nazism after the First World War.[21] For Bloch, the problem lay in the uneven spread of the capitalist mode of production, which meant that members of different layers of society (old/young, rural/urban) had different world views. The persistence of feudalism within developed industrial societies, an 'anachronistic superstructure', was one sign of unequal economic development in the capitalist economy.[22] While the orthodox Marxist view was that capitalism and industrialization drove the standardization of both society and the time which organized it, Bloch suggested that the anger generated by a perception of being left behind threatened social and political stability.

Outside social theory, the idea of anachronistic survival gained purchase in fiction written during the period of European colonial domination. The idea that primitive or distant cultures might offer unexpected access to the past was knowingly taken up in the 1880s in H. Rider Haggard's African adventures *King Solomon's Mines* (documenting the discovery of a quasi-Zulu civilization in the African interior, with Homeric and Spartan resonances) and *She* (whose title-character is a literal survival from classical antiquity). A similarly self-conscious exploitation of the trope was displayed in the 1920s in Edgar Rice Burroughs' Tarzan series, which features not just a feral aristocrat in Africa but also encounters with lost cultures such as an outpost of the Roman empire in a 'little valley of anachronisms' (*Tarzan and the Lost Empire*) and a plateau of Knights and Saracens which is initially mistaken for a film set (*Tarzan, Lord of the Jungle*).[23] As a genre, 'lost world'[24] fiction offers a complicated response to new cultural encounters in the context of colonialism: like Warburg's Hopi Indians, lost cultures can be used to critique technocratic modernity even as they are defined through the lens of that modernity.

The 'lost world' genre offered an extreme variation of a common image in earlier (fictional and non-fictional) travel writing. Journeys from the metropolitan centre to the periphery were often figured as journeys into the past. Walter Scott, for instance, spoke of 'the extreme simplicity as well as unchanging character of eastern manners' in the preface to an 1832 re-issue of his 1825 novel *The Talisman* (set during the Third Crusade). Explaining that these manners 'are taught us early in the enchanting terms which our infancy learns', he expressed the hope that (even without first-hand experience of the Levant) it was possible 'by keeping in generals to avoid any remarkable errors or anachronisms'.[25] Scott made a more dynamic use of anachronistic survival in his depictions of Scottish Highlanders in *Waverley* (set during the 1745 uprising) and of Saxons in *Ivanhoe* (set in the aftermath of the Norman Conquest). The plot of both novels is predicated on the idea of the supersession of the antiquated Highlander or Saxon; both are presented with romantic nostalgia now that they have been incorporated in national narratives of progress. The American Indian is a reference point in Scott's depiction of these anachronistic survivals, and his model influenced in turn the image of American Indians in James Fenimore Cooper's Leatherstocking novels and of Chechens in Tolstoy's novella *Hadji Murat*.[26]

Ideas of anachronistic survival have influenced scholarly writings on classical antiquity since the second half of the nineteenth century. A close interaction of comparative ethnography and classical scholarship is seen in the work on ritual by J. G. Frazer in Britain and by one of Warburg's teachers, Hermann Usener, in Germany.[27] The disciplines were brought together in a series of lectures on *Anthropology and the Classics* at Oxford in 1908, in one of which the Scottish folklorist Andrew Lang (a friend of both Tylor and Rider Haggard) found 'survivals of the barbarian and the savage' (human sacrifice, 'phantasms of the dead') in the epic cycle.[28] More recently, critics have suggested that heroic individualism is presented as anachronistic in works that track the creation of communal values and a new form of social heroism; the moment of transition is variously placed between Homeric epic and Greek tragedy or Virgil, between the *Iliad* and the *Odyssey* or even within individual works, reflecting either a deliberate authorial strategy or different compositional strata.[29] A different image of the 'tragedy of survival' – 'a perennial drama of all complex cultures' – emerges from Thomas Greene's reading of the *Aeneid*. Alluding to a scene at which we glanced earlier (p. 65), where Aeneas encounters Andromache on the shores of the Adriatic making offerings at an empty tomb of Hector, Greene writes that the *Aeneid* 'as the central classic of Western civilization' inscribed 'an awareness of tragic anachronism', an 'ambivalent sympathy', upon the whole Western tradition.[30] While sensitive in his reading of Virgil, Greene's circular definition of that tradition risks making the pathos of survival occlude its politics.

In this chapter we continue to read the surviving remnants of classical antiquity against the changing fortunes of the concept 'anachronism'. As we saw in Chapter 1, it was during the nineteenth century that the meaning of anachronism extended beyond literary retrojections and chronological mistakes to include practices and people deemed out of date. It is this meaning of anachronism that is at stake when historians such as Schiffman deny to the Greeks and Romans a coherent conception of historical difference. We have already seen, however, that ideas of anachronistic survival can be found in ancient accounts of the development of the calendar.[31] In this chapter we explore the ideas of anachronism generated by other developmental schemes in ancient thought; in the next we will see similar processes in play in the treatment of exemplarity.

Anachronistic traces

In 1860 a member of the recently formed Society of Antiquaries of Normandy wrote a letter to the society's bulletin in which he reported on a children's game he had observed in a Normandy village: the children flipped coins, shouting as they did so 'ka pri tcha haut l'navia'. Intrigued, the correspondent, M. Malherbe, discovered that none of the children knew the meaning of the phrase. Enquiring further, he found that the village elders could recall only that they had learnt it in their youth. With further research, however, Malherbe was able to draw a striking conclusion: the strange cry was a survival from a Roman game reported by the fifth-century AD author Macrobius (*Saturnalia* 1.7.22–3). According to Macrobius, the Romans had once had a coin with a head of the god Janus on one side and a ship on the reverse; Macrobius explained that this coin-type had been instituted by Janus when he was ruler in Italy to commemorate the arrival by ship of Saturnus, who brought agriculture to the then 'wild' Italian tribes.[32] As evidence for the old coin, Macrobius cited a game current in his own time, *capita aut navia* ('heads or ships') – the shout uttered by Roman children as they tossed coins, and strangely close to the cry of their counterparts in nineteenth-century Normandy.

Both Macrobius' antiquarian discussion of the Roman coin and Malherbe's learned correspondence bear some similarity to Tylor's idea of survivals. A trace of the past (ships stamped on coins) survives in a children's game even when the cultural feature that gave rise to the practice is defunct. But where Tylor was primarily concerned with survivals of practices from earlier stages of human development (children using bows and arrows as toys), the game Macrobius records is a survival that indirectly attests the emergence of civilization through agricultural technology.

Macrobius' appeal to modern survivals as evidence of ancient practices has roots in the intellectual climate of sophistic Greece more than 800 years earlier. It was in fifth-century Athens that thinkers such as Democritus sketched out views of human development from savagery to civilization.³³ While details of their arguments have to be inferred from later evidence, one type of argument that we know was used in the fifth century was based on the idea that current linguistic usage preserves evidence of earlier technological or social states. Thus Herodotus states that Ionians call papyrus scrolls *diphtherai* (skins) because formerly, when papyrus was scarce, they wrote on the skins of goats and sheep, just as 'many of the barbarians write on such skins still in my time' (5.58.3), while Thucydides supports an argument about early settlement patterns in Attica by noting that the Acropolis is 'up to this time still' known by Athenians as *polis* (city) owing to their early occupation of this area (2.15.6).³⁴ The phrases for 'still in my time' and 'up to this time still', *eti . . . kai to kat' eme* and *mechri toude eti*, are variants on the common *eti kai nun* and *kai nun eti* ('still now'), which, like their Latin equivalents *etiam nunc* and *nunc quoque*, were standard ways of indicating the unexpected survival of a practice. In both authors, moreover, the arguments turn on a vision of historical change. Thucydides is concerned with the stages by which the scattered rural population of Attica was united in a city (the process known as synoecism). Herodotus posits an increase over time of commercial exchange between Ionia and the source of papyrus, Egypt. He also assumes that contemporary practice among non-Greeks was once shared by Ionians. This assumption has been seen as the 'first inkling'³⁵ of the comparative method which, as we shall see, was explicitly elaborated by Thucydides.

That arguments from anachronistic survivals were familiar in the fifth century is shown by their parodic use by the playwright Aristophanes. The Byzantine lexicographer Photius cites a passage from the now lost *Farmers* to illustrate the application of the word *aideis* ('you're singing') to empty or nonsensical speech. One character in the play claims that at one time defendants in court presented their cases singing; as 'proof' (*tekmērion*) he points to the fact that 'still the old men say, while sitting on a jury, whenever someone defends his case ineptly, "you're singing"' (fr. 101a Kastel–Austin). That expression is fancifully taken as a survival of an older cultural practice of song rather than as a proverbial expression of abuse. Further comic play on the notion of survivals appears in a passage in Aristophanes' *Birds* where the leading character Peisetaerus, who has left his native Athens in disgust, seeks to persuade the chorus of birds to help him establish a new city in the sky. Claiming that the birds would be recovering their original status as rulers of the heavens, Peisetaerus lists 'many proofs' (*tekmēria*) of their former position from current linguistic, artistic and social practices: the cock is called the 'Persian bird' and has an upright comb similar to the Persian king's mitre, and can still get people out of bed at dawn; birds sat on rulers' sceptres during the heroic age and are still found on divine images; finally they are invoked in oaths (483–521). In a clever *reductio ad absurdum*, Aristophanes makes Peisetaerus allege that these various features of daily life are survivals of an earlier state of bird power.

The notion of anachronistic survival was not restricted to (pseudo-) antiquarian speculation. It appears frequently in histories of technological and linguistic development. One example appears in the architectural writer Vitruvius, who worked for Augustus. He notes that architects of stone temples drew on functional features of earlier wooden buildings: on the frieze the triglyphs (tablets with three vertical channels) which alternated with metopes (sculptural panels) replaced decorative panels that were previously attached to the cut ends of wooden beams, while *guttae* (droplets) imitated projecting wooden pegs (*On Architecture* 4.2.2–3).[36] Underlying Vitruvius' discussion is a model of development from simple (wooden) to complex (stone) buildings – a pattern also found in accounts of sacred images (see p. 186).

The fullest evidence for the idea of linguistic survival is found in the twelfth-century commentary on the *Iliad* by Eustathius (1.661–2 van der Valk, note on *Iliad* 3.336). Noting that the noun *kuneē* is used for helmets even though they are no longer made of dog-skin (the word's literal meaning), Eustathius offers a long list of parallels drawn from earlier writers. Some of these derivations seem fanciful (for instance, the idea, found also at Athenaeus 11.476a, that the verb *keraō/kerannumi*, used for 'mixing' wine with water, is related to the old use of horns, *kerata*, as drinking-vessels); some are plausible and still accepted by modern scholars (the link, drawn from Plutarch, *Lysander* 17.5, between two types of coin, *obolos* and *drachma*, and the words for a 'spit', used as a form of currency, and a 'handful');[37] some were disputed in antiquity (the alleged Homeric use of *chalkea*, 'bronze', to refer to iron weapons).[38] Latent in these linguistic suggestions are ideas of technological development: horns were regarded as simpler than luxurious vessels of gold and silver (which sometimes imitated their form), and bronze weapons and spits were likewise seen as simpler to make than the iron weapons and coins that replaced them.[39]

Similar links between technological and linguistic development can be traced in earlier authors. The fourth-century BC philosopher Heraclides Ponticus (fr. 160 Wehrli) suggested that lyre-strings were called *linon* (flax) even after *chordē* (originally 'gut' but also the regular word for lyre-strings) came into use; at stake was exegesis of *linon* at *Iliad* 18.570 ('string' or 'Linus-song'?).[40] Again, Censorinus includes in a discussion of public clocks at Rome the information that sundials preceded water-clocks but that the word for sundial, *solarium*, was preserved for the latter (23.7; cf. Cicero, *On the Nature of the Gods* 2.87). A particularly interesting example of this type of argument is provided by a discussion of athletics in one of Plutarch's *Sympotic Questions* (638b–d). One speaker proposes that wrestling must have been the first sport because the word *palaistra* (wrestling-ground) is used for other sports too (he compares the application to pipe-playing of terms such as 'tuning' and 'strokes' which were appropriate for the lyre). Another guest counters that wrestling is too complicated to have been the first sport, 'for necessity produces first what is simple (*haploun*), artless (*atechnon*), and accomplished by force rather than system'. The counter-argument is based on the common assumption that cultures develop from simple to complex.

Striking instances of how language preserves the traces of human development can be found in the etymologies suggested by Varro in *On the Latin Language*. Varro derives, for instance, *panis* (bread) from *pannus*, a cloth woven by women, after the flat sheets in which bread was first baked (5.105), and he links *milites* (soldiers) with *milia* (thousands) on the grounds that Roman legions (in his day 5,000 strong) had been smaller in the past, with 1,000 troops provided by each of the three tribes (5.89). Varro also offers an onomastic tour of the hills of Rome in which he suggests that the toponym Veliae (an area near the Palatine) may derive from the fact that shepherds 'before the invention of shearing, used to pluck (*vellere*) the wool from the sheep, from which the *vellera* (fleeces) were named' (5.54).[41] Varro's explanation here draws on a model of human development which he elaborates in *On the Countryside* (2.1.3–5). Drawing explicitly on the fourth-century philosopher Dicaearchus, author of a work entitled *Life of Greece*,[42] Varro writes of human life 'descending by steps (*gradatim*)': the first stage was 'natural', with humans surviving off the spontaneous produce of the earth; the second was 'pastoral', with nuts, berries, milk and cheese for sustenance; the third stage was 'agricultural' (though many aspects of the previous two stages were maintained). As evidence of the pastoral stage Varro cites the prominence of animals in signs of the zodiac, toponyms (e.g. Bosporus = Ox-ford) and images on early coins,[43] as well as some surviving practices: wild herds can 'even now' be seen in many places (2.1.5), and fines are still assessed 'after the ancient fashion' in oxen and sheep (2.1.9). The name Veliae, then, is evidently linked either with the pastoral stage or with the survival of pastoralism in the agricultural age.[44]

Dream interpretations are another domain where language could be thought to bear traces of obsolete practices. A good example appears in a manual by Artemidorus (who seems to have been based in Ephesus), written in the second or third century AD. Artemidorus lays out the possible implications (depending on the dreamer's sex and status) of an enormous number of dreams, including bedbugs, teeth and incest. When he turns to bathing, he faces the problem that customs, and with them with the meaning of bathing dreams, had changed over time. The oldest writers on dreams did not consider such dreams harmful because people bathed in private tubs. As public baths developed, writers considered dreaming about baths more negatively because they were used irregularly and above all on return from the battlefield or hard labour. Hence it was thought that 'the bath signified on the one hand confusion because of the uproar inside, on the other hand harm because of the secreted sweat, and also mental anguish and fear because the body's colour and appearance is altered in the bath'. But 'some contemporaries', Artemidorus continues, 'offer assessments on the same terms' in error, following 'the old view' rather than 'experience' – that is, current conditions, when there were more public baths and people tended to use them each day, before or after dinner; when the public bath, in short, was 'a path to luxury' (*Interpretation of Dreams* 1.64). With changes in bathing practices, dreams about bathing require a new interpretation, but some interpreters cling to the old association of the word.[45]

Anachronism in the city

When applied by ancient authors to inhabitants of their own communities, the idea of outdatedness was potentially a way of defining marginal groups by contrast with the normative adult male citizen or the citizen-body of which he formed a part. As we shall see, however, while this mode of temporalization was applied as a way of marginalizing groups defined by sex and age, anachronistic survival within the city was often viewed positively, particularly when it was instantiated in ritual.

The notion that old men preserve outmoded values is exploited with some subtlety in the plays of Aristophanes. Aristophanes makes particular comic play of the contrast of fathers and sons. In *Wasps* (422 BC), he opposes the angry juror Philocleon ('Cleon-liker') to his son Bdelycleon ('Cleon-hater'), who has adopted a relaxed, luxurious lifestyle. Bdelycleon convinces his father that, far from being figures of power, old jurors are pawns of powerful politicians such as Cleon. The play seems to be structured around a contrast of stern old morality and easy-going modernity. By a neat reversal, however, when Philocleon follows his son's instruction to party more, he takes to dancing 'those old-fashioned dances which Thespis [an early playwright] used to perform in the contests' and to boasting that he will show up modern tragic performers 'as Cronuses' (as divine ruler before Zeus, Cronus was a figure for the antiquated) (1476–81). Categories of old and modern are reversed in a typical comic fantasy of rejuvenation.

Aristophanes used a similar conception of a 'generation gap'[46] to explore and mock cultural change in *Clouds*, first produced a year before *Wasps*. Alarmed by his son Pheidippides' extravagant expenditure, Strepsiades, the elderly everyman protagonist, resolves to learn the latest ideas from Socrates and his fellow teachers in the hope of winning law-cases against his creditors. Initially Socrates accuses Strepsiades of being a simpleton, 'smelling of the Cronia [a festival of Cronus]' (398). But after his course of philosophical instruction Strepsiades accuses his son of 'archaic thinking' (*archaiika phronein*)[47] in still believing in the Olympian gods (822). Pheidippides is then exposed to sophistic instruction through a contest between the Worse and the Better Argument in which the former repeatedly accuses the latter of being out of date (915, 929, 984–5, 1070). Instructed in modern education, Pheidippides dismisses singing a famous sympotic song by Simonides as 'ancient' (*archaion*), like 'a woman grinding hulled barley' (1355–8); in a final reversal, when his father invokes Zeus, he is dismissed by his son as 'ancient' (*archaios*). Aristophanes' play pokes fun both at the pretention of the son and at the conservatism of the father.

As Strepsiades' comparison with barley-grinding suggests, women, like old men, were often associated with an older and simpler state of society. At Athens, where the sexes were ideologically separated into domains of home and city, the association of women with the old sprang from developmental models in which the household preceded the city and women's lives were seen as more closely connected to nature. The association was especially strong with old women: in the *Republic* Plato presents Socrates complaining that old women transmit to children untrue and dangerous stories about the gods and marking these stories out for destruction through his proposed social and educational reforms (377c).[48] Plato elsewhere, however, makes Socrates put his knowledge of female speech to more positive use: in the *Cratylus* (a dialogue concerned with etymology) Socrates suggests that women are 'the best preservers of ancient language (*archaian phōnēn*)' (418c1), presumably a reflection of the ideology of seclusion, and so that female pronunciation permits the etymology of words to be recognized and their original meanings recovered. Like Tylor, Plato's Socrates is interested both in rooting out irrational and archaic beliefs and in exploiting survivals in order to gain knowledge about the past.

A link between female speech and the past is also developed in Cicero's dialogue *On the Orator* (set in 91 BC). One of the characters in the dialogue, the renowned orator Crassus, claims that when he listens to his mother-in-law Laelia he feels that he is 'listening to Plautus or Naevius' (comic playwrights from the early days of Roman literature) and infers that this was 'how her father and her ancestors used to speak'. As for why 'women more easily preserve antiquity uncorrupted', Crassus explains that they are 'not used to conversation with many people' and so 'always keep what they learnt first' (3.45). Crassus' explanation coheres with the notions of female seclusion found at Athens, but his concern is with the 'unaffected and natural' sound of female speech by contrast with the more artificial attempts of some orators to attain the aura of antiquity.[49] His remarks follow the frequent contrast in Roman ideology between an ancient simplicity and incipient or actual corruption.

The survival of ancient practices was located not just in social groups but also in distinct areas of civil life. Religious cult in particular was seen as an important repository of anachronism – even if in practice it was continually open to adaptation and improvisation.[50] In his tour of the Roman hills, Varro notes that the original division of the Esquiline hill into two, Oppeus and Cespeus, is retained in ritual formulas (*On the Latin Language* 5.50); elsewhere he suggests that the word *tubae* (trumpets) derives from a form *tubi* which is still used at sacrifices (5.117), and discusses words for 'ancient wooden and terracotta shapes' which are still found in sacred vessels (5.121).[51] In addition, sacrificial offerings were interpreted as preserving the diet of early humans, either because they were vegetarian (for instance, the wheat and honey cakes, olive twigs and libations of wine recorded by Pausanias at Elis (5.15.10–11)[52]) or because of the manner of cooking: Athenaeus (14.660e–61d) preserves a fragment of Athenion, a comic playwright of uncertain date, in which a cook boasts that the art of cookery lured early humans away from cannibalism, but that 'people still now, mindful of the past, roast the entrails on the fire for the gods without adding salt' (*Samothracians* fr. 1 Kastel–Austin). Roasting is conceived as temporally prior to boiling, and the lack of salt on the entrails contrasts with the seasoning of the meat which was distributed among the participants in the festival.[53] Plutarch (*Sympotic Questions* 644b) even offers a rationalization of the preservation of the ancient simplicity in sacrifices: unlike luxurious foods with rich sauces, roasted meat can be divided equally, as is required at civic festivals.[54] Besides food, early social conditions were seen in the behaviour of participants at some festivals: at Rome, for instance, the lack of social differentiation found among the first humans was thought to be restored during the Saturnalia (Plutarch, *Numa* 23.11; Macrobius, *Saturnalia* 1.7.26), while the nudity of participants in the Lupercalia, a festival for Faunus (equated with Greek Pan), recalled the bestial way of life among the first inhabitants of Arcadia, from where the festival was thought to derive (Ovid, *Fasti* 2.279–302).

The tendency to preserve old forms in ritual settings can be illustrated from extant objects such as two amphorae given to prize-winning athletes at the Panathenaea (Getty 79.AE.147, 93.AE.55) (Fig. 8). The vases – which carry archon-names dating from 363/2 and 340/39 BC – would have been filled with olive oil produced in the farms of Attica, commemorating the importance of olives and agriculture in Athenian patriotic myth. Their anachronistic traces are constituted by their pictorial technique and lettering. They were produced with black-figure technique long after most pottery had switched to red-figure; the depictions of Athena are archaized; and though separate letters for the long vowels eta and omega were added to the Athenian alphabet at the end of the fifth century BC, the vases retain the old alphabet for the phrase TONATHENETHENATHLON ('from the contests at Athens') but use new letters for the artist's name and for the archon-dating formula.

The preservation of the old in religious settings contrasted with a certain degree of openness to change in some political contexts. In a discussion of the value of political change in his *Politics*, Aristotle noted that the organization of an imaginary *polis* described by the fifth-century town planner Hippodamus of Miletus included the provision that citizens should be rewarded for proposing changes to its laws (1268b22–69a12). While insisting that traditions may have a value in their own right, Aristotle agreed that change has proved valuable in domains such as medicine and physical training and that failure to adopt changes could lead to the survival of outmoded practices. The 'ancient (*archaios*) practices' of the Greeks, he claims, were 'simple (*haplous*) and barbaric (*barbarikous*)' (he cites the practice of carrying arms and 'buying wives from each other', that is by dowry), and 'the remnants' (*ta loipa*) of ancient practices are 'altogether simplistic' (*euēthē*); as an example he cites a law on homicide at Cyme in which the accused is guilty if the prosecutors can find enough witnesses (1268b39–69a3). Aristotle's theoretical defence of change ran counter to the tendency to defend innovations as a means of returning to an ancestral constitution.[55]

Theoretical justifications were offered for conservatism in civic religion too. A speaker in Philostratus' *Life of Apollonius* suggests that the very obscurity of the past is a reason for preserving religious customs even when they lack plausible explanations (6.20.6), while Quintilian explains that hymns which were incomprehensible even to the priests who performed them were preserved because 'what is sacred must be kept in use' (*Oratorical Education* 1.6.39–40). A

Fig. 8 Black-figure and archaized depiction of Athena, Attic Panathenaic amphora, attributed to the Marsyas Painter, Athens, *c.* 330–320 BC, Getty Museum 79.AE.147. Digital image courtesy of the Getty's Open Content Program.

fuller explanation is offered by Dionysius of Halicarnassus in his analysis of Roman religion. He explains that religious rituals provide the best evidence for ancient customs among both Greeks and 'barbarians', neither of whom 'innovate' in these practices because of their fear of the divine anger that such changes might occasion (*Roman Antiquities* 7.70.3). For Dionysius, the only thing that compels people 'to forget or transgress anything that pertains to their rites for the gods' is being overwhelmed by a foreign power and being 'forced' to take on the habits of the conquerors (7.70.4). Dionysius argues that people's desire 'not to forget or transgress' is motivated by a need not to lose a connection with a past in which culturally distinctive relations with the gods were established. This early stage of human development is both a universal structure and something realized in forms particular to each people.

Dionysius' observations form part of an ethically inflected historical analysis. His aim was to show that, far from being 'barbarians', the founders of Rome were Greek settlers who brought with them rituals and other cultural practices which influenced the development of the Roman state. In the field of cultural practices, Dionysius valued the simple and unostentatious over the complex and showy, and argued that manners and conduct have in many respects declined through the course of Roman history. In this schema, rituals that Dionysius claims are still being performed during his own time in exactly the manner in which they were performed when first introduced can appear as anachronistic remnants of a previous age. By being aware of this historical dimension, readers participate in a fuller awareness of how rituals can afford participants an efficacious engagement with the gods. Equally, writing about such rituals enables Dionysius to critique contemporary habits of thought, as in his discussion of the Terminalia, a Roman festival at which sacrifices were offered to ancient boundary stones said to have been set up by the Roman king Numa (2.74). Dionysius comments that 'memory' of these practices is still observed today, but that the festival is undertaken 'for form's sake'. Dionysius' criticism concerns Roman greed and expansionism. He suggests that the Romans should 'observe the motive' that led Numa to 'conceive the boundary stones as gods', by being content with their own possessions and not seeking to appropriate those of others by 'force and trickery'.[56]

Some civic religious rituals met with still more critical responses. Rather than being seen as ancient practices now preserved in form alone, they were regarded as relics from a primitive past. In Aristophanes' *Clouds* (984–5), the Weaker Argument uses as a figure for the antiquated the Athenian Dipolieia festival together with one of its central elements, the Buphonia, in which a team of working oxen were driven up to the Acropolis and the first ox to eat grain spread on an altar was sacrificed.⁵⁷ Similar critiques could be applied to the Roman Lupercalia. In criticizing an adversary for prosecuting a fellow-member of the group that took part in the rite (running through the streets of Rome wearing only a skin of a newly slaughtered goat around their loins), Cicero conjures up an image of the Luperci as a 'a wild and clearly pastoral and rustic association', 'a woodland group established before *humanitas* [here a term for 'civilized' values] and laws' (*For Caelius* 26). Cicero's outrage here is largely a means of attacking his rhetorical opponent, and the festival in fact continued well beyond the arrival of Christianity, as a relic of Roman past(oral).

Anachronism on the periphery

The second part of Adam Ferguson's *Essay on the History of Civil Society* starts with a section 'Of the Informations on this subject which are derived from Antiquity' in which he reviews some of the evidence for the early state of Greece and Italy as well as Greek and Roman perceptions of barbarous peoples. It is here that he offers the comparison (p. 121) between the inhabitants of Britain when first invaded by Rome and present-day natives of North America. Saluting, too, the understanding of human nature shown by the Greek and Roman historians, Ferguson finds a parallel for this comparative method in fifth-century Athens: 'Thucydides, notwithstanding the prejudice of his country against the name of *Barbarian*, understood that it was in the customs of barbarous nations he was to study the more ancient manners of Greece.'⁵⁸ Ferguson here alludes to the theorization of anachronistic survival in the *Archaeology*, an account of the development of Greece that Thucydides placed at the start of his history of the Peloponnesian War.

Thucydides stresses in the *Archaeology* the relative weakness, poverty and lack of centralization in early Greece, insofar as they can be inferred from 'the old poets'. One piece of evidence which he finds in these poets is the prevalence of piracy – an element of the 'old' state of human existence that still survives in the north-western parts of Greece (1.5.3–6.2):

> Up to the present many parts of Greece live in the old way, around the Ozolian Locrians, the Aetolians, the Acarnanians and the mainland thereabouts. The carrying of weapons has survived among these mainlanders from the old habit of pillaging: for all of Greece used to carry weapons because dwellings were unprotected and interactions unsafe, and people made a habit of living with

weapons, just as barbarians do now. That these parts of Greece still live in this way is a sign of the habits that were once similar for everyone.

Thucydides then turns his attention to athletics, arguing that the Greeks had taken up competing naked only recently; previously they wore loincloths, just as 'still among some barbarians nowadays, especially the Asiatic ones, contests in boxing and wrestling are held in which they wear loincloths' (1.6.5). As ancient commentators on Thucydides saw, one of the inspirations for this discussion was the presentation of athletic contests in Homer.[59] Thucydides concludes with the generalization that there are many areas of life where 'the ancient Hellenic' is similar in manner to 'the present barbaric' (1.6.6). Building on a type of argument used already by Herodotus and other sophistic thinkers,[60] Thucydides here maps a process of uneven development: the implication is that movement in space away from central Greece equates to movement backwards in time. As for the cause of this differentiation, the argument of the *Archaeology* suggests that it is rooted in the security and increased interaction provided by centralized naval power, manifested in the fifth century by the Athenian empire. One of the central ironies of Thucydides' work is that the Peloponnesian War undoes progress in Greece through the onset of 'raw' civil faction (3.82.1).[61]

Thucydides detects anachronism, too, in Athens' opponents in the Peloponnesian War. Unlike Athens, Sparta had not been united through synoecism, but remained a dispersed settlement dominating other villages in the surrounding territories. Thucydides claims that Sparta was settled 'in villages in the old style of Greece' (1.10.2), and hints further at a connection between the Spartans' settlement pattern and their character: their Corinthian allies rebuke their practices as 'old-fashioned' (*archaiotropa*, 1.71.2) by contrast with the 'innovative' Athenians (*neōteropoioi*, 1.70.2, cf. 71.4). Sparta's allies are seen as old-fashioned, too, in the way they fight at sea, packing the decks with troops rather than relying on swift skilful manoeuvres (1.49.1). Thucydides prepares the ground for the second great irony of his work: the swift but unstable Athenians will succumb to the slow but steady Spartans.

The spatio-temporal patterning in Thucydides' work is redeployed in the accounts of political development offered by Plato and Aristotle. In Book 3 of the *Laws* (680b1–c1), Plato's Athenian speaker provides a timeline on which different social arrangements can be mapped. After a great flood, only those who lived on the peaks of hills escaped destruction. As they gained in confidence and resources, they moved down from the hilltops to the lower slopes, where they established communities, and eventually to the plains, where they founded cities.

As exemplars of life before the advent of communities, the Athenian cites Homer's Cyclopes, who live in caves in high mountains with 'no advice-bearing councils, no ordinances' and who 'each exercise right over their wives and children, and care nothing for each other' (*Odyssey* 9.112–15); as evidence of the descent, he quotes Homer's account of how the settlers of Troy moved from the hills to the plain (*Iliad* 20.216–18). Plato temporalizes the world of Homer by implying that the remote Cyclopes whom Odysseus encounters on his return from Troy are conceptually prior to Troy itself. At the same time, he links the Cyclopes with a type of patriarchal rule that is 'still now to be found in many parts of Greece and among the barbarians' (680b1–3).[62] A similar picture of the survival of early kingship is found in Aristotle, again with citation of Homer's Cyclopes (*Politics* 1252b19–26). Aristotle posits that the first villages were extensions of households and ruled monarchically by the eldest. In his teleological model, to flourish fully as a human one must be a free citizen in a *polis*, and the failure by 'barbarians' to reach this state is possible evidence that they are natural slaves (and hence incapable of flourishing in a *polis*).

These models of spatially uneven political development are re-shaped in Roman contexts. In a digression Tacitus (*Annals* 3.26) posits an initial state of equality which was displaced by tyrannies (*dominationes*); these tyrannies have been displaced by law in some places, but still remain in many. Tacitus resists the claim that monarchies were the first political form, perhaps as a utopian gesture of resistance to the Roman principate (a constant theme in his work is the maintenance of republican forms as a façade). The Platonic model is more closely followed in a speech that Cassius Dio presents Augustus' sidekick Agrippa making at the time of Augustus' political settlement in 29 BC. Agrippa says that some people 'still now' (*kai nun eti*) live under tyrannies, but that Greek cities moved from monarchy to democracy, and with this change they first accomplished great deeds (52.9.2–3). According to Agrippa, Augustus would be adhering to this model of progress by restoring democracy (that is, the republican constitution) at Rome. But Agrippa is the loser in a constitutional debate in which Maecenas advocates monarchy (52.1) – a political structure that Dio's work suggests is not a relic of the past but (if moderated by the incorporation of elements of a mixed constitution) the only hope of maintaining order in a state of Rome's size. Different models of anachronistic survival are used, then, by Tacitus and Dio as political arguments to highlight the transformation wrought by the Augustan revolution.

The symmetry of the undifferentiated past and the barbarian present is applied in many other domains besides politics. It is a recurrent theme in the ethnographies of the inhabitants of the west and north-west of Europe that Diodorus Siculus offers in Book 5 of his universal history (written in the first century BC, after and during Roman expansion in those areas). Thus he claims that the inhabitants of Britain are said 'to preserve the old (*palaion*) life', explaining that they use chariots for war just like (according to tradition) 'the old Greek heroes in the Trojan War',[63] and that they live in humble dwellings 'mostly constructed from reeds or logs' (5.21.5); this last detail picks up the earlier account of the hardships experienced by the first humans in Egypt, living in reed-houses, a custom 'of which traces still remain among the herdsmen of Egypt' (1.43.4). Diodorus goes on to describe another northern tribe, the Galatae (Gauls), who distribute the best parts of sacrificial meat to 'brave men' as a reward, just as the Achaean leaders honoured Ajax after his single combat with Hector (5.28.4, citing *Iliad* 7.321). Somewhat differently, Diodorus describes the Ligurians as preserving a lifestyle which is 'ancient (*archaion*) and unequipped (*akataskeuon*)', with women as strong as men and men as strong as wild animals (5.39.6). These Ligurians are presented as being at an earlier stage of development than the Gauls and Britons, evidently because they live off hunting in mountains, which were commonly seen as reserves of primitivism.[64] Drawing on the slightly earlier Stoic writer Posidonius, Diodorus focuses throughout partly on social, partly on technological survivals.

A politically charged interest in technological survivals in distant places was shared by many of Diodorus' contemporaries.[65] One of the speakers in Varro's *On the Countryside*, after noting that 'barbarous' peoples such as the Gaetulians and Sardinians use goat-skins as clothing, suggests that 'this usage obtained among the ancient Greeks also', as evidenced by 'the fact that the old men who appear in the tragedies get their name of *diphtheriae* from the goat-skin' (2.11.11).[66] That is, in a move typical of Varro, a word applied to one category of people (old actors) is taken to yield evidence of a once universal practice. A comparable move is made by Vitruvius in a passage of *On Architecture* (2.1.4–5) where he describes how humans emerged from a bestial life through the accidental discovery of fire. Over time, partly through imitation of animals, they began to build the sort of houses (from earth and straw or else daubed with mud) that Vitruvius claims can still be seen in Massilia (in southern France) and on the Areopagus at Athens (evidently a preserved antiquity akin to the hut of Romulus at Rome (p. 186)).[67]

These narratives of technological development involve a vision of early human life as poor and deprived – what George Boas and Arthur Lovejoy in their 1935 study *Primitivism and Related Ideas in Antiquity* term 'hard primitivism', by contrast with the 'soft primitivism' of visions of early life as a golden age. They suggest that changing material conditions and philosophies prompted a move from the 'soft' primitivism seen in works such as Hesiod's *Works and Days* to the 'hard' primitivism of writers who contrast a past of deprivation with the comfortable present. The idea of the golden age nonetheless remained available for use in utopian fictions in distant settings (for instance, the island of Panchaea in the Indian Ocean (Diodorus 5.42–6, from Euhemerus)) or as a metaphor with which to conceptualize political change, notably during the Augustan 'restoration' at Rome.[68]

Religious ritual was another site in which anachronism was attributed to remote peoples. While ancient writers, as we have seen, thought that ritual within the city preserved traces of early stages of human life, in ethnographic contexts this idea was used to define a whole people as antiquated. Two different types of survival are juxtaposed in Dionysius of Halicarnassus' report that human sacrifice in Italy was replaced with a ritual in which human images are thrown into the Tiber, but that it is maintained among the Celts and other 'man-killing' western tribes (*Roman Antiquities* 1.38.2): the continuation of human sacrifice is an index of savageness while the substitution of human images is a survival in the Tylorian sense. Rather differently, Plato in the *Cratylus* has Socrates suggest that the gods still found among 'many barbarians' – 'the sun, moon, earth, stars, and heaven' – were the only ones known to 'the first inhabitants of Greece' (397c8–d1). In context, Socrates' point is etymological: the word *theos* (god) derives from *theein* (run), since the first gods were all moving planets. Underlying this claim is a connection between the primitive and the visible similar to Warburg's reflections on the role of symbols among the Hopi.

Anachronistic survivals in religious practices on the peripheries of the Greco-Roman world could equally denote a praiseworthy simplicity. According to Augustine (*City of God* 4.31), Varro claimed that Rome did not have religious images for 170 years after its foundation and praised the Jews for keeping free of the corruption that such images brought. This moralizing strain was kept up by Christian polemicists such as Tertullian, who looked back to a time when there were no idols, 'before makers of this monstrosity bubbled up', 'just as today in some places traces of antiquity (*vetustatis vestigia*) remain' (*On Idolatry* 3).[69] The opposition of simplicity and corruption is again foremost when Lucan in his epic poem on the civil war between Caesar and Pompey describes a temple in the land of the uncultivated (*inculti*) Garamantians in northern Africa: their god (Jupiter Ammon), Lucan writes, 'is still poor' and 'true to former mores, defends the shrine from Roman gold' (9.519–21). Earlier writers had traced the corruption that wealth brought to Rome through the replacement of terracotta images with Greek statues looted from Syracuse (e.g. Livy 34.4.4). Lucan looks on the Garamantian sanctuary as a survival of early republican probity, the more strongly to condemn the greed and ambition that led to the civil war.

As with anachronistic survivals within the city, there were attempts to explain why ancient practices survived amongst 'remote' peoples. Many writers used a theory of acculturation according to which cultural, mercantile or military interaction led to the adoption of new customs by weaker and less developed peoples.[70] The dynamics of such interaction are illustrated by a story told in Philostratus' *Life of Apollonius* (5.9.2) about the impact of a tragic actor in Baetica (in Spain). The actor was a great success among the 'lesser barbarians' even though they had never heard a Greek tragedy. But when he reached a town called Hispola, the inhabitants were scared by his high boots, elaborate costume and booming voice. While the story concludes with a reflection on the 'ancient' (*archaia*) customs of these western barbarians, there seems to be irony, too, at the expense of the actor's elaborate performance. The model of acculturation also allowed that ancient simplicity could itself be seen as a survival in parts of the Greek world seen as remote: in another work Philostratus describes a hulk of a man who prides himself on having been brought up in the interior of Attica, a district which is 'untainted by barbarians' and hence retains 'the purest strain' of the Attic dialect (*Lives of the Sophists* 2.7.6–7), while Dio Chrysostom in *Oration* 36 describes a visit to a Homer-mad city on the shores of the Black Sea where the inhabitants maintain the long hair of Homeric heroes. Both Philostratus and Dio use spatial distance (whether between city and countryside or between central and peripheral Greek settlements) as a vehicle for fantasies of unmediated contact with the past.[71]

Commercial exchange was regarded as a particularly potent means of accelerating development through acculturation. The first-century AD Roman geographer Pomponius Mela claims in his description of the Black Sea that 'commerce' with other peoples 'softened' the previously savage inhabitants of the Black Sea, so that the sea's name was changed from *Axinus* (Inhospitable) to *Euxinus* (Hospitable) (*Geography* 1.102). Exposure to Roman expansion brought with it the possibility of temporal reclassification: Tacitus notes that Germans 'in the interior' (furthest from contact with Rome) exchange merchandise 'in a simpler and more ancient manner' (*Germany* 5.3),[72] while the geographer Strabo (writing in the Augustan era) posits that conditions in Germany now are evidence for conditions in pre-Roman Gaul (4.4.2). Strabo elsewhere regrets the influence of Roman luxury on previously uncorrupted peoples like the

Scythians – while adding that the Greeks 'even now' like to think of the Scythians as 'the most simple' of peoples in their frugality and self-sufficiency (7.3.7). While in this case it is the assumption of ancient simplicity, rather than simplicity itself, that is the anachronistic survival, the notion that distance in space corresponded with distance in time remained powerful.

Anachronism incorporated

The idealized simplicity of the past was not simply treated with nostalgia or for satire. The possibility of its incorporation in political structures in the present was a recurrent strain in political theories structured around the contrast between simplicity and luxury. Continuing tradition was valued because of its links to the ancient simplicity, while constitutions which were thought to have resisted development into more complex forms were taken up as a means of contemplating alternative forms of social organization: in Athens, for instance, the construction of Sparta, and later Crete, as anachronistic survivals was employed to criticize democracy.[73]

Anachronism could be incorporated, too, through ethical systems focused on individual self-sufficiency. When Plato historicized the simple life of the Cyclopes, he was responding to the Socratic Antisthenes, who suggested that life offered a better route to justice than was possible in cities (*SSR* V A 189A).[74] Owing to his advocacy of the simple life, Antisthenes was later claimed as founder by the Cynics, who presented themselves as rejecting the corruption of the city and returning to the ennobling hardship of the past. Staged encounters between the city and the anachronistic barbarian were one way Cynics developed their critique of luxury. One writer used the voice of the Scythian sage Anacharsis to assert the value of the simple life: 'A Scythian cloak is my covering, the skin of my feet are shoes, the whole earth is bed, milk, cheese and roasted meat are dinner and breakfast, to drink I have water' (*Epistles of Anacharsis* 5).[75] Lucian even places Anacharsis in dialogue with Solon, contrasting the developed practices of Athenian society with the primitive Scythian life. The Scythian sage is bewildered by the exercises performed by youths at the gymnasium and by their lack of weapons (37.34) – a nod to one of the signs of development identified by Thucydides.

Beyond Greek philosophy, the ethnographic construction of anachronism shaped and was shaped by changing relations between Rome and Italy. Comparing the way that Scottish Highlanders came to be valorized in retrospect following the failure of the 1745 uprising, Emma Dench has argued that shifts in Roman perceptions of Italy can be understood in terms of the incorporation of the primitive.[76] Inhabitants of areas such as Samnium, who had initially been marginalized in Roman perceptions as barbarian or primitive, came in the course of the second century BC and especially after the Social Wars at the start of the first to be valued as sturdy farmers, retaining severe ancient customs after these had been abandoned in metropolitan Rome.[77]

The ideological significance of this construction of the Italian is fully realized in Virgil's *Aeneid*. In the catalogue of Aeneas' Italian enemies in Book 7, Virgil offers variations on ethnographic tropes of hardness. One of the Italian leaders, Ufens, is presented as coming from a mountainous area with hard turf and as leading a tribe that is 'especially rough (*horrida*) and used to frequent hunting in the forests': 'The men work the land armed and their pleasure is always to carry off new booty and to live off plunder' (7.746–9). But while Virgil devotes the second half of the poem to the war fought between the hardy Italian and Aeneas' Trojans, he offers, too, a prospective vision of Roman history embossed on the shield of Aeneas in which Augustus is seen 'leading Italians' into battle against Cleopatra and the forces of the East (8.678). Adam Parry suggested in a famous essay on 'The two voices of Virgil's *Aeneid*' that 'the explicit message of the *Aeneid* claims that Rome was a happy reconciliation of the natural virtues of the local Italian peoples and the civilized might of the Trojans'. But he saw, too, in 'the tragic movement' of the poem's closing books hints that Rome's rise involved 'the loss of the pristine purity of Italy'. Tellingly, he compared Virgil's feeling for the 'proud and independent' Italians who 'succumbed inevitably to the expansion of Roman power' with 'what Americans have felt for the American Indian'.[78]

Parry's comparison, like Dench's Highlanders analogy, points to the danger that our own understanding of the anachronistic survival may be shaped by modern re-workings of the trope. Particularly suggestive are the links these comparisons suggest with the fictions of romantic historicism: Scott and Fenimore Cooper looked back admiringly on Highlanders and American Indians firm in the belief that their eclipse was a sign of rational progress. If Scott's model seems the stronger analogy for the *Aeneid* (racial politics prevented the assimilation of Cooper's Indians),[79] it may be no accident that Scott himself was alive to the resonance of Virgil's Italy. He contributed a long introduction to a volume on the antiquities of the Scottish Borders for the epigraph of which he quoted Virgil's address to mountain-dwelling Ufens. Turning to material remains, he compared weapons that had been found in the Borders with those still used by 'the Californian Indians' as well as with those described by Virgil, 'an antiquary and a scholar, as well as a poet'. He singled out for comment the people of Abella, a hilltop town in Campania, whose custom it was to 'whirl boomerangs in the Teutonic manner' (*Aeneid* 7.741). Adopting the mode of thought we have explored throughout this chapter, Scott commented that 'this mountain and rude tribe is described as retaining the ancient customs of the Teutones'[80] – not realizing that 'in the Teutonic manner' has to be understood as an anachronistic simile: it is the northern Teutons (or those of them who survived massacre at the hands of Marius) who, according to Virgil, retain the customs once found in Abella. Despite (or even because of) this slip, Scott points to one further way in which anachronism can be incorporated – through antiquarian scholarship.

This chapter has explored the way in which evidence of different lifestyles in the past and their continuation in the present could be used in debates on important political and philosophical questions as well as in scholarly controversies. The idea of survival was as charged in ancient writing as in modern ideas of development in anthropology and social theory, many of which borrow their basic structures from ancient models even if they offer a different analysis of the mechanisms of change. Anachronistic survival had the potential to serve as an image of superseded primitivism as well as to be taken as exemplary in critiques of modern luxury. As we shall see in our next chapter, the exemplary potential of antiquity was constantly in dialogue with the ethical questions provoked by the realities of historical change.

6

Anachronism and Exemplarity

Exemplarity versus historicism

Following his account of the conquest of Egypt (332 BC) by Alexander of Macedon, the Greek historian Arrian, who wrote an account of Alexander's expedition almost 500 years after the event, compares the administrative arrangements used to govern Egypt by Alexander and those used by the Romans in his own day (*Anabasis* 3.5.7):

> Alexander is said to have distributed rule over Egypt among many men, amazed at the country's physical character and strength, because it did not seem safe to entrust rule over all Egypt to one man. The Romans, in my view, learnt from Alexander to keep a watch on Egypt and to send as governor those classed as Knights and not senators.

Arrian (who was appointed to the Roman senate by the emperor Hadrian) here suggests that Rome learnt from Alexander how to govern Egypt, without any regard for the temporal gap between Alexander's reign and the establishment of a Roman province in Egypt (30 BC). The Romans' successful use of the past conforms to the agenda that Arrian sets out at the close of his account of Alexander. There he suggests that he has praised and criticized Alexander both for the sake of truth and for the utility of humankind: 'it was for this reason that I embarked on this history, myself too [*sc.* like Alexander] not without god's help' (7.30.3).

The gap between past and present that Arrian seems to neglect is very present for the historian Peter Brunt in his edition of Arrian's *Anabasis*. For the passage where Arrian claims the Romans learnt from Alexander how to keep the threat posed by Egypt in check, Brunt offers the laconic note: 'in fact the circumstances and Roman organization were different'.[1] Brunt's rebuke of Arrian speaks to his feeling for the particularities of different historical periods.

For Arrian, by contrast, the idea that the Romans learnt from the past fitted his own adhesion to a distinctive model of exemplarity. He shaped his literary career after the Athenian historian Xenophon (c. 430–c. 350 BC): like Xenophon, he wrote works on hunting, philosophy, and military tactics, and the very title he adopted for his account of Alexander's expedition, *Anabasis* (*March Upcountry*), was modelled on Xenophon's account of the march of the Ten Thousand (already established as a classic in Arrian's time); he even adopted Xenophon as a name.[2]

Arrian's valuation of exemplarity was typical of writers working within the Roman cultural context with which he was familiar. Roman writers carried with them a mental repository of military and domestic figures (both male and female) who could be invoked as either positive or negative paradigms. A passage from the satirist Juvenal suffices to show how the power of an exemplary narrative could be condensed in a bare name. In *Satires* 2, the poet's persona attacks the sexual mores supposedly prevalent at Rome, including the vaunting of same-sex marriages in which men were not ashamed to assume a passive sexual role. Accepting for poetic effect what he calls the childish belief that the dead are able to perceive what is happening in the world above, the poet asks: 'What does Curius feel, and the two Scipios, Fabricius and Camillus' shade?' (153–4). The men mentioned here by name are great military figures from the Roman republic: Marcus Furius Camillus was thought to have saved Rome after the city was sacked by Gallic invaders early in the fourth century BC; Manius Curius Dentatus and Gaius Fabricius Luscinus were heroes of the war against Pyrrhus, King of Epirus, in the first half of the third century BC; while Publius Cornelius Scipio Africanus elder and younger (the latter a grandson by adoption) were seen as responsible for the Roman victories over Carthage in the Second and Third Punic Wars. The names of these men are enough to evoke the manly virtues of the Roman republic that have supposedly been betrayed by Juvenal's contemporaries.

The early history of Rome also provided female exemplars. The exemplary status of women was variously linked to the fulfilment of gender norms. Livy's account of the rape and suicide of Lucretia (1.57–9) begins by presenting her as an exemplary wife, celebrated for domestic activities such as wool-working as well as for chastity and fidelity; as we shall see (p. 165), in her response to her rape Lucretia takes on a much more active role. Active displays by female exemplars were often presented as instances of *virtus*, 'courage' or 'virtue', a word etymologically related to *vir*, 'man', and typically applied to male military heroes (though it came to be used more broadly of the capacity to endure suffering).[3] In adherence to Roman gender norms, such displays were sometimes presented as inspiring for men or else tamed in other ways: thus while Cloelia was widely celebrated for escaping from the Etruscans by swimming or riding across the Tiber, Valerius Maximus presents her as a 'light of *virtus* for men' (3.2.2) and Livy notes her 'decorum' as a hostage in choosing only boys rather than young men to be freed alongside the girls (2.13.9).

For Romans, their abundance of historical examples was a source of pride. When the Roman rhetorician Quintilian (first century AD) makes a distinction between precepts (sayings) and examples (deeds), he concludes with the assertion that 'The Romans are as strong in examples as the Greeks are in precepts, and examples are more important' (*Oratorical Education* 12.2.30). Roman military deeds, he suggests, outdo Greek theorizing.

The ancient attachment to exemplarity has played an important part in discussions of the development of the concept of anachronism. Zachary Sayre Schiffman has suggested that historians in antiquity 'never thought to question the utility of one age's lessons for another – or even to frame the issue in this way', and attributed this failure to the fact that 'they did not have a systematic and sustained idea of anachronism'.[4] Similarly David Lowenthal writes that up to the nineteenth century 'since past circumstances seemed comparable and hence relevant to present concerns, history served as a source of useful exemplars'.[5] This exemplary view of history is often conveyed through the Ciceronian tag *historia magistra vitae* (*On the Orator* 2.36), which suggests a view of the past in which history 'does not yet have the modern sense of a sequential, unitary process but is rather taken as an aggregate of instances designed to serve as guides for behavior and action'.[6]

Historians interested in conceptions of the past often suggest that exemplarity was a stable concept until the Renaissance.[7] An increasing sensitivity to anachronism is thought to have led to the collapse of modes of exemplarity based on the idea of an unchanging human nature. According to many accounts, the hold that exemplarity exercised on the early modern imagination was self-defeating. When people attempted to put the model into practice by imitating the ancients (whether in literature, law or military tactics), the outcome was a stronger appreciation of their historical distance from antiquity.[8] Further weakening of ancient exemplarity arose from objections to non-Christian models and from a recognition of the profusion and complexity of ancient *exempla*. Collections of *exempla* are thought to have led to a sense of their various historical contexts and to have revealed that some individuals were credited with conflicting character traits – a particular problem given that metonymy was one of the dominant modes of exemplarity: if the very name of an ancient figure such as Alexander was shorthand for particular qualities, what to do when those qualities included drunkenness and lust as well as courage and daring?

A second crisis of exemplarity is often located around the time of the French Revolution. On the one hand, the sense felt by contemporaries that the Revolution itself was a break with the old order was marked by the introduction of a new calendrical system. On the other hand, the very fact that the revolutionaries drew so much on the ancient heroic attachment to liberty drew criticism from conservatives, particularly in Britain: the authors of a volume on *Antiquities of Ionia* wrote that 'we cannot but smile at the presumptuous ignorance and temerity of those pretended politicians and philosophers of modern times, who are perpetually recommending their wild and impracticable theories of equal liberty, and pure democracy, by the glorious examples of Athens and Rome'.[9] The revolutionaries' stress on ancient liberty was countered by the spectre of ancient slavery. As during the Renaissance, attempts to replicate antiquity led many to the conviction that such projects were necessarily futile.

These supposed crises of exemplarity have not totally destroyed the power of the exemplary model itself. At one level, the historicist notion of the period can be seen as a continuation of exemplarity by other means. In Alexander Gelley's formulation, 'whereas the classical sense of *historia* envisioned a series of instances linked inductively to produce a conclusion, history in the modern (or at least Hegelian) sense situates particular events in a totalizing schema that assimilates the exemplary function'.[10] With the onset of historicism events or people were themselves seen as representative of a period,[11] and the classical Greek *polis* itself remained exemplary in both academic and popular writing for its supposed integration of private and political realms.[12] This exemplary identification with antiquity is still propagated, moreover, in modern education as well as popular culture. Books and university courses promote the 'leadership lessons' that can be learnt from Xenophon ('Err on the side of self-reliance').[13] Writings by Cicero and his brother are marketed by a university press with the titles 'How to win an argument' and 'How to win an election', with publicity that speaks of 'timeless techniques of effective public speaking from Rome's greatest orator' and quotes a reviewer's soundbite 'I just hope my opponent in the next campaign doesn't get a copy'.[14] Exemplarity remains a popular, powerful and potentially complex model, even if within academic historicist thought it seems an anachronistic survival.

The notion of a modern crisis of exemplarity rests on the belief that exemplarity was a stable system of knowledge within antiquity. Recent treatments of exemplarity by classical scholars, however, have suggested that the notion of a crisis should be stretched back to include antiquity itself. Far from being the product of an enduring commitment to timeless truths, ancient exemplarity should rather, as Christina Kraus suggests, be located within 'the ancient tradition of rhetorical persuasion': '*exempla* are embedded in a system designed to argue both sides of a given question', and 'any exemplary story or figure can be itself the grounds of contested interpretation'.[15] The idea that *exempla* are always open to contestation is supported, too, in recent work by Rebecca Langlands. Langlands aligns exemplarity with what modern philosophers term 'situational ethics', that is, with a sensitivity to the context of actions rather than with an inflexible application of absolute rules.[16] Langlands is also alert to the rhetorical form in which *exempla* were transmitted, in volumes such as Valerius Maximus' *Memorable Doings and Sayings*, a work written under the Emperor Tiberius that enjoyed great popularity during the Renaissance. Valerius' method of grouping disparate anecdotes under the headings of traditional virtues is a way of telling Roman readers 'not simply what to think but *how* to think ethically'.[17] Exemplarity, on Langlands' reading, demands ethical judgement.

Further complexity is introduced into ancient notions of exemplarity once the temporality of *exempla* is taken into account. Matthew Roller has probed the extent to which historicist assumptions can be detected in the Roman use of *exempla*. Roller allows that Roman culture was infused with ideas of development and decline, but suggests that *exempla* kept their power because the same moral framework was felt to obtain over time. He does, however, acknowledge some awareness that exemplary virtues could change with new circumstances: he suggests, for instance, that Roman debate during the Second Punic War over the delaying tactics of Fabius, which were presented as either a cowardly avoidance of battle or a prudent way of saving the state, led to a change in the terms in which military performance was assessed.[18] Our analysis in this chapter will suggest that it may be better to see a dialogue rather than an opposition between exemplarity and historicism.

We can gain a stronger sense of the conversation between exemplary and historicist thought by returning to Arrian's use of Xenophon. Arrian did not simply seek to be another Xenophon, he also attempted to surpass him, in part at least by reflection on his own positioning in time. This sort of reflection is particularly apparent in Arrian's work *On Hunting*. Xenophon had written in his hunting treatise that the hare is 'so graceful' a creature 'that there is no one who would not, at the sight of a hare being tracked, found, chased, caught, forget his own beloved' (*On Hunting* 5.33). Arrian declared that 'on this one point I do not agree with my namesake': to see a hare caught is unpleasant, but 'that other Xenophon should be forgiven if a hare being caught seemed a great sight to him, since he did not know of swift hounds' (*On Hunting* 16.7). Arrian here reverts to one of his justifications for writing a new treatise, namely the fact that Xenophon was unaware of Celtic hounds, an especially fast breed (1.4). Though he implies that Xenophon's treatise was, in our terms, an anachronism, he excuses Xenophon himself on the grounds that it was uncommon for a hare to be caught when he was writing. Rather than working with an unchanging moral compass, he is alert to the earlier conditions.

This chapter will claim that in many other settings, too, the ancient stress on exemplary models was able productively to co-exist with a sense of anachronism. We will explore the temporal complexity in ancient thinking about, and exploitation of, *exempla* as well as the dialectic of exemplarity and historicism. Throughout, we shall see that notions of anachronism affected both the way *exempla* were conceived in theory and the way they were deployed in practice.

Exemplarity in theory

The reason why the idea has taken hold that ancient exemplarity both rested on and inculcated a timeless set of values is not hard to see. It is not just that figures from the classical past are still often cited as exemplars of such values, typically for conservative or racially charged political agendas.[19] An adherence to universal moral concepts is also suggested by programmatic statements in popular authors such as Plutarch, who declares at the start of his life of Aemilius Paullus that he began writing *Lives* to help others and kept at it to help himself, 'trying through history, as with a mirror, somehow to arrange my life and make it resemble the virtues [of my subjects]' (1.1). While Plutarch's *Lives* can be considered biographical narratives, works such as Valerius Maximus' collection presented exemplary anecdotes which operated outside the structures of historical narrative. Anthologies of deeds and sayings drew on great lives and events. Other works were more specialized, such as Frontinus' *Stratagems*, which presented short Greek and Roman military narratives as 'examples (*exemplis*) of counsel and foresight through which their ability to conceive and execute similar deeds may be nurtured' (1.1).

The doctrine of gaining lessons from the past was theorized in many other settings in antiquity. That one could learn by copying an *exemplum* was a central principle of education. Educational examples need not, admittedly, be derived from the past: Horace affectionately portrays his father pointing to the good and bad examples set by acquaintances in his home town (*Satires* 1.4.105–26). But texts that dealt more formally with the moral instruction of the young tended to insist on training through remembering the past as the responsibility of good parents: Plutarch, for instance, argues that 'the memory of past actions is a model (*paradeigma*) of good advice about the future' (*On the Education of Children* 9f). At a later stage, *exempla* played an important part, too, in declamations and *suasoriae* (persuasive speeches), two components of rhetorical education. Speakers were expected to produce allusions to the past that were witty and pointed rather than historically plausible ('but [we are] Spartans, but [we are] at Thermopylae', the elder Seneca records one speaker as saying – an anachronistic appeal to the famous Spartan self-sacrifice placed in a speech encouraging the Spartans to remain at Thermopylae itself (*Suasoriae* 2.18)).

Exemplarity functioned within Roman families in the form of the *imagines*, ancestor-masks displayed in the house and paraded at funerals (Fig. 9).[20] The historian Polybius describes how the funeral itself represents the deceased as an

Fig. 9 Elite Roman holding objects which may represent images of ancestors. Togatus Barberini, *c*. first century AD. MC 2392. Museo Centrale Montemartini, Rome. Alamy.

exemplum to those who succeed him (6.53.2–3); on other occasions, the family member who most closely resembles the commemorated ancestor wears the mask and the honours acquired by that ancestor (6.53.6). Nothing could be more inspiring for the young than the sight of these noble men, Polybius concludes (6.53.10).

The use of *exempla* was explored in theoretical works such as Aristotle's *Rhetoric* (1393a23–94a18). Aristotle divides them into 'speaking of past events' and 'invention', with the latter further divided into the forms of fable (*parabolē*) and comparison. The particular value of invoking past events, he thinks, is that they may provide a pointer to the future: if the King of Persia has previously invaded Greece after being defeated in Egypt, watch out for his activities in Egypt (1393a31–b4). Past events are more informative than fables and provide a better basis for deliberation (1394a5–7). Quintilian deals more directly than Aristotle with the practical steps the aspiring orator should take to achieve success, but he too lays stress on the usefulness of examples: students benefit from writing in praise of good men and from critique of the bad, learning case studies and building their own stocks of *exempla*; they should practice, too, the ability to spot and develop analogies (*Oratorical Education* 2.4.20, 5.11.1–6).

Exemplarity was an important component of historiography. We have already alluded to the famous Ciceronian maxim *historia magistra vitae*: 'As for history, the witness of the ages, the illuminator of reality, the life of memory, the teacher of life, the messenger of antiquity, by whose voice but the orator's is it entrusted to immortality?' (*On the Orator* 2.36). In context, this maxim is from a self-aggrandizing speech by an orator, Antoninus, who deploys eloquence in favour of eloquence (as one of his interlocutors remarks in response). But it represents the sort of claims for utility regularly paraded by historians such as Polybius and Diodorus. Behind such statements lies Thucydides' proud ambition that his work should prove 'useful to all those who will want to see clearly what happened in the past and what will happen again at some time in similar or much the same form in accordance with the human condition' (1.22.4) – a message summed up in a rhetorical treatise later in antiquity by the tag 'history is philosophy through examples' (Ps.-Dionysius, *Rhetoric* 11).

Many readings of literature in antiquity presuppose a timeless approach. There was, for instance, a strong tradition of reading Homeric narrative didactically, even though the lessons extracted are not explicitly foregrounded by the poet himself. Homer himself could be presented variously as a great teacher with an encyclopedic knowledge of human affairs,[21] as a proto-philosopher who encodes in his poetry a profound understanding of the cosmos,[22] or as a master of rhetorical and political theory.[23] Characters within the Homeric poems were similarly open to exemplary readings. Their exemplary status was determined partly by the stable qualities for which they were best known: testimony to the fact that Odysseus continued to be known for cunning (*mētis*) comes from a model speech written in the late fifth century BC by the Athenian philosopher and rhetorician Antisthenes, in which Odysseus extols the qualities he showed during the Trojan War by anticipating the future birth of a 'clever poet' who 'will make me much-enduring (*polutlas*), master of cunning plans (*polumētis*) and full of tricks (*polumēchanos*)' (*SSR* V A 54.14) – the epithets commonly applied to him in the Homeric poems.

There was, then, a widespread practice in antiquity of removing human actions and characters from their temporal nexuses and extracting supposedly timeless truths or models of action, and modern scholars have rightly stressed the divergence of this practice from the historicist awareness of distinctive historical periods. But it would be mistaken to assume that the sort of atemporal approaches outlined so far in this section can themselves be extracted as exemplary. The temporal landscape of exemplarity comes to seem a great deal more rugged if the available evidence is probed more fully.

Against attempts to draw timeless wisdom from the Homeric poems must be set approaches that stressed the contingency or primitivism of his poems. In many biographical traditions Homer was portrayed as a poet singing for his supper, naming characters after people he met during his travels.[24] Within the exemplary realm, a more granular image emerges in the second-century AD moralist Maximus of Tyre, who claims in one of his essays that Homer was an admirable teacher in erotic matters, but 'altogether simple and archaic' in other areas of life, such as medicine, military tactics and chariot-racing (*Dissertations* 18.8). Departing from the view of Homer as a universal sage, he hives off a number of areas where technical advances have rendered the epic poet time-bound; that is, he historicizes the development of wisdom. Homeric examples were similarly dismissed as 'stale and too archaic' by the fourth-century AD rhetorician Themistius (16.205b);[25] conversely, a speaker in Macrobius' *Saturnalia* values the Homeric poems precisely for their age, praising Homeric repetition within catalogues for a 'divine simplicity' that is 'somehow uniquely becoming to Homer ... and worthy of the ancient poet's genius' (5.15.16).

Rhetorical treatises are similarly nuanced in handling the temporality of comparisons. Directly counter to many views of the ancients' naive idea of historical iteration is Aristotle's confession in the *Rhetoric* that 'it is difficult to find similar historical incidents' (1394a3); it is much easier, he writes, to develop likenesses with the current situation through fables or the philosophical use of analogy. Even the one example of a historical situation that Aristotle cites is worth exploring further. In discussing how a Persian attack on Egypt could be taken as a harbinger of an invasion of Greece, Aristotle cites two Persian kings: 'previously Darius did not cross over [from Asia to Greece] until he had taken Egypt, but after taking it, he invaded; again, Xerxes did not attack until he took Egypt, but having taken it, he crossed: thus if [the present king] takes Egypt, he will cross' (1393a31–b4). For modern readers, the allusion to Xerxes is straightforward, since Herodotus expressly states that he put off invading Greece until he had secured Egypt (7.5, 7). It is far from obvious, however, why Aristotle refers to Darius, and it is not likely that his contemporaries would have been any clearer.[26]

The rhetorical tradition was as alive to points of difference as to transhistorical continuities. The author of a fourth-century BC treatise preserved in the Aristotelian corpus writes that 'most actions are partly like and partly unlike one another, so for this reason we shall have a good stock of paradigms and have no difficulty in countering those put forward by the other side' (*Rhetoric to Alexander* 1430a9–11). Similarly, Quintilian suggests that rhetorical appeals to similarity can be met with an argument from dissimilarity, since 'it is not possible that everything should correspond' (*Oratorical Education* 5.13.24). As for the forms of dissimilarity, Quintilian specifies that they may turn on 'kind, manner, time, place' (*genere, modo, tempore, loco*), citing a speech by Cicero where most of these arguments are deployed (5.11.13). What Quintilian means by a difference of 'time' is not a disjunction of two historical periods, in the historicist sense, but rather a situational contrast: thus Cicero in the speech to which Quintilian alludes analyses the force of an *exemplum* in the light of a difference between a time (*tempus*) that was 'quiet and peaceable' and one that was 'disturbed by all the storms of prejudice' (*For Cluentius* 94). The type of difference Quintilian has in mind resembles a distinction made (according to Aulus Gellius 6.3.45–7) by the elder Cato between actions prohibited by the laws of nature or the nations and those prohibited 'by reason of time' (*temporis causa*), that is, in response to a temporary emergency. While differentiating examples by *tempus* may seem less historically nuanced than the historicizing demotion of their use, it is still robust enough to create a sense of anachronism in the deployment of a particular example.

A stronger sense of anachronism emerges from another of the rhetorical strategies that could be used against *exempla*. Quintilian recommends that *exempla* that are 'old' (*vetera*) can be dismissed as 'fabulous' (*fabulosa*); it is those that cannot be doubted on the grounds of antiquity that should be criticized for dissimilarities (5.13.24). Similarly Apsines, a Greek rhetorician of the third century AD, recommended that paradigms should be 'well-known and clear, and not archaic and fabulous' (*Rhetoric* 1.2). The underlying principle that *exempla* are time-bound is expressed by Polybius in a discussion of how speeches should be represented in historical works: he suggests that the historian should vary the sorts of arguments deployed depending on whether a speech was made by contemporaries or in the more distant past, just as he should use different arguments for speakers from different countries (12.25.i.4).

Ancient discussions often presented *historia* as a *magistra* from whom it was quite difficult to learn. Polybius himself was one of the most vocal exponents of the view that studying the past, and particularly the 'calamities of others' (1.1.2), was the best means of education, but he also argues that a broad survey of history, such as that which he constructs, is necessary, as knowledge of a limited range of examples can only provide a partial education (1.4.6–11). He was perhaps in some sense here responding to the distinction Aristotle made in his *Poetics* between history and poetry: history dealt with particulars ('what Alcibiades did or experienced'), poetry with universals ('the kinds of things which it suits a certain kind of person to say or do, in terms of probability of necessity') (*Poetics* 1451b5–11). Polybius elsewhere, nonetheless, disputes whether historical events and characters necessarily generate useful exemplars. In an account of political turmoil in Egypt he describes how a certain Agathocles manoeuvred his way into power as regent for the young son of Ptolemy IV. But his fast rise was followed by a spectacular fall as the people rebelled and destroyed him, his friends and family. Polybius expresses reluctance to relate the events in detail: compared with the improving tale of the successes of Agathocles' namesake, the tyrant of Syracuse, there is nothing to learn from the career of a man whose temporary success was due to the weakness of others rather than any merits of his own (15.34–6).

That the value attached to the past did not preclude complex reflections on temporality is clear, too, in the Roman discourse of exemplarity. The reservoir of past excellence contained in ancestral traditions could be contested; orators might make different claims about what constituted ancestral practice and excellence, while the development of the literary antiquarian tradition by Varro and others provided an alternative source for authoritative information on Roman culture and identity. The antiquarian interest in Roman tradition generated the potential for rupture and change.[27]

Particularly acute reflections on change can be found in the preface of Livy's monumental history of Rome – one of the most famous expressions of an exemplary view of history-writing. Livy there expresses the awareness that he is himself following in the line of many earlier writers on Rome, all of whom hope to surpass their predecessors not just by correcting historical errors but also by improving on 'crude antiquity' (*rudem vetustatem*) in matters of style (*Preface* 2). Earlier writers, then, set an example for Livy in their eagerness to eclipse their less developed forebears, even as Livy hopes to eclipse them. Livy then goes on to praise the value of contemplating the past as a respite from current troubles and as a storehouse of *exempla*. But it is particularly in Rome prior to its moral decline that he claims the greatest treasures are to be found. Livy's views on exemplarity are inseparable from his anxieties about ethical change.

The connection Livy draws in his preface between exemplarity and decline is taken further by Tacitus in a programmatic statement in his account of the civil war at Rome in AD 69 (the Year of the Four Emperors). After telling the story of a common soldier who claimed a reward for killing his own brother in action, Tacitus contrasts this grasping fratricide with the case of a soldier in an earlier civil war (fought between Sulla, Marius and Cinna in 88–87 BC) in which a soldier who had killed his brother by mistake committed suicide. He draws the following moral: 'So much the keener among our ancestors was both the glory of good deeds and regret at disgraceful ones. I shall not unreasonably mention deeds like this, and others from ancient history, whenever the topic or situation demands examples (*exempla*) of the correct action or consolation for the wrong' (*Histories* 3.51). Tacitus here implies that he will insert *exempla* in his work even though he is conscious that they will have no effect in the present. Rather than promoting an idea of timelessness, *exempla* accentuate a sense of difference over time. The past–present contrast is particularly cutting because the glorious past episode is from a civil war. Otho, one of the protagonists in the civil war of AD 69, is made by Cassius Dio (*Roman History* 64.13.2) to say that he 'would choose to be a Mucius, a Decius, a Curtius, or a Regulus' – great Republican *exempla*, known for their self-sacrifice for the state – 'rather than a Marius, a Cinna, or a Sulla' – symbols of the Republic's slide into dissolution. Tacitus more sardonically applies the notion of decline to the participants in civil wars.

The Roman concern with how *exempla* function in times of political decline is matched by Greek authors reflecting on the advent of the *pax Romana* and the concomitant loss of Greek liberty. Acute reflections on the changes made by the Roman conquest can be found in Plutarch's essay *Precepts of Statesmanship*. Plutarch advises that the great themes of the Persian Wars – 'Marathon, Eurymedon, Plataea and other examples which make the masses swell up vainly with pride' – should be left to 'the schools of the sophists'. He does nonetheless recuperate for present use some seemingly less glamorous deeds by the Greeks of old: the statesman can still 'form and correct the characters of contemporaries' by recounting events such as the amnesty at Athens after the downfall of the Thirty Tyrants (814a–c). Just as the great examples of Republican Rome were reconfigured under the Principate, the paradigmatic use of the Greek past underwent a major change after the Roman conquest of Greece.[28]

Particularly penetrating analysis of the periodic impact of war on exemplarity is found in Thucydides' *History*. Furthering his claim that his account of the Peloponnesian War will offer insight into similar events in the future, Thucydides offers a sketch of the harm inflicted by civil strife on the cities of Greece – 'as happens and always will do so while human nature remains the same'. This universal claim is tempered by recognition that 'the degree and kind of the damage may vary in each case according to the particular circumstances'. But a far greater threat to the exemplary model comes when Thucydides turns to the effect of peace and war on human character: 'in peace and good circumstances cities and individuals alike show better judgement' – but 'war is a violent teacher' which 'takes away the ease of daily life' and 'assimilates passions to circumstances' (3.82.2). Thucydides does not simply underline, like many historians after him, the difficulty of learning from the past. He roots that difficulty in a psychological model according to which human judgement is moulded by material circumstances and by the passions unleashed by conflict. If, as Thucydides asserts, 'men exchanged the customary evaluation of words in relation to deeds' (3.82.4), then the ethical system on which timeless paradigms were based was at the mercy of changing political pressures.

We have seen that in ancient theoretical writing on exemplarity, a conception of *exempla* understood as predicated on similarities, between one story and another, between past and present situations, is balanced by a sensitivity to the complex relations between exemplary narratives and temporal change. Similar balance is required to do justice to the subtlety with which *exempla* are employed in ancient literature.

Exemplarity in action

Exemplarity often seems to function in a timeless way in ancient works which invoke specific examples as illustrations of general truths or else to recommend a certain course of action. Aristotle, for instance, lists numerous psychological or structural causes of civic conflict in his discussion in the fifth book of the *Politics* (fear or contempt of one group for another, for instance, or the presence of additional settlers), and for each type of cause he adduces a number of specific instances. What his dense argumentation lacks is any attention to the temporal setting of the various examples; his lack of attention to chronology itself supports his overall project of offering generalized political truths.

Similarly ahistorical in their presentation were the exemplary lists employed in the ethical essays of the younger Seneca and of Maximus of Tyre. In an essay on bodily and spiritual sickness, Maximus offers no chronological anchoring as he moves between characters from Homer, the supposedly debauched Assyrian king Sardanapallus, and figures such as Alcibiades and Critias who lived during the Peloponnesian War (7.6–7). As with Aristotle's use of achronic political data, Maximus' indifference to chronology seems to contribute to the use of such stories as examples to be imitated or avoided.[29]

The apparently timeless exploitation of *exempla* can be traced right back to the beginnings of Greek literature. The *Iliad* draws to a powerful close with the Trojan king Priam travelling to Achilles' hut to ransom the corpse of his son Hector. Priam invokes Achilles' absent father and the two men gaze at each other in mutual recognition of their suffering. Achilles then appeals to the old man to eat with him, drawing on an unusual paradigm: 'Even lovely-haired Niobe was mindful of food, though her twelve children had been killed in her house, six daughters and six sons in the prime of youth' (24.602–4). Niobe had boasted that she had more children than Leto, mother of Apollo and Artemis, and in due course was punished by the gods she had offended. Achilles' use of Niobe as an *exemplum* follows the same structure of exemplarity we have observed in Aristotle and Maximus of Tyre. Although her story belongs in the past, there is no attempt to clarify how far in the past it belongs and no sense that its pastness detracts from its exemplary power.

The way Achilles' rhetoric develops, however, suggests that *exempla* were employed not just as vehicles for unchanging truths, but as means of reflecting on and responding to the processes of temporal change. Niobe, Achilles continues, endures now in Mount Sipylus, where 'though a stone, she nurses sorrows from the gods' (24.617). Achilles here alludes to a geographical feature that would have been known by repute, if not by sight, to Homer's audience: a distinctively shaped rock in Lydia which would seem to weep when rain water trickled down it. Niobe's metamorphosis removes her from ordinary human experience. At the same time, the intensity of her pain is attested by its continuance even in her new rocky form. If Niobe, who grieves even as a rock, took food, all the more reason for Priam to do so.

The *Iliad*'s closing reflection on how temporal change can boost the logic of exemplarity returns to a theme established in its very first *exemplum*. Agamemnon demands that Briseis, an enslaved princess, be taken from Achilles and given to him. When Achilles objects, the two heroes flare into quarrelling. Attempting to conciliate, Nestor, the old king from Pylos, steps forward. Before advising them to patch up their dispute for their mutual benefit, Nestor reflects on his own position (1.259–62, 267–8): 'But listen to me, since you are both younger than I. For once upon a time I associated with men greater than you, and they never made light of me. Such warriors I have not seen since and will not see again ... mighty were they, and they battled with the mighty mountain-dwelling centaurs, and destroyed them terribly.' Nestor's assertion of his exemplary status as an ideal counsellor is based on his superior experience, but also on temporal change. Because men of the past were greater than those today, and because even they took him seriously, his present claim to respect should be heeded. Warfare in the past is also subtly differentiated from its present counterpart. Earlier men battled with centaurs rather than with other men. Together with the centaurs' position beyond human society, the strong language used of this combat (the phrase 'destroyed them terribly' (*ekpaglōs apolessan*) occurs only here in the *Iliad*) suggests that it was more violent and less rule-governed than the fighting of the Trojan War. Both decline and development therefore inform the history that Nestor constructs, and give point to his argument. The former implies in passing that Achilles and Agamemnon should not think too highly of themselves, while the latter emphasizes the importance of the social codes that regulate human behaviour.

Nestor's speech in the opening book of the *Iliad* points to a use of exemplarity as dynamic and open to change rather than as a static reification of an achronic historical field. In listening to Nestor mould his speech, we eavesdrop on the processes by which *exempla* are shaped to meet the demands of a specific situation; in listening to Achilles and Agamemnon reject his plea for reconciliation, we find that the present may not find *exempla* drawn from the past to its liking.

The workings of these specific *exempla* are true to the narrative logic of the *Iliad* as a whole. The poem presents a complex, temporally evolving mixture of actions, mistakes, evasions, changes of mind, and decisions. Characters are exemplary not as symbols, but as fully-fledged agents. Thus Aristotle commented that Achilles was a paradigm of both virtue and harshness (*Poetics* 1454b14–15), and numerous later writers, ranging from Sappho to Gorgias, responded to the ambivalent portrayal of Helen.[30] Even before Aristotle and his contemporaries had formulated the notion of the 'paradigm', Homer created characters who transcend simple notions of what it is to be paradigmatic.

Homeric epic was itself a vital influence on the formation of historical writing in antiquity, and it is no surprise that the Homeric linking of exemplarity and change was picked up by the earliest practitioners of the new genre. A particular motif in the ancient historians is the malleability of *exempla* in rhetorical traditions. In Herodotus, the story of the tyrannicides Harmodius and Aristogiton is invoked, with a self-conscious allusion to memorialization, in the Athenian general Miltiades' appeal to the polemarch Callimachus before the battle of Marathon (6.109.3) – even though Herodotus' own account had brought out that their actions, far from bringing an end to the tyranny, had in fact made it worse (5.55, 62.2). Later, in his account of the run-up to the battle of Plataea, Herodotus presents a debate over which Greek city should hold the left wing in which Athenian speakers invoke the battle of Marathon as a great victory won by themselves 'alone' (9.27.5–6). The Athenian speech is probably an anachronistic echo of the tradition of Athenian patriotic oratory that developed over the course of the fifth century (see p. 67). But again the *exemplum* deployed in the speech runs counter to Herodotus' own account, which had mentioned the presence of the Plataeans at the battle (6.108). The changeability of the past in speeches boosts the authority and importance of the historian's own account while hinting, too, at its fragility.

It is not just through rhetorical manipulation that *exempla* are subject to temporality. In that same debate at Plataea, the Athenians start by telling of the great deeds of their ancestors. They draw various examples from what we regard as myth: the Athenians saved the destitute descendants of Heracles, ensured that the Seven against Thebes received burial, and fought off an Amazon invasion; they were even, so they claim, as good as any who fought at Troy (despite Homer's almost complete silence about their role). Herodotus' Athenians go on to argue, however, that 'there is not much point in mentioning these events': 'people who were good then might be worse now, and people who were bad then might be better now' (9.27.4). Instead they appeal, as we have seen, to their recent achievements at Marathon. In keeping with the principles formulated by later rhetoricians, claims on the distant past are replaced by claims made on (a distorted version of) the more recent past.

Historians also explore how the wisdom of attempts to draw lessons from the past is subject to re-assessment with new circumstances. Livy, for instance, following the stress in his preface on the usefulness of his historical enterprise, continues to engage with exemplarity when he turns to describe Rome's eventful history. He makes overt comments on the exemplary value of particular deeds and shows characters using the past in an exemplary fashion in both speech and action. If on the surface he seems to fit the model of *historia magistra vitae*, analysis of the way *exempla* are used over the course of his work cuts against this characterization. It is not just that they are subject (as we would expect) to rhetorical manipulation by speakers, it is also that they have a life span: speakers are consistently shown prioritizing recent over more distant *exempla*.[31]

Livy also probes the form in which exemplary models were relayed. A story about the early years of the Roman Republic that was much repeated in antiquity told how the patricians sent a spokesman, Agrippa Menenius, to conciliate the *plebs*, who had seceded to a nearby mountain. Menenius proceeded to tell a fable of how the other parts of the body revolted against the belly, aggrieved that they did all the work while the belly reaped all the rewards. In the version of this speech by Livy, Menenius' use of a fable is described by the adjectives *priscus* and *horridus*, 'old-time' and 'rough' (2.32.8) – the former a word frequently applied to the old institutions of Rome, the latter (literally 'bristling') evoking an image of shaggy antiquity, the bearded figures on Roman *imagines*. Livy's characterization of the speech is particularly striking after his explanation that Menenius was sent on the mission as an 'eloquent' speaker – a judgement that, like many in Livy's account of early Rome, is presumably to be read against the standards of the time he is describing rather than those of his own day. The eloquent Menenius uses a mode of communication that is hardly to be taken as exemplary; citing his example, Quintilian regarded fables as suitable only for pleasing 'uneducated rustics' (*Oratorical Education* 5.11.19).

The contrast of past and present is central to the discourse of exemplarity in many other Roman authors. We noted above the important collection of *exempla* composed by Valerius Maximus in the first century AD. Throughout his work, Valerius plays on an (at times explicit but more often implicit) sense of contrast with the present. Tensions result, however, when the offsetting of past against present confronts the need to flatter the current regime: thus in his preface to his second book, Valerius promises an account of the 'old and memorable institutions' of Rome, with the aim of showing 'the elements of this happy life we lead under the best of emperors, so that a retrospect of them may in some way profit present-day manners'. The conventional idealization of the present ruler is undercut by the potential for amelioration from *exempla* drawn from the Republican past.

Elsewhere Valerius Maximus draws attention to another way in which exemplarity is implicated in temporality – namely through the chronological gap between exemplary actions and the words which are required to commemorate them. 'Overwhelmed by the weight of the praise which you have deserved,' he writes at one point in one of his frequent addresses to dead heroes, 'I represent more the weakness of my own talent than your virtue' (2.7.6). (His addressees here, Postumius Tubertus and Manlius Torquatus, are both credited by Valerius with executing victorious sons for disobeying orders; Livy, by contrast, rejects the tradition about Postumius as an anachronism, on the grounds that the proverbial phrase 'Manlian orders' would not have arisen had there existed the prior example of Postumius (4.29.5–6).) Later Valerius notes the severity of the censors who struck the distinguished Cornelius Rufinus off the senatorial register for having ten pounds' worth of silver plate: 'Good lord! the very letters of our era seem to me to be astonished when they are forced to apply themselves to recording such severity, and to be afraid that they be thought to be commemorating the acts of a city that is not our own.' The sense of the past as a foreign city is generated here by the relative scale of Rufinus' luxury: the amount of silver that led to his expulsion would now be seen as 'the most contemptible poverty' (2.9.4).

The gap between Republic and Principate is fundamental to Roman authors' exploration of the temporality of *exempla*. Evidence of the power of Republican *exempla* is offered by Cassius Dio's account of an epochal event in Roman history: Octavian's settlement of the constitution in 27 BC (the occasion when he took the name 'Augustus'). Dio presents him making a long speech to the senate in which he hails his own renunciation of autocratic rule as more glorious than all the military conquests that either he himself or his adoptive father, Julius Caesar, achieved, and greater even than his resolution of the civil war against Antony. His speech nonetheless betrays an anxiety that he might be compared unfavourably with old-time Romans who laid down their lives for the good of the state (53.8.3–4):

> If Horatius, Mucius, Curtius, Regulus, the Decii consented to face danger and die to gain the reputation of having done a great and noble deed, why should I not desire even more to do something through which I will surpass in glory while alive both those men and all others too? Let none of you think that the Romans of old desired excellence and renown, but that now manliness has become wholly extinct in the state.

Dio here pointedly makes Augustus use a word with a strong historiographical resonance: 'extinct' (*exitēlon*) occurs in Herodotus' opening promise to preserve the great and admirable deeds performed by Greeks and non-Greeks alike (1 proem). Augustus adapts the Herodotean model by claiming that his own noble deeds militate against a sense of decay. The way he sets about combatting a spirit of defeatism about the present nonetheless confirms that the heroes of Rome exemplified as much an idea of *past* greatness as the particular qualities for which they were renowned.

It is not just the move from Republic to Principate that explains why the contrast of past and present is so powerful an element in thinking about exemplarity at Rome. Another distinctive feature of Roman exemplarity, as we have seen, is that it was tied closely with the histories of a limited number of families. The potential of these exemplary Roman families to inspire reflection on historical change was in turn brilliantly realized in Cassius Dio's account of the reign of Nero. Dio reports that Nero forced senators and other high-class Romans to participate in games at Rome as actors and musicians or even as gladiators: 'People at that time saw the great families – the Furii, the Horatii, the Fabii, the Porcii, the Valerii, all the rest whose trophies and temples were to be seen – standing below them and doing things some of which they would not have seen even being performed by others' (61.17.4). Dio's withering account of the sight of exemplary names in action in the arena reverses Polybius' theoretical focus on the patriotic spectacle of the aristocratic funeral.

Exempla in their time

The preceding sections have suggested that *exempla* are not just exposed to the passing of time, but themselves often self-consciously invite reflection on the specific circumstances in which they are re-worked. They are as much subject to as shaped by a concern with historical change. A similar self-consciousness, we shall now see, can be found in relation to the times in which *exempla* themselves are located.

The status of exemplary heroes can be modified by suggesting that the qualities that made them exemplary are representative of the age in which they lived rather than indicative of virtues that distinguish the heroes themselves. A good example of this move is found in Cicero's treatment in *On Duties* of Marcus Atilius Regulus, a Roman consul taken prisoner during the Second Punic War who was sent to Rome supposedly to negotiate peace, but when he got there argued against the peace and returned to die in Carthage rather than break his oath and stay in Rome (3.111):

> That he returned now seems amazing to us, but in those times he could not have done otherwise. Therefore that praise belongs not to the man, but to the times; for our ancestors wanted no bond to bind faith more tightly than an oath. This is shown by the laws in the Twelve Tables, by the sacred laws and by the treaties by which our faith is pledged even with an enemy.

Here Cicero draws on surviving legal documents as evidence of the tenor of the times in which they were drawn up, while accentuating the sense of distance from his own present by the language of amazement (*admiratione dignum*), which is often found in ethnographic treatments of remote peoples.[32]

While Cicero re-directs praise from the exemplary hero to his times, a stronger form of historical relativism is used to deflate the famous *exempla* of the past in Lucan's epic on the civil war between Caesar and Pompey. Lucan concludes a catalogue of the luxuries of Alexandria, Cleopatra's capital city, by berating the queen's folly in putting on an elaborate banquet, with fine gold and silver dishes, for Caesar (10.149–54): 'Even though it were not Caesar, prepared in abominable warfare to seek wealth by the world's ruin – place here the old-time (*priscos*) leaders and the names of a poor age, Fabricii and stern Curii; or let that consul, brought dirty from his Etruscan plough, recline here, and he will wish to lead for his country a triumph like this.' The two men named here were, as we saw earlier, renowned Roman leaders of the first half of the third century BC; they were often paired by Cicero as models of austerity. They are followed by an allusion to a figure from the early years of the Republic, Cincinnatus, who was ploughing his small farm when envoys arrived to summon him back to Rome in a crisis. The thrust of Lucan's argument is that these exemplary figures were able to maintain their frugality only because they were not exposed to the temptations that Caesar encountered in Egypt.

Lucan's argument is particularly cutting because both Fabricius and Curius were famous for resisting offers of lavish gifts. Pyrrhus admired Fabricius so much that he attempted to buy his services, while Curius told Samnite envoys who found him roasting turnips that he preferred ruling over people who possessed gold than possessing it himself. Even figures who could resist the wealth offered by Pyrrhus or the Samnites, it is implied, would succumb to the wealth of Cleopatra.

Lucan at the same time hints at a traditional picture of Roman decline by imagining Cincinnatus reclining at Cleopatra's court. This anachronistic banquet evokes an ideologically charged narrative of Roman dining customs: according to Isidore of Seville (*Etymologies* 20.11.9), Varro reported that Romans did not eat reclining in the past. Isidore's citation does not reveal whether Varro gave precise information on when or why the custom of reclining began – though it is likely that the influence of Greek customs was held accountable. The narrative's ideological charge lies in the claim that Roman women still sat at dinner. The implication is that Roman men policed in women the retention of strict ancient customs they had themselves abandoned.[33]

The idea that the virtues of an exemplary hero may reflect the character of the times in which that hero lived is found in the satirist Juvenal. In one of his poems Juvenal depicts the misfortunes of the Roman nobility at the hands of tyrannical rulers such as Domitian. Seeing the wealthy condemned to an early death by avaricious emperors, one young noble, Juvenal claims, even became a gladiator in the hope that this career would increase his life expectancy – but his attempted deception proved futile. Juvenal then contrasts his misfortune with the ruse adopted by Lucius Junius Brutus, leader of the Romans' uprising against their final king, Tarquin the Proud: 'who marvels at that old-time (*priscum*) cunning of yours, Brutus? Fooling a bearded king is easy' (4.102–3). The cunning to which Juvenal alludes is Brutus' pretended dumbness: having avoided thereby making himself suspect to the ruling family, Brutus revealed his true character after one of the younger Tarquins raped Lucretia. The implication is that Brutus got away with his ruse only because of the naivety of his royal opponents – here symbolized by their beards.

Juvenal's historicist slant is strengthened by his re-working of Livy's narrative of Brutus' conspiracy. The story told by Livy is that Lucretia commits suicide in front of her father and husband after making them promise to take vengeance on her behalf, and that Brutus then takes the lead while the others are overwhelmed by grief. The link with Juvenal comes through the language of the marvellous. Livy relates that Lucretia's father and husband are 'dumbfounded at this marvel (*miraculo rei*): where did this new spirit in Brutus' breast come from?'; and that the people then gather in the forum, 'attracted, as happens, by the marvellous new event (*miraculo . . . rei novae*)' (1.59.2–3). For contemporaries, Livy suggests, the miracle lies in the change observable in Brutus. Juvenal's riposte 'who marvels (*miratur*) . . .?' suggests that, from the perspective of his present, there is nothing surprising in the fact that Brutus got away with his deception.

The debunking of exemplarity at the hands of Lucan and Juvenal attests to a declamatory culture at Rome which took *exempla* as rhetorical material for displays of wit. But their reworking of the tropes of exemplarity does not just spring from a desire to seem clever. Serious thought about the operations of historical memory are compatible with (indeed, an essential part of) their cleverness. In the passages analysed above, the implication is that exemplarity is necessarily tinged with anachronism: Lucan suggests that the myth of Roman frugality arises retrospectively from the notion of decline, while Juvenal destabilizes conventional admiration for Rome's liberator by framing his actions as time-bound. By showing *exempla* in their time, they suggest that those *exempla* are out of time now – and so no longer *exempla* at all.

We may conclude this section by looking at the complex engagement with the historicity of *exempla* found in a political case from the late Republic: Cicero's defence speech for his former intern, the young Roman *eques* (knight) Marcus

Caelius, which was delivered in 56 BC in front of seventy-five jurors and a crowded forum. The charges against Caelius (attempted murder and poisoning) related in part to the aristocratic Roman matron Clodia, whose lover he had at one time been. Cicero's defence of Caelius is based on the insinuation that Clodia is the malicious inspiration for the prosecution. He proceeds to denigrate Clodia and defend Caelius by manipulation of the rhetoric of exemplarity.

Cicero's engagement with *exempla* in *For Caelius* involves self-conscious exploitation of negative and positive gender stereotypes. Early in the speech, he hints at the presence of a 'Palatine Medea' controlling the case (18) – as if the barbarous poisoner familiar from Greek and Roman tragedy has relocated to Rome. Later, turning to Clodia, Cicero asks whether she prefers him to deal with her 'severely, seriously and in an old-fashioned way (*prisce*), or in a relaxed, gentle and urbane manner', and suggests that if she prefers the 'austere way', he 'must summon from the dead one of those bearded men, not with the sort of small beard she delights in, but with that rough type we see on old statues and busts' (33). He then addresses her in the voice of her ancestor Appius Claudius Caecus (an important political figure in Rome in the late fourth and early third centuries BC), who is indignant that Clodia has neglected the distinguished examples set by her male and female forebears.

Cicero places Caecus in his time by identifying him with one prominent physical characteristic, his beard (the feature Juvenal uses to mark out the simplicity of the regal period). By a cynical balancing act, Cicero condemns Clodia through Caecus' assumed moral outrage while holding up Caecus himself to slight ridicule as an exponent of a rigid moral code that is as outmoded as his appearance.

Cicero then turns to defend Caelius from the implied charge that his associations with Clodia are a sign of degeneracy. He starts by suggesting that any man able to live without occasional relaxation must be endowed with 'some sort of divine virtues': 'Of this sort I think were those Camilli, Fabricii, Curii and all those who made Rome so great from being so small. But virtues of this kind are now not found in our manners, and scarcely even in our books' (39). Cicero here suggests that the great figures from the early Republic are no longer meaningful *exempla*, and perhaps even that the growth of Roman power that their virtues enabled renders those same virtues impossible. While Clodia is condemned for a luxuriousness that removes her from the revered simple past, Caelius is permitted to inhabit a different social regime from his ancestors without losing contact with their virtues.

The self-consciousness of Cicero's historicizing of exemplarity is further shown by his distinction between theory and practice. The theory of exemplarity,

Cicero suggests, is derived from books – and Greek books at that. And the reason the virtues of old-time austerity and poverty are no longer to be found in books is that Greek philosophy itself has changed: 'precepts of another kind have arisen now that times have changed for Greece' (40). The paradox is that the change in Greece to which Cicero alludes is its conquest by Rome. With some rhetorical bravura, Cicero allows a relativizing view of Greek moral philosophy to undercut further the moral virtues that supposedly ensured Rome supremacy over Greece. He hints that those austere Roman virtues are the creation of a theoretical framework derived from a subject people who no longer support that moral code themselves. It is but a short step from this assault on the Greek experts in exemplary theory to the final blow Cicero strikes against the timeless virtues of the Romans of old – the claim that dalliances with courtesans were not just the sort of behaviour tolerated in the permissive present but accepted among the ancestors too (48). So much for the quasi-divine Fabricii and Curii.

Cicero's masterly exploitation of the temporal domain of *exempla* in his speech for Caelius gains further resonance when read alongside surviving representations of one of the speeches actually made by Appius Claudius Caecus, the bearded hero whom Cicero summons up to berate his descendant Clodia. Cicero makes Caecus proudly allude to a speech he made appealing against peace with Pyrrhus – a speech that received its canonical form in the *Annales* by the second-century BC poet Ennius. A section of the Ennian version of the speech (199–200 Skutsch) is quoted in Cicero's treatise *On Old Age*, in a passage where the elder Cato holds Appius up as an example of the possibility of an old man pursuing a political life (16): 'when opinion in the senate was inclining towards peace and a treaty with Pyrrhus, Appius did not hesitate to say what Ennius put into verse: "Where have your minds, that previously used to stand upright, turned aside in madness?"' When we read this Ennian version alongside the rhetorical fireworks of Cicero's invective against Clodia, we can see that the decline that the Appius of *For Caelius* sees between his own time and Clodia's was already present in Appius' own day. Even then Appius was in danger of seeming an anachronism.

Cicero's misogynistic play with exemplary models in *For Caelius* confirms the picture we have seen throughout this chapter. The Greek and Roman devotion to paradigms and *exempla* did not presuppose a static or unchanging view of the ethical landscape. From the start, *exempla* were deployed flexibly and with sensitivity to the way in which past and present mutually define each other. Far from being a sign of temporal flattening or inert taxonomic thinking, Greek and

Roman tropes of exemplarity were guided by a perception of contrast between past and present and by apprehensions of further change in the future. They were constantly re-moulded by self-conscious reflection about rhetorical principles and by the perpetual striving for innovation.

What of the opposition between exemplarity and historicism with which we began? One of the core features of historicism is generally thought to be an adhesion to the particular: Gelley, as we have seen, suggests that history in the post-classical sense 'situates particular events in a totalizing schema', while in a major study Frederick Beiser writes of the historicist's belief that 'the essence, identity or nature of everything in the human world is made by history, so that it is entirely the product of the particular historical processes that brought it into being'.[34] Our analysis has shown that the ancient model of exemplarity, too, drew its power from the fact that it was rooted in the particular. It involved a careful scrutiny of points of difference and similarity between discrete historical events. This dialectical approach was fully compatible with a sense of anachronism: *exempla* could become out of date owing to their distance in the past or as a result of new political constellations. The particularity of the exemplary viewpoint also lent itself to relativizing or historicizing approaches; the virtues of exemplary figures could be seen as shaped not so much by their distinct choices as ethical agents as by the character of the age in which they lived, and the character of their times could be understood through models of historical development (above all, the move from simplicity to complexity discussed in Chapter 5). By contrast with modern historicisms, however, ancient exemplarity did embrace the possibility of renewal. Old *exempla* could become salient again with new twists in the order of things, sometimes at the very moment they were dismissed as antiquated. Rooted in the needs of the present, constantly re-shaping the past, projected towards the future, they provide eloquent evidence for an ancient sense of multitemporality whose contours will emerge in our next chapter.

Interlude: Ariadne on Naxos

Two famous Ariadne moments. First, the words with which Johann Joachim Winckelmann (1717–68), author of an influential *History of the Art of Antiquity*, begins to draw his work to a close:

> I could not keep myself from gazing after the fate of works of art as far as my eye could see. Just as a beloved stands on the seashore and follows with tearful eyes her departing sweetheart, with no hope of ever seeing him again, and believes she can glimpse even in the distant sail the image of her lover – so we, like the beloved, have as it were only a shadowy outline of the subject of our desires remaining. But this arouses so much the greater longing for what is lost, and we examine the copies we have with greater attention than we would if we were in full possession of the originals.[1]

The unnamed figure to which this passage gestures is (we may suppose) the Cretan princess Ariadne, abandoned by Theseus on the island of Naxos (and later picked up by the god Dionysus and turned into a constellation). For Winckelmann, Ariadne's gaze after her departing lover is a fitting image both of his own longing for the lost plenitude of ancient art and of the deepened attention occasioned by no longer having direct access to this plenitude.

Second, *The Soothsayer's Recompense*, a painting by the modernist Giorgio de Chirico (1888–1978), born in Greece of Italian parents (Fig. 10). A statue of a woman lies in the sunlight in an empty piazza. Her body is poised between two shadows, one that reaches out from the plinth on which she rests, the other imposingly cast by a gabled building (a railway station or palace?) with arched frontage that looms behind her. In the distance beyond a low wall, a steam train and two palm trees, framed by another arched structure on the right (or is it the other building seen from a different angle?). As we look at the statue, we are struck by the incongruity of its environment. We seem to be looking down at it from a height but the flat planes of the painting are not anchored to a single perspective. The grand building behind the statue has a clock that shows (roughly) ten minutes to two, but the deep shadows suggest that it is much later in the afternoon; if we

Fig. 10 Giorgio de Chirico, *The Soothsayer's Recompense*, 1913, Philadelphia Museum of Art, The Louise and Walter Arensberg Collection, 1950-134-38, © 2009 Artists Rights Society (ARS), New York / SIAE, Rome.

look more closely, we see that the clock itself has only eleven hour-numbers. No less strange is the way in which the statue itself emerges from this environment. It is the only visible human presence in the scene, its faintly languorous pose the only reminder of emotion and sensation in an otherwise bleakly anonymous world. Dwarfed by modern architecture, it seems out of place, abandoned, unmoored in any of the usual frames for such a figure. Its loneliness is enhanced by its positioning in the series of similar paintings produced by de Chirico in 1912–13,[2] soon after his arrival in Paris, all featuring variations on the sleeping figure, a famous statue in the Vatican museum which was identified as Cleopatra after its discovery in the Renaissance century and as a nymph by Winckelmann, but since the late eighteenth century has generally been regarded as Ariadne.[3] And the sense of solitude is further enhanced when the painting is read against a prose poem, 'The Statue's Desire', that the artist wrote in French at the same time:

> 'I desire at all costs to be alone', said the statue with the eternal look …
>   It *desires*.
>   Silence.

> It loves its strange soul. It has *vanquished*.
> And now the sun has stopped on high at the centre of the sky; and the statue in eternal happiness drowns its soul in contemplation of its shadow.[4]

Two Ariadne moments, then, but each has its own temporal positioning, each a different sense of anachronism. Winckelmann's discussion is attentive to historical change even as it insists on the value of the ancient art that is seen sailing away. In his account of Greek art as a whole, he plots a development from archaic hardness to the graceful beauty of the classical period; he is concerned with the conditions under which this transformation was achieved and with the prospects for imitating the exemplary works of Greek genius in the modern world. Now, as he closes his work, he makes clear his personal investment in the passage from antiquity to the present. He imagines himself back into the role of the lonely, abandoned Ariadne, assimilating his desire for the vanishing past with hers for the departing Theseus. And through this imaginative leap (across time, across genders) he makes us confront the high stakes in our confrontations with the antique. His closing flourish continues: 'we often are like individuals who wish to converse with spirits and believe they can see something where nothing exists. The word *antiquity* has become a prejudice, but even this bias is not without its uses. One always imagines that there is so much to find, so one searches much to catch sight of something.'[5] Paradoxically, he goes on to suggest, the very poverty of the material survivals from antiquity leads to a heightened historical sense.

As with Winckelmann, the words and images of de Chirico introduce a sense of the timeless (the statue's 'eternal look' and 'eternal happiness') while being sensitive to historical change. But to Winckelmann's image of the past slowly sailing away de Chirico introduces a discordant clash of temporalities. Displacing Ariadne's statue to a modern environment, he stages even more insistently than Winckelmann a series of questions about the temporal relationship between antiquity and modernity. Is the statue's isolation a sign that the force that the remnants of ancient culture once had to shape the imaginative lives of viewers can now only manifest itself in fragmentary, diminished encounters? Or is Ariadne a reminder of the potential for sensuous life that can be partially recaptured by recourse to Greek art and myth, even as it is assailed by modern culture? Or does the painting match its play with visual perspective by shortening, or even abolishing, the distance between antiquity and modernity?

The pieces of de Chirico's puzzle suggest different answers to these questions. The palm trees evoke a desert island, but also perhaps the Egypt of the queen whom the statue was previously thought to represent (it was at one time displayed in the Vatican with a decorative palm backdrop). The clock and train may together gesture to the standardization of world time (expanding railway networks were a major impetus towards the creation of standard time zones; an International Conference on Time, devoted to creating accurate and uniform time signals, was held in Paris in 1912).[6] The train could be read, too, as a substitute for the departing Theseus' ship; other paintings in the series show both a train and a ship, at the same time emblems of departure and arrival (but which is which?) and a poignant vignette of technological development (de Chirico himself wrote in a 1920 essay that the 'romanticism of modern life' could be found in 'the nostalgia of railroad stations, of arrivals and departures'[7]). Differently, we might see the abandonment visited on the statue as enhancing that visited on the character Ariadne by Theseus. On this view, Ariadne's statue could be seen as a paradigm of the fate of ancient culture, uprooted and displaced in time. But rather than gradually slipping from our vision like a departing traveller, ancient culture here rejoices in its solitude. It has vanquished – modernity?

The temporal juxtapositions in de Chirico's painting do not simply interrogate the opposition of antiquity and modernity and the mediating presence of earlier receptions. They raise, too, questions about the temporal positioning involved in individual acts of viewing or recreating an ancient sculpture. Belying its static form, the painting suggests different modes of movement, both by means of representation and through the narrative it implies. We see the train shuffling gouts of steam, and are invited to juxtapose their fleeting shapes with the statue's permanence. More locally, we imagine shadows inching across the ground, and the small changes wrought thereby on the appearance of the statue. (Compare de Chirico on the effect of sunlight on an arched Roman wall: 'The Roman arcade is a fatality. Its voice speaks in enigmas filled with a strangely Roman poetry; shadows on old walls and a curious music, profoundly blue, having something of an afternoon at the seaside, like these lines of Horace . . .'[8]) The sculpture itself is a synecdoche of the painting's condensation of temporalities, as hard, durable marble and the incidental, impermanent time of the body meet. Form freezes a particular imagined moment, a specific extension of the arm and knee, into a monumental stillness.

The engagement with antiquity and the moment in *The Soothsayer's Recompense* is mediated through German romantic philosophy. In one of his writings, de Chirico invoked Schopenhauer's call to 'isolate oneself from the world for a few moments so completely that the most commonplace happenings appear to be new and unfamiliar'.⁹ But it is above all de Chirico's obsession with Nietzsche that the painting reveals. Its title alludes to the figure of the soothsayer in *Thus Spake Zarathustra*, against whose proclamations of emptiness Zarathustra reacts with an affirmation of will. The statue evokes Nietzsche's frequent invocation of Ariadne in his self-projection as Dionysus, for instance in the poem 'Ariadne's Lament' in *Dithyrambs of Dionysus*. De Chirico himself wrote that 'the Nietzschean method' was 'to create previously unknown sensations ... to see everything, even man, in its quality of *thing*', and that Nietzsche's statement that he was 'surprised' by Zarathustra contains 'the whole enigma of sudden revelation'.[10]

The Soothsayer's Recompense can be viewed as an experiment by de Chirico in this 'Nietzschean method' of representation. The blanched bare earth, impending shadows and evacuation of human presence build an atmosphere of threat. Yet the painting's surreal assemblage includes momentary phenomena (steam and shade) that potentially enrich our experience of the statue. It rejects thereby what Nietzsche in the second of his *Untimely Meditations* dismissed as *Monumentalgeschichte* (monumental history), that is, a type of history that satisfies the optimistic human aspiration that 'a long-ago moment shall be ... still living, bright and great'.[11] Instead, the sculpture takes on a more temporally layered significance, open to the dialectical tension between the momentary and the monumental.

Like Winckelmann's self-projection as Ariadne, then, de Chirico's painting invites reflection on the gap between ancient and modern culture. *The Soothsayer's Recompense* moves us away from Winckelmann's concern with the imitation of the antique, with all its difficulties, to a use of an ancient myth to ground aesthetic modes foreign to antiquity itself. If Winckelmann displays a sense of anachronism as historical change, de Chirico's use of the statue of Ariadne as a paradigm of temporal complexity showcases a modern sense of anachronism as multitemporality.

7

Anachronism Now: Multitemporal Moments

Theorizing multitemporality

A black-figure painting by the renowned artist Exekias (active *c.* 540 BC) shows the Achaean warrior Ajax leaning forward, crouched and with his head bent over, intent on the ground under his face (Fig. 11). His right hand is carefully placing an upright sword into a little mound of earth; his left hand pats the earth down. The verticality of the sword contrasts both with the hunched warrior and with two spears which lean at an angle against an assemblage of armour – a crested helmet perched on the rim of a figure-of-eight shield, its empty frame eerily gazing down at the human figure. Behind the warrior, a palm tree, isolated, its branches curving down as if to caress the naked back, the only witness to the impending suicide.

Exekias' painting is unique in its handling of its topic. Ajax, second in fighting prowess to Achilles among the Achaean warriors at Troy, had lost a contest with Odysseus for the arms of Achilles and then attempted to gain vengeance on Odysseus and other leaders of the army at Troy. Exekias shows the aftermath of Ajax' failure. But whereas other ancient depictions show Ajax as a corpse, penetrated by the sword, he captures Ajax just before he falls on the sword, with the rest of his weapons stacked up as a reminder of his recent humiliation as well as of the military successes that brought him glory (he was particularly renowned for his shield).

The temporal tensions caught in Exekias' painting chime with a prominent strand in recent thinking about time in a number of disciplinary frameworks: its irreducible multiplicity. For the French philosopher Michel Serres (1930–2019), a particular concern is the multitemporality of the instantaneous moment. He introduces ideas about the dynamic behaviour of fluids to reconstruct the poet Guillaume Apollinaire's idea of a flowing river ('Sous le pont Mirabeau coule le Seine') as a metaphor for the unidirectional passage of time: 'he hadn't noticed the countercurrents or the turbulences'. Like much of Serres' thinking, this

Fig. 11 Ajax preparing his suicide. Black-figure amphora attributed to Exekias, Athens, sixth century BC, 558.3, Musée Communale, Boulogne-sur-Mer. © Philippe Beurtheret.

comment connects to his fundamental claim that Lucretian atomism and contemporary physics describe the same phenomenon of the chaotic movements of atoms within fluids.[1] Lucretius and modern physicists should not be seen as separated by unbridgeable time: in place of linear temporality and differentiated periods, Serres views every historical era as 'multitemporal', consisting of 'a time that is gathered together, with multiple pleats', like a crumpled handkerchief in which apparently distant points touch each other.[2] He offers the example of two elderly brothers mourning a youthful corpse – the preserved body of their mountain-guide father, rediscovered decades after he had gone missing in the high mountains when the brothers were children. Serres offers this scene, 'precisely an anachronism', as a metaphor for the relationship between writers – their thought preserved in time – and critics;[3] the metaphor encapsulates his goal of unsettling everyday assumptions about linear temporality.

Other disciplines where human experience has been analysed as multitemporal include psychoanalysis, cognitive science, memory studies and narrative theory. Psychoanalysts from Freud to Fédida have spoken of the 'anachronism' or 'anachronic' structure of the subconscious, signifying the capacity of memory to retain and re-order traces of the past and its resistance to linear structuring.[4] Cognitive theorists such as Evelyn Tribble and John Sutton approach temporal multiplicity through the workings of the human mind. They argue that views of the past as a realm that can be definitively separated from the present oversimplify how time is experienced, and see the presence of multiple, perhaps conflicting, ways of making sense of time at any given moment as a constant of human existence rather than as the product of acculturation. To capture this sense of multiplicity they have recourse to the language of anachronism, which they describe as 'intrinsic to human experience'.[5] The classical scholar Glenn Most similarly suggests that people experience their own lives by 'ordinary empirical anachronisms ... in the form of the narratives they recount to one another and, above all, to themselves' – anachronistic narratives that are far more complex, according to Most, than anything to be found even in Proust.[6] Again, philosophers of history interested in the capacity of narrative to represent history have presented a layered image of human experience, involving a blend of past, present and future,[7] while historians interested in cultural memory have paradoxically aligned the anachronistic with the synchronic (given that memory brings together different times in the present) rather than seeing the terms as antithetical.[8]

As we noted in Chapter 1, an important inspiration for the reconfiguration of the language of anachronism is found in Alexander Nagel and Christopher Wood's *Anachronic Renaissance*. Rejecting the notion that linear chronology is 'the inevitable matrix of experience and cognition', Nagel and Wood substitute the term 'anachronic' for 'anachronistic' as a means of naming artworks' peculiar concatenation of remembering, anticipation and belatedness, but one which is free from the historicist assumption that the artwork is 'a witness to its times'. They conceive of artworks as temporally plural, simultaneously pointing forward to their future recipients and commenting on the historicity of their own creation, whether by placing themselves within a substitutionary chain of earlier works that looks back to a remote origin or by styling themselves as authorial performances that anticipate later responses. The anachronic, in their formulation, is not so much what an artwork is but what it *does*.

Scholars have also in recent years paid attention to the varied ways in which the anachronic nature of time can be grasped through human engagement with material objects and literary representations of objects. A good example of this scholarly approach is Jonathan Gil Harris' 2009 study of Elizabethan theatre, *Untimely Matter in the Age of Shakespeare*. Partly through the influence of Serres and another French philosopher, Bruno Latour, Harris resists attempts to understand objects within their immediate contexts of production or use, or to construct cultural biographies in which objects are understood as having different values at different temporal moments.[9] Instead Harris proposes that multiple temporal traces inhere in objects and can be opened up to understanding in unpredictable ways. His analysis promotes sensitivity to how 'things chafe against the sovereignty of the moment-state' by being used in multiple contexts, and also by folding multiple times together as a precondition of their existence:[10] 'materiality ... articulates temporal difference', but 'in collating traces of past, present and future, it also pluralizes and hence problematizes the time of the object'. Harris employs 'multitemporality' to name the process by which an object 'can prompt many different understandings and experiences of temporality'.[11] Objects, in other words, do not simply reflect temporal experience, but promote particular means of comprehending it.

As we shall see in this chapter, analysis of material objects and their representation in literary works points to an awareness of temporal multiplicity in antiquity. We will discuss the role of objects in narrative genres such as epic and historiography as well as their use as props in theatrical performance (Sophocles' version of the suicide scene depicted on Exekias' vase). First, however, we set this use of objects in context by analysis of the apprehension of the multitemporal moment suggested by literary and philosophical writings in antiquity.

Seizing the moment

Let us consider first two Roman attempts to capture the history of recent rhetorical performances. Cicero in his dialogue *Brutus* (c. 46 BC) sketches the leading practitioners of forensic oratory at Rome in the closing decades of the Republic, carefully placing each figure within his own 'age' (*aetas*). As the account approaches Cicero's present, the gap between these 'ages' grows shorter and shorter, and orators are increasingly frequently positioned in overlapping generations. Time seems to become faster and, in Serres' terms, more folded. A more phenomenological sense of multiplicity is found in an account of declamations in the rhetorical schools that was written by the elder Seneca in old age at the request of his sons. Seneca begins the work with reflections on the distortions of memory (*Controversiae* 1 preface 3–5):

> Whatever I deposited in memory as a boy or young man, it brings out without delay as if recent and just heard. But things I have entrusted to it these last years it has lost and mislaid so that even though they are often dinned into me, I nonetheless hear them each time as new (*quasi nova*). ... I must ask you not to want me to follow a strict order in drawing my thoughts together; I must ... grasp whatever occurs to me. I shall perhaps put in several different places *sententiae* which were actually spoken in one declamation.

Seneca here to some extent anticipates the view of cognitive theorists that memory is 'animated by plural temporalities and by rhythms other than those of linear succession'.[12] But he presents the wavering of memory as a failing of old age rather than as inherent in human consciousness. The difference of perspective exemplifies the capacity of subjects to enrich their experience of time by their own reflections of it.

The most profound ancient investigation of the human consciousness of time is often thought to be that conducted by the Christian theologian Augustine of Hippo (354–430) in Book 11 of his *Confessions*.[13] Part of Augustine's discussion turns on the meaning of the past (which exists no longer) and the future (which does not yet exist): 'our present intention draws the future into the past: as the future diminishes, the past grows, until the future is spent and everything is the past'. The stress in 'intention' on human mental activity is reinforced as Augustine affirms that it is 'mind' that 'looks forward, and is aware, and remembers': 'what it looks forward to shifts through what it is aware of into what it remembers'. Past and future, then, are wrapped together in the present – which itself 'passes in an instant', while 'attention endures'. Augustine then clarifies what is meant by the common expressions 'a long future' and 'a long past', namely 'a long expectation of the future' and 'a long memory of the past' (11.27-8).

Augustine's conception of time is frequently characterized as a radical departure from non-Christian temporal perspectives. But while Christianity did shape Augustine's division of history (with 'six ages of the world' of 1,000 years followed by a seventh age of rest), his account of time as shaped by memory of the past and anticipation of the future in the fleeting present is foreshadowed in earlier philosophical writings. The poet Lucretius, for instance, expresses a similar sense of the moment in a passage where, in line with Epicurean doctrine, he denies the existence of entities other than atoms and void: 'Time also exists not of itself, but from things themselves is derived the sense of what has been done in the past, then what thing is present with us, further what is to follow after'; 'a sense of time', he concludes, is inseparable from the movement of atoms (*On the Nature of Things* 1.459-64). Aristotle, too, reached his definition of time as the 'number of movement in respect of the before and after' (*Physics* 220a25–6) by considering the human experience of time passing. For theologian, poet and philosopher alike, past and future are grasped through human perception in the present.

This tripartite model of time is found in non-philosophical writings too. Rhetorical theories of narrative divided time into 'what has gone by, what is present, what is going to be' (Theon, *Exercises* 78) – a division Quintilian thought too trivial to require further discussion (*Oratorical Education* 4.2.3). The same division surfaces right at the outset of the Greek literature: Calchas is introduced in the first book of the *Iliad* as 'the best of augurs, who knew what is, and what will be, and what was before' (1.69–70). Homer, admittedly, does not specify that past and future exist only as perceived through memory and expectation, but his praise of Calchas' seercraft implies something along those lines: Calchas can exploit his special skill at times when ordinary mortals have to act on the basis of a much dimmer apprehension of what is not immediately present. There is a strong case, moreover, for claiming that the tripartite model of time is inherent in the structure of narrative as well as other human interactions. Whether or not they offer explicit reflections on time, narratives present characters acting in their present on the basis of their recollections of the past and their desires for the future. Thus the *Iliad* starts with a priest of Apollo coming to the Achaean camp at Troy with a plan for the future (ransoming his daughter) based on his knowledge of a past event (his daughter's capture). Thwarted by Agamemnon, the priest then prays to Apollo for help with a new plan (revenge), invoking as he does so, with a conventional formula, his past services to the god (1.12–13, 37–42). While this tripartite model is distinct from an experience of time as multitemporal, texts such as the *Iliad* create situations that become multitemporal for readers by drawing the three times together. Readers experience as simultaneity what the rhetoricians divide.

The anachronicity of the present moment emerges still more powerfully in some ancient reflections on its evanescence. A memorable expression of the multitemporal moment appears in a chapter of Censorinus' *On the Birthday* in which time is divided into units such as 'day', 'month', 'the turning year', 'the great year' (the period between repeated conjunctions of different planets), 'era' (*saeculum*) and 'eternity' (*aevum*), which is defined as 'the single greatest time', 'immeasurable, without origin, without end', and the same for all humans. It is in treating this final category (rather than units with culturally specific divisions, such as 'day' or 'month') that Censorinus elaborates on past, present, and future (16.4):

Of these, the past lacks a beginning, the future an end; the present, which is the middle, is so exiguous and incomprehensible that it has no length and seems to be nothing other than a conjunction of the transacted and the future. It is so unstable that it is never in the same place, and it plucks (*decerpit*) whatever runs through from the future and adds it to the past.

The present as slippery meeting place of past and present stands in dialectical opposition to the infinite time of the *aevum*, a time so immense that any unit of finite time is, in comparison with it, 'not equal to one winter's hour' (16.6).

Perhaps no other ancient writer is as celebrated as Horace for giving poetic shape to this sense of fleetingness. 'Pluck the day' (*carpe diem*) is the best-known phrase in the whole Horatian corpus, often translated 'seize the day' and taken to express a recommendation to live for the moment. What has been less noticed, however, is that the poem which contains that soundbite (*Odes* 1.11) invites readers to form a subtle understanding of what a 'moment' entails. It does so through its evocation of a specific time and place and through its use of tenses:

> Do not ask – knowing is impermissible – what end the gods have given to you, what to me, Leuconoe, and do not meddle with Babylonian numbers. How much better to endure whatever will be, whether Jupiter has allotted us more winters, or this is the last that now weakens the Tyrrhenian Sea against pumice rocks. Be prudent: strain the wine, and cut back long hopes within a small space. While we talk, grudging time will have fled. Pluck the day, trusting as little as possible to the future.[14]

Horace is at the seaside with a lover, but he leaves us to imagine the dynamics of their past relationship, which have made Leuconoe turn to astrology in the hope of discovering the future. He focuses instead on the present, creating with the phrase 'that now (*nunc*) weakens the Tyrrhenian Sea against pumice rocks' a powerful instance of what Jonathan Culler calls 'the special "now" of lyric articulation'.[15] The line achieves an arresting condensation of times: the sea breaking against the rocks belongs to the *longue durée*, but the waves' repeated collapse is also open to human apprehension. Horace's 'nunc' folds together these two time scales: winter now acts as a synecdoche for winter in general.

The surprising image of a storm 'wearing out' the sea locates the poem in a particular setting. David West has noted that volcanic pumice is found by the sea in Italy only in the Bay of Naples (an area known in antiquity for its relaxed sexual mores).[16] On West's reading, the image is not one of sea crashing into cliffs, but of waves rolling back pumice pebbles on a beach; it is the porosity of pumice that weakens the sea. Horace's phrase pinpoints the specific, and repeated, moment at which waves weaken and come apart, hushed into foam and spray. Combining the momentary and the repetitive, the seasonal and the sweep of cosmic time, the lyric present constructed here opens up a perception of the multitemporal by which readers are enabled to step beyond the limited view of human temporality that holds sway over the user of 'Babylonian numbers' (horoscopes). This way of thinking, Horace implies, reduces the experience of time to a finite series of vacancies, a subject for calculation rather than a scene of emotion and self-reflection.

To this calculative manner, the poem opposes its multitemporal attitude. The multiplicity of times suggested by the storm crashing against the seashore is expanded through Horace's exhortations to his companion. Horace is telling Leuconoe to make the most of the present (by having sex?). But his present-tense observation 'while we talk' is followed by the unsettling future-perfect in 'grudging time will have fled' (*fugerit*: we expect 'time is fleeing'). The effect is to configure the 'now' (*nunc*) of the winter scene not simply as an evanescent immediacy, but as capable of being grasped retrospectively from a point in the future. And the 'time' (*aetas*) whose flight is experienced both in the present and in the future is itself multiple: it is at once a semi-personified vehicle of envy, the supra-human time of the cosmos, and the measure of a brief conversation ('while we talk') which forms part of that larger timescale. Crucially, the fleeting moment is given depth and significance by these relations. It is not only to be enjoyed through the senses (as *carpe diem*, with its implications of grape-plucking, intimates), but the means of an enriched reflection on what makes a moment meaningful as a time in which joy is felt more intensely through an awareness of its transience. The prudence ('be wise') that the poem recommends and enables is partly a matter of pursuing contentment unencumbered by fruitless dwelling on the future. But it also involves a simultaneous grasp of the present's connections to past and future, and of the multiple dimensions of the present itself, that renders the apprehension itself an enactment of human finitude and self-awareness.

Objects in time

We turn now to the multitemporality of material objects, starting with a necessarily speculative reconstruction of possible responses to a painting (Fig. 12) on a psykter (wine-cooler) attributed to the Athenian vase-painter Oltos (active c. 525–500 BC). The psykter shows an ostensibly surreal scene: hoplites in battle array, carrying shields and spears, ride on the backs of dolphins. When used at a symposium, the psykter would have stood in water to keep the wine cool, creating a congruence between use and image. The water around the base of the psykter would have taken on the appearance of the sea, on which the dolphins would have appeared to ride, bobbing with the movements of the water. This interaction between object and setting makes the transformative powers that are at work in the image itself (men borne out to sea on the backs of dolphins) radiate out into the environment in which it is used. It enacts the notion of the symposium as a space of psychological and emotional transformation.[17]

So much for the fit between object and environment. But how is the odd scene that the psykter depicts to be understood? Scholars have tended to interpret the scene as a symbolic depiction of a choral dance:[18] dolphins are often associated with choral dance in Greek poetry because of their love of music and

Fig. 12 Hoplites riding on dolphins; the devices on their shields suggest the symposium, as in the kylix shown on the right-hand shield here. Red-figure psykter attributed to Oltos, c. 520–510 BC. 1989.281.69, Metropolitan Museum of Art, New York.

their tendency to follow ships on which auloi (instruments similar to oboes) were being played.[19] This analysis might well be correct, but the psykter also repays being read against the kind of experience drinkers at symposia would often have had. Conjoining hoplites and dolphins, the image literalizes the process by which different aspects of a man's identity meet in symposiastic revelry. A man who serves in an ordered group of hoplites now drinks and listens to the aulos. In so doing, he takes on something of the dolphin's intuitive response to music. More metaphorically still, he and his friends are assimilated to a group of dolphins which moves together in a different sort of harmony. Yet they retain their identity as men: the hoplites ride on, rather than become, dolphins. The image metaphorizes the new type of order that the men enact in the symposium, condensing thereby their activities as hoplites, dancers and listeners, and producing a new kind of coherence even as it draws attention to the temporal segmentation of these varied activities.

We approach here Harris' elaboration of the ways in which an object 'can prompt many different understandings and experiences of temporality'. The object's viewers could have understood the scene as a metaphorical representation of the energies released in choral dancing, energies that might have conjured up their own memories of choral performance. Equally, they could have read the scene as related to their immediate sympotic experiences. On either reading, the image both enforces the realization that different relations to and inhabitations of time can intersect within a given moment and calls attention to the differentiation that makes such folding meaningful.

While Oltos' psykter illustrates how artworks from antiquity are capable of foregrounding the relationship between their static form and the temporal multi-layeredness of the phenomena they present, ancient writers were interested in the experiences generated by the re-use of material objects in time periods other than those in which they were first manufactured. We focus here on ancient discussions of some object-groups which reveal a perspective incipiently similar to that developed by critics such as Nagel and Wood.

The first objects are bronze statues of the Athenian lovers Harmodius and Aristogiton, known as the 'tyrannicides' for their assassination of Hipparchus, son of the earlier tyrant Pisistratus (Thucydides (6.54.2) suggested that it was Hipparchus' brother Hippias who was actually tyrant at the time of the assassination).[20] Statues of the lovers by Antenor were set up in the Athenian agora at some point after the expulsion of the Pisistratids, but removed by the Persians when they sacked Athens in 480 BC. The Athenians soon commissioned a new statue-group, with gestures (arm raised about to strike) thought either to be modelled on, or themselves to have influenced, representations of Theseus, who was revered at Athens as a founding figure (p. 64). The originals were, however, recovered by Alexander the Great when he captured Susa, and the historian Arrian (second century AD) states that they 'are now positioned at Athens in the Ceramicus [used in his time for the agora too], where we go up to the acropolis (*es polin*[21])'; he implies, too, that they were visible to those visiting Athens, as high-status Romans often did for cultural prestige (*Anabasis* 3.16.7–8). Further details are added by the reports of other authors in the imperial period. Pausanias reports seeing both the original and the replacement groups (identified by their sculptors' names) at Athens (1.8.5), while Cassius Dio mentions that the Athenians set up bronze statues of Caesar's assassins near the tyrannicides, 'suggesting that Brutus and Cassius had emulated them' (47.20.4).

The tyrannicide statues are, in Nagel and Wood's term, anachronic artworks. Arrian's account pointedly juxtaposes four distinct times, that of the tyrant-slaying for which the statues were originally constructed, Xerxes capturing the statues, Alexander recapturing them, and the present in which the statues can be viewed in a new setting itself of political import. He presents the statue-group as part of a narrative spanning symbolic episodes in Athens' past, suggesting that its meaning had changed along with the city's political transformations: in Nagel and Wood's terms, it was not simply 'a witness to its times', but accrued significance from these temporal displacements. Pausanias and Cassius Dio, on the other hand, speak to the distinction Nagel and Wood draw between 'authorial performance' and 'substitution' as models of artistic creation: authorial performance 'cuts time into before and after' through the element of agency, and 'asserts punctual difference against repetition and continuity', while 'substitution proposes sameness across difference'.[22] Pausanias' attention to the names of the sculptors promotes a view of the statues as authorial performance; he was writing at a time when the replacement statues – 'the craft (*technē*) of Critius', in Pausanias' terms – and not the 'old/original' (*archaious*: the adjective can mean either) ones made by Antenor had been widely copied across the Roman Empire. Cassius Dio, by contrast, attributes to the Athenians something closer to a substitutional view: as an act of political self-assertion, and in negotiation of their complex relationship with Rome, the Athenians present the statues of Caesar's assassins, and by extension the assassination itself, as part of a chain with Athenian origins, linking those fighting to preserve the Roman republic with the heritage of Athenian democracy. This substitutional view may have been enhanced by the status enjoyed by the replacement statue-group as well as by the visual link with depictions of Theseus.

Our second example concerns a statue of the penultimate Roman king, Servius Tullius, which was placed in a temple of Fortuna at Rome built by Tullius himself and later, during the Second Punic War, survived a fire that destroyed the rest of the temple. The episode is recounted in various authors: Livy merely notes the fire in passing without mentioning the statue (24.47.15); Valerius Maximus hails the statue's survival as a miracle (1.8.11); and Ovid attributes its survival to Tullius' supposed father, the god Vulcan (*Fasti* 6.625–6). Most detailed and complex is the account in Dionysius of Halicarnassus' *Roman Antiquities*. Dionysius looks ahead to the fire immediately after recounting Tullius' death (4.40.7):

> In the temple of Fortune which he himself constructed a gilded wooden statue of Tullius alone remained unharmed by the fire when there was a conflagration and everything else was destroyed. And still now, while the temple and everything in it, all that was restored to the old/original arrangement (*archaion kosmon*) after the conflagration, are clearly of modern craftsmanship (*kainēs technēs*), the statue is, as previously, archaic (*archaikē*) in construction; for it still remains an object of reverence for the Romans.

The main point of the anecdote is that the statue's survival offers a proof of the favour shown the king by the gods. But the story also reveals a consciousness of the multiple temporal perspectives that can be prompted by a given object. For Dionysius, both the 'old/original' form of the restored temple and the 'modern' craft that produced it can be apprehended simultaneously; or rather, to apply Nagel and Wood's suggestion that 'the original was the creature of the replica',[23] the idea of the temple's *archaios* condition depends on the act of restoration. Dionysius' account suggests further that the statue of Tullius gains from its position in the restored temple: it is described by the adjective *archaikos*, which (unlike the cognate *archaios*) always conveys a sense of period style; and while that adjective can be used of deliberate archaisms, here it emphasizes that the statue is a survival of a previous age, and in doing so enhances its numinousness.

Nagel and Wood themselves illustrate their ideas of original and replica with another Roman structure described by Dionysius, the Casa Romuli. This was a hut on the Palatine alleged to be that in which the twins Romulus and Remus were reared by a shepherd and his wife. Dionysius notes that the hut survives 'even in my time' (1.79.11), is treated as 'holy' and is repaired when damaged 'in as similar a way to before as is possible'. As Nagel and Wood note, the original hut was probably constructed long after the time of its supposed inhabitants, but its presence on the Palatine (as that of a rival hut on the Capitoline) created a sense of connection to Rome's past, even as its surroundings were re-shaped with buildings of marble.[24]

Epic mo(nu)ments

In the last two sections of this chapter we turn to imaginary objects in Greek tragedy and (to start with) Greek and Roman epic. While epic typically has a broad spatial and temporal canvas, three illustrative scenes will show how epic poets were capable of making characters' engagement with material objects serve as a vehicle for reflection on the multitemporality of the moment.

First, a distant time and space, as evoked in the *Argonautica*, written in the third century BC by Apollonius of Rhodes. The passage describes how the Argonauts in the course of their voyage around the Black Sea encounter a place used by the Amazons for sacred rites (2.1169–76):

> They all went together to Ares' temple to sacrifice sheep, and they stood around the altar eagerly, which was outside the roofless temple, made of pebbles. Within a black rock had been fixed, holy, to which once all the Amazons prayed; and it was their custom, whenever they came from the mainland, not to burn sacrifices of sheep or bulls upon the altar, but they slaughtered horses prepared for a year's length.

The black rock juts uncannily into the Argonauts' world, and that of the reader. Unworked, housed in a simple 'roofless' temple, it appears as a relic of an unspecified past. Veneration is paid to it seemingly in virtue of its pure objecthood. Apollonius' terse account enforces its mysteriousness.

Apollonius' primordial rock is nonetheless surrounded with hints of different temporalities. The contrast between two types of sacrificial victim (sheep and horses) evokes conventional Greek views of the differences between Greek and barbarian, hinting perhaps at a contrast between the 'primitivism' of the nomadic, horse-rearing Amazons and the more 'advanced' Greeks. A more subtle mechanism is the verb-form Apollonius uses for the 'fixing' of the rock in the temple, *ērēreisto*. This form of the verb appears in Apollonius (here and at 2.1105) for the first time in extant poetry since his most important stylistic model, the *Iliad*, where it is used four times, always in the same metrical position as in Apollonius (with heavy long syllable in the fifth foot of the hexameter), and always of a spear being 'fixed' in a 'much-decorated breastplate' as a warrior falls in battle (3.358, 4.136, 7.252, 11.436). The echo of this violent literary past is as uncanny as the experience of seeing the stone. The primeval quality of the rock is captured by means of a self-conscious reversion to Homer, a linguistic gesture that twins belatedness and remembering. Borrowing again the language of Nagel and Wood, we might say that Apollonius translates the black rock from anachronism to anachrony. An object that, perceived in isolation, might seem a left over from a distant past becomes a means of experiencing and reflecting on the multitemporal nature of our intellectual constitution as readers. At the same time, the momentary experience of coordinating Apollonius' recollection of Homer contrasts forcefully with the enduring qualities of the rock that it describes.[25]

We turn now forward in heroic, but back in literary, chronology to a famous moment in the ninth book of the *Iliad*. Achilles has withdrawn from battle because Agamemnon has taken away from him Briseis, a woman captured and given to Achilles as a slave when he sacked the city of Lyrnessus and awarded to him in recognition of his valour. Three envoys are sent to woo him back: 'They found him delighting his mind with the clear-toned lyre, fair and elaborate, and on it was a silver bridge, which he had taken from the spoils when sacking Eetion's city; with this he delighted his heart and sang the great deeds of men' (9.186–9). Through the lyre's history, Homer evokes a specific past: Eetion was ruler of Lyrnessus, the city where Briseis was captured, and father of Hector's wife Andromache, who earlier in the poem has recalled in a pathetic speech his killing at Achilles' hands (6.414). The story attached to the lyre shows that Achilles is still gripped by anger at Agamemnon's recent wrongs; its continuing presence contrasts with the absence of Briseis. It invites us, too, to contrast the lyre's permanence with the transience of Eetion's city and to reflect on its varying performance history: it was once used to celebrate, perhaps, quite different deeds. The use Achilles makes of the lyre points at the same time to the future. By singing of 'the great deeds of men' (*klea andrōn*), he evokes the 'undying fame' (*kleos aphthiton*) for which the warrior undergoes the danger of battle, for which Achilles himself accepts an early death (9.413). Even without knowing the details of what Achilles sings about, we apprehend the lyre as a device in which different times fold.

Achilles singing on his lyre offers an oblique model for Homer's own practice. In inviting listeners to hear two songs simultaneously, Homer's own and what Achilles is imagined as singing, the scene is paradigmatic for the *Iliad*'s poetics. In addition to foregrounding parallelism of theme (the *Iliad* too celebrates 'the great deeds of men'), the lyre captures the way in which the *Iliad* collapses distinct times while allowing listeners to reflect on their differences. Like Apollonius' unworked rock, the crafted lyre transcends the moment in which it appears in the narrative and becomes an anachronic object.

The capacity of material objects to crystallize the folding of the present moment in the lasting literary monument is nowhere exploited more remarkably than at the very end of the *Aeneid*. Virgil presents Aeneas on the battlefield, pondering whether to spare the Rutilian king Turnus (Italian Hector to his Achilles). As Turnus pleads with him, Aeneas suddenly sees that he is wearing on his shoulder a baldric ripped from the corpse of Pallas, the young son of Aeneas' ally Evander; consumed with fury, he 'buries' (*condit*) his sword in Turnus' body (12.950). The verb used here for the act of killing is, as critics have noted, regularly used for the founding of cities; the *Aeneid* itself starts by stressing Aeneas' multiple sufferings in war and journeying 'until he should found (*conderet*) a city' (1.5). The poem folds back on itself, inviting readers to reflect on the connection between this killing of one man and the creation of Rome. Multiple times converge even more startlingly in the description of the baldric (with a standard poetic use of the plural) as 'monuments (*monimenta*) of savage grief' (12.945): in Don Fowler's words, 'it is a reminder to Aeneas *of* the pain that Pallas suffered, it is a reminder that causes savage pain *in* him at this point, it will cause him to bring about savage pain in Turnus, and it is a monument representing a scene of pain' (the baldric has depicted on it the slaughter of their husbands by the daughters of Danaus on their wedding night).[26] The present folds together past and future as well as the perpetuation of suffering in art. As with Achilles' lyre, moreover, the momentary focus on Pallas' baldric thematizes poetics: 'monuments of savage grief' is an apt description of the *Aeneid* itself, and so a further instantiation of Virgil's self-reflexive engagement with different temporalities.

The literary objects that we have explored in this section emblematize the complex relations that exist between the time of events and the time of their recipients. By focusing attention on the difference between these two times, they point to audience time as a domain in which readers are able to articulate for themselves a distinct form of synoptic, retrospective temporal consciousness. The rock, the lyre and the baldric do not simply open up a local understanding of time's passing conceived in relation to particular events. The poems themselves provide frames for coordinating the different temporalities presented within them. They make available not a unified theorization of temporality, but an expanded understanding of what it is to live in time.

Anachronic Ajax

Our discussion of anachronism in tragedy in Chapter 3 focused on the retrojection of post-heroic practices to the heroic world. At issue here is a different manifestation of the genre's creative capacities, namely the use of objects as a way of putting on show a multitemporal understanding of human agency. We focus here on the most famous telling of the story portrayed on the vase-painting with which we began this chapter: Sophocles' *Ajax* (composed perhaps in the 440s BC), a play that is distinctive in the connection it forges between multitemporality and its thematic focus on change and resistance to change.

How was the climactic moment of Ajax's suicide portrayed in Sophocles' play? Objects in tragedy may be physically present (as props on stage) or captured solely by language; for the former we rely in any case (in the absence of stage directions) on characters' words for clues not just about objects' meaning but even about their very presence. In *Ajax*, Sophocles used both types of object anachronically to elicit reflection on the significance of the hero's suicide.

A striking tableau towards the start of the play presents Ajax surrounded by visible evidence of the previous night's carnage (maddened by Athena, he had slaughtered some of the army's livestock under the illusion he was killing his enemies).[27] Apparently set on suicide, he calls for his son Eurysaces, asserting that the child 'will not be frightened to look on this newly-spilt blood' (545–6), and then bids him to 'take the thing from which you take your name' – 'my shield unbreakable, of seven hides, wielding it by its well-sewn thong' (574–6: 'Eurysaces' means 'broad-shielded'). The shield (which may or may not be present on stage) is a disconcertingly multitemporal object: the resonant 'of seven hides' alludes to Ajax's shield as it is known from the *Iliad*, but while that large Iliadic shield was attached to the body by a leather strap, the tragic version has a hand-grip (*porpax*) like contemporary hoplite shields, but one made of leather rather than metal.[28] The slight rupture introduced by this technological anachronism contrasts with the shield's function as emblem of continuity from father to son. This sense of continuity is both reinforced and complicated by Ajax's confident assertion that his son will be undaunted by the sight of gore – in marked contrast with the emotional Iliadic scene where Hector's young son Astyanax cowers before his father's nodding helmet, 'frightened by the bronze and the crest of horse-hair' (6.469). The complication introduced by the Homeric intertext is typical of Attic tragedy's tendency to take elements of the epic ethos (here inherited fearlessness) and push them to uncomfortable extremes.

The presence onstage of the suicide weapon is first attested in the famous 'deception speech' in which Ajax seems to suggest that he has decided not to kill himself: 'I will go where I can find untrodden ground, and hide this sword of mine, most hated of weapons, digging a place in the ground where none will see it.... since I received this gift from Hector, my deadliest enemy, I have never experienced anything good from the Argives' (657–63). Ajax here alludes to his exchange of gifts with Hector after their duel in the *Iliad*, which was left unresolved owing to the arrival of night (7.303–5); he now identifies that exchange as the beginning of his misfortunes. Later in the play, in a soliloquy before he does kill himself, Ajax returns to the same scene, starting with a personification of the sword itself (which is probably placed behind a screen which will conceal Ajax's actual death): 'The slaughterer stands where it will be sharpest, if one has leisure to calculate – a gift of Hector, of all foreigners to me most hateful, most fell to see' (815–18). He proceeds to announce that he has 'fixed' the sword 'in Troy's hostile earth ... on an iron-consuming whetstone newly-sharpened' (819–20), and to offer prayers that his half-brother Teucer may find him 'fallen on this newly-dripping sword' (828) and that the god Hermes may convey him to the underworld, 'ribs broken by this sword with a swift, spasm-less leap' (833–4). Ajax here attempts to exert a measure of imaginative control over his fate by successively paring down his figuration of the sword, moving from personification to detailed description to simple reference.

Ajax's recollection of Hector's gift has been seen as linking him with the world of Homeric epic.[29] This reading is in keeping with a common interpretation of the play as a whole: Ajax is often interpreted as an anachronistic character, attached to the stubborn individualism and pride of the epic hero, an individualism that is now seen to yield to the flexibility shown by Odysseus, who pleads that Ajax should be allowed burial, thereby showing himself ready to ignore personal slights.[30] Like a hero in an American Western, on this reading the Homeric Ajax cannot survive in the settled civic world.

Interpretations of Ajax's character as anachronistic subscribe to a misleading linear understanding of temporality of the sort that is contested by the critics canvassed earlier in this chapter. The goddess Athena attributes to Ajax the intellectual qualities which Thucydides (1.138.3, 2.65.6) praises in the leading fifth-century Athenian generals Themistocles and Pericles – 'foresight' and skill at 'seizing opportunities (*kairia*)' (119–20). Ajax's attempted murder of the army's leaders would in any case have been as problematic in Homeric ethics as it is from the civic perspective of fifth-century Athens. The Homeric poems themselves continued to exercise an immense (though not unchallenged) influence on Athenian education and culture; they were capable of framing ethical and political questions even in the changed conditions of a democracy.[31]

Ajax's sword appears in the play not as an anachronistic relic of epic but as an object of his multitemporal consciousness. In his closing self-address, Ajax's initial reference to Hector's gift links its present role to its provenance. Next, the resonant compounds 'newly-sharpened' and 'newly-dripping' offer glimpses of the immediate past (Ajax's preparations since his last appearance on stage) and future (the sword's appearance after his death); the latter recalls too the 'newly-spilt blood' (546) on which Ajax called his son to look. Finally, the sparse reference to falling on 'this sword' expresses Ajax's self-assertion. Throughout the speech, he layers the object with temporal significance, allowing listeners to perceive its past and future aspects folded into its present appearance at the same time as he attempts figuratively to displace its agency with his own.

The temporal implications of the allusion to Hector's gift repay closer examination. In the 'deception speech', Ajax expresses through the sword his fixed hostility towards Hector: 'the saying of men is true: the gifts of enemies are evil gifts and bring no benefits' (664–5). And yet the rest of that speech is full of images of alternating change, in which the cyclical patterns of the cosmos are offered as an ethical paradigm: 'For even terrible and most mighty things yield to prerogatives: snow-footed winters turn to crop-filled summer, night's dread sphere stands aside for day's white-foaled light to blaze' (669–73). Ajax draws the lesson that 'my enemy should be hated as one who will sometime become a friend; while as for a friend, I shall aim to help and assist him this far, as one who will not remain so for ever' (678–82). Ajax wavers, then, between seeing human relations as fixed and inflecting the present moment with a sense of their mutability.

Ajax's engagement with his physical surroundings creates an equally powerful expression of multitemporality. While he began his final speech by addressing his sword, he closes it by turning aside from his present concerns to address the landscape and the cosmos: 'O light, o sacred plain of native Salamis, o ground of my father's hearth, and famous Athens, and your kindred race, and these springs and rivers and the Trojan plain, you I address: farewell, my nourishers.' This is the last word Ajax speaks: 'other things I address to those in Hades below' (859–65). The address' pathos is intensified by the way it balances various temporalities. In addressing himself to rivers, plains and light, phenomena removed from the time of human inhabitation, he projects himself into an imagined community with a supra-human order while underlining his own fragility. This sense of fragility is further suggested by the narrative progression adumbrated in Ajax's address: he moves from his origins in Salamis and Athens (both present in his consciousness alone) to his situation in Troy, and from the 'light' of life to 'Hades'. The temporal tensions come to a head, finally, as he first uses his own name ('Ajax speaks'), 'seeing himself *sub specie aeternitatis*, like the preceding objects of the landscape',[32] before reverting to the first person as he ponders his future in the underworld.

Ajax should be interpreted as an anachronic rather than an anachronistic hero. What he does through his final speeches is to offer a self-reflexive exploration of his own temporal consciousness. To the deception speech's rendering of simple alternations, his final speech adds a more complex notion of temporality in which objects with different histories are folded together. It challenges spectators (in the modern world as much as in fifth-century Athens) by presenting a collage of experiences of time out of which they can shape their own understanding of temporal processes.

Coda: Ariadne at Cumae

A further Virgilian moment. Aeneas has finally arrived in Italy. In keeping with instructions from the ghost of his father Anchises, he makes for Cumae to seek help from the Sibyl. There he finds a temple founded by Daedalus in his flight from Crete. On it are gilded images, among them Cretan scenes: Pasiphae and her offspring, the Minotaur, 'monuments (*monimenta*) of unspeakable lust' (*Aeneid* 6.26); the labyrinth Daedalus created to house the monster; and Daedalus himself, helping Ariadne unlock its secrets with a thread 'in pity for the queen's great love' (6.28). *Monimenta* again folds time: it signifies the Minotaur himself as memorial of and warning against sexual excess and also the temple door on which he is now depicted. By portraying Ariadne, moreover, Daedalus repeats in exile the gesture of pity he made when he helped her in Crete. But he does so now in metal, and now (as we know even if Daedalus himself does not) as a premonition of the still greater pity that the abandoned Ariadne will evoke. Daedalus' artwork points, too, to the limits of art: twice Daedalus tried to portray the 'fall' (*casus*, 6.32) of his son Icarus, twice his hands 'fell' (*cecidere*, 6.33); and Aeneas' own viewing is cut short as the priestess tells him that 'this is not the time for these spectacles' (6.37). He must instead find the dark grove within which shines a golden bough that will open a path to the underworld where he is to see his father and have unfolded before him a pageant of future Roman heroes.

Interlude: Aeneas in the Underworld

The golden bough in hand, Aeneas is led by the Sibyl down through a cave to the underworld. They arrive at a river bank which is thronged by men and women of all ages, all begging to be allowed to cross – as the Sibyl explains, the unburied dead. Transported across the Styx by the ferryman Charon, Aeneas encounters various groups in the underworld (suicides, women who have died through passion, men who have died in war), gazes at the grim walls of Tartarus, and then enters the pleasant pastures of Elysium, where his father Anchises offers a glimpse of Roman history through the sight of souls awaiting their new life in the world above. Aeneas finally departs with the Sibyl through the gates of ivory, through which false dreams are sent to the world above.

Virgil's account of Aeneas' experiences in the sixth book of the *Aeneid* is part of a long literary tradition in which the underworld is the site of a conversation across and about time and history.[1] Among its predecessors are (now lost) poems on the underworld descents of Heracles and Orpheus. The most important influence, however, is Odysseus' account of his journey to the entrance of the underworld in the eleventh book of the *Odyssey*. Odysseus' goal was to receive advice from the seer Tiresias about his return to Ithaca. To converse with Odysseus, Tiresias first has to drink from a trench filled with the blood of a sacrificed sheep. Other shades flock to drink too: some are known to him – his mother Euryclea and his former companions at Troy, Agamemnon and Achilles (Ajax resolutely refuses); besides them, famous women from earlier generations, including Tyro, Phaedra and Ariadne, approach (in some sort of chronological order[2]) and offer brief sketches of their lives. And though Odysseus (unlike Aeneas) seemingly does not move from the entrance into the underworld proper, he sees other famous figures: Minos giving judgments; Orion hunting; Tantalus and Sisyphus being punished; finally a phantom of the deified Heracles, who recalls his own journey to the underworld to fetch Cerberus.

Odysseus' conversations with the shades are themselves in dialogue with other poetic traditions.[3] They fill in some of the aftermath of the *Iliad* while offering a partial re-appraisal of human life from the perspective of the dead: Achilles glories in his son Neoptolemus' successes, but famously expresses a preference for the lowliest life on earth to the highest honours in the underworld. The account gestures, too, in both form and content to the genre of catalogue poetry. It has the repetitive paratactic structure typical of catalogues, above all in its descriptions of the famous women ('After her I saw Antiope ... After her I saw Alcmene ... And I saw the mother of Oedipus ...') and men ('And I saw Tityos ... And I saw Tantalus ... And I saw Sisyphus too ...') from earlier generations; the account of women may even draw on a forerunner of the (later and now largely lost) Hesiodic *Catalogue of Women*, which charted a path through Greek heroic traditions by means of genealogy.[4] Homer's underworld, then, offers a wider picture of both mythographic and poetic traditions.

Virgil similarly uses the underworld to evoke and reflect on tradition. He alludes to the two great wars of Greek epic when he describes Aeneas seeing figures from the Theban War as well as warriors from both sides who fell at Troy. Like Homer, he re-visits in a new setting characters from his own epic (Aeneas addresses Dido, who is unmoved, like 'hard flint or Marpessian rock' (6.471)) and has his hero encounter a series of famous women such as Phaedra, Pasiphae and, by a twist, Caeneus, now restored to her original female form (6.445–9). But Virgil also departs from the Homeric model. Whereas Odysseus first does his business with his mother and Tiresias and then enjoys leisurely encounters with the other shades, Aeneas' climactic meeting with Anchises evokes a distinct sense of national history and purpose. This climax, moreover, involves a startling rupture, as Anchises explains the presence of the souls through Orphic-Pythagorean and Stoic beliefs that are hard to reconcile with the earlier underworld scenes (703–51).[5]

Virgil's use of the underworld as a stage for Roman history exerted a strong influence on the later epic tradition. Lucan in his *Civil War* (on the conflict of Caesar and Pompey) has a Thessalian sorceress revive a dead Pompeian soldier who reveals the impact of the war in the underworld – the despair of the virtuous Romans of old, the joy of Catiline – while Pluto 'prepares punishment for the victor' (6.784–820). Again, Silius Italicus in his *Punic War* allows Scipio Africanus to see by means of necromancy members of his family and other great figures, male and female, from the Roman past, as well as Homer and the heroes of Homeric epic (13.615–895).[6] Virgil's own inspirations may have included the *imagines* of ancestors displayed in Roman homes and funerals (p. 151) and the statue groupings of Roman heroes in the Capitol and the Forum Romanum.[7] Whatever Virgil's sources, the pageant of Roman heroes fundamentally re-shapes the dialogue between past and present established in the *Odyssey*. In keeping with the Homeric background, there is still a strong stress on individuals and martial valour, but the underworld has become the scene for a national story.

Anachronism plays an important part in Virgil's creation of the underworld. Given the varied eschatologies on which it draws, the encounters with heroes from different ages are not in themselves strictly anachronisms. But anachronistic Roman touches do make themselves felt. The account of the punishment allotted to sinners mentions, as a category, those who 'cheated a client' (6.609) and, among individual victims, one man who 'sold his country for gold and set over it a powerful master, set up laws and abrogated them for a price' and another who 'entered his daughter's bedchamber and its forbidden union' (6.621-2). Partly following Servius, modern scholars detect specific allusions to Antony and Catiline, both apparently paying the penalty for their crimes centuries before they were born.[8]

In his account of the parade, Virgil draws attention to points of both contrast and continuity between past and present. Listing Italian towns such as Gabii and Fidenae that will be founded in the future, Anchises tells Aeneas that 'these will then be names, now they are lands without name' (6.776) – but these words have an edge for Virgil's contemporaries, familiar with these towns' recent decline.[9] Caesar and Pompey are presented as harmonious boys, the better to magnify the contrast with their later quarrel (6.826-35). Other figures (for instance, the populist Ancus at 6.815-16) already display the character they will have in their lifetimes. The most pointed continuity is stressed by a breach in the chronological presentation of the future Romans. After Romulus, the founder of Rome, Virgil introduces with a flourish Augustus, the founder of a new golden age in the present (6.792-3), whose military reach exceeds that of Hercules and Bacchus (6.801-5). The juxtaposition and comparisons connect Augustus with three deified figures, thereby promising him the same fate.

The temporal complexity is magnified when Anchises addresses the souls of Fabius Maximus (famous for his delaying tactics in the Second Punic War (p. 149)) and Augustus' nephew Marcellus (who had died aged nineteen in 23 BC). Turning to Fabius, Anchises quotes from Ennius' *Annals* what was already a famous description of his achievement: 'You are that Maximus, the one man who restores the state by delaying' (6.845-6). While Anchises tends to use the future tense for the deeds of other Romans, Fabius is already fixed in (Ennius' description of) his role in Roman history. For Marcellus, by contrast, Anchises creates an identity defined by potential and pathos: 'Alas for his piety, alas for his old-fashioned (*prisca*) fidelity ... Alas pitiful boy ... You will be Marcellus' (6.882–3). Marcellus is anachronistically defined by the virtues of the early Republic; Anchises' foresight extends to knowledge of how a past that lies in his future will be idealized in hindsight.

The anachronism of Virgil's underworld peaks in the famous lines (placed in between the addresses to Fabius and Marcellus) in which Anchises defines Rome's imperial mission:

> Others will beat out bronzes breathing more softly (I believe so), draw living faces from marble, plead cases better, describe with a rod the movements of the heavens with a pointer and tell of the rising stars. Do you remember, Roman, to rule over peoples in nations (these will be your skills) and to impose habit on peace, to spare the defeated and subdue in war the proud.
>
> 6.847–53

'Do you remember, Roman ...' (*tu ... Romane, memento*) – but who is the Roman that is addressed? If it is (the Trojan) Aeneas, who is standing by Anchises' side, then the implication may be that Aeneas already contains in himself the whole Roman race 'in embryo'.[10] James Zetzel, however, complains that 'Aeneas is not, and never will be, a Roman' and that 'there is no parallel in the poem for so striking an anachronism'; he allows that Anchises' vocative is an 'anachronism', but suggests that it is directed to 'the future citizen of the Roman state, and the readers of the *Aeneid* itself'.[11] With either of these readings, *Romane* involves an anachronism: with the first, in the form of his address; with the second, in the identity of his addressees. Perhaps there is no need to choose between them.[12] As an address to both Aeneas and future readers, *Romane* encapsulates the dialogue with and through anachronism that pervades the *Aeneid* and has made it so amenable to later imperial re-working.

8

Anachronistic Dialogues

Anachronism and the *School of Athens*

Two men wrapped in conversation are walking beneath a grand vaulted ceiling modelled on the ruins of the grand imperial baths and triumphal arches in Rome (Fig. 13). The elder of them, bald and bearded, is pointing upwards; the younger, also bearded, gestures ahead and slightly downwards. Their identities are suggested by the (Italian) titles of the books in their left hands: on the left, with *Timeo* (*Timaeus*), is Plato (*c.* 428–348 BC); beside him, holding *Etica* (*Nicomachean Ethics*), is his greatest pupil, Aristotle (384–322 BC). To their sides many further figures, all male, some of them clearly identifiable, spread out over the floor and steps: some are simply onlookers; others converse in groups; some are absorbed in writing. This group of men could not have come together in this way at any single moment in history, but together they are the masters and pupils in the fresco that since the seventeenth century has been known as the *School of Athens*. Painted by Raphael between 1508 and 1512 for the Stanza della Segnatura, one of the rooms of Pope Julius II's private apartment in the Vatican (probably a library), it has come to be seen as the most famous instance of the artistic use of anachronism in the construction of an image of antiquity. As such, it forms an appropriate starting point for our explorations in this chapter of the use of dialogue across time (among philosophers, among the dead, and between writers and readers) as a vehicle for the formation of intellectual communities that transcend human temporality.

Viewing the scene portrayed in the *School of Athens* as an anachronism is itself the result of changing critical fashions. In his life of Raphael (first published in 1550), the painter and art historian Giorgio Vasari (1511–74) claims that the image depicts sages reconciling theology with philosophy and astrology. He pays no attention at all to the temporality of the figures, though he names eight of them: Plato and Aristotle; the fourth-century BC cynic Diogenes lying on the central steps; the apostle St Matthew writing on the left; the Persian sage

Fig. 13 Raphael, *School of Athens* (*c*. 1510), Stanza della Segnatura, Vatican.

Zoroaster (dates uncertain) on the right side, holding a globe with his back to the viewer; and three of Raphael's contemporaries – the young Federigo II, Duke of Mantua; the architect Bramante bent over a compass; and Raphael himself.[1] A century later, by contrast, the French scholar Fréart de Chambray observes in his *An Idea of the Perfection of Painting* that the painting mixes times, notably through the figure (Vasari's Zoroaster) that he identified as the second-century AD astronomer and geographer Ptolemy. Significantly, Fréart cites the painting by the title *School of Athens* and pays attention to space as well as time: he justifies naming one figure as the Athenian Epicurus (341–270 BC) on the grounds of when and where he lived, and he explains that Raphael has preserved the philosophers' tranquillity by removing the 'corporal exercises' such as wrestling and fencing that would take place in ancient gymnasia.[2]

The first writer to apply the term 'anachronism' itself to the *School of Athens* seems to have been the painter and biographer Giovanni Pietro Bellori (1613–96). Bellori wrote in a 1695 treatise on Raphael's Vatican frescoes that the artist had intended to bring together 'the schools of the most illustrious philosophers, not of one age alone, but of the most celebrated ages of the world', and in doing so he had made use of 'anachronism or the reduction of the periods in which they lived'.³ 'Reduction' (*riduzione*) here has the obsolete sense of a 'bringing back' of later figures into an earlier time (as we have seen, the Greek equivalent *anagōgē* and its cognates were used in the same way). But 'reduction' in its normal sense captures, too, the way in which Raphael's fresco has been received as an icon of classicism. Implicit in that reception is a collapsing of multiple periods into a single, seemingly timeless, image of the classical.

Bellori justified his claim of anachronism by identifying sixteen of the human figures in the fresco. He concurred with seven of Vasari's list of eight, but inferred from the mathematical images on a tablet held by his companion that Vasari's St Matthew was actually Pythagoras (sixth century BC) – an identification followed by almost all scholars since.⁴ Besides Pythagoras, one other of Bellori's identifications has received general assent: the figure conversing in a small group to the viewer's left, though portrayed here as younger than Plato, unmistakably recalls ancient busts of Plato's mentor Socrates (*c*. 470–399 BC). There is still much uncertainty, however, over many of the other figures. Bellori suggested that the dashing young man in armour with whom Socrates is conversing is Alcibiades, but a few years later this pair of figures was used as an illustration of Socrates and Xenophon.⁵ Among other names added by Bellori were a cluster of writers and thinkers from Sicily and Italy whom he linked with Pythagoras, namely Empedocles, Epicharmus and Archytas; as later scholars filled up the picture, they were joined by the leaders of the philosophical schools that claimed descent from Socrates, Plato and Aristotle (the nineteenth-century German painter Johann David Passavant offered names for as many as fifty of the figures).⁶ While the project of making such identifications has been attacked,⁷ it is still clear that the painting depicts a chronologically impossible group, gathering together founders, students and successors of important philosophical schools.

Ever since Raphael's chronological mixture was first identified, its aesthetic propriety has been disputed. While Bellori found it 'very appropriate', Fréart de Chambray accepted that Ptolemy's presence was permitted by artistic licence (with an appeal to the treatment of Dido by 'the incomparable Virgil'), but was scornful of Vasari's identification of Zoroaster, 'an old Scythian king' and 'magician' of whom 'assuredly Raphael had never heard', and who 'came into the world almost 2,000 years before Plato, and in a country extremely distant from his'.⁸ A century later Robert Bromley, a British clergyman who wrote a treatise on aesthetics, followed Fréart's normative approach, criticizing Raphael for breaking the principle that the artist 'shall not transport us by anachronismal fictions beyond the period in which the scene is laid'; in Bromley's view, to 'bring together upon the same spot those who are known to have lived ages asunder' is 'to destroy all the effect at once, by telling us we were imposed upon and deceived'. While he acknowledged that in scenes in heaven figures can 'mix together in the same groups, whatever may be the distance of their ages', what he found inadmissible in the *School of Athens* was the inclusion of living figures alongside the dead.[9]

But is the *School of Athens* an anachronism at all? The painting is cited in a philosophical discussion of anachronism by Annette Barnes and Jonathan Barnes. They argue that if Raphael does not imply that Socrates was actually alive at the same time as an old Plato, then 'there would not be any anachronism': 'Whether a given representational work contains an anachronism depends upon the kind of representation it is and this in turn depends upon how we interpret the work.'[10] While Barnes and Barnes appeal to the authority of Ernst Gombrich in support of the view that the *School of Athens* is not the kind of representation that can contain an anachronism, a similar view was already presented by the French critic Roger de Piles (1635–1709) in his *Principles of Painting*. De Piles suggested that Raphael meant to represent not 'a simple history' but 'an allegory where the diversity of times and countries does not hinder the unity of the subject', and that he had done so because 'it was only by the succession of times that philosophy reached the degree of perfection in which we see it'.[11] On one view, then, it is the 'anachronism'[12] of (one interpretation of) the title *School of Athens* that creates the 'anachronism' of the assemblage – as well as the spatial error (the inclusion of 'Scythian' Zoroaster) to which Fréart objected.[13] But others would claim that the multitemporality creates anachronism whatever Raphael's intentions.

However it is defined, the sort of multitemporal dialogue that Raphael portrays and critics such as Bromley deplore is an artistic commonplace. An example from Bromley's own era is Nicolas-André Monsiau's *Aspasia Conversing with the Most Illustrious Men of Athens*, which was shown at the Paris Salon in 1806. Besides being anachronistic in its suggestion of a modern literary salon, the painting includes Sophocles, Euripides, Socrates, Phidias and Pericles alongside some men who were born at around the time Pericles died (Plato, Xenophon, Isocrates, the painter Parrhasius). The anachronistic grouping offered an idealized image of Athens at its political, poetic and artistic peak. A possible ancient parallel to Raphael's technique is the 'Mosaic of the Philosophers' discovered in Pompeii, which shows seven men at leisure, one of them apparently instructing the others in the use of a (possibly anachronistic) armillary sphere. The mosaic has been variously identified as a representation of the Seven Sages (themselves a group whose membership was not clearly established), of Plato's Academy, of philosophers from a later school, or perhaps of all three at once.[14]

While that mosaic shows figures interacting, there was also an ancient tradition of grouping isolated figures from different times: a hemicycle of statues set up at Memphis in the third century BC included Homer in the centre with Hesiod, Thales, Heraclitus, Protagoras, Plato and Demetrius of Phalerum among those shown on either side.[15] This tradition continued in the medieval era with representations of the 'Nine Worthies', three pagan (Hector, Alexander and Julius Caesar), three Jewish and three Christian.[16] Particularly important for understanding the *School of Athens* is the tradition in medieval art of placing a group of exemplary figures beneath the abstraction that they exemplify. Raphael follows this tradition by including a personified figure of Philosophy above the *School of Athens*, but he introduces a striking innovation by placing it on the ceiling rather than on the same plane as the philosophers and by transforming isolated exemplars into small groups engaged in dialogues with which viewers can imaginatively engage.[17]

The sense of dialogue in Raphael's fresco is intensified by its placement in the Stanza della Segnatura. Philosophy is joined on the ceiling by allegories of Poetry, Theology and Justice, each overseeing an anachronistic picture on the wall below. Beneath Poetry is the *Parnassus* (Fig. 14), which depicts Apollo and the Muses gathered in song on the top of a mountain, flanked by classical and modern

Fig. 14 Raphael, *Parnassus* (*c.* 1510), Stanza della Segnatura, Vatican.

poets as well as by one artist (Raphael again). As in the *School of Athens*, the identity of some figures is uncertain (Sappho alone is explicitly named), but the groupings that can be identified (Homer gazing upwards as Dante and Virgil look on) are connected more by poetic affinity than by date. Under Theology, facing the *School of Athens*, is the *Disputation of the Sacrament*, a fresco split in two layers, with Christ, the Virgin and biblical figures on the upper level, and some church fathers, popes and other figures below, gesturing or just looking at an altar which holds the sacrament, symbol of Christ's intercession on earth. Finally, below Jurisprudence on the fourth wall are three allegorical figures (Virtues or Graces) and reliefs of Justinian and Gregory XI.

The *School of Athens* invites comparison above all with the *Parnassus*. Both paintings portray harmonious gatherings of figures we would call classical, medieval and Renaissance (Raphael's contemporaries). Some elements in the *Parnassus* nonetheless seem to appeal to the idea of a succession of distinct historical times. As we noted in Chapter 2, Raphael places a modern *lira da braccio* in Apollo's hands – the deliberate anachronism with which Panofsky concluded his study of the differences between medieval and Renaissance art. Another iconographic innovation is Apollo's upturned gaze: as Luba Freedman points out, in classical art Apollo looks straight ahead or downwards, never heavenwards. Freedman reads Apollo's glance as intimating that 'the authority of the classical deity ... has waned'.[18] Apollo may well be acknowledging a higher force, but Raphael still had good reason for wanting him to retain much of his power. Apollo was interpreted in Raphael's time as a typological precursor of Christ.[19] He was also associated with poetic and prophetic inspiration: above the *Parnassus* the depiction of Poetry includes a motto, NVMINE AFFLATVR, 'inspired by divine power', that is modelled on Virgil's description (*Aeneid* 6.50) of the Sibyl, who drew her prophetic power from Apollo. A statue of Apollo was prominent, too, in the Belvedere courtyard, towards which the window in the Stanza della Segnatura looked; the statue was displayed there along with other newly found statues (including the *Ariadne* that inspired de Chirico, at that time interpreted as a *Cleopatra*) that spoke of the greatness of Rome, and the entrance to the Courtyard was itself capped by another quotation from Virgil's account of Aeneas' revelatory journey to the underworld (*Aeneid* 6.258: *procul este profani*, 'be far away, those who are profane'). On one reading, *Parnassus* celebrates the establishment of a new Augustan era in the Rome of Julius II, with Raphael himself as Julius' Virgil.[20]

A similar typological scheme can be seen at work in the *School of Athens* when it is interpreted in its setting in the Stanza della Segnatura. On the wall opposite is *Disputa*, a fresco which imitates in its general structure the apse of a medieval church and which has as its focal point the sacrament, emblem of the light of divine revelation.[21] In the *School of Athens*, then, Plato and Aristotle are walking as if through the nave of an open church towards the sacrament in the apse across the room. The whole anachronistic assemblage can be read, moreover, as supporting the Renaissance ideal of philosophical and theological concord. Many Renaissance humanists supported the proposition that the views of the idealist Plato and the empiricist Aristotle could be reconciled; Raphael's depiction attends to their differences (reflected in Plato's upwards and Aristotle's downwards gestures) while hinting at the possibility of harmonious resolution. Another tenet held by some humanists (especially Neoplatonists such as Marsilio Ficino, Pico della Mirandola and Egidio da Viterbo) was the compatibility of Greek philosophy with Christianity; that Raphael's painting promotes this idea is suggested by the work in Plato's hands, *Timaeus*, whose account of the creation of the cosmos by a divine demiurge was often read in the Renaissance as a precursor of Christian belief.[22]

The Stanza della Segnatura has gained a further place in the history of anachronism from its discussion by Nagel and Wood in the final chapter of *Anachronic Renaissance* – itself a self-conscious tribute to its place in Panofsky's conception of the Renaissance (with the acknowledgement that 'in a deep sense our reasons are not so different'). For Nagel and Wood, the *School of Athens* – 'a picture of sociable interaction, so harmonious and so inviting that one easily forgets the basic impossibility, the anachronism, of the scene' – is an 'instant fiction' that tears 'the substitutional web'. That is, it is an artistic performance that proclaims its own innovation, gesturing to the tradition of the stable centre found in many Church paintings, but instead portraying diversity, 'the ceaseless circuitry ... of intellectual discourse' that spreads from the harmonious pairing of Plato and Aristotle, and in the process spatializing temporal difference along the surface of the wall. Central to Nagel and Wood's interpretation is the position of Raphael's Vatican frescoes at the moment when print culture emerges, enabling the seamless reproduction of images. They read the various paintings as thematizing in different ways tensions between unitary origin and dispersed transmission and between unmediated speech and mediated writing.[23]

Nagel and Wood open up fresh ways of reading the anachronistic dialogue portrayed in the *School of Athens*. Even as context suggests ways in which the paintings can be integrated into the political program of Julius II, their very form realizes and makes available an asynchronous time in which what the classical (or what comes to be identified as such) recurs and can be variously attended to as an object of significance in its own right. Perpetuation guarantees the unpredictability of such recurrences: different generations will come to the painting with an intellectual variousness that matches, perhaps exceeds, that of Raphael's philosophers. At the same time, the radiant precision with which the figures are pictured, the depth of care that they bestow on their activities and which is answered by Raphael's craftsmanship, encourages viewers to take pleasure and intellectual stimulation from them, in a manner that resists any simple narrative recuperation.

Philosophical dialogues across time

When Raphael portrayed ancient philosophers conversing together, he (or whoever was responsible for the conception) was drawing on a long literary tradition of using chronologically impossible philosophical dialogue to represent intellectual connections and hierarchies. One of the most famous examples is the grand scene in Plato's *Protagoras* which portrays the assembly of sophists and their followers that Socrates and Hippocrates find when they visit the home of the wealthy Athenian Callias (314e–315b). Like the *School of Athens*, the dialogue lacks firm chronological anchoring: to cite just one inconsistency, a dramatic date of 420 BC is suggested by the fact that Pherecrates' comedy *Wild Men* is at one point said to have been staged 'last year', but those present at the scene include the sons of Pericles, who died in the plague at Athens a decade earlier.[24] This 'carefree anachronism', along with the ambience of Plato's description, has led to the suggestion that the *Protagoras* scene directly inspired Raphael's design.[25]

Anachronism was a common feature of philosophical dialogue in antiquity. In Plato's Socratic dialogues, it takes a number of forms: some works (such as the *Protagoras* and also the *Gorgias*) have incompatible chronological indications;[26] the *Symposium* describes a party celebrating the tragedian Agathon's first dramatic victory in 416 BC, but includes references to later events, including events after Socrates' death in 399 BC; the *Menexenus*, unlike the *Symposium*, does not have quite such a precise occasion, but includes a speech by Socrates which refers to events after Socrates' death; and other dialogues show Socrates engaging in dialogue with figures who seem either too early (*Parmenides*) or too late (*Euthydemus*). To look beyond Plato, Socrates also appears in anachronistic dialogues such as Xenophon's *Symposium*, in which Xenophon himself (born c. 428 BC), or at least a narrator-figure who resembles him, is present as an adult at a party commemorating an athletic victory in 422 BC; and in the *Aspasia* by another fourth-century Socratic, Aeschines of Sphettus, in which Socrates relates a conversation between Aspasia and Xenophon's wife (though Xenophon probably married only after Socrates' death).[27] Non-Socratic parallels include a short dialogue on alchemy between Ostanes (a possibly legendary Persian magus, dated by Pliny to the time of the Persian Wars) and Cleopatra, and Athenaeus' *Deipnosophists*, which gestures to anachronism through participants (Galen, Plutarch and Ulpian) with the same names as famous but asynchronous intellectual figures from the Roman imperial period (only Galen is unquestionably the celebrity himself).[28]

Anachronisms in philosophical dialogues were discussed by a number of ancient critics.[29] The chronological inconsistencies in the *Symposium* and *Menexenus* are examined in two works by the second-century AD rhetorician Aelius Aristides (3.577–82, 4.50–1), while those in *Protagoras*, *Gorgias*, *Parmenides* and Xenophon's *Symposium* are discussed by speakers in Athenaeus (5.216c–18e, 11.505f–6a). Both authors pay close attention to chronological indications such as archon-dates, and they may well have drawn their material from a second-century BC treatise *Against the Admirer of Socrates* by the grammarian Herodicus of Babylon. For both, chronological criticism was not an end in itself, but motivated by a desire to impugn Plato's reliability more generally, in Aristides' case as a response to Plato's attacks on rhetoric and to the critique of Athenian politicians in the *Gorgias* (515b–519b), in Athenaeus' as an exercise in self-definition against a canonical fellow-writer of sympotic dialogue.[30] Assuming that the dialogues were meant to be reports of actual conversations, Aristides dismisses them as 'fictions' (3.586), while Athenaeus' speaker claims that philosophers 'lie about everything and do not realize that much of what they write goes against the times (*para tous chronous*)' (5.216c). It is even suggested in Athenaeus that two characters in Plato's dialogues, Gorgias and Phaedo, rejected the ideas attributed to them by Plato (11.506e) – a suggestion that is itself probably an anachronism. Plato's loose handling of time was felt to be emblematic of his other alleged distortions of the thought of the characters depicted in his dialogues.

The importance of accurate chronology in the dramatic setting of dialogues was also stressed by Cicero. In his dialogue *Brutus* (on the history of oratory), a writer of consular rank, C. Scribonius Curio, is criticized for depicting a conversation in which the characters discuss a meeting of the senate supposedly held during Julius Caesar's first consulship while the actual details of the discussion relate to his subsequent campaigns in Gaul (218–19). Again, in a section from a lost speech, *For Gallius*, which is cited by Jerome (*Epistles* 52.8.3), Cicero laments the popularity of a staged work, *Conversations of Poets and Philosophers*, in which at one point Euripides and Menander, and at another Socrates and Epicurus, converse – men 'whose lives we know were separated not by years but by centuries'.[31] Besides criticizing anachronisms in others, Cicero wrote dialogues on ethical and philosophical themes (notably *Republic* and *Laws*) which strongly engage with Plato's dialogues and yet avoid their anachronistic cast-lists.

Despite the criticisms of Cicero and others, anachronisms in philosophical dialogues could be defended as a feature of the genre. The fifth-century AD Roman writer Macrobius appeals overtly to Platonic precedent to defend his own anachronistic presentation of the characters gathered at the discussion he depicts in his *Saturnalia* (set in the early AD 380s): 'It should not be viewed as dishonest if one or two of those whom the gathering brought together reached maturity later than the age of Praetextatus [a high-standing official in the imperial service who is one of the dialogue's principal characters].' He mentions the *Protagoras* and *Timaeus* (the latter not discussed by Aristides or Athenaeus), but appeals particularly to the *Parmenides*, whose title character 'was so much older than Socrates that Socrates' boyhood hardly coincided with the other's old age, and yet their discussion is about difficult issues' (1.1.5–6). Just as Plato in that dialogue introduced a young Socrates (see below), Macrobius presents a young character who went on to play an important role in Roman intellectual culture and who speaks already with the authority his scholarship would later gain for him: the grammarian Servius, whose commentary on Virgil's *Aeneid* identified many of its anachronisms.[32]

While the ancient critical attitude to anachronistic dialogues is largely negative, modern scholars have tried to show their constructive potential. One of the most successful examples of this approach is M. M. McCabe's discussion of Plato.[33] Countering the tendency of readers in the tradition of analytical philosophy to extract arguments from their dialogic context, she observes that it can be impossible to separate argument, dialogue and dramatic setting, and that we should use the presences, absences and connections that the dialogue form offers to help us read the arguments that Plato is presenting. Plato, on her reading, was concerned above all with the communication of ideas and arguments and with their relationships to each other. His dialogues are intellectual engagements that go beyond immediate conversations with those present.

Plato's use of anachronism is shown in different ways in *Euthydemus*, *Parmenides* and *Menexenus*. The cast of characters in *Euthydemus* includes

Socrates, his friend Crito, and two sophists, the brothers Dionysodorus and Euthydemus. The two brothers are not historical characters, but caricature fourth-century 'eristic' philosophers, who engaged in a combative form of argument based on the aggressive identification and use of fallacies and errors. Although such argument had its roots in the work of fifth-century philosophers, by retrojecting a later and more developed form of this philosophical method to Socrates' lifetime, Plato creates a dramatized encounter that leads the reader through the process of analysing the arguments themselves.[34] Towards the end of the dialogue, moreover, Crito reports a conversation he has had with a 'man who thinks that he is extremely wise' (304d5) whom commentators often identify with Plato's rival educator Isocrates; by leaving this character unnamed Plato avoids an explicit anachronism.[35] The use of anonymous and imagined speakers is one way in which Plato manages the impact of anachronism, especially in his later dialogues.

Anachronism operates differently in *Parmenides*, one of Plato's most austere and philosophically difficult works. Plato uses a setting common in dialogues, a religious festival (in this case, the Panathenaea), to bring non-Athenian characters into the city and in contact with each other – here, at a reading of Zeno's book (127c–d). The anachronistic element lies in the appearance of both people and ideas at the wrong time. This is the only Platonic dialogue to represent Socrates as a youth, while Parmenides is described as 'very old' (in his sixties) at the time of their meeting (127a7–b6). Debra Nails, who has catalogued the dramatic settings for all Plato's dialogues, argues for a dramatic date for this discussion of 450 BC, but notes that there is a great deal of circularity involved in this identification, with the dates for Parmenides' life often being inferred from Plato's text.[36] It is in fact unclear whether the meeting is historically possible at all:[37] Diogenes Laertius (9.23) gives an earlier date for Parmenides that would preclude his having visited Athens during Socrates' youth.[38] Whether or not the conversation could have taken place, the proleptic depiction of Socrates' philosophical talent emphasizes his future importance,[39] while the arguments he presents for Parmenides to criticize are the metaphysical theory of Forms, normally associated with Plato himself. The young Socrates, Parmenides suggests, is trying to develop his theory 'too early' in his intellectual career (135c), signposting Plato's deliberate anachronism in voicing his own later ideas through him. Such interventions may signal authorial recognition of the artificiality of the dialogue. Plato lends a further layer of multitemporality to all the Socratic dialogues by leaving unspoken the extent to which he makes Socrates the mouthpiece for his own ideas.

The anachronisms in *Menexenus* relate (on the surface at least) more to history and rhetoric than to philosophy. The dialogue portrays Socrates offering his companions a civic funeral speech prepared by Aspasia, the partner of Pericles, constructed of parts left out of the speech she is represented as having written for Pericles (presumably that presented by Thucydides). As Aelius Aristides carefully calculated, its narrative of Athenian history goes down to the King's Peace in the archonship of Theodotus (387/6 BC), at which time Socrates has been dead for thirteen years and Aspasia was probably dead too. Within the dialogue, there are hints of the anachronism: Socrates claims that orators prepare funeral speeches in advance so that they are not tied to the context of their delivery (235d), and when he turns to events after his own lifetime he flags them as 'not ancient' (244d2). The anachronism itself has been variously interpreted. Some scholars suggest that Aspasia's funeral speech is a parodic distortion of Athenian patriotic rhetoric, designed to highlight by contrast the superiority of philosophical discourse or to critique the legacy of Pericles' leadership.[40] Others read the anachronism against the dialogue's pervasive concern with death. It is not just that the dialogue is one of 'ghosts' (Pierre Vidal-Naquet's phrase).[41] The theme of death is highlighted too by Socrates' claim that he imagines he is living on the Isles of the Blessed (the traditional posthumous home of noble heroes) when he listens to Athenian patriotic speeches (235c) and by a section in Aspasia's speech in which dead Athenian soldiers address their sons from the underworld (246d–7c). The imagery of death has suggested to some critics another way in which philosophy trumps rhetoric: Socrates' example remains more alive than the gullible and vainglorious Athenians.[42]

Death is a motif in many other philosophical dialogues in antiquity. Plato's *Phaedo* dramatizes the death of Socrates, while many of his other dialogues are set in the period leading up to that event; in his version of Socrates' defence speech, moreover, he presents Socrates expressing his hopes for the underworld, where he will meet and argue with many great figures of the past, writers and heroes alike (*Apology* 41a–c), entering into dialogue with the ultimate anachronistic community. Cicero's *Republic* presents a conversation that took place just a week before the death of its main speaker, the consul and victor of the Third Punic war Scipio Aemilianus in 129 BC, while his *On Old Age* is set in 150 BC, a year or two before the death of the elder Cato. Athenaeus' *Deipnosophists* (which starts with an echo of *Phaedo*) and Macrobius' *Saturnalia* are similarly set just before the deaths of their leading characters Ulpian and Praetextatus.[43]

The theme of death can also be suggested by literary allusion alone. In *Protagoras*, Plato has Socrates describe his response to the sophists present in Callias' house through quotations from Odysseus' account of his sight of heroic figures from the past (see p. 195): first Socrates introduces Hippias with 'after him I saw' (315b), the start of a line in which Odysseus describes catching sight of Heracles (*Odyssey* 11.601); then he continues '"And I saw Tantalus" – for Prodicus of Ceos was in town too' (315c, quoting *Odyssey* 11.582). The effect is to present the crowd scene as a vision of the underworld. The trope was picked up, too, in Aelius Aristides' critique of Plato: he complains that in *Symposium* Plato 'advances the years' in a manner that is impossible 'unless the symposium was put together in the Elysian Field' (3.579–80) and that in *Menexenus* he 'contrives that the dead are together with one another as if they are alive' (4.50).

The recurrent motifs of death and the underworld are intimately connected with the use of anachronism to create a sense of intellectual community. Macrobius' *Saturnalia* presents a cast of 'nobles and other learned men' discussing the ancient traditions of Rome during the final stages of pagan culture at Rome a few decades earlier.[44] Cicero's *Republic* is set during a political crisis that he identified as the beginning of the troubles the Roman Republic now faced. Scipio's reminiscences, moreover, enable him to bring in some further characters from the more distant past, such as Masinissa, king of the Numidians, and, famously, a dream (6.12–33) in which he converses with his relative by adoption, Scipio Africanus, victor of the Second Punic War, who had died in 183 BC when the younger Scipio was only two years old.[45] In the dream (a possible model for Anchises' speech in the sixth book of the *Aeneid* (pp. 196–8)), Scipio receives a prophecy of his own future while being granted a vision of the harmonious structure of the cosmos and with it of the insignificance of human achievements when viewed from space. Particularly suggestive is the use of anachronism in the scene from Plato's *Protagoras* with which we began this section. While the presentation of the underworld as a place of individual existence is challenged elsewhere by Plato, in the *Protagoras* Socrates' joking assimilation of two of the sophists at Callias' house to Heracles and Tantalus as seen by Odysseus in the underworld may be read as a comment on the fact that many of the dialogue's characters were long dead when Plato wrote the dialogue. If Raphael was inspired by this scene to portray the harmonious conjunction of Platonism and Aristotelianism, Plato himself creates through anachronism a picture of the intellectual milieu of Athens during Socrates' lifetime, the better to differentiate Socrates himself.

Dialogues with the dead

We saw in our Prelude that Lucian sends the ferryman Charon up from the underworld to gaze on human folly in the world above. Travel between the lower and upper worlds is a plot device that he exploits for satirical and philosophical purposes in several of his other works too. In his dialogue *Fisherman* it is a group of philosophers who are presented as returning to life. The reason for their return emerges from the opening exchange, where Socrates encourages the other philosophers (all leading figures from the fifth, fourth or third centuries BC, including Empedocles, Plato, Aristotle, Diogenes, Epicurus and Chrysippus) to throw stones and lumps of earth at a man who has attacked them. Their enemy turns out to be one Parrhesiades ('Son of Frankness') – and a live ringer for Lucian himself: like Lucian, Parrhesiades is originally from Syria (28.19), and he has written a work strongly resembling Lucian's *Auction of the Lives*, which depicted philosophers being sold as slaves (27.4). The philosophers plan to kill Parrhesiades straightaway, but relent when Parrhesiades proclaims his innocence. Socrates suggests that they summon an embodiment of Philosophy, and she in turn persuades them to try Parrhesiades on the Acropolis. Parrhesiades is in due course acquitted after defending himself with the plea that his attacks were made not against the old philosophers but against modern imposters who affect to follow austere philosophical doctrines while in fact pursuing money and fame. Their fakery is then staged as one after another they are caught with a fishing line (hence the dialogue's title) and brought up to the Acropolis to be examined. The dead philosophers are forced to accept that their ideals and the intellectual communities bound by them have not persisted across time. The dialogue closes with Philosophy sending them back to Hades and Parrhesiades descending to the lower city to continue his investigations.

The contrast of past and present established by the anachronistic dialogue in *Fisherman* is strongly mediated through various parts of the literary tradition.[46] The plot – a comic writer being tried by philosophers – is a reversal of Plato's *Apology*, where Socrates identifies comic poets as his 'old accusers' (19c), alluding to his portrayal in Aristophanes' *Clouds* (which is itself referenced in Lucian's dialogue (28.25)). In addition, the opening arrival of angry philosophers recalls the entrance of the chorus in plays such as Aristophanes' *Acharnians* and *Knights*, and the sequence that follows (a contest followed by a series of tests) is a typical structure in Old Comedy too. A further literary layer consists in the lines of verse that the characters trade: after Socrates' initial appeal that the philosophers 'all join shields together against him' (28.1, evoking the tradition that Socrates showed courage in battle as a hoplite), his hexameter appeal 'that pouch give aid to pouch, and staff to staff' (alluding to the typical apparatus of a Cynic philosopher) is a mock-epic variant on Nestor's appeal to the Achaeans in the *Iliad* (2.363: 'that clan give aid to clan, and tribe to tribe').

Lucian also draws on comic antecedents for the plot-device of raising the dead as a way of bringing past and present into an anachronistic dialogue. *Demes*, a play composed by Eupolis in the late fifth century BC which now only survives in fragments, includes in its cast politicians from different stages of Athenian history – Solon, Miltiades, Aristides and Pericles. The surviving fragments show that the drama made much of the meeting of worlds enabled by having figures from the past interact with, and criticize, the habits of contemporary society. In one fragment, for instance, Aristides 'the Just' is shown arguing with an informant; the two men represent their respective ages, Aristides that of the time of Athens' greatness around the Persian wars, the informer the corrupt present (fr. 99.78–120 Kastel–Austin).

Another possible inspiration for Lucian is the contest in the Underworld staged in Aristophanes' *Frogs* between tragedians of different generations. Performed in 405 BC, soon after the deaths of Sophocles and Euripides, and at a time when Athens' military fortunes were low, the play shows Aeschylus and Euripides competing for the throne of tragedy in the Underworld – with Sophocles ready to challenge Euripides if he should win. The contest fortuitously coincides with the arrival of the god Dionysus, who has journeyed to Hades to fetch Euripides because he misses him so much. Throughout, Aristophanes plays on the contrast of old and new: Aeschylus' grand style and themes match the greatness of Athens at the time of the Persian Wars; Euripides represents the vocal and volatile Athenian democracy of the final years of the Peloponnesian War.[47] Though the pay ends with Dionysus declaring Aeschylus the victor and returning with him to the world above in order to save Athens, Aristophanes does much to overturn any simplistic nostalgia for the old days through the close and loving attention he pays to Euripides' sophisticated mannerisms and the 'new music' he espouses. Bringing Aeschylus back to life is not going to help Athens win the war.

It would be equally rash to take Lucian's anachronistic group of philosophers in *Fisherman* as a serious reflection on the history of philosophy. The contrast of past and present is undercut by divisions among the old philosophers: at the outset Socrates rebukes Aristippus and Epicurus for slacking – evidently a hit at their hedonist philosophies (28.1). As we shall see, moreover, in some of his other works Lucian does attack some of the philosophers who are persuaded to acquit Parrhesiades; indeed *Auction of the Lives*, the work which has upset the philosophers, can easily be read as satirizing the founders of the philosophical schools rather than their modern followers, as Parrhesiades disingenuously claims.

Lucian reverses the direction of travel between the worlds above and below to similar satirical effect in another of his works, *Menippus or Oracle-consultation in Hades*. The title-character was a third-century BC Cynic philosopher and satirist Menippus, a predecessor of and inspiration to Lucian (in *Fisherman* Diogenes complains that he has betrayed his fellow-philosophers by not taking part in the attack on Parrhesiades (28.26)). The extent of Menippus' influence on Lucian is hard to determine since none of his works survives, but they did evidently include encounters with the dead (one was called *Necyia* (*Underworld Visit*) after the title of *Odyssey* Book 11); a report survives, too, that Menippus himself would assume the guise of a Fury, with a grey tunic reaching to his feet, and proclaim that he had come from the Underworld as an inspector of wrongdoings (Suda phi 180 Adler).[48] Menippus' Underworld concerns can also be glimpsed through his influence on the versatile Varro, who (besides his historical works) wrote 150 (largely lost) books of *Menippean Satires*. These books included one work certainly set in the underworld, *On Suicide*, in which Hannibal was quizzed on his suicide (fr. 407 Astbury), and another entitled *Tomb of Menippus*.[49]

Lucian's dialogue *Menippus* starts with the title-character returning to the upper world after a visit to the dead, spouting lines of verse. After telling his startled friends that he has just been 'keeping company with Euripides and Homer' and has 'somehow become infected with their poetry', he explains that he was driven to visit the underworld because he had reached an intellectual *impasse*: as a boy he had been delighted by the tales of the poets; he had then turned to philosophers – and been confused and disenchanted by their disagreements. So he had decided to travel to Babylon to consult a magus, and with his help he was able to visit the Underworld so as to consult Tiresias on the best path to philosophy.

While Menippus' sketch mirrors some ancient accounts of the development of the human race as a move from poetry to philosophy,[50] Lucian's portrayal of his experiences in the underworld militates against any notion of intellectual ascent. Comedic inspiration is drawn from a vision of the underworld as a place where all social and physical distinctions are collapsed. Menippus cannot tell apart Nireus and Thersites – the most beautiful and ugly of the characters in the *Iliad* – now that they are just bones (38.15). The rich and powerful are indistinguishable from the other inhabitants of the underworld: the likes of the Persian kings Xerxes and Darius and the Samian tyrant Polycrates could be seen begging at crossroads (38.17). Lucian does allow that (as in Raphael's frescoes) like-minded groups from different eras may converse, as Socrates does with the equally loquacious Palamedes, Nestor and Odysseus (38.18). As he concludes from the sight of the dead that life is but a pageant of shifting roles arranged by Fortune (38.16), Menippus is ready to receive the secret truth that Tiresias whispers to him: the disputes of philosophers can be safely ignored; best is the life of ordinary people, living for the present, taking nothing too seriously (38.21).

Lucian returns to many of the themes and figures of *Menippus* in his *Dialogues of the Dead*, a series of short dialogues set in the underworld. In the opening dialogue, Diogenes the Cynic asks Polydeuces, who returns to life every other day, to summon Menippus to the underworld, where he will find even more to mock than he does in the world above (Menippus' previous underworld knowledge is ignored). The ensuing dialogues show the arrival of Menippus, now properly dead, and his initial meetings with some of the underworld's inhabitants, including philosophers such as Pythagoras and Socrates (77.8). As in *Menippus*, dialogue with the dead opens up the possibility of contrasting past and present – but here decline from the Socratic peak is already seen with Aristippus and Plato (77.6.5). Again as in *Menippus*, the underworld is free from distinctions: a transtemporal group of rich Asiatic kings, Croesus, Sardanapallus and Midas, is subjected to Menippus' mockery (77.3), and former beauties such as Narcissus and Helen are indistinguishable skulls (77.5.1). This 'equality of status' is given a political spin by the ex-god Chiron, who praises it as 'for the people' (*dēmotikē*). But Menippus responds with the same message of contentment with one's lot that Tiresias had expressed in *Menippus*. Chiron had abandoned immortality because of the lack of variety, but Menippus warns him that he may get bored by the repetitiveness of existence in the underworld too (77.8.2).

Lucian's virtuosity is kept up in subsequent dialogues as he lets his writerly imagination play in new ways on this very repetitiveness. Some feature people (portrayed by Homer as) alive at the time of the Trojan War (77.23, 26, both set in the immediate aftermath of Odysseus' visit to the underworld). Others include Alexander and contemporaries (77.12, 13) or invented stereotypes (77.16–20). But Lucian does also continue to play with asynchronous groupings of peers. In one dialogue, the Cynic philosophers Diogenes, Antisthenes and Crates, realizing they are at leisure, go off to mock newcomers (77.22). In another, Lucian, dropping the theme that distinctions are unimportant in the underworld, presents Alexander and Hannibal arguing over who was the better general (77.25), with Scipio Africanus (like Sophocles in Aristophanes' *Frogs*) as middle-man, prepared to stand aside for Alexander but not for Hannibal (77.25).

Lucian's underworld experiments have had an extraordinary influence in Western Europe since the Renaissance. One early exponent was Erasmus, who wrote in 1529 a short *Charon* in which the ferryman is preparing a large new ship to ferry all those killed in the wars plaguing Europe at the time.[51] Erasmus here signals a contrast with the age of Lucian, who has Charon complain of the lack of custom owing to the spread of peace, a common theme of imperial Greek literature – though Lucian adds the twist that people die of gluttony or because they are murdered for their money (77.14.2). A different direction for the genre was heralded by Ulrich von Hutten's *Arminius* (c. 1520), in which the eponymous character, leader in the first century AD of a German revolt against Rome, pleads before Minos, with Tacitus (who describes the revolt in his *Annals*) to support him and with Alexander, Hannibal and Scipio all present. The dialogue played an important part in the emergence of Arminius as a figurehead for German nationalism.

Dialogues of the Dead were particularly popular in France and Britain during the 'quarrel of ancients and moderns' at the end of the seventeenth and start of the eighteenth centuries.[52] Fontenelle, who sided with the moderns, published in 1683 a collection of *New Dialogues of the Dead*, explaining in a programmatic epistle to Lucian that he had 'suppressed Pluto, Charon and Cerberus, and everything that was worn-out (*usé*) in the Underworld'.[53] The collection itself was divided into three sections, ancient, ancient and modern, and modern, with the first and third including anachronistic dialogues (e.g. Anacreon and Aristotle; Paracelsus and Molière) as well as conversations between contemporaries. Fontenelle thus pays tribute to Lucian as founder of the genre while marking his distance as an ancient. Conversely William King, a follower of the 'ancients', satirized one of the 'moderns', the classical scholar Richard Bentley, under the name Bentivoglio, with frequent allusions to Bentley's arguments that letters attributed to the sixth-century BC Sicilian tyrant Phalaris were later forgeries; Phalaris appears in person, disputing with a Sophist who claims to have written the letters.[54] Other practitioners, including Fenelon in France and Lord Lyttelton in Britain, took over from Lucian not just the format but also the fondness for literary allusion. Just as Lucian included Menippus in his dialogues, Lucian himself becomes a character in later dialogues, conversing with Herodotus in Fenelon and with Rabelais in Lyttelton, and similary Fenelon converses with Plato in Lyttelton.[55]

Later imitators tend to exploit the form of the anachronistic dialogue in a rather different way from Lucian. For Fontenelle and William King, as we have noted, the ancient form is exploited in a dialogue about the meaning of antiquity itself. Many other dialogues, too, engaged with the difference of antiquity. Lucian's *Dialogues of the Dead* include just one sentence spoken by a female speaker, and she is a goddess (Persephone).[56] In the modern genre, by contrast, women play a large role: Fontenelle, for instance, includes a dialogue between Dido and Stratonice, wife of the Seleucid king Antiochus, in which Dido complains of Virgil's anachronism, of which she has learnt from listening to Virgil himself.[57] The contrast of ancient and modern in the treatment of women is overtly thematized in a dialogue by Lady Mary Wortley Montagu that Lyttelon included (anonymously) in his collection. Montagu's dialogue features Plutarch in conversation with a modern bookseller. Plutarch is upset to discover from the bookseller that buying a stock of his works had proved to be a financial disaster, but is relieved by the thought that people's morals must have improved so much that they no longer need his guidance. The bookseller assures him that that assumption is far from the truth: people now prefer to read *Lives of the Highwaymen* or *Lives of Men that Never Lived* (that is, novels). And when Plutarch regrets not writing a life of Lucretia for women at least, the bookseller assures him that they would read it only if Lucretia had actually been caught in the arms of a slave.[58]

Another difference in the modern genre lies in the way that issues of ethnic and national self-definition are treated. Whereas von Hutten's *Arminius* recuperated an ancient opponent of Rome, later the anachronistic dialogue became a forum for debate on the inheritance of ancient Greece. One eighteenth-century version (possibly written by Voltaire) portrays Pericles in conversation with a modern Greek and a Russian. Pericles is astonished that the modern Greek knows nothing of him or of other Athenian heroes; he does not even know that he lives in part of ancient Athens.[59] While this hapless figure conforms to stereotypes of Greek degeneracy under the Ottoman Empire, the Russian by contrast tells Pericles that he is a descendant of the Scythians – but knows the history of Greece and can read ancient Greek. The debate is re-phrased in *The New Lucian*, a collection by a Victorian author, H. D. Traill, which includes a dialogue between Plato and the earlier nineteenth-century writer Walter Savage Landor, who had used Diogenes as a mouthpiece for criticisms of Plato in one of his *Imaginary Conversations*. Traill presents Plato as initially dismissive of his 'barbarian' critic, but Landor himself rejects the culture of his contemporaries as either Persian or Scythian – that is, given over either to the 'pursuit of pleasure' or to the 'pleasure of pursuit' (hunting) – and making a claim instead for the 'immortal' Greek spirit: 'no man's birth into its service can be an anachronism. A Greek cannot be born out of due time.'[60] Greekness is here a figure both of timelessness ('immortal') and of extreme timeliness.

That Lucian's *Dialogues of the Dead* avoid overt comparisons of the Greeks of his own day with their forebears should not be attributed to a deficient sense of historical consciousness. It reflects, rather, a deliberate choice (shared with many of the writers of his day) to engage with the Greek past as a literary phenomenon, filtered through the words of Homer and other classic authors. It is through this commitment to a literary canon that he transmits and interrogates the labile constructions of Greek cultural identity.

The same varied engagement with canonicity and death is found in Lucian's still more inventive and influential *True Histories*. Here a narrator figure, who is at the end identified with Lucian, recounts with ironic proclamations of truthfulness his remarkable adventures on the moon, inside a whale and in other strange settings. At one point he is driven over the seas and stumbles on the Isles of the Blessed (14.4–29), where he finds gathered together the epic and cultural heroes of the Greek tradition, and even Persians like the two Cyruses (who doubtless owe their presence to Xenophon). Through this fiction Lucian is able to mock traditional scholarly themes – chronological difficulties are set aside as Theseus and Menelaus compete for Helen – and to parody the ultimate sort of anachronistic dialogue, the dream of unmediated access to the author: Lucian converses with Homer directly, but, unable to escape the banal scholarly tradition, he fluffs his chance with tedious queries about Homer's place of origin (Babylon!) and the (mistaken) interpolations detected by the likes of Aristarchus (14.20).[61]

Reading communities

Lucian's encounter with Homer on the Isles of the Blessed offers a fantastic transfiguration of the way in which the dialogue between reader and author was often configured in antiquity. A good example is provided by Vitruvius' extensive discussion of the experience of reading in the preface to Book 9 of *On Architecture*. While the book itself is devoted to sundials (and thus to the measurement of passing time), the preface offers a rich panegyric of the transtemporal encounters that are made possible by intellectual exertion. By contrast with the short-lived bodily splendour of the athlete, Vitruvius hails the discoveries that have brought lasting benefit to the human race while creating the possibility for individuals to engage with wise figures from the past (9 preface 17):

> Many people born in our memory will seem to discuss the nature of the world with Lucretius as if in person, or the art of rhetoric with Cicero, and many of our posterity will converse with Varro on the Latin language, and similarly many scholars as they deliberate over many things with Greek sages will seem to be having private conversations with them; in sum, the opinions of wise writers, absent in body but flourishing with age, when they are present in our counsels and discussions, all have greater authority than those who are actually present.

When Vitruvius figures reading as a 'private conversation', he develops an idea that occurs frequently when ancient authors conceptualize interactions with their predecessors. Authors are addressed in the second person in poems such as Simias' epigram for Sophocles (5 Gow–Page) and in works of literary criticism;[62] as we have seen, the trope continued beyond antiquity in the letters that Petrarch addressed to classical authors (p. 39).

A subtle exploration of this conception of literary community is found in Dio Chrysostom's dialogue *On Socrates and Homer*. The dialogue starts on the question of who (if anyone) taught Socrates. When Dio himself offers the answer 'Homer', he is met with the obvious response: 'how can one say that a man who never met Homer nor ever saw him, but lived so many years later, was a pupil of Homer' (55.3). Dio stresses against this chronological pedantry that learning is a matter of imitation and attention, not seeing and associating. As proof of Socrates' attention he points to the similarity of the two men's intellectual projects. Even the difference between the genres in which they worked is less important than the aims they shared. Dio suggests that Socrates has engaged in a transtemporal conversation with Homer, and his own dialogue, by drawing out and accentuating the shared qualities and forms of thought on which this conversation depended, allows his readers to participate in this dialogue for themselves.

Dio elaborates a slightly different perspective in his account of a day spent comparing the Philoctetes plays by Athens' three greatest tragedians, Aeschylus, Sophocles and Euripides. His perception of them is in some ways conventional: in keeping with the image found in Aristophanes' *Frogs*, he stresses the 'magnanimity and ancient flavour' of Aeschylus and the political focus of Euripides, while placing Sophocles in the middle (52.4, 11, 15). At issue here, however, is the way he stages reading as the self-conscious practice of anachronism. Dio realizes that he is in a position that was unavailable to those who lived in the fifth century BC: as he explains, Sophocles competed as a young man with Aeschylus and as an old man with Euripides, while Aeschylus and Euripides never competed with each other; the tragedians, moreover, rarely competed with each other with plays on the same subject (52.3). In Dio's study, however, the three authors jostle together in an almost timeless domain of learned comparison. Almost, but not quite. Before embarking on his examination of the three plays, Dio draws attention to the circumstances that shaped his reading. He was suffering from an illness; he began reading after some light exercise, a ride in his carriage, breakfast (52.1). He notes, with a hint of self-depreciation, that his planned reading constitutes 'quite an indulgence and a novel solace for illness' (52.3). His encounter with the great tragedians does not take place on a plane of timeless intellectual contemplation, therefore, but in the time of the body, a time measured out by eating, regimented movements, recuperation from illness. At the same time as his utterance, as a written document, pulls away into timelessness, the detail with which he locates his thinking in time makes his reading irreducibly individual. His aspiration to critical reflections that transcend temporal setting arises precisely from an anxiety about the all-too timely, corporeal frame from which these reflections emerge.

The asynchronous elements of the reading experience are captured by the language Dio employs. Because the opportunity to read the three plays alongside one another is so precious, he says, 'I played the producer (*echorēgoun*) for myself most dazzlingly, and tried to pay close attention, as if I were a judge of the foremost tragic choruses' (52.4). Dio is projected out of his own time and situation as he acts out the historically situated role of the *chorēgos* (the individual who paid as a public liturgy for the production of a play). Despite this imaginative investment, he cannot but read and act conditionally, in the mode of the 'as if'. He oversees the production of critical judgements rather than performances, arranging a virtual 'competition' which enables him to examine literary affiliations (between Homer and Euripides, for instance) and observing the evolution of a genre. Reading becomes a means of scrutinizing the complex temporal structure of the 'present'.

A different kind of dialogue with the past emerges in Dionysius of Halicarnassus' treatise *Demosthenes* (22). Reflecting on the various emotions ('disbelief, anguish, terror, contempt, hatred, pity, goodwill, anger, envy') he experiences while reading Demosthenes, Dionysius suggests that the speeches themselves delineate their emotional structure so clearly that they serve almost as stage directions for readers: 'the words themselves show how one should enact them, feigning now irony, now indignation, now rage, now fear'. His emotional response leads him in turn to reflect on how much greater the affective force generated by Demosthenes' rhetoric must have been for those who heard the orator himself speaking: 'given that we, so far separated in time and unconnected with the events, are carried away and overcome in this way and journey wherever the speech leads us, how must the Athenians and the other Greeks have been led on at that time by the orator on real and personal issues'. Reading Demosthenes prompts an attempt to form a psychological commonality with listeners in the past, whose reactions are imagined as an intensity of involvement ('how must [they] have been excited'). But Dionysius can only sense rather than fully participate in the emotions felt by Demosthenes' contemporaries. The combination of dialogue and distance that reading occasions is registered in his description of the experience of reading as bringing him closer still to the sensations felt by participants 'in the Corybantic dances and the rites of the Mother-Goddess, and other similar ceremonies', no matter whether those celebrations are 'inspired by the scents, sights, or sounds or by the influence of the deities themselves'.[63] The two distinct communities ('the Athenians and the rest of the Greeks' and the ritual agents) against which Dionysius measures his experience differ markedly: the audiences are located in a specific time and place and called on to make decisions on the basis of the speeches; the practitioners of ritual, by contrast, partake of a recurring experience that can be forged anywhere, and their actions are defined in terms of the emotions and senses. By forging simultaneous and differing affiliations to these experiential communities, Dionysius accentuates the unpredictably anachronic character of the communities created in reading.

Like the second-person address to authors, Dionysius' use of ritual as a figure for reading finds echoes beyond antiquity. At the end of a lecture on Greek historical writing delivered in 1908, the renowned German classicist Ulrich von Wilamowitz-Moellendorff turned to reflect on the labours involved in the historical reconstruction of antiquity. After evoking the spirit of research through the 'indispensable' Mr Dryasdust, he suggested that something further was needed to revivify dead tradition – the use of 'our free formative imagination'. Finally, to illustrate the work required of the imagination, he turned to the underworld scene in the *Odyssey* that since antiquity has been one of the most important templates for the anachronistic dialogue:

> We know that ghosts cannot speak until they have drunk blood; and the spirits which we evoke demand the blood of our hearts. We give it to them gladly; but

if they then abide our question, something from us has entered into them; something alien, that must be cast out, cast out in the name of truth! For Truth is a stern goddess...[64]

That 'something alien' is glossed by a modern scholar as 'anachronism'[65] – and however much Wilamowitz insists on the possibility that the historian can be something other than a ventriloquist, it is the poetic force of his evocation of scholarship as re-animation that lingers.[66]

The various types of anachronistic dialogue on which we have eavesdropped in this chapter all welcome that alien element that Wilamowitz strives in vain to exclude. We have, it is true, seen evidence of a desire to remain faithful to the historical moment even in its fleetingness. The *School of Athens* allows us to imagine a diverse range of conversations even as it intimates the possibility that conflicting discourses can be reconciled. Plato brilliantly evokes specific moments of intellectual conversation, and critics in antiquity took him to task for his occasional willingness to disregard the limits imposed by those moments. And yet something of the liveliness of Raphael, Plato and Lucian does lie in the way they in their different ways use dialogue across time as a way of transcending historical difference and constructing a sense of ethical or cultural communality – a sense that is necessarily fragile and fantastic, and can all too easily run the risk of being exclusionary; but one that is part all the same of a new dialogue across and never quite beyond time.

Epilogue: Crowning the Victors

Spanning an entire wall in the Great Room in the Royal Society for the Encouragement of Arts, Manufactures and Commerce in London is an ornate painting of a classical Greek landscape with figures (Figs. 15–17). The painting – *Crowning the Victors at Olympia* by the Irish artist James Barry (1741–1806) – shows a sort of frieze of figures (all of them male) framed by large statues to left and right and with a hilltop temple in the background; most of the figures stand in small groups, but there are also two men on horseback, one in a chariot, three on a sculpted dais, and one, an old man, held aloft by two youths. Unlike in Raphael's Vatican frescoes (an important influence on Barry),[1] most of the figures are carefully identified in a guide written by the painter himself. Some are victors at the games, including (in the chariot) Hiero, tyrant of Syracuse, and (raising their aged father) the sons of Diagoras of Rhodes, who was himself an Olympic champion (and reportedly died of joy on his sons' success (Aulus Gellius 3.15.3)). Others are spectators, consisting, Barry explained, 'for the most part ... of all those celebrated characters of Greece, who lived nearly about that time, and might have been present on the occasion'.[2] The names he supplied are a roll call of the leading cultural and political figures of classical Greece: among them, the poet Pindar (complete with lyre); the dramatists Sophocles, Euripides and Aristophanes; the military and political leaders Cimon and Pericles; and various protagonists in the Greek intellectual revolution, including the philosophers Anaxagoras and Democritus, the medical writer Hippocrates and the historian Herodotus.

While Barry's guide offers the impression that the painting shows with some verisimilitude a possible gathering at Olympia, some of his contemporaries did wonder just how much chronological artifice was involved in the vision he presented. Susan Burney (sister of the novelist Fanny), who visited the artist while he was at work on the painting, found it a 'very fine Performance' which 'to we fair sex appeared extremely well executed'. She did profess herself, however, unable to determine 'Whether He may not have committed some anachronisms'.[3]

Fig. 15 Hiero, tyrant of Syracuse, Pindar and the artist as Timanthes: left-hand section of James Barry, *Crowning the Victors at Olympia* (1777–83), Royal Society of Arts. © RSA, London, UK / Bridgeman Images.

Fig. 16 William Pitt as Pericles, Diagoras of Rhodes with his sons: central section of James Barry, *Crowning the Victors at Olympia*, Royal Society of Arts. © RSA, London, UK / Bridgeman Images.

Fig. 17 Herodotus and the Olympic judges: right-hand section of James Barry, *Crowning the Victors at Olympia*, Royal Society of Arts. © RSA, London, UK / Bridgeman Images.

Another of Barry's acquaintances raised directly with the painter the objection that Pericles was depicted with the features of the Earl of Chatham (William Pitt the Elder) – but, according to Barry's account at least, 'a little reflexion soon convinced him that this was no Anachronism', there having been no model for Pericles' head at the time he was painting.[4] The sensitivity to anachronism shown by these incidental comments was picked up by the clergyman Robert Bromley in his treatise on aesthetics. Bromley, as we noted in Chapter 8, found Raphael guilty of anachronism in the *School of Athens*, but he was prepared to acquit Barry of the same charge: 'not a single anachronism or unnatural blending is to be found, all the characters introduced are of the same age'. And yet, despite this verdict, the clergyman confessed to being 'not quite satisfied with the head of Chatham put upon the shoulders of Pericles'.[5]

The varied responses to the chronology of Barry's painting seem to suggest that anachronism is in the eye of the beholder. Some viewers were alert to the possibility of anachronism, and yet prepared, it seems, to ignore the ancient evidence. Hiero was, according to all our sources, victor in the chariot race in the seventy-eighth Olympiad (468 BC), and it was five Olympiads later that the sons of Diagoras of Rhodes were victorious on the same day. Nor do the chronological complications of the painting lie simply in its depiction of victories twenty years apart as if they happened at the same games. Similar problems are posed by some of the spectators: Aristophanes stands close to Cimon, who died before Aristophanes was born. Aristophanes, moreover, is said by Barry to be 'attentive to nothing but the immoderate length of Pericles's head, at which he is ridiculously pointing and laughing'[6] – a clear allusion to the attacks on Pericles (and the shape of his head) in Aristophanes' plays. But those attacks were posthumous: Pericles died in 429 BC, when Aristophanes was about sixteen. A further problem is created by the figure who, Barry explains, is declaring 'the Olympiad, and the name, family, and country of the conqueror'. Barry here nods to the fact that 'the Greek chronology was regulated by those games',[7] but, as we saw in Chapter 4, this chronological use of Olympiads began at the earliest c. 400 BC; there is no evidence for any sort of Olympic record-keeping prior to that time. Finally, on the far left, cut off slightly from the other figures, a man sits with an easel, staring directly out at the viewer. This artist is identified in Barry's account as Timanthes, who lived in the fourth century BC, well after the other figures in the painting, and is said to be painted here, 'from a vanity not uncommon amongst artists',[8] with the features of Barry himself.

The *Olympia* painting was one of a series of six paintings depicting 'The Progress of Human Knowledge and Culture' created by Barry for the walls of the Great Room between 1777 and 1784 (with occasional subsequent alterations). The series reflected his ambitions for public art in Britain. Thwarted in a proposal to fill St Paul's Cathedral with historical paintings, Barry persuaded the Society of Arts to let him paint the Great Room in return for expenses and proceedings from an exhibition, with the unusual stipulation that he be allowed to choose his theme himself. He made little money from his years of work, but he used his artistic freedom to forge what is on the surface a strong Enlightenment story of progress.

The first painting in the series shows the musician Orpheus as a civilizing figure 'in a wild and savage country, surrounded by people as savage as their soil'; their savage state is illustrated in Barry's guide with quotations from Lucretius' evolutionary account of early human life.[9] Next in the series is *A Grecian Harvest Home, or Thanksgiving to the Rural Deities, Ceres, Bacchus & c.*, an agricultural scene fittingly supported in the guide by a quotation from Virgil's *Georgics*. The third painting, the scene at Olympia, marks a further stage in the path of progress and seemingly a culmination within Greece itself. The Enlightenment model then continues with two British scenes, *Commerce, or the Triumph of the Thames* and *The Distribution of Premiums in the Society of Arts* (an event that took place in the very room in which Barry was painting). Alongside this model of progress, however, as the art historian William Pressly has demonstrated, is a parallel Christian (and specifically Catholic) narrative: Orpheus is iconographically linked to St John the Baptist; the harvest scene includes a nativity modelled on images of the birth of Christ; the introduction of Bacchus and Ceres, wine and bread, is an allegory of the eucharist; the elderly Diagoras held aloft is modelled on images of papal processions; and the three judges stand for the Trinity.[10] The *Olympia* picture picks up, moreover, parallels drawn in eighteenth-century scholarship between Greek athletic festivals and Catholicism.

The religious theme is openly suggested in the final painting in the series, *Elysium, or the State of Final Retribution*. Filling the whole wall opposite *Crowning the Victors*, it depicts a mass of figures in period clothing, most of them carefully identified by Barry: the philosophers Shaftesbury and Locke talk to Plato and Aristotle, while Thales and Archimedes are grouped with Roger

Fig. 18 William Penn showing his law code to the ancient law-givers Lycurgus, Solon, Numa and Zaleucus. Detail from James Barry, *Elysium* (1777–1801), Royal Society of Arts. © RSA, London, UK / Bridgeman Images.

Bacon and Descartes; William Penn shows his law code to the ancient law-givers Lycurgus, Solon, Numa, and Zaleucus (Fig. 18); and above them Homer sits with his lyre next to Milton, with Sappho and Alcaeus nearby (the latter conversing with Ossian). Barry in this way fulfilled his wish 'to bring together in Elysium, those great and good men of all ages and nations, who were cultivators and benefactors of mankind', as 'a kind of apotheosis, or more properly a beatification of those useful qualities which were pursued through the whole work'.[11]

The painting of *Elysium* seems to have excited some of the same worries as *Crowning the Victors*, even though it purports to display a scene in the afterlife. An abridgement of Barry's guide to the series added the claim that 'this sublime Picture' is 'without any of those anachronisms which tarnish the lustre of other very celebrated performances'.[12] The extra clause suggests a certain defensiveness, as if the very attempt to avoid anachronism in the depiction of costumes exposed the anachronism of the painting's corporeal encounters.

Barry's series and the debates to which it gave rise captures many of the themes which we have explored throughout this book: definitions of anachronism (what latitude is allowed before a chronological breach of an 'age' is felt as such?); anachronism in creative works (Barry's inclusion of his own and Chatham's features may even have been inspired by Phidias' inclusion of himself and Pericles on Athena's shield on the Athenian acropolis (p. 59)); the history of chronology; narratives of human development and historical change; conceptions of exemplarity; the capacity of artworks to embrace multiple temporalities. The series even allows reflection on the way anachronism is implicated in the dialectical relationship of antiquity and modernity. The anachronism of the *Olympia* scene creates a sense of the classical Greek past as cohesive and whole, and yet as necessarily superseded, its very wholeness dependent on its pastness. The modern artist uses the anachronism of hindsight to crown the victors of antiquity.

Classical antiquity itself can easily be seen as another of the victors crowned by historical hindsight. It has been hived off as an idealized space, a point of origin for 'Western' political and intellectual concepts such as democracy, liberty and even history itself, as well as for numerous artistic and literary traditions. In part the position that antiquity has enjoyed reflects the choices that thinkers and creative artists and writers have made to rework the material and literary remains of the Greeks and Romans, while attaching themselves at the same time to a chain of intermediaries. This form of adherence to Greco-Roman antiquity has necessarily been at the expense of other cultures – sometimes wilfully so. The neglect or suppression of alternative points of origin is particularly regrettable in accounts of the development of historical consciousness, which typically neglect the well-documented peoples of the Ancient Near East by whom the Greeks themselves were undoubtedly influenced.

Classical antiquity, too, has paid a price for its success. While fifth-century Greece is the starting place for many modern narratives about the creation of a sense of history, it is often defined in these narratives in terms of absence. The Greeks, it is thought, lacked a sense of anachronism, and this alleged lack acts in turn as an *a fortiori* justification for dismissing the claims of other cultures to a sophisticated sense of historical difference. Paradoxically, however, such narratives of absence are themselves (as we saw in Chapter 2) the product of an anachronistic application and reification of later conceptions of history.

'One must look to the end of every affair, to see how it turns out.' How does Solon's advice to Croesus seem at the end of our anachronistic tour of antiquity? The wisdom (and not just the chronology) of Solon's advice was debated in antiquity: can one really not regard someone as happy until they are dead?[13] Our concern here is with Solon's reflections on hindsight rather than on happiness. We have used anachronism in this book in part to explore the richness of ancient thought on temporality, in part to explore the constructedness of classical antiquity itself. Both of these investigations have repeatedly drawn attention to the fact that antiquity is the product of hindsight with its accompanying emotions of desire and disdain. Our goal has been to replace the binary narrative of before and after with a more varied and dynamic picture of the workings of temporal consciousness among (and between) the Greeks and Romans, a picture that does justice to the surviving evidence in its varied multiplicity. Throughout, the texts and images we have studied have spoken to a robust sense of historical difference. As we look back from the end, antiquity itself turns out to have been among the most enduring anachronisms of modernity. But we can also see that the storehouse of ancient thought on anachronism which we have explored in this book did much to form the temporal imagination that continues to give antiquity its contours.

Notes

Prelude: Look to the End

1. Gibbon (1972) 365 (marginalia), alluding to Voltaire (1786) 38.271 (article 'Bien, souverain bien' from *Dictionnaire philosophique*).
2. Wallace (2016), however, argues that Croesus' reign started in the 580s.
3. For general orientation see Bowie (1970) and Whitmarsh (2001); on *Charon*, Favreau-Linder (2015). See further pp. 212–16 on Lucian's *Dialogues of the Dead*.
4. See p. 98.
5. See e.g. Callimachus' first *Iamb*, with Kerkhecker (1999) 11–48; Diogenes Laertius 1.27–33, 82. Andron of Ephesus (*FGrH Cont.* 1005; fourth century BC) wrote a whole book on the Seven Sages entitled *The Tripod*.
6. Thales is the only sage whom Diogenes makes the founder of a philosophical tradition (1.122). Plutarch similarly introduces a minor rupture into the synchronous Seven when he claims that Solon is 'too simple and archaic' in his handling of physics, while Thales alone of the sages 'carried his speculations beyond necessity' (*Solon* 3.6–8).
7. E.g. Moles (1996).

Chapter 1

1. Wilde ([1890] 2000) 252.
2. Dinshaw (2007) 107, 108.
3. Dinshaw (2012) 105.
4. Carroll (2014) 2, 273.
5. Clark (2015) 62.
6. Miller (2010).
7. Didi-Huberman ([1990] 2005) xxiii.
8. Nagel and Wood (2010) 13.
9. See Chapter 7.
10. Lowenthal (1985) title of chapter 7; Greene (1986) 221.
11. Robertson (1996) 142 (on camp); Bal (2016) 290.
12. Bal (2016) 292.
13. Kalter (2012) 53.

14 Luzzi (2009) 71 n. 6; Nagel and Wood (2010) 13.
15 Nagel and Wood (2010) 13.
16 Rancière ([1996] 2015) 22–3.
17 See Chapter 4 n. 36.
18 Now joined by a previously unattested noun *anachronia* in a new edition of the scholia to Euripides' *Hippolytus* (Cavarzeran (2016), scholion on 231). The ancient terms are surveyed by Stemplinger (1956).
19 An eighteenth-century successor dismissed the anachronism: 'as the remark is no less obvious than true, we need not be surprised to find it quoted as proverbial, even in the earliest ages' (Francklin (1758–9) 2.95).
20 Messeri and Pintaudi (2002) 232–7 (Ostraca Medinet Madi 272). Thanks to Amin Benaissa for discussion.
21 Boak, Husselman and Edgerton (1933–44) 2.287–8.
22 Luzzi (2009) 71 n. 6.
23 Burke (2001) 173.
24 Grazia (2010) 20, 15.
25 Ibid. 20–1, 30–1.
26 Burke (2001) 173; Luzzi (2009) 71 n. 6.
27 Wilson ([1992] 2017) 30–1.
28 Ricchieri (1542) 423.
29 For his sources see pp. 72, 81.
30 Castelvetro ([1570] 1978–9) 2.198, 260 ((1984) 262, 292). The *ana-* prefix has lost its force in these coinages; Castelvetro himself offers the gloss *trastemporaneamento* for *anachronismos*.
31 Mazzoni (1587) 515–25, citing (516) Valerius Maximus 9.8.ext.1, Pomponius Mela 2.116 and Servius on *Aeneid* 3.411 for the cape's naming after Hannibal's steersman, hence later than the First Punic War context of Polybius 1.11.6.
32 Heller (2014) 282.
33 Fielding (1766) 9.263 n.; Barthélemy ([1787] 1793–4) 5.210.
34 Gregory (1649) 174 (from *De Æris & Epochis*).
35 Lisle (1623) 15.
36 Hales (1617) 36–7.
37 Blount (1656) n.p.
38 Ralegh (1614) n.p. We have found no other seventeenth-century instances of the form.
39 See p. 94. Ebeling 1937 suggests that Scaliger introduced the word itself and that it first appeared in the posthumous 1629 edition; both claims have been frequently repeated.
40 Ralegh (1614) n.p. For the Julian Period see further p. 103.
41 See pp. 94–5.
42 Blasco (1578) 59.

43 Heinsius (1639) 869; (1623) 147 (trans. from Gale (1669) 371).
44 Grazia (2010) 19.
45 Grey (1754) 2.112. This remark was quoted a century later by the historian George Grote with the dismissive comment that 'such a supposed chronological discrepancy would hardly be pointed out in any commentary now written' – that is, now that the scholarly field had been transformed by the separation of legend and history (Grote ([1846–56] 1888) 1.432 n. 2).
46 See e.g. Martindale and Martindale (1990) 121; Ruthven (2004) 354.
47 Bolingbroke (1752) 1.9.
48 P. 238 n.23.
49 E.g. Lucian 45.80, where it is used with *metachronos* of the errors of a mime-dancer.
50 Gregory (1649) 174.
51 Drayton (1612) A2.
52 E.g. Athenaeus 5.216c; scholia on Euripides, *Hecuba* 573, *Andromache* 734. Some dictionaries from the eighteenth century onwards define 'parachronism' (by contrast with 'anachronism') as placement too *late* (Petit (1985) 32–3); this definition is not justified by earlier usages or etymology.
53 Montagu (1642) 3.186.
54 See Torzi (2000) 61–117 for the word's use by grammarians and exegetes; Lacombe (1930) 50 (Langton); *OED* s.v. 'prolepsis' (Calvin, Holland). *Anticipatio* is used with a similar sense (e.g. Servius on *Aeneid* 6.359). Other terms applied to anachronism are *kakoplastos* 'flawed in invention' (Hermogenes, *On Issues* 1.1; scholion on Lycophron 592; Heath (1995) 254) and *para tēn historian* 'against history' (Athenaeus 5.218e).
55 Rancière ([1996] 2015) 22–3.
56 Bentley (1697) 32.
57 Robertson (1788) 160, 168 (prochronism); 166, 167 (parachronism). See Fig. 6.
58 Vico ([1744] 1999) 333. The first edition lists five kinds of anachronism (Vico ([1725] 2002) 128–30). On the Varro passage see p. 107.
59 Coleridge (1969–2002) 6.43.
60 De Quincey (1862–83) 9.202 n.
61 Hegel ([1835] 1975) 1.278.
62 Grumach (1949) 212.
63 Pope (1871–89) 6.115; cf. *OED* s.v. 'high' 18.
64 Gough (1786–96) 1.7 (inspired by Warton (1778–81) 2.97 on Lydgate's 'anachronistic improprieties'). The title page captures a sense of period style by moving down from Gothic to Roman fonts.
65 Waugh (1962) 9.
66 Eastman (1926) 22–3.
67 Robinson (1912) 265.

68 Stern (1970) 187; Coulanges ([1864] 1980) 3–4.
69 Sorel (1891) 8.
70 Febvre ([1942] 1985) 5.
71 Blaas (1978) 244–5.
72 Butterfield ([1931] 1973) 30.
73 Skinner (1969) 40.
74 Blaas (1978) 280.
75 Rancière ([1996] 2015).
76 Loraux (1993).
77 Loraux ([1997] 2001) 136–7.
78 See further https://anachronismandantiquity.wordpress.com/2016/11/28/anachronism-and-analogy/.
79 'Anachronistic' has often carried a stronger sense of periodicity than words such as 'obsolete' (dated by the *OED* to 1579), 'outdated' (1616), 'antiquated' (1623) and 'stale' (1550 for the metaphor).

Chapter 2

1 Borges ([1939] 1970) 69–71.
2 Koselleck ([1979] 2004) 10, 11, 22; also 255–75 on experience and expectation.
3 Levy (1967) ix, 7–8.
4 E.g. Panofsky ([1960] 1970) 227 n.
5 Ibid. 262.
6 Hay (1977) 196 n. 10.
7 Panofsky ([1960] 1970) 262–3, ([1955] 1970) 205.
8 Ritter (1986) 12.
9 Bury (1909) 240, 248–9.
10 Finley (1959) 18.
11 Pocock ([1957] 1987) 1, 150.
12 Haddock (1980) 2.
13 Burke (1969) 138–41. Cf. Bury (1920) 10; Collingwood (1946) 20–1.
14 See Momigliano (1966); Möller and Luraghi (1995).
15 Schiffman (2011) 3–4, 71, 5, 6, 273.
16 Cervantes ([1605–15] 1992) 77.
17 Ibid. 536.
18 Ibid. 376–81. Cf. Hale (1994) 99–100.
19 Burke (1969) 21.
20 Grazia (2007).
21 Fantham (2017) 2.470–4 (text and translation).

22 Greene (1982) 8.
23 E.g. Burke (1969) 50; Ritter (1986) 11; Kelley (1998) 132.
24 Nota and Dotti (2002–13) 5.71–83 (text); Bernardo et al. (1992) 621–5 (translation).
25 Borchardt (1975) 423.
26 Petrarch is nonetheless right: Pinkster (2015) 1120 notes that 'the first instances of the use of the so-called plural of majesty … by dignitaries to underline their authority are found in the third century AD. This … becomes quite common in the fifth century.' Caesar does in his surviving works use first-person plural forms in his role as historian, in phrases such as 'as we have shown'.
27 Fantham (2007) 2.498–9. A similar anachronism at Ovid, *Heroic Women* 2.83.
28 Bernardo et al. (1992) 625.
29 In the twelfth century Pope Innocent III had drawn up five prescriptions for detecting forgery, but placed more emphasis on seals as a means of authentication than on composition or script (Hiatt (2004) 26).
30 Kelley (1998) 132.
31 Bowersock (2007) for text and translation.
32 Wilamowitz's suggestion that Valla wrote the treatise once he had been schooled in historical method by his translation of Thucydides is disproved by the chronology (Wilson ([1992] 2017) 86–7).
33 Delph (1996).
34 Compare Valla's *commenticiam fictamque* with Cicero's *fictam et commenticiam*.
35 Hiatt (2004) 164–7.
36 Kalter (2012) 53.
37 Grazia (2010) 22–3.
38 Black (1995).
39 Valla (1511) 16 verso, praising as a 'beautiful prolepsis' the use of the cognomen 'Creticus', which Sallust applies to Quintus Metellus even prior to his capture of Crete.
40 Bowersock (2007) 183.
41 Bowersock (2007) 198 n. 21.
42 Fussner (1969) 376 complains that Levy (1967) 'thinks of "the concept of anachronism" as a commodity, which can be imported and exported like cheese, wine, or cigars': 'If we are told that Pericles used a wrist watch to time his funeral oration, we dismiss this statement as an anachronism – not because we have a "concept of anachronism", but because we have the facts.'
43 Borchardt (1975) 423.
44 Schlegel ([1805] 1959) 118–20 ((1988) 67–72).
45 Koselleck (1979) 17–18 ((2004) 9–10).
46 Pocock (1999–2016) 3.98–150.
47 Koselleck (1979) 18–19 ((2004) 10).

48 Cary (1956) Plate VI; Hale (1990) 186.
49 Pfeiffer (1993).
50 Ronen (1993).
51 E.g. Curtius Rufus, *History of Alexander* 3.3.19.
52 Goldberg (1994) 253–62; West (2007).
53 Nagel and Wood (2010) 14.
54 Eschenburg (1979); on Aventinus, see Strauss (1963).
55 West (2007) 207.
56 Noll (2016).
57 Schlegel ([1805] 1959) 118 ((1988) 68). Partly owing to the misleading English translation, Koselleck has often been taken as suggesting that Schlegel sees Altdorfer himself, not the battle as he depicts it, as chivalrous.
58 Schlegel ([1815] 1818) 1.326.
59 Schlegel ([1805] 1959) 119.
60 Strauss (1963) 128.
61 Schlegel ([1805] 1959) 120 ((1988) 69).
62 Schlegel ([1805] 1959) 123 ((1988) 72), with n. 8 for the re-working of the passage for Schlegel's 1823 collected works.
63 Ruehl (2015) 138–49.
64 Schlegel ([1805] 1959) 119 ((1988) 68–9).
65 See Koselleck (2018). While his theoretical model resists periodization, Koselleck re-inscribes it through his readings of the origins of the separate strata (for instance, in discussing the differences between Herodotus and Thucydides).
66 Rudolf similarly adopted an ancient Roman gem in his seal (Grzęda (2016) 132–3).
67 Hiatt (2004) 53.
68 Schiffman (2011) 6, 111, 140–1, 261; Montesquieu ([1734] 1999) 23.
69 Guynn and Stahuljak (2013) 14.
70 Veyne ([1971] 1984) 5.
71 Ibid. 6.
72 Ibid. 129, 141.
73 Gilmore (1963) 7.
74 E.g. Plato, *Protagoras* 322b1; Diodorus, *Historical Library* 3.56.3.

Chapter 3

1 Sandbach (1965–6) 33; cf. Horsfall (2016) 135–44.
2 Mastronarde (2002) 210.
3 Knox (1957) 61.

4 Taplin (1986) 171–2. 'Newfangled' is from D'Angour (2011) 147. The Anaxagorean link is picked up in the scholia and in Satyrus, *Life of Euripides* (fr. 37 col. 3 Schorn).
5 Stricker (1880) 125; Schwenk (1895) 3.
6 Easterling (1985) 5–6, 9.
7 Easterling (1985) 9. On tragic temporality see also Vernant and Vidal-Naquet ([1972] 1988) 23–8; Pelling (1997), (2000) 164–7; Sourvinou-Inwood (2003) 15–25.
8 Schironi (2018). On ancient scholarship see Montanari et al. (2015), Zetzel (2018).
9 Including dowries: see Schmidt (1976) 240–6 on how the Homeric scholia bring out complexities better than the *Medea* scholia cited above.
10 For context see Braund and Wilkins (2000), Holford-Strevens ([1988] 2003), König and Woolf (2013).
11 Cf. pp. 184–5 on Theseus.
12 See on this topic Nünlist (2012).
13 Parker (1998) argues that *turannos* is Phrygian in origin.
14 Conversely a choral passage in Aeschylus' *Agamemnon* evoking the return from Troy of ashes in exchange for men (433–44) is seen as a deliberate anachronistic allusion to a new Athenian practice (e.g. Jacoby (1944) 44).
15 For further use of anachronism in textual arguments, see scholion T on *Iliad* 23.825 (Aristarchan emendation, cf. scholion AT on *Iliad* 7.304); scholion T on *Iliad* 24.476 (interpolation); and (on the same passage) Athenaeus 1.12b (emendation). Similar arguments were used to dismiss physical relics from the heroic period: see Pausanias 8.14.7–8, 9.41.1, 10.38.5–7 (on bronze statues); Pliny, *Natural History* 13.88 (on a papyrus letter); Higbie (2017); also https://anachronismandantiquity.wordpress.com/2018/01/18/anchoring-innovation/. Conversely, claims by Ephorus (*FGrH* 70 F42) and Posidonius (fr. 284 Edelstein-Kidd), both of whom held sages responsible for all human inventions, that the Scythian sage Anacharsis invented the potter's wheel were refuted with evidence from Homer, who was older than Anacharsis (Strabo 7.3.9; Seneca, *Epistles* 90.31).
16 For arguments from anachronistic allusions to historical events, see Diogenes Laertius 2.39 (citing Favorinus) on Polycrates' defence speech for Socrates; Athenaeus 3.116d, on a poem *On Saltfish* attributed to Hesiod; Dionysius of Halicarnassus, *Dinarchus* 11, 13, *Lysias* 12; and the scholia on Aristophanes, *Wealth* 173, 179 and 1146, which suggest that anachronisms were inserted from Aristophanes' second version of the play (392 BC), under the mistaken impression that they were commenting on his first version (408 BC). For lexical or etymological arguments, see Galen's commentary (Kühn 15.172–3) on the Hippocratic *On the Nature of the Human Being*, and Macrobius, *Saturnalia* 1.12.13 (citing Varro). Cf. arguments from dialect at Diogenes Laertius 1.112 and from letter-forms at Theopompus *FGrH* 115 F154; Plutarch, *Aristides* 1.6; and in general Grafton (1990).

17 E.g. in a famous law suit at Athens in 330 BC (Aeschines 2.89–92; Demosthenes 18.225), or in Cicero's attacks on Antony's supposed forgery of documents after Caesar's assassination (*Philippics* 2.97; cf. Cassius Dio 45.32.4).
18 Logue (2015) 126; Oswald (2011) 36, 72.
19 Oswald (2015).
20 The reference to 'Achaemenes' (ancestor of the Persian royal line) reflects the common assimilation of Parthians and Persians (they were separate Iranian peoples).
21 More on anachronistic trumpets at scholia on Aeschylus, *Eumenides* 556–9; Euripides, *Phoenician Women* 1377 (trumpet taken as a simile, with 'misplaced pedantry about the chronology of the use of trumpets', according to Mastronarde (1994) 534); and Lycophron 250 (on Lycophron's misplaced pedantry in avoiding mention of trumpets), both with reference to *Iliad* 18.219 (also cross-referenced in scholion T on *Iliad* 24.480–2).
22 Horse-riding is elsewhere mentioned in a simile at *Odyssey* 5.371 and exceptionally in the night-time *Doloneia* (*Iliad* 10, often suspected as a later insertion), where the scholiasts comment that the riding is 'out of necessity', i.e. for a swift escape (scholion bT on *Iliad* 10.513; also scholion PQT on *Odyssey* 5.371).
23 See also scholion T on *Iliad* 24.480–2. The late Byzantine astronomer Theodorus Meliteniotis marked a simile at *Iliad* 5.5 as an instance of *metachronismos*.
24 Taplin (2007) 182.
25 Easterling (1985) 9.
26 See further Nünlist (2009) 122–4, 282–98.
27 Now Gaeta, where Cy Twombly had a studio.
28 Hinds (1998) 109 n. 14.
29 Overly accurate prophecies could come under suspicion as forgeries after the event: cf. Strabo 13.1.53, arguing against an emendation of *Iliad* 20.307–8 which created an allusion to the Roman empire; Lucian 42.28 on 'metachronic' oracles; and Porphyry of Tyre, *Against the Christians* fr. 43 von Harnack on the prophecies in the Book of Daniel as written in the reign of Antiochus Epiphanes.
30 Stok (2016) 426–7.
31 See Nünlist (2009) 117. Ancient critics identified at least four different cities called Ephyre (Strabo 8.3.5).
32 Fr. 819 *TrGF*, with notes *ad loc.* on the interpretative problems.
33 Easterling (1985) 8–9.
34 A mistake for 'Spartan'.
35 Hesychius kappa 4343 Latte comments on anachronistic references to the lot in Sophocles' (lost) *Meleager* and *Inachus*.
36 The comparison would be exact only if the scholiasts were suggesting that Hippolytus' horses came from the area later inhabited by the Enetians; but this does

not seem to be the case. Support for Easterling can be found in a scholion on Sophocles, *Electra* 62: 'he guarded against naming the man' (*à propos* a supposed allusion to Pythagoras).
37 Eustathius' citation of Stephanus alludes to 'Enetian mares', evidently among the Paphlagonian Enetians. He explains, too, that the Enetians moved from Paphlagonia to the Adriatic, stopping off in Thrace on the way.
38 Van der Valk *ad loc.*
39 E.g. the Hellenistic paradoxographer Antigonus of Carystus (Leigh (2013) 187).
40 *Idion* is used in the discussion of *turannos* in the hypothesis to *Oedipus the King* (see above), but there it refers to a linguistic feature shared among several different poets.
41 For *plasma* in the scholia see Papadopoulou (1999).
42 Burkert (1972) 125–32, 180–3.
43 Lefkowitz ([1981] 2012) 87–103.
44 Cf. Aulus Gellius 15.20.8, citing Alexander of Aetolia (fr. 19 Lightfoot). The counter-claim could have been based on scenes such as Heracles' appearance in the *Alcestis*, which is denounced in the scholia (on 780) as a breach of probability (*ouk eulogōs*) on the curious grounds that Euripides presents him philosophizing while drunk.
45 Robortello (1555) 250; Castelvestro ([1570] 1978–9) 2.193–8 ((1984) 260–2).
46 Similarly Suda s.v. *proschēma* (pi 2853 Adler).
47 Cf. the use of the cognate noun *alogia* of an anachronism at scholion V on Aristophanes, *Wealth* 1146.
48 Thus Easterling (1985) 8. See Christesen (2007) 179–202 on traditions about the games.
49 Hornblower (1991–2008) 1.521–2.
50 Stricker (1880) 124–5.
51 Dover (1978) 197.
52 See pp. 195–8.
53 Seneca in *Suasoriae* 2.22 points out the anachronism. The Spartan's goal was to ensure that Xerxes could not utter those words.

Interlude: Dido *versus* Virgil

1 Scott ([1823] 2007) 4, 11.
2 Scott ([1814] 1985) 96; ([1820] 1996) 505.
3 Scott ([1818] 2008) 3.
4 This version is found e.g. in Timaeus and Jerome, *Against Jovinian* 1.43. The story may have appeared earlier in Naevius' historical epic *Bellum Punicum* (Horsfall ([1973] 1990)).

5 Hearne (1705) 8, defining anachronism as 'a civil Expression of an Error' by contrast with 'the rude Charge of Falshood'; Button (1740) xv.
6 Diderot (1751–72) 1.395; Johnson (1755) 1.129.
7 Mazzoni (1587) 518.
8 Tasso ([1594] 1964) 118, (1973) 58–9. These debates are echoed in the novelist Manzoni's discussion of historical fiction (([1850] 1996) 53).
9 A glance at Lucian's *Dialogues of the Dead*, where this trio does converse – in the underworld (p. 216).
10 Segrais (1668) 27–35.
11 Todd and Bowden (1998) 146–59.
12 *Verdicts of the Learned* ([1697] 1814) 8.
13 Dryden (1697) n.p.
14 Kalter (2012) 62.
15 Womersley (1997) 213.
16 Ibid. 245.
17 Chateaubriand (1811) 3.129–30.
18 Cf. *Anthologia Graeca* 16.151, an epigram in Dido's voice denouncing Virgil's falsehood, and its Latin adaptation, Ps.-Ausonius, *Epigrams* 118.
19 Fantham (2017) 1.405–7 for text and translation.
20 Desmond (1994).
21 Mazzoni (1587) 518.
22 Tasso ([1594] 1973) 58; contrast the *Discourses on the Poetic Art* (written 1560s, published 1587), where Tasso discusses the episode without the term 'anachronism' ((1964) 17–18). A 1721 French dictionary does use Dido to illustrate *anachronisme* by contrast with *parachronisme* (Petit (1985) 32; cf. Chapter 1 n. 52).
23 Examples of *anachronismos* and related phrases in the scholia occasionally indicate the extent of the anachronism by years (scholion on Sophocles, *Electra* 47) or generations (scholion on Euripides, *Phoenician Women* 854), but mostly use phrases such as 'not yet' (e.g. scholia on Aeschylus, *Seven against Thebes* 277, *Prometheus Bound* 411, 669; Euripides, *Phoenician Women* 6) or 'later' (e.g. scholia on Pindar, *Nemean* 7.56; Euripides, *Rhesus* 502; Apollonius of Rhodes, *Argonautica* 4.552–6).
24 Marolles (1662) 25–36.
25 Newton (1728) 32.
26 Gibbon: Buchwald and Feingold (2012) 418–19. Monstrous: Sale et al. (1736–44) 6.659.
27 Scaliger (1598) 'Prolegomena' ε1 recto; Ralegh (1614) 1.466; Helvicus ([1609] 1629) 48–9; Hearne (1698) 8.
28 Hardie (2012) 109–10.
29 Giusti (2018) 170–4.

Chapter 4

1. Bickerman ([1968] 1980) 88; cf. Mosshammer (1979) 38.
2. Pattison ([1860] 1889) 1.132.
3. See Grafton (1983–93); Nothaft (2012) 1–9, 271–6; Hardy (2018) esp. 131–41.
4. Botley and van Miert (2012) 2.161.
5. Scaliger (1598) 'Prolegomena' γ6 recto (cf. γ3 verso, γ4 verso), 'Notae' ix.
6. Scaliger (1606) *Isagogici chronologiae canones* 117 ('depravatio tituli temporis, vel luxatio Epochae'; '*parastrophē epochēs kata aphairesin*, quando minus dicitur'; '*parastrophē epochēs kata prosthesin*, quum plus dicitur'); see p. 22 for John Gregory's inversion of the terms. For the metaphor, cf. Hamlet's (more or less synchronous) 'Time is out of joint'.
7. Grafton and Williams (2006) 133–77.
8. Scaliger (1606) *Animadversiones in Chronologica Eusebii* 100. Editions of Eusebius/Jerome often differ slightly over the precise year to which each historical entry should be attached.
9. Nothaft (2012) 263 (explaining how Apianus opted for the wrong eclipse).
10. Scaliger also aligns *kata aphairesin* with George Syncellus' phrase (198.1 Mosshammer) *kata elattōsin* ('through lessening').
11. Shaw (2003) 25. Cf. Wilcox (1987), discussed at https://anachronismandantiquity.wordpress.com/2018/12/15/time-episodic/.
12. On which see also Livy 1.18.1–4; Dionysius of Halicarnassus, *Roman Antiquities* 2.59.1–4; n. 69 below.
13. For the Greco-Roman tradition see Christesen (2007), Clarke (2008); for Near Eastern and Christian traditions, Adler (1989), Dillery (2015); on time-reckoning generally, Samuel (1972), Hannah (2009).
14. Scaliger (1583) 1.
15. Scaliger (1583) 1. For their fragments see *FGrH* 256, 250, 257 and 241.
16. Scaliger (1583) 1, 2. For this metaphorical use of *eruere* cf. Varro, *On the Latin language* 6.2; Ovid, *Fasti* 1.7, 4.11.
17. Scaliger (1606) *Historiōn sunagōgē* 317–54; Scheibel (1852), with Grafton (1983–93) 2.548–59.
18. Glareanus (1531) a2 verso (= Erasmus (1974–) 17.231). The labyrinth metaphor is developed from Jerome (*Chronicle* 5.10 Helm) and echoed by Bodin ([1566] 1945) 303.
19. Scaliger (1583) 47, 133; cf. Grafton (1983–93) 2.145–67.
20. Scaliger (1598) 57–8.
21. Evans and Berggren (2006) 180 n. 17.
22. Wilson ([1992] 2017) 89–94; Botley (2006).
23. For *ataxia*, 'disorder', as a feature in such accounts see e.g. Critias DK 88 B25; Diodorus 1.8.1.

24 Cf. Censorinus 19.5 (the Arcadians 'established the year before it was matched in Greece to the moon's course'); another explanation was that the Arcadian Endymion discovered the moon's periods (scholion on Apollonius of Rhodes 4.264).
25 The month length is similarly not indicated in Herodotus' reference to the Greek calendar at 2.4.1 (where he stresses the superiority of the Egyptian system).
26 Scaliger (1583) 50.
27 Aligned by some with a ten-month Homeric year, according to Aulus Gellius 3.16.16.
28 Scaliger (1583) 117, 126.
29 Ovid draws on Varro (cited by Censorinus 22.11); cf. also Plutarch, *Roman Questions* 268b.
30 Cf. Plutarch, *Caesar* 59 with Pelling (2011).
31 Scaliger (1583) 157.
32 See Chapter 5.
33 Feeney (2007) 194.
34 Stern (2012).
35 Feeney (2007), 198–201, 156–7. To put it another way: Roman precision about measurement (where have all the hours gone?) created a sense of Greek imprecision (wrong time passing).
36 Cf. Stern (2003) 91–8. For time as river, cf. Horace, *Odes* 2.14.1–2, 3.29.33–40; Ovid, *Metamorphoses* 15.179–80.
37 Scaliger (1606) *Animadversiones* 99; similarly Casaubon (1600) 238.
38 Scheibel (1852) 73.
39 Scaliger (1583) 50, (1606) *Animadversiones* 99 (Thucydides' 'two months' are compressed into 'a few days').
40 This decision helps Scaliger claim a prochronism in Eusebius' Macedonian king-list, albeit on the basis of a passage of Athenaeus (5.217e) where, as Casaubon (1600) 244 had recognized, a sentence has dropped out.
41 Cf. his criticism of Hellanicus for being 'inaccurate in his dates' (1.97.2).
42 As Scaliger (1583) 46 noted, selectively citing the second pair of dates to support an argument that the two cities started their calendar cycles at different lunar positions.
43 Cf. (from the Second Punic War) 21.15 (with Levene (2010) 52–61) and 25.11.20.
44 E.g. Livy 6.1.2; Plutarch, *Fortune of the Romans* 323e, 326a; Censorinus 20.1.
45 Similarly Strabo 8.6.2.
46 Scaliger (1583) 208.
47 Scaliger (1606) *ICC* 339, 273.
48 The symbol H, which originally indicated aspiration, was anachronistically preserved for 'hundred' (*hekaton*) even though it indicated the letter eta in the Ionic alphabet adopted at Athens in 403 BC (cf. Scaliger (1606) *Animadversiones* 105).
49 Rotstein (2016).

50 Feeney (2007) 29–32.
51 Rood (2007) 173–4.
52 Scaliger (1606) *Animadversiones* 119, 133. Dates in this section are in relation to the birth of Abraham unless otherwise indicated.
53 Ibid. 47, cf. 44, 273.
54 Ibid. 35, 98.
55 Ibid. 229.
56 Ibid. 77.
57 Grafton (1983–93) 2.134.
58 Livy's protest may reflect his use of the Roman year: the deaths could have fallen in the same Olympic year (Walbank (1957–79) 3.235–9).
59 Scaliger (1606) *Animadversiones* 44.
60 Scaliger here had Eusebius' Greek as cited by Syncellus (297.23 Mosshammer); he noted an identical report in Diodorus (12.31.1) for the third year of the eighty-fifth Olympiad.
61 Vico ([1744] 1999) 477.
62 Cf. p. 67.
63 Scaliger (1606) *Animadversiones* 95.
64 For the variants on Terpander and Lycurgus see Mosshammer (1979) 173–92, 227–32; Shaw (2003) 71–3, 85–6.
65 Scaliger (1606) *Animadversiones* 129.
66 For old age as a criterion for rejecting a military chronology cf. Dionysius of Halicarnassus, *Roman Antiquities* 6.11.
67 Cf. Aristotle *Politics* 1274a25–31 (on claims that the lawgivers Lycurgus and Zaleucus were pupils of Thales, and Charondas of Zaleucus); Suetonius, *On Grammarians* 7. Conversely a teacher–pupil relationship could be cited against a chronology (Pliny, *Natural History* 35.61).
68 Scaliger (1606) *Animadversiones* 25.
69 Similar issues of cultural influence are at work in the Numa–Pythagoras synchronism (p. 95): Cicero's rejection of this tradition (*Republic* 2.28–9) supports his thesis of the internal development of the Roman constitution.
70 For a second Hercules, cf. Herodorus *FGrH* 31 F14. Positing duplicates was a popular way to avoid anachronism: other instances include Pythagoras (Plutarch, *Numa* 1.4), Telamon (Pausanias 8.15.7), Lycurgus (Timaeus *FGrH* 566 F127), Orpheus (Herodorus *FGrH* 31 F42), Ariadne (Plutarch, *Theseus* 20.8–9) and Homer (Hesiod T2 Most (Tzetzes)). Other doublets were seemingly invented to fill chronological gaps (the second Cecrops and Pandion in the Athenian king-list; the second Kainan inserted by the Septuagint between Arphaxad and Sela).
71 For the Greek habit of placing events in Egypt too late, cf. Herodotus 2.134 (rejecting a claim that a pyramid had been built by a Greek *hetaera*, Rhodopis).

72 Scaliger (1606) *Animadversiones* 1.
73 Ibid. 3.
74 See Vannicelli (2001) on Egypt's importance in Herodotus' chronology.

Chapter 5

1 Michaud ([1998] 2007) 301.
2 Warburg (1995); Gombrich ([1970] 1986) 88–92, 216–27; Michaud ([1998] 2007) 171–228; Didi-Huberman ([2002] 2017) 231–9.
3 Warburg (1995) 38.
4 Ibid. 17.
5 Ibid. 51–4.
6 Farago ([2002] 2009) 212.
7 Farago (2006).
8 Fabian (1983) 31–2.
9 Pagden ([1982] 1986); Hartog (2005).
10 Teng (2004) 78.
11 Meek (1976); Pocock (1999–2016) 2.258–365.
12 Ferguson ([1767] 1995) 75.
13 Ibid. 185–8.
14 Didi-Huberman ([2002] 2017) 27–32.
15 Tylor (1871) 1.21, 16.
16 Ibid. 1.16, 73.
17 Ibid. 2.453. See further Burrow (1966); Stocking (1987).
18 Hegel ([1837] 1975) 196–208.
19 Marx and Engels (1975–) 35.7–11.
20 Ibid. 24.370–1 (from 1881 'Letter to Vera Zasulich'). Cf. Tomba (2013) 159–86.
21 Bloch ([1935] 1991) 97. Cf. p. 52 on Koselleck.
22 Ibid. 106.
23 Burroughs (1929) 72; (1928) 102.
24 Named after Arthur Conan Doyle's *The Lost World* (with dinosaurs alive on a plateau in South America).
25 Scott (2012) 2.394.
26 Green (1979).
27 Csapo (2005) 10–79; Schlesier (1994).
28 Lang (1908) 44.
29 Tragedy: see p. 191; Virgil: Galinski (1996) 239; *Odyssey*: Griffin ([1987] 2004) 90–4; strategy: Clauss (1993) on Heracles and Jason in Apollonius; strata: Seaford (1994) 144–90 on the *Iliad*.

30 Greene (1986) 221, 225.
31 See p. 101.
32 The explanation follows the Euhemerist view that (some) gods were deified culture-heroes. For the game cf. Ps.-Aurelius Victor, *Origin of the Roman People* 3.4–5.
33 Cole (1967); Blundell (1986).
34 Cf. Plutarch, *Pelopidas* 18.1.
35 Sikes (1914) 10; Hodgen (1964) 476.
36 Sluiter (2016) 29.
37 LSJ s.v. *obolos*, with Seaford (2004) 104 for reservations.
38 Scholia on Hesiod, *Works and Days* 150, with West (1978). Cf. Aristotle's observation (*Poetics* 1461a30) that iron-workers are called 'bronzesmiths'.
39 Cf. 2.132, 4.260 van der Valk (notes on *Iliad* 5.487–8, 18.570). For similar arguments in Plato's *Cratylus* see p. 139; Sedley (2003).
40 A scholion *ad loc.* compares the use of *lithos* 'stone' for 'anchor' even when metal anchors had replaced stones.
41 Cf. *On the Countryside* 2.11.9, with the addition 'some people pluck the wool even today'.
42 Nelsestuen (2017).
43 Cf. Plutarch, *Publicola* 11.6 on how words for money and images on coins retain the old use of animals as a form of currency; also Cicero, *Republic* 2.16 and Ovid, *Fasti* 5.280–1.
44 Other linguistic examples at *On the Latin Language* 5.42, 43, 166; *On the Countryside* 2.11.5.
45 Price (1986) 27 notes the lack of 'social or political anachronisms' in Artemidorus.
46 Forrest (1975).
47 Later a proverb, with 'archaic' glossed by 'simple' (*euēthika*) (Diogenianus, *Proverbs* 3.40).
48 Buxton (1994) 18.
49 Clackson (2015) 124–34. Crassus also links ancient language with the countryside (3.42); cf. p. 140.
50 North (1976).
51 See also 5.106, 122, 123, 130, 6.82. For earthenware ladles or cups as survivals of ancient practice see Pliny, *Natural History* 35.158; Athenaeus 11.483c.
52 Cf. e.g. Dionysius of Halicarnassus, *Roman Antiquities* 2.25.2; Athenaeus 4.137e.
53 Detienne (1979) 74–9.
54 For the survival of the ancient at festivals see Diodorus 1.14.2, 1.43.2, 5.4.7; Ovid, *Fasti* 4.369–72, 6.169–80, 6.533–4; Plutarch, *Symposium* 158a; Kearns (2012).
55 Atack (2010).
56 See further https://anachronismandantiquity.wordpress.com/2018/01/07/dionysius/.
57 Parker (2005) 187–91.

58 Ferguson ([1767] 1995) 80.
59 The scholia on Thucydides 1.6.5 cite *Odyssey* 18.30.
60 Cf. Ps.-Hippocrates, *On Ancient Medicine* 5.7–12.
61 Koselleck (2002) 222; Rood (2015), (2016).
62 Cf. Strabo on the 'Cyclopean' life of Albanians by the Caspian Sea (11.4.3).
63 Cf. 'archaic' chariots at 5.45.3.
64 Buxton (1992).
65 Rawson (1985) 250–67; Clarke (1999); Woolf (2011).
66 Cf. Seneca, *Epistles* 90.16.
67 Cf. Pliny, *Natural History* 7.206 (on British ships). For 'bestial' early life see Guthrie (1971) 80; for 'bestial' survivals see e.g. Polybius 6.5.9 and Pliny, *Natural History* 18.74.
68 Gantz (1967); Wallace-Hadrill (1982); Perkell (2002).
69 On aniconism see Gaifman (2012).
70 For the effect of conquest cf. p. 134 (Dionysius).
71 Swain (1996) 79–85; Whitmarsh (2001) 105–8.
72 Cf. Maximus of Tyre 36.3 for a contrast between equal heroic exchange and post-heroic profit-driven commerce.
73 Morrow (1960); Long (2013) 139–60.
74 Prauscello (2017).
75 The author and date of this fictional letter are unknown, but it was circulating among scholars in the late Roman Republic (Cicero, *Tusculan Disputations* 5.90).
76 Dench (1995) 91–2.
77 See e.g. Plutarch, *Marius* 3.1 (rustic upbringing as 'similar to the old Roman'); Tacitus, *Annals* 16.5.
78 Parry (1963) 68.
79 Cf. Adam Parry's unequal opposition between 'Americans' and 'the American Indian'.
80 Scott (1814–17) 1.ix–xi. Thompson (1911) xii compares the romantic feeling for geography in Virgil and Scott.

Chapter 6

1 Brunt (1976–83) 1.237 n. 6.
2 Rood (2011) 136.
3 For gendered images of death see Edwards (2007) 179–206.
4 Schiffman (2011) 178.
5 Lowenthal (2015) 4.
6 Gelley (1995) 5, drawing on Koselleck ([1979] 2004) 26–42.
7 For discussion see Rigolot (1998) and other contributions to the same issue.
8 Pocock ([1957] 1987) 4; Vlassopoulos (2007) 18.
9 Society of Dilettanti (1797) viii.

10   Gelley (1995) 5.
11   Chandler (1998) 171–4.
12   For these tropes in inter-war Germany see Näf (1986), esp. 85–6 on Max Pohlenz, and Marchand (1996) 302–40.
13   E.g. Hedrick (2007), a paraphrase of the *Education of Cyrus* in the voice of Cyrus, with a cover quote from the management thinker Peter Drucker.
14   Freeman (2012); May (2016).
15   Kraus (2005) 186.
16   Langlands (2011), (2018).
17   Langlands (2008) 160.
18   Roller (2018) esp. 17–23, 153–63 (on Gaius Duilius), 163–97 (on Fabius).
19   See e.g. Rood (2010) on the appropriation of Greek military figures in the United States.
20   Flower (1996).
21   E.g. by the rhapsode Ion in Plato, *Ion* (his beliefs are attacked by Socrates).
22   E.g. Ps.-Plutarch, *Life of Homer* 94–111; Heraclitus, *Homeric Problems* 36, 43–51.
23   E.g. Ps.-Plutarch, *Life of Homer* 161–98.
24   E.g. Ps.-Herodotus, *Life of Homer* 26.
25   He proceeds to use a Homeric example anyway.
26   Tuplin (1991) 266.
27   Wallace-Hadrill (2008) 231–7.
28   The change was not permanent: for the revival of Persian Wars rhetoric during the third-century AD Gothic invasion, see https://anachronismandantiquity.wordpress.com/2017/09/26/thermopylae/.
29   Cf. Hedrick (2006) 55, with the conclusion that '"anachronism" is a vice only to modern historians, with our concern for precise dating and contextualization'.
30   For the use of Helen in Sappho 16 see https://anachronismandantiquity.wordpress.com/2017/06/08/sapphos-memories/.
31   Chaplin (2000).
32   There is similar distancing of exemplary Regulus in Horace, *Odes* 3.5, where an anachronistic simile compares his departure from Rome with a lawyer leaving for his rural retreat (Arieti (1990) 219).
33   For anachronistic survivals among women see pp. 130–1.
34   Beiser (2011) 2.

Interlude: Ariadne on Naxos

1   Winckelmann ([1764] 2006) 351.
2   Taylor (2002).
3   Haskell and Penny (1981) 184–7.
4   De Chirico (2008) 435.

5   Winckelmann ([1764] 2006) 351.
6   Kern (1983) 13, 23.
7   Soby (1955) 55.
8   Ibid. 247 (citing *Epodes* 1.1–2, 'You, friend, will go on Liburnian galleys among the lofty superstructures of ships').
9   Ibid. 251.
10 Ibid.
11 Nietzsche ([1873–6] 1997) 68.

Chapter 7

1   Serres ([1977] 2000) 3–7, 158–64.
2   Serres and Latour ([1992] 1995) 45, 58–60.
3   Ibid. 61. Cf. Deleuze ([1968] 2014) on the synthesis of time; Clayton (2012).
4   Freud (1957) 178 (letter of 1896); Fédida (1985).
5   Tribble and Sutton (2012) 588.
6   Most (2004) 297.
7   Carr (1986), (2014).
8   Pollmann (2017) 48.
9   Ibid. 8–9.
10 Harris (2009) 2.
11 Ibid. 3–4.
12 Tribble and Sutton (2012) 588.
13 Grethlein (2013) 313–42; Kennedy (2013) 1–42.
14 'Tu ne quaesieris, scire nefas, quem mihi, quem tibi / finem di dederint, Leuconoe, nec Babylonios / temptaris numeros. ut melius, quidquid erit, pati, / seu pluris hiemes seu tribuit Iuppiter ultimam, / quae nunc oppositis debilitat pumicibus mare / Tyrrhenum: sapias, vina liques, et spatio brevi / spem longam reseces. dum loquimur, fugerit invida / aetas: carpe diem, quam minimum credula postero.'
15 Culler (2015) 226.
16 West (1995) 50–1.
17 For which see e.g. Fearn (2018).
18 See e.g. Kowalzig (2013).
19 See e.g. Pindar fr. 140b with Steiner (2016).
20 Azoulay ([2014] 2017) offers an account of the statue-group and its reception.
21 Literally 'to the city' (p. 126), a deliberate archaism (the phrase was old-fashioned by the fourth century).
22 Nagel and Wood (2010) 14–16.
23 Ibid. 25.

24 Ibid. 51.
25 For a different reading see Gaifman (2012) 110–13.
26 Fowler (2000) 213.
27 In the first performance at Athens the actor playing Ajax would have been wheeled out of the stage-building on a wooded platform (*ekkuklēma*).
28 Finglass (2011) 306–7.
29 See Mueller (2016) 19–34, 134–54, and Weiberg (2018) for different emphases.
30 Knox (1961).
31 Gould (2001) 165–7.
32 Finglass 2011 (389), citing M. Davies.

Interlude: Aeneas in the Underworld

1 Ekroth and Nilsson (2018) trace the narrative trope through to Byzantium. Virgil also draws on Ennius' account of his dream of Homer and on the Dream of Scipio in Cicero's *Republic*, in both of which national and cosmic themes are combined (Hardie (1986) 66–83).
2 At least with the mothers and wives of Neleus (Tyro, Chloris) and Heracles (Alcmene, Megara).
3 Most (1992).
4 West (1985).
5 Bremmer (2009).
6 Hardie (2011) 396–7.
7 Burke (1979).
8 In the first instance, the allusion is mediated through a quotation (noted by Macrobius, *Saturnalia* 6.1.39) from the poem *On Death* by Virgil's friend Varius Rufus as well as through echoes of Cicero's polemics against Antony; see Hollis (1977), Berry (1992).
9 Feeney (1986) 7–8.
10 Hardie (2011) 390. Aeneas has been drawn into a Roman orbit when Anchises points out to him Augustus along with 'your Romans' (6.789: *Romanosque tuos*).
11 Zetzel (1989) 278.
12 E.g. Kennedy (2013) 70.

Chapter 8

1 Vasari ([1550] 1998) 312–17.
2 Fréart de Chambray (1662) 108–16 ((1668) 111–18). For the title's resonance, see Most (2006).

3 Bellori (1695) 15 ((1997) 48–9).
4 Vasari's identification is defended by Kempers (1998) 160; for its relation to prints of the fresco see Wood (1988).
5 See the frontispiece of Anderson (1974), taken from a 1703 edition of Xenophon (Luuk Huitink noted this link).
6 Hall (1997) 32.
7 E.g. Williams (2017) 91.
8 Bellori (1695) 15 ((1997) 48); Fréart de Chambray (1662) 115 ((1668) 118).
9 Bromley (1793) 2.65–6. On Bromley see Phillips (2013) 62–5.
10 Barnes and Barnes (1989) 257.
11 De Piles (1708) 62 ((1743) 48). Aristotle portrays a similar developmental view of the history of philosophy in *Metaphysics* 1.
12 Rijser (2012) 111.
13 An 'anatopism', in Castelvetro's terms (p. 17).
14 See https://anachronismandantiquity.wordpress.com/2017/03/31/of-sundials/.
15 Mentioned by Brilliant (1984) 2 *à propos* Raphael.
16 Keen (1984) 121–3.
17 Gombrich (1972) 85–101; Hall (1997) 9–11; Most (1996).
18 Freedman (1997) 24.
19 Rowland (1997) 104.
20 Rijser (2005).
21 Klienbub (2011) 46–69.
22 See further O'Malley (1977), who publishes a 1508 sermon according to which Julius II's library restores Athens in Rome; Rowland (1997), (2018), who suggests Egidio and the librarian Tomasso Inghirami as influences on the design; Joost-Gaugier (2002); Taylor (2009); Rijser (2018).
23 Nagel and Wood (2010) 346–65.
24 Denyer (2008) 66.
25 Most (1996) 164. Lloyd (1866) 20 compared the scenes without suggesting direct influence.
26 Dodds (1959) 17–18.
27 See Cicero, *On Invention* 1.51–3 for the dialogue's discussion of themes relating to marriage and the household; given that similar themes are treated by Xenophon in works which post-date Socrates' death, it is as much a conversation between Aeschines and Xenophon as Socratics. The scenarios in both *Symposium* and *Aspasia* are possible on the *floruit* date for Xenophon offered by Diogenes Laertius 2.55, but see Huitink and Rood (2019) 9.
28 König (2012) 106; cf. 64 on Plutarch's *Sympotic Questions*.
29 Zeller (1873); Graham (2007).
30 Flinterman (2000–2001) 42–4; Trapp (2000).

31 Peta Fowler drew this passage to our attention.
32 Cameron (2011) 239.
33 McCabe (2000) 3–6.
34 Although Burnyeat (2002) 51–5 argues that the brothers' exposition of 'how not to argue' shows that they have 'no philosophical beliefs at all' and cannot be taken as representatives of any of Plato's rivals.
35 Jackson (1990) 394 n. 88.
36 Nails (2002) 217, 309.
37 Hermann (2010) 8–11. Plato alludes to meetings between Parmenides and Socrates also at *Theaetetus* 183e and *Sophist* 217c.
38 Cf. Strabo 6.1.1; Plutarch, *Reply to Colotes* 1126a–b.
39 Plato accords the same treatment to the mathematician Theaetetus in the dialogue of that name.
40 Coventry (1989) 4; Monoson (1998) 489–95.
41 Loraux ([1981] 1986) 466 n. 303.
42 Dean-Jones (1995).
43 Davidson (2000); Cameron (1966) 28–9.
44 Cameron (2011) 231.
45 The dream is largely preserved through Macrobius' commentary on it.
46 MacLeod (1991) 258–63.
47 Cf. pp. 77, 83.
48 Diogenes Laertius 6.102 tells the story of Menedemus, presumably a mistake for Menippus. On Menippean satire see Hall (1981) 64–105; Relihan (1993); Weinbrot (2005).
49 The underworld may have appeared in *Ulixes-and-a-half*, which used the *Odyssey* as model for a narrative of Varro's longer absence from Rome on military service; cf. Horace, *Satires* 2.5, where a consultation between Ulixes and Tiresias in the underworld refers to the experiences of Roman soldiers in the Civil Wars. Varro experimented with time and morality in other ways too: in *Sixty-year Old* a character falls asleep aged ten and awakens aged sixty to discover that morals at Rome have greatly declined during his long sleep.
50 E.g. Plutarch, *The Oracles at Delphi No Longer Given in Verse*. Cf. Horace, *Epistles* 2.2.55–7, 144.
51 Erasmus (1974–) 40.818–30.
52 Keener (1973); Robinson (1979); Marsh (1998) 42–75, 105–10.
53 Fontenelle (1683) n.p.
54 King (1699). See p. 23. Cf. Hardinge (1782), a dialogue between Chatterton and his forged medieval poet Rowley, including appearances by Bentley and Pseudo-Phalaris.
55 Fenelon (1700) 52–5; Lyttelton (1760) 231–40, 16–22.

56 Female speakers are found in other types of dialogue, e.g. Lucian's *Dialogues of Courtesans* and Methodius' *Symposium*, a Christian all-female discussion of chastity.
57 Fontenelle (1683) 27–38.
58 Lyttelton (1760) 306–20.
59 Voltaire (1765–75) 5.270–6; also attributed to Jean-Baptiste-Antoine Suard (Robinson (1979) 156).
60 Traill (1884) 60.
61 Kim (2010) 156–74; Ní Mheallaigh (2014) 206–60. Lucian is the inspiration for the necromantic island in *Gulliver's Travels*, where Gulliver wants to see Homer conversing with the commentators Didymus and Eustathius, but finds that they are in hiding because of all their mistakes (Swift ([1726] (1940) 210); and again for the underworld scene in Fielding's *A Journey from this World to the Next* ((1766) 5.235) where Homer is encountered with his French translator Madame Dacier on his lap, waiting for Pope to arrive.
62 Bréchet (2015).
63 Plato's Corybantic imagery (on which see Wasmuth (2015)) is probably Dionysius' inspiration. Cf. Bacchic language of Demosthenes at Eratosthenes *FGrH* 241 F32.
64 Wilamowitz-Moellendorff (1908) 25.
65 Kennedy (2018) 209.
66 For the image, cf. the maxim 'Descent into Hades' by Wilamowitz's former philological adversary Nietzsche ([1878] 1996) 299.

Epilogue: Crowning the Victors

1 Pressly (2014) 23–5.
2 Barry (1809) 2.329.
3 Quoted by Pressly (2014) 78.
4 Barry (1809) 2.438 (from a 1793 account).
5 Bromley (1793) 2.47, 63.
6 Barry (1809) 2.329.
7 Ibid. 2.328.
8 Ibid. 2.331.
9 Ibid. 2.324.
10 Pressly (2014) 207–30, esp. 210–11 on Dughet's Orpheus-like painting of St John the Baptist, 213 on the peacock as nativity symbol, 214 on the eucharist (mediated through Christian appropriations of Virgil).
11 Barry (1809) 2.361.

12 Barry (1803) 6. The abridgement, made by the Society's secretary, was originally published in 1785 and subsequently re-issued; the clause cited here was added in the 1803 edition, which had new input from Barry himself (Pressly (2014) 366 n. 10).
13 See Aristotle, *Nicomachean Ethics* 1100a10–1101a21.

References

Adler, W. (1989) *Time Immemorial: Archaic History and its Sources in Christian Chronography from Julius Africanus to George Syncellus* (Washington, DC).
Anderson, J. K. (1974) *Xenophon* (London).
Arieti, J. (1990) 'Horatian philosophy and the Regulus Ode (*Odes* 3.5)', *Transactions of the American Philological Association*, 120: 209–20.
Atack, C. (2010) 'Ancestral constitutions in fourth-century BCE Athenian political argument', MPhil thesis, University of Cambridge.
Atack, C. (2019) *The Discourse of Kingship in Classical Greece* (London).
Azoulay, V. ([2014] 2017) *The Tyrant-slayers of Ancient Athens*, trans. J. Lloyd (New York).
Bal, M. (2016) 'Long live anachronism', in L. Brozgal and S. Kippur (eds), *Being Contemporary* (Liverpool) 281–304.
Barnes, A. and J. Barnes (1989) 'Time out of joint', *Journal of Aesthetics and Art Criticism*, 47: 253–61.
Barry, J. (1803) *A Description of the Series of Pictures painted by James Barry* (London).
Barry, J. (1809) *The Works of James Barry* (London).
Barthélemy, J.-J. ([1787] 1793–4) *Travels of Anacharsis the Younger in Greece*, trans. W. Beaumont (London).
Beiser, F. (2011) *The German Historicist Tradition* (Oxford).
Bellori, G. P. (1695) *Descrizzione delle quattro immagini dipinte da Raffaelle* (Rome).
Bellori, G. P. (1997) 'The image of the ancient *Gymnasium of Athens*, or *Philosophy*', trans. A. S. Wohl, in M. Hall (ed.), *Raphael's 'School of Athens'* (Cambridge) 48–56.
Bentley, R. (1697) *Dissertations on the Epistles of Phalaris* (London).
Bernardo, A. S., S. Levin and R. A. Bernardo (1992) (trans.) *Francis Petrarch: Letters of Old Age* (Baltimore).
Berry, D. (1992) 'The criminals in Virgil's Tartarus', *Classical Quarterly*, 42: 416–20.
Bickerman, E. J. ([1968] 1980) *Chronology of the Ancient World* (London).
Blaas, P. B. M. (1978) *Continuity and Anachronism* (The Hague).
Black, R. (1995) 'The Donation of Constantine', in A. Brown (ed.), *Language and Images of Renaissance Italy* (Oxford) 51–85.
Blasco, C. (1578) *Diatriba de Joanna papissa, seu de eius fabulae origine* (Naples).
Bloch, E. ([1935] 1991) *Heritage of Our Times*, trans. N. Plaice and S. Plaice (Oxford).
Blount, T. (1656) *Glossographia* (London).
Blundell, S. (1986) *The Origins of Civilization in Greek and Roman Thought* (London).
Boak, A. E. R., E. M. Husselman and W. F. Edgerton (1933–44) (eds) *Papyri from Tebtunis* (Ann Arbor).

Boas, G. and A. O. Lovejoy ([1935] 1997) *Primitivism and Related Ideas in Antiquity* (Baltimore).
Bodin, J. ([1566] 1945) *Method for the Easy Comprehension of History*, trans. B. Reynolds (New York).
Bolingbroke, H. St. J. (1752) *Letters on the Study and Use of History* (London).
Borchardt, F. L. (1975) 'Petrarch: The German connection', in A. Scaglione (ed.), *Francis Petrarch Six Centuries Later* (Chapel Hill) 418–31.
Borges, J. L. ([1939] 1970) 'Pierre Menard, author of the *Quixote*', trans. J. E. Irby, in id., *Labyrinths* (Harmondsworth) 62–71.
Botley, P. (2006) 'Renaissance scholarship and the Athenian calendar', *Greek, Roman, and Byzantine Studies*, 46: 395–431.
Botley, P. and D. van Miert (2012) (eds) *The Correspondence of Joseph Justus Scaliger* (Geneva).
Bowersock, G. W. (2007) (ed., trans.) *Lorenzo Valla: On the Donation of Constantine* (Cambridge, MA).
Bowie, E. L. (1970) 'Greeks and their past in the second sophistic', *Past and Present*, 46: 3–41.
Braund, D. and J. Wilkins (2000) (eds) *Athenaeus and His World* (Exeter).
Bréchet, C. (2015) '"Parle avec eux": le dialogue avec les auteurs classiques', in S. Dubel and S. Gotteland (eds), *Formes et genres du dialogue antique* (Bordeaux) 155–64.
Bremmer, J. (2009) 'The golden bough', *Kernos*, 22: 183–208.
Brilliant, R. (1984) 'Intellectual giants', *Source*, 3: 1–12.
Bromley, R. A. (1793) *A Philosophical and Critical History of the Fine Arts* (London).
Brunt, P. A. (1976–83) (ed., trans.) *Arrian: Anabasis of Alexander and Indica* (Cambridge, MA).
Buchwald, J. Z. and M. Feingold (2012) *Newton and the Origin of Civilization* (Princeton).
Burke, P. (1969) *The Renaissance Sense of the Past* (London).
Burke, P. (2001) 'The sense of anachronism from Petrarch to Poussin', in C. Humphrey and W. M. Ormrod (eds), *Time in the Medieval World* (Woodbridge) 157–74.
Burke, P. F. (1979) 'Roman rites for the dead and *Aeneid* 6', *Classical Journal*, 74: 220–8.
Burkert, W. (1972) *Lore and Science in Ancient Pythagoreanism*, trans. E. Minar (Cambridge, MA).
Burnyeat, M. F. (2002) 'Plato on how to speak what is not', in M. Canto-Sperber and P. Pellegrin (eds), *Le style de la pensée* (Paris) 40–66.
Burroughs, E. R. (1928) *Tarzan, Lord of the Jungle* (London).
Burroughs, E. R. (1929) *Tarzan and the Lost Empire* (London).
Burrow, J. W. (1966) *Evolution and Society* (Cambridge).
Bury, J. B. (1909) *The Ancient Greek Historians* (London).
Bury, J. B. (1920) *The Idea of Progress* (London).
Butterfield, H. W. ([1931] 1973) *The Whig Interpretation of History* (Harmondsworth).
Button, E. (1740) *Rudiments of Ancient History* (London).

Buxton, R. G. A. (1992) 'Imaginary Greek mountains', *Journal of Hellenic Studies*, 112: 1–15.
Buxton, R. G. A. (1994) *Imaginary Greece* (Cambridge).
Cameron, A. (1966) 'The date and identity of Macrobius', *Journal of Roman Studies* 56: 25–38.
Cameron, A. (2011) *The Last Pagans of Rome* (New York).
Carr, D. (1986) *Time, Narrative, and History* (Bloomington, IN).
Carr, D. (2014) *Experience and History* (Oxford).
Carroll, K. von Z. (2014) *Art in the Time of Colony* (Farnham).
Cary, G. (1956) *The Medieval Alexander* (Cambridge).
Casaubon, I. (1600) *Animadversionum in Athenæi Dipnosophistas libri XV* (Lyon).
Castelvetro, L. ([1570] 1978–9) *Poetica d'Aristotele vulgarizzata e sposta*, ed. W. Romani (Rome).
Castelvetro, L. ([1570] 1984) *Castelvetro on the Art of Poetry*, trans. A. Bongiorno (Binghampton, NY).
Cavarzeran, J. (2016) (ed.) *Scholia in Euripidis Hippolytum* (Berlin).
Cervantes, M. de ([1605–15] 1992) *Don Quixote*, trans. C. Jarvis (Oxford).
Chakrabarty, D. (2000) *Provincializing Europe* (Princeton).
Chandler, J. (1998) *England in 1819: The Politics of Literary Culture and the Case of Romantic Historicism* (Chicago).
Chaplin, J. (2000) *Livy's Exemplary History* (Oxford).
Chateaubriand, F.-R. de (1811) *Itinéraire de Paris à Jérusalem et de Jérusalem à Paris* (Paris).
Christesen, P. (2007) *Olympic Victor Lists and Ancient Greek History* (Cambridge).
Clackson, J. (2015) *Language and Society in the Greek and Roman Worlds* (Cambridge).
Clark, T. (2015) *Ecocriticism on the Edge* (London).
Clarke, K. J. (1999) *Between Geography and History* (Oxford).
Clarke, K. J. (2008) *Making Time for the Past* (Oxford).
Clauss, J. J. (1993) *The Best of the Argonauts* (Berkeley).
Clayton, K. (2012) 'Time folded and crumpled', in B. Herzogenrath (ed.), *Time and History in Deleuze and Serres* (London) 31–49.
Cole, T. ([1967] 1990) *Democritus and the Sources of Greek Anthropology* (Atlanta).
Coleridge, S. T. (1969–2002) *Collected Works*, ed. K. Coburn (London and Princeton).
Collingwood, R. G. (1946) *The Idea of History* (Oxford).
Conan Doyle, A. (1912) *The Lost World* (London).
Coulanges, N.D. Fustel de ([1864] 1980) *The Ancient City*, trans. W. Small (Baltimore).
Coventry, L. J. (1989) 'Philosophy and rhetoric in the *Menexenus*', *Journal of Hellenic Studies*, 109: 1–15.
Csapo, E. (2005) *Theories of Mythology* (Malden, MA).
Culler, J. (2015) *Theory of the Lyric* (Cambridge).
D'Angour, A. (2011) *The Greeks and the New* (Cambridge).
Davidson, J. (2000) 'Pleasure and pedantry in Athenaeus', in D. Braund and J. Wilkins (eds), *Athenaeus and His World* (Exeter) 292–303.

De Chirico, G. (2008) 'Tutte le poesie', *Metafisica*, 7–8: 423–507.
De Piles, R. (1708) *Cours de peinture par principes* (Paris).
De Piles, R. (1743) *The Principles of Painting* (London).
De Quincey, T. (1862–83) *The Works of Thomas de Quincey* (Edinburgh).
Dean-Jones, L. (1995) 'Menexenus – Son of Socrates', *Classical Quarterly*, 45: 51–7.
Deleuze, G. ([1968] 2014) *Difference and Repetition*, trans. P. Patton (London).
Delph, R. K. (1996) 'Valla Grammaticus, Agostino Steuco, and the Donation of Constantine', *Journal of the History of Ideas*, 57: 55–77.
Dench, E. (1995) *From Barbarians to New Men: Greek, Roman, and Modern Perceptions of Peoples of the Central Apennines* (Oxford).
Denyer, N. (2008) (ed.) *Plato: Protagoras* (Cambridge).
Desmond, M. (1994) *Reading Dido: Gender, Textuality, and the Medieval Aeneid* (Minneapolis).
Detienne, M. (1979) *Dionysos Slain*, trans. M. and L. Muellner (Baltimore).
Diderot, D. (1751–72) (ed.) *Encyclopédie, ou dictionnaire raisonné des sciences, des arts et des métiers* (Paris).
Didi-Huberman, G. ([1990] 2005) *Confronting Images*, trans. J. Goodman (University Park, PA).
Didi-Huberman, G. ([2002] 2017) *The Surviving Image*, trans. H. Mendelsohn (University Park, PA).
Didi-Huberman, G. (2003) 'Before the image, before time', in C. J. Farago and R. Zwijnenberg (eds), *Compelling Visuality* (Minneapolis) 31–44.
Dillery, J. (2015) *Clio's Other Sons: Berossus and Manetho* (Ann Arbor).
Dinshaw, C. (2007) 'Temporalities', in P. Strohm (ed.), *Middle English* (Oxford) 107–23.
Dinshaw, C. (2012) *How Soon is Now?* (Durham, NC).
Dodds, E. R. (1959) (ed.) *Plato: Gorgias* (Oxford).
Dover, K. J. (1978) *Greek Homosexuality* (London).
Drayton, M. (1612) *Poly-Olbion* (London).
Dryden, J. (1697) (trans.) *The Works of Virgil* (London).
Düring, I. (1941) *Herodicus the Cratetean* (Stockholm).
Easterling P. E. (1985) 'Anachronism in Greek tragedy', *Journal of Hellenic Studies*, 105: 1–10.
Eastman, C. (1926) 'British women fire the first gun in their second suffrage battle', *Equal Rights*, 13: 22–3.
Ebeling, H. L. (1937) 'The word "anachronism"', *Modern Language Notes*, 52: 120–1.
Edwards, C. (2007) *Death in Ancient Rome* (New Haven).
Ekroth, G. and I. Nilsson (2018) (eds) *Round Trip to Hades in the Eastern Mediterranean Tradition* (Leiden and Boston).
Erasmus, D. (1974–) *Collected Works* (Toronto).
Eschenburg, B. (1979) 'Altdorfers *Alexanderschlacht* und ihr Verhältnis zum Historienzyklus Wilhelms IV', *Zeitschrift des Deutschen Vereins für Kunstwissenschaft*, 33: 36–67.

Evans, J. and J. L. Berggren (2006) (eds, trans.) *Geminos's Introduction to the Phenomena* (Princeton).
Fabian, J. (1983) *Time and the Other* (New York).
Fantham, E. (2017) (ed., trans.) *Francesco Petrarca: Selected Letters* (Cambridge, MA).
Farago, C. J. ([2002] 2009) 'Silent moves: on excluding the ethnographic subject from the discourse of art history', in D. Preziosi (ed.), *The Art of Art History* (Oxford) 195–212.
Farago, C. J. (2006) 'Re(f)using Art: Aby Warburg and the ethics of scholarship', in C. J. Farago and D. Pierce, *Transforming Images* (University Park, PA) 259–74.
Favreau-Linder, A.-M. (2015) 'Le *Charon* de Lucien', in S. Dubel and S. Gotteland (eds), *Formes et genres du dialogue antique* (Bordeaux) 197–209.
Fearn, D. (2018) 'Materialities of political commitment?', in F. Budelmann and T. Phillips (eds), *Textual Events* (Oxford) 93–113.
Febvre, L. ([1942] 1985) *The Problem of Unbelief in the Sixteenth Century*, trans. B. Gottlieb (Cambridge, MA).
Fédida, P. (1985) 'Passé anachronique et present reminiscent', *L'Ecrit du temps*, 10: 23–45.
Feeney, D. C. (1986) 'History and revelation in Virgil's Underworld', *Proceedings of the Cambridge Philological Society*, 32: 1–24.
Feeney, D. C. (2007) *Caesar's Calendar* (Berkeley).
Fenelon, F. de Salignac de La Mothe (1700) *Dialogues des morts* (Paris).
Ferguson, A. ([1767] 1995) *An Essay on the History of Civil Society* (Cambridge).
Fielding, H. (1766) *The Works of Henry Fielding* (London).
Finglass, P. J. (2011) (ed.) *Sophocles: Ajax* (Cambridge).
Finley, M. I. (1959) (ed.) *The Greek Historians* (London).
Flinterman, J.-J. (2000–1) 'Aelius Aristides on Plato's dialogues', *Ancient Narrative* 1: 32–54.
Flower, H. I. (1996) *Ancestor Masks and Aristocratic Power in Roman Culture* (Oxford).
Fontenelle, B. Le Bouvier de (1683) *Nouveaux dialogues des morts* (Paris).
Forrest, W. G. (1975) 'An Athenian generation gap', *Yale Classical Studies*, 4: 37–52.
Fowler, D. P. (2000) *Roman Constructions* (Oxford).
Francklin, T. (1758–9) (ed.) *The Tragedies of Sophocles* (London).
Fréart de Chambray, R. (1662) *Idée de la perfection de la peinture* (Paris).
Fréart de Chambray, R. (1668) *An Idea of the Perfection of Painting*, trans. J. Evelyn (London).
Freedman, L. (1997), 'Apollo's glance in Raphael's *Parnassus*', *Source*, 16: 20–5.
Freeman, P. (2012) (trans.) *Quintus Tullius Cicero: How to Win an Election* (Princeton).
Freud, S. (1957) *The Origins of Psychoanalysis* (New York).
Fussner, F. S. (1969) Review of Levy, *Tudor Historical Thought*, *History and Theory*, 8: 371–87.
Gaifman, M. (2012) *Aniconism in Greek Antiquity* (Oxford).
Gale, T. (1669) *Court of the Gentiles* (Oxford).
Galinski, K. (1996) *Augustan Culture* (Princeton).
Gantz, B. (1967) *Weltalter, Goldene Zeit und sinnverwandte Vorstellungen* (Hildesheim).

Gelley, A. (1995) *Unruly Examples* (Stanford).
Gibbon, E. (1972) *The English Essays of Edward Gibbon*, ed. P. B. Craddock (Oxford).
Gilmore, M. P. (1963) *Humanists and Jurists* (Cambridge, MA).
Giusti, E. (2018) *Carthage in Virgil's Aeneid* (Cambridge).
Glareanus, H. (1531) *En ... damus amice lector T. Liuii ... quicquid hactenus fuit æditum ... Addita est Chronologia Henrici Glareani* (Basel).
Goldberg, G. (1984) 'La bataille d'Alexandre le Grand contre le Roi Darius III', in *Altdorfer et le réalisme fantastique dans l'art allemand* (Paris) 245–70.
Gombrich, E. H. ([1970] 1986) *Aby Warburg* (Oxford).
Gombrich, E. H. (1972) *Symbolic Images* (London).
Gough, R. (1786–96) *Sepulchral Monuments in Great Britain* (London).
Gould, J. (2001) *Myth, Ritual, Memory, and Exchange* (Oxford).
Grafton, A. T. (1983–93) *Joseph Scaliger: A Study in the History of Classical Scholarship* (Oxford).
Grafton, A. T. (1990) *Forgers and Critics* (Princeton).
Grafton, A. T. and M. Williams (2006) *Christianity and the Transformation of the Book* (Cambridge, MA).
Graham, A. J. (2007) 'Plato's anachronisms', in N. Sekunda (ed.), *Corolla Cosmo Rodewald* (Gdansk) 67–74.
Grazia, M. de (2007) 'The modern divide', *Journal of Medieval and Early Modern Studies*, 43: 453–67.
Grazia, M. de (2010) 'Anachronism', in B. Cummings and J. Simpson (eds), *Cultural Reformation* (Oxford) 13–32.
Green, M. (1979) *Dreams of Adventure, Deeds of Empire* (New York).
Greene, T. M. (1982) *The Light in Troy* (New Haven).
Greene, T. M. (1986) *The Vulnerable Text* (New York).
Gregory, J. (1649) *Posthuma* (London).
Grethlein, J. (2013) *Experience and Teleology in Ancient Historiography* (Cambridge).
Grey, Z. (1754) *Critical, Historical, and Explanatory Notes on Shakespeare* (London).
Griffin, J. ([1987] 2004) *Homer: The Odyssey* (Cambridge).
Grote, G. ([1846–56] 1888) *History of Greece* (London).
Grumach, E. (1949) (ed.) *Goethe und die Antike* (Berlin).
Grzęda A. (2016) 'Reconsideration of the portrait of Rudolf IV', in U. Fleckner and T. Hensel (eds), *Hermeneutik des Gesichts* (Berlin) 123–40.
Guthrie, W. K. C. (1971) *The Sophists* (Cambridge).
Guynn, N. D. and Z. Stahuljak (2013) 'Introduction', in eid. (eds), *Violence and the Writing of History in the Medieval Francophone World* (Cambridge) 1–17.
Haddock, B. A. (1980) *An Introduction to Historical Thought* (London).
Hale, J. R. (1990) *Artists and Warfare in the Renaissance* (New Haven).
Hale, J. R. (1994) *The Civilization of Europe in the Renaissance* (New York).
Hales, J. (1617) *A Sermon preached at St Maries in Oxford vpon Tuesday in Easter Vveeke* (Oxford).

Hall, J. (1981) *Lucian's Satire* (New York).
Hall, M. (1997) 'Introduction', in ead. (ed.), *Raphael's 'School of Athens'* (Cambridge) 1–47.
Halliwell, S. (2008) *Greek Laughter* (Cambridge).
Hannah, R. (2009) *Time in Antiquity* (London).
Hardie, P. R. (1986) *Cosmos and Imperium* (Oxford).
Hardie, P. R. (2011) 'Strategies of praise', in G. Urso (ed.), *Dicere laudes* (Pisa) 383–99.
Hardie, P. R. (2012) *Rumour and Renown* (Cambridge).
Hardinge, G. (1782) *Rowley and Chatterton in the Shades* (London).
Hardy, N. J. S. (2018) *Criticism and Confession: The Bible in the Seventeenth Century Republic of Letters* (Oxford).
Harloe, K. (2013) *Winckelmann and the Invention of Antiquity* (Oxford).
Harris, J. G. (2009). *Untimely Matter in the Time of Shakespeare* (Philadelphia).
Hartog, F. ([2003] 2015) *Regimes of Historicity*, trans. S. Brown (New York).
Hartog, F. (2005) *Anciens, modernes, sauvages* (Paris).
Haskell, F. and N. Penny (1981) *Taste and the Antique* (New Haven).
Hay, D. (1977) *Annalists and Historians* (London).
Hearne, T. (1698, 1705) *Ductor historicus* (London).
Heath, M. (1995) (ed., trans.) *Hermogenes: On Issues* (Oxford).
Hedrick, C. (2006) *Ancient History* (Malden, MA).
Hedrick, L. (2007) *Xenophon's Cyrus the Great: The Arts of Leadership and War* (New York).
Hegel, G. W. F. ([1835] 1975) *Aesthetics: Lectures on Fine Art*, trans. T. M. Knox (Oxford).
Hegel, G. W. F. ([1837] 1975) *Lectures on the Philosophy of World History*, trans. H. B. Nisbet (Cambridge).
Heinsius, D. (1623) *Laus asini* (Leiden).
Heinsius, D. (1639) *Sacrarum exercitationum ad Novum Testamentum libri XX* (Leiden).
Heller, W. (2014) 'Opera between the Ancients and the Moderns', in H. M. Greenwald (ed.), *The Oxford Handbook of Opera* (New York) 275–95.
Helvicus, C. ([1609] 1629) *Theatrum historicum, sive Chronologiae systema novum* (Marburg).
Hermann, A. (2010) *Plato's Parmenides* (Las Vegas).
Hiatt, A. (2004) *The Making of Medieval Forgeries* (London).
Higbie, C. (2017) *Collectors, Scholars, and Forgers in the Ancient World* (Oxford).
Hinds, S. (1998) *Allusion and Intertext* (Cambridge).
Hodgen, M. T. (1964) *Early Anthropology in the Sixteenth and Seventeenth Centuries* (Philadelphia).
Holford-Strevens, L. ([1988] 2003) *Aulus Gellius* (Oxford).
Hollis, A. (1977) 'L. Varius Rufus, *De Morte* (frs. 1–4 Morel)', *Classical Quarterly*, 27: 187–90.
Hornblower, S. (1991–2008) *A Commentary on Thucydides* (Oxford).

Horsfall, N. M. ([1973] 1990), 'Dido in the Light of History', in S. J. Harrison (ed.), *Oxford Readings in Vergil's Aeneid* (Oxford) 127–44.
Horsfall, N. M. (2016) *The Epic Distilled* (Oxford).
Huitink, L. and T. C. B. Rood (2019) (eds) *Xenophon: Anabasis Book III* (Cambridge).
Hunter, R. L. (2012) *Plato and the Traditions of Ancient Literature* (Cambridge).
Hurd, R. (1762) *Letters on Chivalry and Romance* (London).
Jackson, R. (1990) 'Socrates' Iolaos', *Classical Quarterly*, 40: 378–95.
Jacoby, F. (1944) '*Patrios Nomos*', *Journal of Hellenic Studies*, 64: 37–66.
Johnson, S. (1755) *A Dictionary of the English Language* (London).
Joost-Gaugier, C. L. (2002) *Raphael's Stanza della Signatura* (Cambridge).
Kalter, B. (2012) *Modern Antiques* (Lewisburg, PA).
Kearns, E. (2012) '"Remembering the ancient way of life"', in J. Marincola, L. Llewellyn-Jones and C. Maciver (eds), *Greek Notions of the Past in the Archaic and Classical Eras* (Edinburgh) 301–16.
Keen, M. (1984) *Chivalry* (New Haven).
Keener, F. M. (1973) *English Dialogues of the Dead* (New York).
Kelley, D. R. (1998) *Faces of History* (New Haven).
Kempers, B. (1998) 'Words, images and all the Pope's men: Raphael's Stanza della Segnatura and the Synthesis of Divine Wisdom', in I. Hampsher-Monk (ed.), *History of Concepts* (Amsterdam) 131–65.
Kennedy, D. K. (2013) *Antiquity and the Meanings of Time* (London).
Kennedy, S. (2018) *T.S. Eliot and the Dynamic Imagination* (Cambridge).
Kerkhecker A. (1999) (ed.) *Callimachus: Book of Iambi* (Oxford).
Kern, S. (1983) *The Culture of Space and Time 1880–1918* (London).
Kim, L. Y. (2010) *Homer between History and Fiction in Imperial Greek Literature* (Cambridge).
King, W. (1699) *Dialogues of the Dead* (London).
Klienbub, C. K. (2011) *Vision and the Visionary in Raphael* (University Park, PA).
Knox, B. M. W. (1957) *Oedipus at Thebes* (New Haven).
Knox, B. M. W. (1961) 'The *Ajax* of Sophocles', *Harvard Studies in Classical Philology*, 65: 1–37.
König, J. (2012) *Saints and Symposiasts* (Cambridge).
König, J. and G. Woolf (2013) (eds) *Encyclopaedism from Antiquity to the Renaissance* (Cambridge).
Koselleck, R. (1979) *Vergangene Zukunft* (Frankfurt).
Koselleck, R. (2002) *The Practice of Conceptual History*, trans. T. S. Presner, K. Behnke and J. Welge (Stanford).
Koselleck, R. (2004) *Futures Past*, trans. K. Tribe (New York).
Koselleck, R. (2018) *Sediments of Time*, trans. S.-L. Hoffmann and S. Franzel (Stanford).
Kowalzig, B. (2013) 'Dancing dolphins on the wine-dark sea', in B. Kowalzig and P. J. Wilson (eds), *Dithyramb in Context* (Oxford) 31–58.

Kraus, C. S. (2005) 'From exempla to exemplar?', in J. Edmonson, S. Mason and J. Rives (eds), *Flavius Josephus and Flavian Rome* (Oxford) 181–200.

Lacombe, G. (1930) 'Studies on the commentaries of Cardinal Stephen Langton', *Archives d'histoire doctrinale et littéraire du Moyen Age*, 5: 5–151.

Lafitau, J.-F. (1724) *Mœurs des sauvages ameriquains, comparées aux mœurs des premiers temps* (Paris).

Lang, A. (1908) 'Homer and anthropology', in R. R. Marett (ed.), *Anthropology and the Classics* (Oxford) 44–65.

Langlands, R. (2008) '"Reading for the moral" in Valerius Maximus', *Cambridge Classical Journal*, 54: 160–87.

Langlands, R. (2011) 'Roman exempla and situation ethics', *Journal of Roman Studies*, 101: 1–23.

Langlands, R. (2018) *Exemplary Ethics in Ancient Rome* (Cambridge).

Lascaris, J. (1518) *Commentarii in septem tragedias Sophoclis* (Rome).

Lefkowitz, M. R. ([1981] 2012) *The Lives of the Greek Poets* (London).

Leigh, M. (2013) *From Polypragmon to Curiosus* (Oxford).

Levene D. S. (2010) *Livy on the Hannibalic War* (Oxford).

Levy, F. J. (1967) *Tudor Historical Thought* (San Marino, CA).

Lisle, W. (1623) *A Saxon Treatise Concerning the Old and New Testament* (London).

Lloyd, W. W. (1866) *Philosophy, Theology, and Poetry, in the Age and the Art of Rafael* (London).

Logue, C. (2015) *War Music* (London).

Long, A. G. (2013) *Conversation and Self-sufficiency in Plato* (Oxford).

Loraux, N. ([1981] 1986) *The Invention of Athens*, trans. A. Sheridan (Cambridge, MA).

Loraux, N. (1993) 'Éloge de l'anachronisme en histoire', *Le genre humain*, 27: 23–39.

Loraux, N. ([1997] 2001) *The Divided City*, trans. C. Pache and J. Fort (New York).

Lowenthal, D. (1985) *The Past is a Foreign Country* (Cambridge).

Lowenthal, D. (2015) *The Past is a Foreign Country Revisited* (Cambridge).

Luzzi, J. (2009) 'The rhetoric of anachronism', *Comparative Literature*, 61: 69–84.

Lyttelton, G. (1760) *Dialogues of the Dead* (London).

MacLeod, M. D. (1991) (ed.) *Lucian: A Selection* (Warminster).

Maiorano, N. (1542–50) *Eustathiou archiepiskopou Thessalonikēs Parekbolai eis tēn Homērou Iliada kai Odysseian* (Rome).

Malherbe, J. (1860) 'A M. Charma', *Bulletin de la Societé des Antiquaires de Normandie*, 1: 273–5.

Manzoni, A. ([1850] 1996) *Del romanzo storico*, in id., *Scritti teorici* (Catania) 25–76.

Marchand, S. (1996) *Down from Olympus* (Princeton).

Marolles, M. de (1662) *Traité du poème épique, pour l'intelligence de l'Énéide de Virgile* (Paris).

Marsh, D. (1998) *Lucian and the Latins* (Ann Arbor).

Martindale, C. and M. Martindale (1990) *Shakespeare and the Uses of Antiquity* (London).

Marx, K. and F. Engels (1975–) *The Collected Works of Marx and Engels* (New York).
Mastronarde, D. (1994) (ed.) *Euripides: Phoenissae* (Cambridge).
Mastronarde, D. (2002) (ed.) *Euripides: Medea* (Cambridge).
May, J. M. (2016) (trans.) *Marcus Tullius Cicero: How to Win an Argument* (Princeton).
Mazzoni, J. (1587) *Della difesa della commedia di Dante* (Cesena).
McCabe, M. M. (2000) *Plato and His Predecessors* (Cambridge).
Meek, R. L. (1976) *Social Science and the Ignoble Savage* (Cambridge).
Messeri, G. and R. Pintaudi (2002) 'Ostraca greci da Narmouthis', *Chronique d'Égypte*, 77: 209–37.
Michaud, P.-A. ([1998] 2007) *Aby Warburg and the Image in Motion*, trans. S. Hawkes (New York).
Miller, J. H. (2010) 'Anachronistic reading', *Derrida Today*, 3: 75–91.
Moles, J. L. (1996) 'Herodotus warns the Athenians', *Papers of the Leeds International Latin Seminar*, 9: 259–84.
Möller, A. and N. Luraghi (1995) 'Time in the writing of history', *Storia della storiografia* 28: 3–15.
Momigliano, A. (1966) 'Time in ancient historiography', *History and Theory*, 6: 1–23.
Monoson, S. (1998) 'Remembering Pericles: the political and theoretical Import of Plato's *Menexenus*', *Political Theory*, 26: 489–513.
Montagu, R. (1642) *The Acts and Monuments of the Church before Christ Incarnate* (London).
Montanari, F., S. Matthaios and A. Rengakos (2015) (eds) *Brill's Companion to Ancient Greek Scholarship* (Leiden and Boston).
Montesquieu, C. L. de Secondat, Baron de ([1734] 1999) *Considerations on the Causes of the Greatness of the Romans and their Decline*, trans. D. Lowenthal (Indianapolis).
Morrow, G. R. (1960) *Plato's Cretan City* (Princeton).
Mosshammer, A. A. (1979) *The Chronicle of Eusebius and Greek Chronographic Tradition* (Lewisburg, PA).
Most, G. W. (1992) 'Il poeta nell'Ade', *Studi italiani di filologia classica*, 85: 1014–26.
Most, G. W. (1996) 'Reading Raphael', *Critical Inquiry*, 23: 145–82.
Most, G. W. (2004) 'Anachronisms', *Scientia Poetica*, 8: 294–7.
Most, G. W. (2006) 'Athens as the School of Greece', in J. Porter (ed.), *Classical Pasts* (Princeton) 377–88.
Mueller, M. (2016) *Objects as Actors* (Chicago).
Näf, B. (1986) *Von Perikles zu Hitler?* (Bern and New York).
Nagel, A. and C. Wood (2010) *Anachronic Renaissance* (New York).
Nails, D. (2002) *The People of Plato* (Indianapolis).
Nelsestuen, G. A. (2017) 'Varro, Dicaearchus, and the history of Roman *Res rusticae*', *Bulletin of the Institute of Classical Studies*, 60: 21–33.
Newton, I. (1728) *The Chronology of Ancient Kingdoms Amended* (London).
Ní Mheallaigh, K. (2014) *Reading Fiction with Lucian* (Cambridge).
Nietzsche, F. ([1873–6] 1997) *Untimely Meditations*, trans. R. J. Hollingdale (Cambridge).

Nietzsche, F. ([1878] 1996) *Human All Too Human*, trans. R. J. Hollingdale (Cambridge).
Noll, T. (2016) 'The visual image of Alexander the Great', in M. Stock (ed.), *Alexander the Great in the Middle Ages* (Toronto) 244–63.
North, J. (1976) 'Conservatism and change in Roman religion', *Papers of the British School at Rome*, 44: 1–12.
Nota, E. and U. Dotti (2002–13) (eds) *Pétrarque: Lettres de la vieillesse* (Paris).
Nothaft, C. P. E. (2012) *Dating the Passion* (Leiden and Boston).
Nünlist, R. (2009) *The Ancient Critic at Work* (Cambridge).
Nünlist, R. (2012) 'A chapter in the history of Greek linguistics', *Rheinisches Museum*, 155: 152–65.
O'Malley, J. W. (1977) 'The Vatican Library and the School of Athens', *Journal of Medieval and Renaissance Studies*, 7: 271–87.
Oswald, A. (2011) *Memorial* (London).
Oswald, A. (2015) 'Unleashing a forgotten kind of energy', *Daily Telegraph*, 23 December 2015, 29.
Pagden, A. ([1982] 1986) *The Fall of Natural Man* (Cambridge).
Panofsky, E. ([1955] 1970) *Meaning in the Visual Arts* (Harmondsworth).
Panofsky, E. ([1960] 1970) *Renaissance and Renascences in Western Art* (London).
Papadopoulou, T. (1999) 'Literary theory and terminology in the Greek tragic scholia', *Bulletin of the Institute of Classical Studies*, 43: 203–10.
Pappas, N. and Zelcer, M. (2014) *Politics and Philosophy in Plato's Menexenus* (London).
Parker, R. C. T. (2005) *Polytheism and Society at Athens* (Oxford).
Parker, V. (1998) '*Turannos*: the semantics of a political concept from Archilochus to Aristotle', *Hermes*, 126: 145–72.
Parry, A. (1963) 'The two voices of Virgil's *Aeneid*', *Arion*, 2: 66–80.
Pattison, M. ([1860] 1889) 'Joseph Scaliger', in id., *Essays* (Oxford) 1.132–95.
Pelling, C. B. R. (1997) (ed.) *Greek Tragedy and the Historian* (Oxford).
Pelling, C. B. R. (2000) *Literary Texts and the Greek Historian* (London).
Pelling, C. B. R. (2011) (ed.) *Plutarch: Caesar* (Oxford).
Perkell, C. (2002) 'The Golden Age and its contradictions in the poetry of Vergil', *Vergilius*, 48: 3–39.
Petit, A. (1985) *L'Anachronisme dans les romans antiques du XIIe siècle* (Université de Lille III).
Pfeiffer, W. (1993) 'Zur Ikonographie der Alexanderschlacht Albrecht Altdorfers', *Münchner Jahrbuch der bildenden Kunst*, 44: 73–97.
Phillips, M. S. (2013) *On Historical Distance* (New Haven).
Phillips, T. R. (2020) *Untimely Epic: Apollonius Rhodius' Argonautica* (Oxford).
Pinkster, H. (2015) *Oxford Latin Syntax* (Oxford).
Pocock, J. G. A. ([1957] 1987) *The Ancient Constitution and the Feudal Law* (Cambridge).
Pocock, J. G. A. (1999–2016) *Barbarism and Religion* (Cambridge).

Pollmann, J. (2017) *Memory in Early Modern Europe, 1500–1800* (Oxford).
Pope, A. (1871–89) *The Works of Alexander Pope* (London).
Potts, A. (1994) *Flesh and the Ideal* (New Haven).
Prauscello, L. (2017) 'Plato *Laws* 3.680B–C: Antisthenes, the Cyclopes and Homeric exegesis', *Journal of Hellenic Studies*, 137: 8–23.
Pressly, W. L. (2014) *James Barry's Murals at the Royal Society of Arts* (Cork).
Price, S. R. F. (1986) 'The future of dreams', *Past and Present*, 113: 3–37.
Ralegh, W. (1614) *The History of the World* (London).
Rancière, J. ([1996] 2015) 'The concept of anachronism and the historian's truth', trans. T. Stott and N. Fitzpatrick, *InPrint*, 3: 21–48.
Rawson, E. (1985) *Intellectual Life in the Late Roman Republic* (London).
Relihan, J. C. (1993) *Ancient Menippean Satire* (Baltimore).
Ricchieri, L. C. (1542) *Lectionum antiquarum libri triginta* (Basel).
Rider Haggard, H. (1885) *King Solomon's Mines* (London).
Rider Haggard, H. (1887) *She* (London).
Rigolot, F. (1998) 'The Renaissance crisis of exemplarity', *Journal of the History of Ideas*, 59: 557–63.
Rijser, D. (2005) 'Fedra and the "Phaedrus"', *Bruniana & Campanelliana*, 11: 345–63.
Rijser, D. (2012) *Raphael's Poetics* (Amsterdam).
Rijser, D. (2018) 'Tradition and originality in Raphael' in K. A. E. Enenkel and K. A. Ottenheym (eds), *The Quest for an Appropriate Past in Literature, Art and Architecture* (Leiden and Boston).
Ritter, H. (1986) *Dictionary of Concepts in History* (New York).
Robertson, J. (1788) *The Parian Chronicle* (London).
Robertson, P. (1996) *Guilty Pleasures* (London).
Robinson, C. (1979) *Lucian and his Influence in Europe* (London).
Robinson, J. H. (1912) *New History* (New York).
Robortello, F. (1552) *Scholia in Aeschyli tragoedias omnes* (Venice).
Robortello, F. (1555) *In librum Aristotelis de arte Poëtica explicationes* (Basel).
Roller, M. B. (2018) *Models from the Past in Roman Culture* (Cambridge).
Ronen, A. (1993) 'The chariot of Darius', *Münchner Jahrbuch der bildenden Kunst*, 44: 99–117.
Rood, T. C. B. (2007) 'Polybius', in I. J. F. de Jong and R. Nünlist (eds), *Time in Ancient Greek Narrative* (Leiden and Boston) 165–81.
Rood, T. C. B. (2010) *American Anabasis* (London).
Rood, T. C. B. (2011) 'Black Sea variations', *Cambridge Classical Journal*, 57: 135–61.
Rood, T. C. B. (2015) 'The reception of Thucydides' *Archaeology*', in N. Morley and C. M.-W. Lee (eds), *A Handbook to the Reception of Thucydides* (Malden, MA) 174–92.
Rood, T. C. B. (2016) 'Mapping spatial and temporal distance', in E. T. E. Barker, C. B. R. Pelling, S. Bouzorovski and L. Isaksen (eds), *New Worlds out of Old Texts* (Oxford) 101–20.
Rotstein, A. (2016) *Literary History in the Parian Marble* (Cambridge, MA).

Rowland, I. (1997) 'The intellectual background of the *School of Athens*', in M. Hall (ed.), *Raphael's 'School of Athens'* (Cambridge) 131–70.
Rowland, I. (2018), 'Raphael's eminent *philosophes*', in J. Miller (ed.), *Diogenes Laertius: Lives of the Eminent Philosophers* (Oxford) 554–61.
Ruehl, M. A. (2015) *The Italian Renaissance in the German Historical Imagination, 1860–1930* (Cambridge).
Ruthven, K. K. (2004) 'Preposterous Chatterton', *English Literary History*, 71: 345–75.
Rykwert, J. (1972) *On Adam's House in Paradise* (New York).
Sale, G., G. Psalmanazar, A. Bower, G. Shelvocke, J. Cambell and J. Swinton (1736–44) *An Universal History, from the Earliest Account of Time to the Present* (London).
Samuel, A. E. (1972) *Greek and Roman Chronology* (Munich).
Sandbach, F. H. (1965–6) 'Anti-antiquarianism in the *Aeneid*', *Proceedings of the Virgil Society*, 5: 26–38.
Scaliger, J. J. (1583) *Opus nouum de emendatione temporum* (Paris).
Scaliger, J. J. (1598) *Opus nouum de emendatione temporum*, 2nd edn (Leiden).
Scaliger, J. J. (1606) *Thesaurus temporum* (Leiden).
Scheibel, E. (1852) *Iosephi Scaligeri Olumpiadōn anagraphē* (Berlin).
Schiffman, Z. S. (2011) *The Birth of the Past* (Baltimore).
Schironi, F. (2018) *The Best of the Grammarians* (Ann Arbor).
Schlegel, F. von ([1805] 1959) 'Dritter Nachtrag alter Gemälde', in id., *Ansichten und Ideen von der Christlichen Kunst*, ed. H. Eichner (Munich, Paderborn and Vienna) 116–52.
Schlegel, F. von ([1815] 1818) *Lectures on the History of Literature, Ancient and Modern*, trans. S. J. G. Lockhart (Philadelphia).
Schlegel, F. von (1988) 'From Descriptions of Paintings from Paris and the Netherlands in the Years 1802 to 1804', trans P. Wortsman and G. Schiff, in G. Schiff (ed.), *German Essays on Art History* (New York) 59–72.
Schlesier, R. (1994) *Kulte, Mythen und Gelehrte. Anthropologie der Antike seit 1800* (Frankfurt).
Schmidt, M. (1976) *Die Erklärungen zum Weltbild Homers und zur Kultur der Heroenzeit in den bT-Scholien zur Ilias* (Munich).
Schwenk, R. (1895) *De anachronismis apud Euripidem obviis* (Hof).
Scott, W. ([1814] 1985) *Waverley* (Harmondsworth).
Scott, W. (1814–17) *Border Antiquities* (London and Edinburgh).
Scott, W. ([1818] 2008) *Rob Roy* (Edinburgh).
Scott, W. ([1820] 1996) *Ivanhoe* (Oxford).
Scott, W. ([1823] 2007) *Peveril of the Peak* (Edinburgh).
Scott, W. (2012) *Introductions and Notes from the Magnum Opus*, ed. J. H. Alexander, P. Garside and C. Lamont (Edinburgh).
Seaford, R. (1994) *Ritual and Reciprocity* (Oxford).
Seaford, R. (2004) *Money and the Early Greek Mind* (Cambridge).
Sedley, D. (2003) *Plato's Cratylus* (Cambridge).
Segrais, J. R. de (1668) *Traduction de l'Eneïde de Virgile* (Paris).

Serres, M. ([1997] 2000) *The Birth of Physics*, trans. J. Hawkes (Manchester).
Serres, M. and B. Latour ([1992] 1995) *Conversations on Science, Culture, and Time*, trans. R. Lapidus (Ann Arbor).
Shaw, P.-J. (2003) *Discrepancies in Olympiad Dating and Chronological Problems of Archaic Peloponnesian History* (Stuttgart).
Sikes, E. E. (1914) *The Anthropology of the Greeks* (London).
Skinner, Q. (1969) 'Meaning and understanding in the history of ideas', *History and Theory*, 8: 3–53.
Sluiter, I. (2016) 'Anchoring innovation', *European Review*, 25: 20–38.
Soby, J. T. (1955) *Giorgio de Chirico* (New York).
Society of Dilettanti (1797) *Antiquities of Ionia* (London).
Sorel, A. (1891) 'Notice sur les travaux de Fustel de Coulanges', *Séances et travaux de l'Académie des Sciences Morales et Politiques*, 135: 5–44.
Sourvinou-Inwood, C. (2003) *Tragedy and Athenian Religion* (Lanham, MD).
Steinberg, M. P. (1995), 'Aby Warburg's Kreuzlingen lecture', in A. Warburg, *Images from the Region of the Pueblo Indians of North America* (Ithaca) 59–114.
Steiner, D. (2016) 'Harmonic divergence', *Journal of Hellenic Studies*, 136: 132–51.
Stemplinger, E. (1956) 'Antike Anachronismen', *Altertum*, 2: 103–6.
Stern, F. (1970) (ed.) *The Varieties of History* (London).
Stern, S. (2003) *Time and Process in Ancient Judaism* (Oxford).
Stern, S. (2012) *Calendars in Antiquity* (Oxford).
Stocking, G. (1987) *Victorian Anthropology* (New York).
Stok, F. (2016) 'Storie a anacronismi nell'esegesi serviana', in A. Garcea, M.-K. Lhommé and D. Vallat (eds), *Fragments d'érudition* (Hildesheim, Zurich and New York) 415–34.
Strauss, G. (1963) *Historian in an Age of Crisis* (Cambridge, MA).
Stricker, J. A. (1880) *De tragicorum anachronismis* (Amsterdam).
Swain, S. (1996) *Hellenism and Empire* (Oxford).
Swift, J. ([1726] 1940) *Gulliver's Travels* (London).
Taplin, O. (1986) 'Fifth-century tragedy and comedy', *Journal of Hellenic Studies*, 106: 163–74.
Taplin, O. (2007) 'Some assimilations of the Homeric simile in later twentieth-century poetry', in B. Graziosi and E. Greenwood (eds), *Homer in the Twentieth Century* (Oxford) 177–90.
Tasso, T. ([1587, 1594] 1964) *Discorsi dell' Arte poetica e del Poema eroico*, ed. L. Poma (Bari).
Tasso, T. ([1594] 1973) *Discourses on the Heroic Poem*, trans. M. Cavalchini and I. Samuel (Oxford).
Taylor, M. R. (2002) (ed.) *Giorgio de Chirico and the Myth of Ariadne* (London).
Taylor, P. (2009) 'Julius II and the Stanza della Signatura', *Journal of the Warburg and Courtauld Institutes*, 72: 103–41.
Teng, E. J. (2004) *Taiwan's Imagined Geography* (Cambridge, MA).

Thompson, A. H. (1911) (ed.) *John Dryden: Virgil's Aeneid* (Cambridge).
Todd, W. B. and A. Bowden (1998) *Sir Walter Scott: A Bibliographical History, 1796–1832* (New Castle, DE).
Tomba, M. ([2011] 2013) *Marx's Temporalities*, trans. P. D. Thomas and S. R. Farris (Leiden).
Torzi, I. (2000) *Ratio et usus* (Milan).
Traill, H. D. (1884) *The New Lucian* (London).
Trapp, M. (2000) 'Plato in the *Deipnosophistae*', in D. Braund and J. Wilkins (eds), *Athenaeus and his World* (Exeter) 353–63.
Tribble, E. B. and J. Sutton (2012) 'Minds in and out of time', *Textual Practice*, 26: 587–607.
Tuplin, C. J. (1991) 'Darius' Suez canal and Persian imperialism', in H. Sancisi-Weerdenburg and A. T. Kuhrt (eds), *Achaemenid History VI* (Leiden) 237–83.
Tylor, E. B. (1871) *Primitive Culture* (London).
Valk, M. van der (1971) *Eustathii archiepiscopi Thessalonicensis Commentarii ad Homeri Iliadem pertinentes* (Leiden).
Valla, L. (1511) 'Commentarii', in *Hoc in volumine haec opera continentur omnia: C. Crispi Salustii vita, etc.* (Venice).
Vannicelli, P. (2001) 'Herodotus' Egypt and the foundations of universal history', in N. Luraghi (ed.), *The Historian's Craft in the Age of Herodotus* (Oxford) 211–40.
Vasari, G. ([1550] 1998) *Lives of the Artists*, trans. J. C. and P. Bondanella (Oxford).
Verdicts of the Learned concerning Virgil and Homer's Heroic Poems ([1697] 1814) in W. Scott (ed.), *A Collection of Scarce and Valuable Tracts on the Most Interesting and Entertaining Subjects* (London) 12.1–19.
Vernant, J.-P. and P. Vidal-Naquet ([1972] 1988) *Myth and Tragedy in Ancient Greece*, trans. J. Lloyd (New York).
Veyne, P. ([1971] 1984) *Writing History*, trans. M. Moore-Rinvolucri (Manchester).
Vico, G. ([1725] 2002) *The First New Science*, trans. L. Pompa (Cambridge).
Vico, G. ([1744] 1999) *New Science*, trans. D. Marsh (London).
Vlassopoulos, K. (2007) *Unthinking the Polis* (Cambridge).
Voltaire (1765–75) *Nouveaux mélanges philosophiques, historiques, critiques* (Geneva).
Voltaire (1786) *Oeuvres complètes de Voltaire* (Gotha).
Walbank, F. (1957–79) *A Historical Commentary on Polybius* (Oxford).
Wallace, R. W. (2016) 'Redating Croesus', *Journal of Hellenic Studies*, 136: 168–81.
Wallace-Hadrill, A. (1982) 'The Golden Age and sin in Augustan ideology', *Past and Present*, 95: 19–36.
Wallace-Hadrill, A. (2008) *Rome's Cultural Revolution* (Cambridge).
Warburg, A. (1995) *Images from the Region of the Pueblo Indians of North America*, ed. M. P. Steinberg (Ithaca).
Warton, T. (1778–81) *The History of English Poetry* (London).
Wasmuth, E. (2015) '*Hōsper hoi Korubantiōntes*: the Corybantic rites in Plato's Dialogues', *Classical Quarterly*, 65: 69–84.
Waugh, E. ([1932] 1962) *Black Mischief* (London).

Weiberg, E. L. (2018) 'Weapons as friends and foes in Sophocles' *Ajax* and Euripides' *Heracles*', in M. Mueller and M. Telò (eds), *The Materialities of Greek Tragedy* (London) 63–77.
Weinbrot, H. D. (2005) *Menippean Satire Reconsidered* (Baltimore).
West, A. (2007) 'Exemplary painting of Hans Burgkmair the Elder', in R. C. Head and D. Christensen (eds), *Orthodoxies and Heterodoxies in Early Modern German Culture* (Leiden) 197–225.
West, D. (1995) (ed.) *Horace: Odes III* (Oxford).
West, M. L. (1978) (ed.) *Hesiod: Works and Days* (Oxford).
West, M. L. (1985) *The Hesiodic Catalogue of Women* (Oxford).
Whitmarsh, T. J. G. (2001) *Greek Literature and the Roman Empire* (Oxford).
Wiater, N. (2019) 'Experiencing the past', in R. L. Hunter and C. C. de Jonge (eds), *Dionysius of Halicarnassus and Augustan Rome* (Cambridge) 56–82.
Wilamowitz-Moellendorff, U. von (1908) *Greek Historical Writing and Apollo*, trans. G. Murray (Oxford).
Wilcox, D. J. (1987) *The Measure of Times Past* (Chicago).
Wilde, O. ([1890] 2000) 'The Critic as Artist', in *The Major Works*, ed. I. Murray (Oxford) 241–97.
Williams, R. (2017) *Raphael and the Redefinition of Art in Renaissance Italy* (Cambridge).
Wilson, N. G. ([1992] 2017) *From Byzantium to Italy* (London).
Winckelmann, J. J. ([1764] 2006) *History of the Art of Antiquity*, trans. H. F. Mallgrave (Los Angeles).
Womersley, D. (1997) (ed.) *Augustan Critical Writing* (Harmondsworth).
Wood, J. (1988) 'Cannibalized prints and early art history', *Journal of the Warburg and Courtauld Institutes*, 51: 210–20
Woolf, G. (2011) *Tales of the Barbarians* (Malden, MA).
Zeller, E. (1873) 'Über die Anachronismen in den platonischen Gesprächen', *Abhandlungen der Königlichen Akademie der Wissenschaften zu Berlin*, 79–99.
Zetzel, J. E. G. (1989) '*Romane memento*: justice and judgement in *Aeneid 6*', *Transactions of the American Philological Association*, 119: 263–84.
Zetzel, J. E. G. (2018) *Critics, Compilers, and Commentators* (New York).

Index

Abraham 94
　year of 95, 110
Achilles 69–70, 84, 107, 158–9, 175, 188–9, 195–6
Aeschines (1.142–50) 84, (2.89–92) 238 n.17
Aeschines of Sphettus 207
Aeschylus 16–17, 64, 79, 83–4, 213, 220
　Agamemnon (433–44) 237 n.14
　Cabiri 79
　Libation-bearers 80
　Myrmidons 84
　Philoctetes 219–20
Aesop, Life of (G32) 60
Aetius, *On the Opinions of Philosophers* (880e) 77–8
agriculture 87, 102, 121, 125, 128, 132, 226
Agrippa, Marcus Vipsanius 137
Agrippa Menenius Lanatus 161
Ajax 67, 70, 138, 175–6, 190–3, 195
Alexander of Aetolia (fr. 19) 239 n.44
Alexander III of Macedon 18, 21, 38, 43, 45–7, 50–1, 89, 97, 145, 147, 185, 203, 215–16
Alexander Romance 48, 49
Alexandria 12, 63, 97, 164
Altdorfer, Albrecht 45–52, 62
Amazons 15, 59, 187
America, indigenous peoples 119–21, 123, 124, 142–3
Anacharsis 141, 237 n.15
Anacharsis, Epistles of (5) 141
anachronic 10–12, 29, 88, 189, 193, 221
Anachronic Renaissance (Nagel and Wood) 10–12, 177, 184, 185, 186, 188, 205
anachronicism 19–20
anachronism
　and authorial licence 3–4, 18, 21, 71–2, 77, 88–91, 201–2
　and authorial persona 76–80
　character vs narrator perspectives 18, 69–71, 72–3, 85

　conscious and unconscious 35, 45, 48, 50, 55, 87, 92, 219
　etymology 11–15
　history of the word 6–7, 9–31, 35, 59, 91, 94, 124
　vs linear time 10
　necessary 26, *passim*
　practical 25, 31
　of reading 33, 38–9, 218–22
　see also chronology; hindsight; historicism; multitemporality; past, the; philology; retrojection; survival, anachronistic; textual criticism
anaprosōpismos 17
anatopismos 17, 250 n.13
anatropismos 17
Anaxagoras 61, 115, 223
Anchises 193, 195–8, 211
anchors 60, 76, 245 n.40
Andron of Ephesus, *The Tripod* 231 n.5
Annales school 28, 29
Antenor (sculptor) 184–5
Anthologia Graeca (16.151) 240 n.18
anthropology 30, 120–1, 124, 143
antichronism 22
anticipatio 233 n.54
Antigonus of Carystus 239 n.39
antiquarianism 3, 48, 63, 87, 125, 127, 143, 155
Antisthenes 141, 153, 215
Antony, Mark 162, 197, 238 n.17
Apianus, Petrus 95
Apollo Belvedere 204
Apollodorus of Athens (*FGrH* 244) 108, (F32) 114
Apollonius of Rhodes
　Argonautica 244 n.29, (2.1169–76) 187–8, 189
　see also Scholia on Apollonius of Rhodes
Appian, *Punic Wars* (1) 88

Arcadia 99–100, 132
archaeology 97
archaic 4, 33, 130, 153, 155, 171, 186, 246 n.63
archaism 132–3, 186, 248 n.21
architecture 3, 26, 35, 49, 50, 60, 69, 127, 138, 170, 186–7
Ariadne 169–73, 193, 195, 204, 243 n.70
Aristarchus 63, 66–7, 72, 83, 218
Aristides (Athenian) 213
Aristides, Aelius (3.577–82, 4.50–1) 207, 210, 211
Aristophanes 64, 83, 223, 226
  Acharnians 212
  Birds (483–521) 126–7
  Clouds 130, 212, (607–26) 103, (984–5) 134
  Farmers (fr. 101a) 126
  Frogs 213, 216, 219, (890, 952, 959–61) 64
  Knights 212
  Wasps (1476–81) 129–30
  Wealth 237 n.16
Aristotle 89, 199, 201, 205, 212, 216, 227
  Metaphysics (Book 1) 250 n.11
  Nicomachean Ethics 199, (1100a10–1101a21) 253 n.13
  Physics (220a25–6) 179–80
  Poetics (1449a15–18) 100, (1451b5–11) 155, (1454b14–15) 159, (1460a28–32) 17, 80–1, 82–3, (1461a30) 245 n.38
  Politics (1252b19–26) 137, (1268b22–69a12) 132, (1274a25–31) 243 n.67, (Book 5) 157–8
  Rhetoric (1375b29–30) 67, (1393a23–94a18) 152, 153–4
Arminius 216, 217
Arrian
  Anabasis (3.5.7) 145, (3.16.7–8) 185, (7.30.3) 145
  On Hunting (1.4) 150, (16.7) 149–50
  and Xenophon 146, 149–50
Arriphon of Triconium 66
Artemidorus, *Interpretation of Dreams* (1.64) 128–9
artworks, *see* Mosaic of the Philosophers; painting; statues
Asconius 23

Aspasia 207, 210
Athenaeus, *Deipnosophists* 63, 85, 207, 208, 210, (1.12b) 237 n.15, (1.17) 79, (3.116d) 237 n.16, (4.137e) 245 n.52, (4.183c) 100, (5.216c–18e) 207, 233 nn.52, 54, 242 n.40, (10.428f) 79, (11.476a) 127, (11.483c) 245 n.51, (11.505f–6a) 207, (14.635e–f) 113–14, (14.660e–61d) 131
Athenion, *Samothracians* (fr. 1) 131
Athens, city of
  acropolis 126, 134, 185, 212, 228
  agora 59, 184–5
  Ceramicus 185
  Stoa Poikile 59
Athens, history of
  amnesty 30, 157
  empire 5, 136
  Sicilian Expedition 95–6, 110, 114
  see also democracy, Athenian
athletics 128, 132, 136, 207, 219
  festivals 227; *see also* Delia; Olympic games; Pythia
Atticus (*FRHist* 33) 40, (F8) 111
Augustine 56
  City of God (4.31) 139
  Confessions (1.13) 91, (11.27–8) 179
Augustus 40, 84, 101, 103, 127, 137, 142, 162, 197, 249 n.10
Aurelius Victor, Ps.-, *Origin of the Roman People* (3.4–5) 245 n.32
Ausonius, Ps.-, *Epigrams* (118) 240 n.18
Aventinus (Johannes Turmaier) 49, 51

Bacchus, *see* Dionysus
Baronio, Cesare 94
Barry, James 223–8
Barthélemy, Jean-Jacques 18
battering rams 60
battles, *see* Gaugamela; Issus; Marathon; Plataea; Thermopylae
Bellori, Giovanni Pietro 200–10
Bentley, Richard 23, 216, 251 n.54
Berossus 23, 94
Bible
  Daniel 47, 49, 238 n.29
  Genesis 94
  Judges 21

Judith 94
New Testament 41, 94
Revelation 34, 47
Septuagint 23 n.70
Bion of Borysthenes (fr. 3) 80
Bloch, Ernst 123
Blount, Thomas 19, 20
Bolingbroke, Lord (Henry St John) 21–2
boomerangs 143
Borges, Jorge Luis 33, 38
bows and arrows 122
Britain 21, 28, 52, 121, 135, 138, 148, 223–6
    empire 10
    see also Scotland
Bromley, Robert 201–2, 225
Brunt, Peter 145
Brutus, Lucius Junius 43, 67, 165
Brutus, Marcus Junius 185
Buphonia 134–5
Burke, Peter 15, 16, 37, 39
Burney, Susan 223
Burroughs, Edgar Rice 123
Bury, J. B. 36–7
Busiris 110, 115
Butterfield, Herbert 28
Button, Edward 88

Caeneus 107, 196
Caesar, Gaius Julius 40–1, 48, 52, 53, 85, 101–2, 139, 185, 197, 203, 207
Caieta 72
calendars 98–103
    Athenian 98, 102, 103, 104, 105, 109
    Egyptian 103, 242 n.25
    intercalation 4, 98–100, 102
    Kalends 44, 101
    month names 101
    Roman 99–102, 104
    Spartan 105
Callias 206, 211
Callimachus, *Iambs* (1) 231 n.5
Callisthenes 81
Calvin, John 19, 23
Canopus Decree 103
Capua, foundation of 110, 112–13
Carneia 110, 113
Carthage 88–92, 114, 146, 163
Cassius Longinus, Gaius 185

Cassius Dio, *Roman History* (45.32.4) 238 n .17, (47.20.4) 185, (52.1, 9) 137, (53.8.3–4) 162, (61.17.4) 163, (64.13.2) 156
Castelvetro, Lodovico 17–18, 80–1
Castor of Rhodes (*FGrH* 250) 97, 106
Catiline (Lucius Sergius Catilina) 196, 197
Cato the Elder (*FRHist* 5) 154, 167, 210, (F52) 112–13, (F64) 65
Censorinus, *On the Birthday* (16.4) 180–1, (18, 19) 100, (20.1) 242 n.44, (21) 107, (22.8) 101, (22.11) 242 n.29, (23.7) 127–8
Cervantes, Miguel de 33, 38
Chakrabarty, Dipesh 10
chariots 48, 138, 223
    racing 17, 69, 80–2, 153, 225
Charles IV (Holy Roman Emperor) 40
Charon 2, 195, 212, 216
Chateaubriand, François-René de 90
Chatham, Earl of (William Pitt the Elder) 225, 228
Chechens 124
childhood 64, 112, 119, 122, 125, 130, 190
chivalry 3, 26, 38, 48, 50–1
chronography 81, 93, 94–5, 97, 103, 106–7, 115
chronology
    archon dates 104, 106, 107, 108, 109, 132, 207, 210
    chronological errors 1–2, 3–4, 14–15, 18–22, 24, 87–92, 110–16, 225–6
    comparative 94, 116–17
    consul dates 44, 104, 106, 107, 111, 112
    dating systems 103–10
    generational dating 15, 91, 107, 115, 240 n.23
    history of the word 97
    king-lists 94, 106, 107, 243 n.70
    Olympiad dating 74, 95, 97, 103, 104, 106, 107, 108, 109, 111, 113, 226
    regnal years 13, 40, 95, 106, 109, 110
    tables 19–20, 95–7, 109
Cicero 23, 39, 40, 42, 148, 164
    Brutus 178, (72–3) 114, (218–19) 207
    For Caelius 165–7, (26) 135
    For Cluentius (94) 154
    For Gallius 208
    Laws 208

On Duties (3.39) 42, (3.111) 163–4
On Invention (1.51–3) 250 n.27
On the Nature of the Gods (2.87) 128
On Old Age 210, (16) 167
On the Orator (2.36) 147, 152, (3.42) 245 n.49, (3.45) 130–1
Philippics 249 n.8, (2.97) 238 n.17
Republic 208, 210, (2.16) 245 n.43, (2.28–9) 243 n.69, (6.12–33) 211, 249 n.1
Tusculan Disputations (5.90) 246 n.75
Cincinnatus, Lucius Quinctius 164
Clement of Alexandria 116
  Miscellanies (1.117) 113
Cleopatra 142, 164, 170, 204, 207
Cloelia 146–7
clothing 3, 47-8, 55, 121, 126, 135, 136, 138, 227
cognitive science 10, 177, 179
coins 41, 121, 125, 127, 128
Coleridge, Samuel Taylor 25, 31
Collingwood, R. G. 37
Comedy, Old 61, 83, 212
commentaries (*hupomnēmata*) 12, 20–1, 23, 31, 44, 62–5, 82, 84, 97, 103, 104; *see also* Eustathius; scholia; Servius
commerce 114, 121, 126, 140, 226
Constantine, Donation of 3, 42–5, 52, 53
Conversations of Poets and Philosophers 208
Cooper, James Fenimore 124, 142
Coulanges, N. D. Fustel de 27–8
countryside 100, 122, 123, 128, 135, 140, 161, 226, 247 n.32
Crete 141, 193, 235 n.39
Critias (DK 88) 78, 148, (B18) 102, (B25) 241 n.23
Croesus 1–6, 13, 55, 95, 98, 116, 215, 229
Cromwell, Henry 26
Cronus 130
Crusades 50, 89, 123
Curius Dentatus, Manius 146, 164
Curtius Rufus, *History of Alexander* (3.3.19) 236 n.51
Cyclopes 25, 137, 141
Cynics 112, 141, 213, 214, 215
Cyrus 1–3, 5, 218, 247 n.13

Dacier, Anne 252 n.61
Daedalus 107, 193

dancing 129, 221, 233 n.49
Dante 18, 54, 204
Darius I 21, 154, 215
Darius III 21, 47, 48
De Acosta, José 121
De Chirico, Giorgio 169–73, 204
declamation 41–2, 85, 151, 165, 178–9
Delia 81–2
democracy 28, 30, 137, 141, 228
  Athenian 4, 59, 61, 64, 102, 148, 185, 192, 213
  Roman 137, 185
Democritus 125, 223
Demosthenes 60, 220–1, (18.225) 238 n.17
Dennis, John 89–90
De Piles, Roger 202
De Quincey, Thomas 25
development
  bestial to rational 24, 131–2, 138, 226–7
  disorder to order 99
  Marxist theories of 122–3
  simple to complex 57, 63, 99, 101, 103, 127, 128, 168
  simple to corrupt/luxurious 43, 80, 131, 139
  small to big 100
  sporadic to global 57
  stadial theories of 25, 121
  uneven 99, 117, 119–25, 136–7
  see also luxury; simplicity, ancient
Dexippus (*FGrH* 100) 106
Diagoras of Rhodes 223–4, 226, 227
dialect 66, 140, 237 n.16
dialogues, anachronistic 1–6, 18, 95, 199–218
Dicaearchus, *Life of Greece* 128
Diderot, Denis 88
Didi-Huberman, Georges 10–11, 120
Dido 196; *see also* Virgil, Dido/Aeneas anachronism
Didymus 252 n.61
Dipolieia 134–5
Dinshaw, Carolyn 9–10
Dio Chrysostom (36) 140, (52) 219–20, (55) 219
Diodorus, *Historical Library* 95, 104, 106, 108, 110, 152, (1.8.1) 241 n.23, (1.14.2, 43.2) 245 n.54, (1.43.4) 138,

(3.56.3) 236 n.74, (5.4.7) 245 n.54,
  (5.21.5, 28.4, 39.6) 138, (5.42–6)
  139, (12.31.1) 243 n.60, (12.38) 103
Diogenes (cynic) 18, 28, 199, 212, 214,
  215, 217
Diogenes Laertius, *Lives of the*
  Philosophers 115, (Book 1) 5,
  (1.27–33) 231 n.5, (1.33) 5, (1.48)
  67, (1.82) 231 n.5, (1.112) 237 n.16,
  (1.122) 231 n.6, (2.39) 239 n.16,
  (2.43) 41, (2.55) 250 n.27, (2.79) 80,
  (6.102) 251 n.48, (9.23) 209
Dionysia 64, 220
Dionysius of Halicarnassus
  Demosthenes (22) 220–1
  Dinarchus (11, 13) 237 n.16
  Lysias (12) 237 n.16
  Roman Antiquities 77, 108, (1.38.2) 139,
    (1.79.11) 186–7, (2.25.2) 245 n.52,
    (2.59.1–4) 241 n.12, (2.74) 134,
    (4.40.7) 186, (5.17.4) 67–8, (6.11)
    243 n.66, (7.70) 134
Dionysius, Ps.-, *Rhetoric* (11) 152
Dionysus 64, 116, 119, 169, 173, 213, 226
dolphins 182–4
Donatus 63
dreams 44, 112, 128–9, 195, 211, 249 n.1
drinking 79, 84
Dryden, John 88, 89
Dürer, Albrecht 51

Easterling, Pat 62, 70, 73–5
ecocriticism 10
education
  ancient 85, 130, 150–5, 192
  modern 148
Egidio da Viterbo 205
Egypt 12, 13, 56, 98, 100, 103, 115–17, 126,
  138, 145, 152, 154–5
Elpinice 59
Empedocles 114, 201, 212
empires
  succession of 22, 47, 50, 52
  see also Athens, history of; Britain;
    Holy Roman Empire; Persia; Rome,
    history of; Turks
Enetians 73–5
Enlightenment 25, 34, 36, 121, 226

Ennius, *Annales* 197, 249 n.1, (79–81) 69,
  (199–200) 167
Ephorus (*FGrH* 70) (F42) 237 n.15
Ephyre 71, 73, 238 n.31
epic 69, 75–6, 89, 124, 153, 159, 164, 187–9,
  196, 213; *see also* Apollonius of
  Rhodes; Ennius; Homer; Statius;
  Virgil
epic cycle 124
Epicurus 200, 208, 212, 213
Erasmus 16–17, 97, 216
Eratosthenes (*FGrH* 241) 81, 97, 107, (F19)
  114, (F52) 252 n.63
eschatology 34, 47, 197
etymology 11–16, 101, 130, 139, 237 n.16
Eudoxus of Cnidus 100
Euhemerus 139
Eunapius (F1) 105–6
Euphranor (painter) 63
Eupolis 114
  Demes 213
Euripides 64, 75, 76–9, 83–4, 202, 208, 213,
  214, 219–20, 223
  Hecuba (254–5) 77
  Hippolytus (231) 74–5, (952–4) 78
  Medea (232–3) 60–1
  Palamedes 78
  Philoctetes 219–20
  Phoenician Women 14–15
  Phrixus 73
  Sisyphus 78
  Suppliant Women 67–8, (787–8) 102
  Trojan Women (886, 889) 61, 64
  see also Scholia on Euripides
Eusebius of Caesarea 94–7, 104, 108–16
Eustathius 12, 17
  Commentary on Dionysius the Periegete
    (378) 75
  Commentary on the Iliad (1.567–8)
    73–7, (3.785) 70
Eutropius 111
Exekias (painter) 175–8
exemplarity 34, 38, 145–68, 228
  women as *exempla* 43, 49, 146–7,
    165–8, 217

Fabius Maximus, Quintus 197
Fabricius Luscinus, Gaius 146, 164
Favorinus 237 n.16

Febvre, Lucien 28
Fédida, Pierre 177
Feeney, Denis 101–2
Fenelon, F. de Salignac de La Mothe 216–7
Fenestella (*FRHist* 70) 114
Ferguson, Adam 121, 135
festivals, *see* athletics, festivals; Buphonia; Carneia; Dipolieia; Dionysia; Lupercalia; Panathenaea; Terminalia
Ficino, Marsilio 205
Fielding, Henry 18, 252 n.16
Finley, Moses 36–7
Florus 40
Fontenelle, B. Le Bovier de 216–7
food 70, 78–9, 131, 138, 141
forgery 3, 40–5, 52–3, 216, 235 n.29, 238 nn.17, 29
France 30, 54, 89, 90, 138, 216–18
    French Revolution 27, 31, 34, 50, 52, 148
Frazer, J. G. 124
Fréart de Chambray, R. 200, 201
Freud, Sigmund 177
Frontinus, *Stratagems* (1.1) 150
funerals 4, 66–7, 151, 163, 196
    funeral orations 67–8, 210, 235 n.42

Gaetulians 138
Galen 207, (15.172–3 Kühn) 237 n.16
Garamantians 139
Gaugamela, Battle of 48
Gauls 48, 54, 138
Gaza, Theodore, *On Months* (7) 99
Gellius, Aulus, *Attic Nights* 23, 63, (3.15.3) 223, (3.16.16) 242 n.27, (6.3.45–7) 154, (10.16) 72, (14.6.4) 71, (15.20.8) 239 n.44, (17.3) 66, (17.21.16) 103
Geminus, *Introduction to the Phenomena* (8.26) 99, (8.26–59) 100
gender 111–12, 122, 130–1, 146–7, 164, 166, 223; *see also* exemplarity, women as *exempla*
genealogy 107, 196
genre 53–6, 73, 77, 79, 178, 190, 219, 220; *see also* chronography; Comedy, Old; declamation; dialogues; epic; historiography; lost world fiction; satyr plays; tragedy

Germany 11, 25, 34, 45–52, 122, 123, 124, 172
Gibbon, Edward 1, 92
Goethe, Johann von 26
Gombrich, E. H. 202
Gorgias 159, 206–7
Gothic
    art 26, 50
    invasion 247 n.28
Grafton, Anthony 93–4
Grazia, Margreta de 15–16, 21, 43
Gregory, John 18, 22
Grey, Zachary 21
Grote, George 233 n.45

Hales, John 19–20
Hannibal 89–90, 110–11, 214, 216
Hapsburgs 40, 46–7
Harmodius and Aristogiton 160, 184
Harris, Jonathan Gil 177–8, 184
Hartog, François 34, 52
Hearne, Thomas 92
Hecataeus (*FGrH* 1) 107, 115
Hector 69, 124, 138, 158, 191–2, 203
Hegel, G. W. F. 25–6, 122
Heinsius, Daniel 21
Hellanicus (*FGrH* 4) 104, (F85a) 113, (F168a) 112
Helvicus, Christopher 92
Henry IV (Holy Roman Emperor) 40
Heracles 13, 72, 81, 112, 115–6, 160, 195, 211, 239 n.44
Heraclides Ponticus (fr. 160) 127
Heraclids, return of the 106
Heraclitus, *Homeric Problems* (36, 43–51) 247 n.22
Hermippus of Smyrna (*FGrH* Cont. 1026) (F13) 5
Hermogenes, *On Issues* (1.1) 233 n.54
Herodicus of Babylon 207
Herodorus (*FGrH* 31) (F14, F42) 243 n.70
Herodotus 107, 113, 217, 223, 225, 236 n.65, (1 proem) 162, (1.5–6) 55, (1.29–33) 1–6, (1.29.1) 55, (1.32) 98–9, 100, 102, (1.82) 3, (2.4.1) 102, 242 n.24, (2.43) 116, (2.53) 113, 116, (2.134) 243 n.71, (2.143) 115, (2.145) 115–16, (3.40–3) 3, (5.55, 62.2) 160, (5.58.3) 126, 136, (6.108, 109.3) 160, (7.5, 7) 154, (9.27) 160

Herodotus, Ps.-, *Life of Homer* 113, (26) 247 n.24
heroic age 50, 57, 59–71, 74, 76–81, 83–5, 91, 107, 124, 127, 196
Hesiod 67, 113, 116, 203
   Works and Days 139, (43–6) 68, 74
   see also Scholia on Hesiod
Hesiod, Ps.-
   Catalogue of Women 107, 196
   On Saltfish 237 n.16
Hesychius (kappa 4343) 238 n.35
Hiero 223–4
Hieronymus, *On Citharodes* (fr. 33) 113
hindsight 6, 27–9, 85, 198, 228–9
Hippias (*FGrH* 6) 95, 211, (F6) 66, 83
Hippocrates, Ps.-, *On Ancient Medicine* (5.7–12) 246 n.60
Hippodamus of Miletus 132
historicism 10, 31, 34–5, 53, 64, 103, 142
   and exemplarity 145–50, 166, 168
historiography 27–30, 34–7, 55–6, 147, 152
history
   of art 10, 35–6
   New 27
   patterning of 57, 136
   periodization of 24, 30, 52–7, 62, 107
   as process 24–7, 36–7, 49–50, 52, 93, 116, 147, 178
   universal 88, 138
   Whig view of 28, 55
   see also development
Hoecke, Gaspar van den 2
Holland, Philemon 23
Holy Roman Empire 34, 40, 45–52, 122
Homer
   ancient and Byzantine criticism and reception of 14, 63, 64, 66–7, 79, 84, 85, 105, 107, 112, 113, 116, 127, 140, 152–3, 158, 159, 190–2, 196, 203, 214, 218, 219, 220, 237 n.15, 242 n.27, 243 n.70, 247 n.25, 249 n.1
   Iliad 26, 51, 69, 124, 159, 187, 190, 195, 214, (1.12–13, 37–42, 69–70) 180, (1.259–68) 159, (2.135) 66, (2.363) 213, (2.519) 71, (2.557–8) 67, (2.852) 73–4, 75, (3.336) 27, (5.487–8) 245 n.39, (6.152) 73, (6.414) 188, (6.469) 190, (7.303–5) 191, (7.321) 138, (9.186–9) 188–9, (11.244) 62, (18.219) 238 n.21, (18.570) 127, (20.216–18) 137, (20.307–8) 238 n.29, (23.262–652) 81, (24.602–4) 158
   Odyssey 26, 79–80, 124, 251 n.49, (5.371) 238 n.22, (9.112–15) 137, (Book 11) 195–7, 211, 214, 215, 221–2, (18.30) 136, (20.299–300) 79
   post-Byzantine criticism and reception of 39, 41, 50, 69, 89, 121, 123, 204, 228, 252 n.61
   see also Eustathius; Scholia on Homer
Homeric Hymn to Apollo 81–2
Hopi 119–21, 139
Horace
   Art of Poetry (202–19) 100
   Odes (1.11) 181–2, (2.14.1–2) 242 n.36, (3.5) 247 n.32, (3.19.1–3) 95–6, (3.29.33–40) 242 n.36
   Epistles (1.2.28) 79–80, (2.5.55–7, 144) 251 n.50
   Epodes (1.1–2) 172
   Satires (1.4.105–26) 150, (2.5) 251 n.49
horses 74–5
   horse-riding 70
   see also chariots
hunting 138, 142, 146, 149–50, 218
Hurd, Richard 51
Hutten, Ulrich von 216–17
Hyginus 72, 84
hysterosis 18–19, 22

imagery
   darkness 39, 106
   labyrinth 97, 193
   religious 28–9
   travel 18, 106, 121, 123, 172, 214
imagines 151, 161, 196
Isidore of Seville, *Etymologies* (20.11.9) 164
Isles of the Blessed 210, 218
Isocrates 202, 209
   Busiris (*hypothesis*) 78, (7–8, 36–7) 115
Issus, Battle of 45–51
Italians, ancient 142–3

Jerome
   Against Jovinian (1.43) 239 n.4
   Chronicle 95–6, 114, 208, (5.10) 241 n.18
   Epistles (52.8.3) 208

Jesus Christ 9–10, 56, 204, 227
John the Lydian, *On Months* (3.1) 99–100
Johnson, Samuel 88
Josephus 94
    Against Apion (9) 91
Julian Period 20, 103
Julius Africanus (F34) 95, 106
Julius II, Pope 199, 204–5
Justin, *Epitome of Pompeius Trogus' Philippic Histories* (18.6.9) 88
Juvenal, *Satires* (2.153–4) 146, (4.102–3) 164–5, 166

Kempe, Margery 10
King, William 216–17
Knox, Bernard 61
Koselleck, Reinhart 34–6, 45–52

Lactantius 42
Lafitau, Joseph-François 121
Landor, Walter Savage 217–18
Lang, Andrew 124
Langlands, Rebecca 149
Langton, Stephen 23
language
    anachronistic 40–1, 42–3, 55–6, 65–6, 125, 126–9, 131, 237 n.16
    see also dialect; etymology; names, anachronistic
Laodice 59
Lascaris, Janus 17
leadership lessons 148
Lisle, William 18–19
Livius Andronicus 114
Livy, *From the Foundation of the City* 39–40, 41, 56–7, 97, 160–1, (Preface) 155–6, (1.18.1–4) 241 n.12, (1.56–7) 146, (1.59.2–3) 165, (2.13.9) 147, (2.21.4) 106, (2.32.8) 161, (4.29.5–6) 161–2, (6.1.2) 242 n.44, (21.15) 242 n.43, (24.47.15) 186, (25.11.20) 242 n.43, (34.4.4) 140, (39.52.1–3) 111
Logue, Christopher 69
Loraux, Nicole 29–30
lost world fiction 123–4
Lovejoy, A. and G. Boas 138–9
Lucan, *Civil War* 26, 41, (6.784–820) 196, (9.519–21) 139–40, (10.149–54) 164–5

Lucian (42.28) 238 n.29, (45.80) 233 n.49
    Anacharsis 141
    Auction of the Lives 212, 214
    Charon 2–3, 212
    Cock 112
    Dialogues of Courtesans 252 n.56
    Dialogues of the Dead 112, 215–18, 240 n.9
    Fisherman 212–14
    Menippus 214–15
    True Histories 218
Lucretia 43, 49, 146, 165, 217
Lucretius, *On the Nature of Things* 176, 219, 226, (1.459–64) 179
Lupercalia 131, 135
luxury 80, 127, 128–9, 131, 140–1, 143, 162, 164, 166
Luzzi, Joseph 11, 15–16
Lycophron, *see* Scholia on Lycophron
Lydgate, John 26
lyres 35, 188–9, 204
Lyttelton, Lord 216–17

Macrobius
    Commentary on the Dream of Scipio 251 n.45
    Saturnalia 208, 210–11, (1.1.5–6) 208, (1.7.22–3) 125, (1.7.26) 131, (1.10.2) 101, (1.12.13) 237 n.16, (1.13.1) 100–1, (1.14.13–15) 101, (5.15.16) 153, (5.17.5) 91, (6.1.39) 249 n.8
Maitland, F. W. 28
Manlius Torquatus, Titus 161–2
Manzoni, Alessandro 26
Marathon, Battle of 68, 156, 160
Marcellinus, *Life of Thucydides* (22) 115
Marcellus, Marcus Claudius 197–8
Marolles, Michel de 91
marriage 60, 61, 132, 200 n.27
Marx, Karl 122–3
Maximilian I (Holy Roman Emperor) 46–7, 49
Maximus of Tyre, *Dissertations* (7.6–7) 158, (18.8) 153, (36.3) 246 n.72
Mazzoni, Jacopo 17–18, 88–9, 91
medicine 132, 153, 246 n.60
medievalism 9–10, 37, 50, 54–5, 203–5
Menippus 214–16
metachronism 19, 22, 95, 97, 104, 110–14

metachronismos 22, 238 n.23
Metellus Creticus, Quintus 235 n.39
Methodius, *Symposium* 252 n.56
Meton of Athens 100
Millar, John 25
monarchy 41, 64, 89, 137; *see also* chronology, king-lists
monimentum 189, 193
Monsiau, Nicolas-André 202
Montagu, Lady Mary Wortley 217
Montagu, Richard 23
Montesquieu, C. L. de Secondat 54
Mosaic of the Philosophers 203–4
Moses 21, 116
mountains 45, 137–8, 176
multitemporality 10, 30, 175–93, 202–4, 209
music 64, 81–2, 100, 113, 163, 183–4, 213; *see also* lyres; Orpheus
mythical period 107
mythologies, anachronistic 29

Naevius 131, 239 n.4
names, anachronistic 17, 23, 40, 42, 44, 71–6, 101, 131, 138
numerals, acrophonic 108–9, 242 n.48
Napoleon I 45, 50, 52
Neoclassicism 50
Nepos, Cornelius, *Hannibal* (13.1) 111
Nero 21, 40–1, 52–3, 163
Newton, Isaac 91–2
Nietzsche, Friedrich 172–3, 252 n.66
Nine Worthies, the 203
Numa 95, 100, 134, 228

old age 114, 126, 129–30, 138, 167, 176, 178–9
Oltos (painter) 182–4
Olympic games 223–6; *see also* chronology, Olympiads
Orosius 40, 111
Orpheus 78–9, 115, 195, 226–7
Ostanes 207
Oswald, Alice 69
Otto of Freising 47
Ovid
  Fasti (1.7) 241 n.16, (1.29) 101, (2.279–302) 131–2, (3.79–80, 155–6) 101, (4.11) 241 n.16, (4. 369–72) 245 n.54, (5.280–1) 245 n.43, (6.169–80, 533–4) 245 n.54, (6.625–6) 186
  Heroic Women (2.83) 235 n.27
  Metamorphoses (14.156–7) 72, 84, (15.179–80) 242 n.36
Oxford English Dictionary 18–20, 25, 26, 233 n.54, 234 n.79

painting, classical 9, 100; *see also* Euphranor; Polygnotus; Timanthes; vase painting
painting, post-classical 36, 53, 56; *see also* Altdorfer, Albrecht; Barry, James; Burgkmair; De Chirico, Giorgio; Dürer, Albrecht; Raphael
Panathenaea 132, 209
Panofsky, Erwin 10–11, 35–6, 204
parachronism 22–3, 240 n.22
Parian Marble 23–4, 108–9
Parmenides 209
Parry, Adam 142
Passavant, Johann David 201
past, the
  as different 3, 6, 16, 31, 33–57, *passim*
  single vs multiple 37
  see also development; history; simplicity, ancient
Pausanias, *Description of Greece* (1.3.3) 63–4, 67, 68, 77, (1.8.5) 185, (2.37.3) 66, (3.24.11) 107, (4.5.10) 108, (5.15.10–11) 131, (7.17.7) 71, (8.14.7–8) 237 n.15, (8.15.7) 243 n.70, (9.30.3) 113, (9.41.1) 237 n.15, (10.7.5) 81, (10.7.6) 82, (10.17.4) 107, (10.36.5) 71–2, (10.38.5–7) 237n.15
pederasty 4, 84
Peloponnesian War 77, 82, 95, 103–4, 110, 135–6, 157, 158, 213
Pericles 59, 161, 202, 206, 210, 213, 217, 223–6, 228
Persia 55, 152, 154, 238 n.20
  empire 47
  headwear 47-8, 126
  see also Cyrus; Darius; Xerxes
Persian Wars 6, 156, 207, 213, 247 n.28; *see also* Marathon; Plataea; Thermopylae

Petrarch 39–45, 53, 54, 56–7, 91, 219
Phalaris, Epistles of 23, 216
Pherecrates, *Wild Men* 206
Phidias 59, 202, 228
Philammon 66
Philistus (*FGrH* 556) (F47) 88
Philochorus (*FGrH* 328) (F221) 78
philology 22, 35–6, 40–1, 43, 59–85, 124, 221–2; *see also* antiquarianism; chronology; commentries; textual criticism
Philopoemen 111
Philostratus
    Life of Apollonius (2.22.4) 100, (5.9.2) 140, (6.20.6) 132
    Lives of the Sophists (2.7.6–7) 140
Phlegon of Tralles (*FGrH* 257) 97, (F4.6–10) 106–7
Photius 126
Pico della Mirandola 205
Pindar 223–4, (fr. 140b) 248 n.19, (fr. 159) 102
    Pythian Odes (4.191–2) 76
    see also Scholia on Pindar
Pisistratus 4, 67, 184
plasma 77
Plataea, Battle of 156, 160
Plato 5, 18, 37, 85, 91, 114, 199, 201–3, 205, 212, 215, 217, 222, 227, 252 n.63
    Apology (19c) 212
    Cratylus (397c8–d1) 139, (418c1) 130
    Euthydemus 208–9
    Gorgias 207
    Ion 247 n.21
    Laws 208, (680b1–c1) 136–7, 141
    Menexenus 206, 207, 210, 211
    Parmenides 207, 208–9
    Phaedo 210
    Phaedrus 23
    Protagoras 206–7, 208, 211, (322b1) 236 n.74
    Republic 42, 115, 208, (377c) 130
    Sophist (217c) 251 n.37
    Symposium 206, 207, (180a) 84
    Theaetetus 251 n.39, (183e) 251 n.37
    Timaeus 99, 199, 205, 208
Plautus 131
Pliny the Elder, *Natural History* 63, 207, (7.206) 246 n.67, (7.207–8) 100, (13.88) 237 n.15, (18.74) 246 n.67, (35.61) 243 n.67, (35.158) 245 n.51
Plutarch 207, 217
    Aemilius Paullus (1.1) 150
    Aristides (1.6) 237 n.16
    Banquet of the Seven Sages 4
    Caesar (59) 242 n.30
    Cimon (4.6) 59
    Fortune of the Romans (323e, 326a) 242 n 44
    Lycurgus (1.1) 114
    Lysander (17.5) 127
    Marius (3.1) 246 n.77
    Numa (1.4) 243 n.70, (1.6, 8.21) 95, (18.1) 99, (23.11) 131
    On the Education of Children (9f) 151
    On the Malignity of Herodotus (857f) 4
    The Oracles at Delphi 251 n.50
    Pelopidas (18.1) 245 n.34
    Pericles (31.3) 59
    Precepts of Statesmanship (814a–c) 156–7
    Publicola (11.6) 245 n.43
    Reply to Colotes (1126a–b) 251 n.38
    Roman Questions (268a–b) 101, 242 n.29
    Solon (1.4–5) 4, (3.6–8) 4, 231 n.6, (10.2–3) 67, (27.1) 3–4, 95
    Symposium of the Seven Sages (158a) 245 n.54
    Sympotic Questions 250 n.28, (638b–d) 128, (644b) 131
    Syncrisis of Theseus and Romulus (6.1) 112
    Themistocles (2.5) 115
    Theseus (1.1) 106, (20.8–9) 243 n.70, (31.1) 112
Plutarch, Ps.-
    Life of Homer (94–111) 247 n.22, (161–98) 247 n.23
    see also Aetius
Pocock, J. G. A. 36
politics, *see* democracy; monarchy; voting
Pollard, A. F. 29
Polybius, *Histories* 109–10, (1.1.2, 1.4.6–11) 155, (1.11.6) 18, (4.28) 109, (5.30.8–33) 105, (6.5.9) 246 n.67, (6.53) 151–2, 163, (12.25.i.4) 155, (14.12.4–5) 105,

(15.24a) 105, (15.34–6) 155, (23.13) 111, (28.16.5–11) 105, (32.11.2–7) 105
Polycrates 3, 115, 215
Polygnotus (painter) 59
Pompey (Gnaeus Pompeius Magnus) 41, 139, 164, 196, 197
Pomponius Mela, *Geography* (1.102) 140, (2.116) 232 n.31
Pope, Alexander 26, 89–90
Porphyry of Tyre, *Against the Christians* (fr. 43) 238 n.29
Posidonius 138, (fr. 284) 237 n.15
Postumius Tubertus, Aulus 161–2
Praetextatus, Vettius Agorius 208, 210
Pressly, William 227
primitivism, hard and soft 138–9, 143, 153, 187
priscus 161, 164, 165, 166, 198
prochronism 22, 23, 94–5, 97, 110
Proclus 68
Prodicus 78, 211
progress, *see* development; history, as process
prolepsis 23, 31, 44, 65, 73, 107
prophecy 15, 72, 211, 238 n.29
P.Tebt. (2.413) 13–14
Punic Wars
    First 232 n.31
    Second 41, 111, 146, 149, 163, 186
    Third 114, 146, 210
Pythagoras 78, 95, 112, 201, 215, 239, 243
Pythia 82

Queer Theory 9–10
Quintilian, *Oratorical Education* 41, (1.6.39–40) 132, (2.4.20) 152, (4.2.3) 180, (5.11.1–6) 152, (5.11.13) 154, (5.11.19) 161, (5.13.24) 154, (12.2.30) 147

Rabelais, François 28–9, 217
Ralegh, Walter 19–20, 92
Rancière, Jacques 12, 23, 29
Raphael 35, 199–206, 211, 223
Reformation 34–5, 45, 47–9
Regulus, Marcus Atilius 156, 162, 163, 247
relics 237 n.15

religion
    anachronistic 131–2, 134–5, 138, 139–40, 187
    Christian 34, 94, 117, 227
    evolution of 119–20
    pagan 40–1, 44, 119–20, 221
    see also chronology, comparative; Dionysus; festivals; imagery, religious
Renaissance 3, 10–11, 15–20, 35–7, 54, 85, 147–9
retrojection 5, 6, 12–13, 16–18, 24, 30, 40–1, 48, 59–83, 161–2, 197, 226
rhetoric 20, 23, 43, 85, 149, 152–5, 160–1, 165, 180, 207, 210; *see also* Antisthenes; Apsines; Aristides, Aelius; Aristotle; Cicero; declamation; Dionysius, Ps.-; Quintilian; Themistius; Theon
Ricchieri, Lodovico 17
Rider Haggard, Henry 123–4
Robertson, Joseph 23
Robertson, William 25
Robinson, James Harvey 27–8
Robortello, Francisco 17, 80
Roller, Matthew 149
Rome, city of
    Capitol 44, 187, 196
    Casa Romuli 186
    Esquiline 131
    forum Romanum 165, 166, 196
    Palatine 128, 186–7
    Vatican 171–2, 199–206
Rome, history of
    early 67–9, 99–101, 106, 128, 131, 134–5, 139–42, 146–8, 186–7, 197
    empire 3, 84, 97, 117, 122–3, 185, 198, 238 n.29
    Principate 25, 137, 146, 156–7, 162–3,
    Republic 57, 106, 146, 162, 164–6, 178, 185, 198, 211
    Republic vs Principate 161–2
Romulus 69, 99–101, 138, 186, 197
Royal Society of Arts 223
Rudolf IV (Duke of Austria) 40, 44, 53, 236 n.66
ruins 90

Sallust 44, 85, 235
Sallust, Ps.-, *Letters to Julius Caesar* 85

Santra (grammarian) 114
Sappho 159, 204, 228
Sardanapallus 158, 215
Sardinians 138
satyr plays 79–80
Satyrus, *Life of Euripides* (fr. 37) 237 n.4
Scaliger, Joseph 20–2, 82, 93–101, 103–4, 107, 110–16
Scheibel, Ewald 97, 103
Schiffman, Z. S. 37, 53–4, 57, 125, 147
Schlegel, Friedrich von 45–52, 62
scholia 12, 63
Scholia on Aeschylus
    Eumenides 84, (556–9) 238 n.21, (723) 17
    Prometheus Bound (362, 723) 15, (411, 669) 240 n.23
    Seven against Thebes (277) 65, 240 n.23
Scholia on Apollonius of Rhodes (4.264) 242 n.24, (4.552–6) 73, 240 n.23
Scholia on Aristophanes, *Wealth* (173, 179, 1146) 237 n.16, (1146) 239 n.47
Scholia on Euripides
    Alcestis (780) 239 n.44
    Andromache (150) 77, (734) 77, 233 n.52
    Hecuba (254) 77, (573) 233 n.52
    Hippolytus (231) 74–5, 232 n.18, (957–9) 78
    Medea (232, 233) 62
    Orestes (371) 77
    Phoenician Women (6) 73, 240 n.23, (854) 14–15, 240 n.23, (1377) 238 n.21
    Rhesus (502) 240 n.23
Scholia on Hesiod, *Works and Days* (45–6) 68, (150) 245 n.38
Scholia on Homer
    Iliad (2.570) 73, (5.5) 238 n.23, (7.304) 237 n.15, (7.334–5) 66–7, (9.395) 66, (10.513) 238 n.22, (15.679) 70, (16.595) 66, (18.219) 70, (18.570) 245 n.40, (21.362) 70, (23.683) 67, (23.825) 237 n.15, (24.476) 237 n.15, (24.480–2) 238 nn.21, 23
    Odyssey (5.371) 238 n.22
Scholia on Lycophron (250) 238 n.21, (592) 233 n.54

Scholia on Pindar
    Nemean Odes (7.56) 240 n.23
    Olympian Odes (6.106a) 76
    Pythian Odes (hypothesis) 81–2, (4.191–2, 11.26) 76
Scholia on Sophocles
    Ajax (449) 74, (1285) 74
    Electra (47) 81, 240 n.23, (62) 238 n.36, (682) 81
    Oedipus the King (391) 65
    Trachinian Women (1) 13, 17
Scholia on Thucydides (1.6.5) 246 n.59, (8.109) 115
Schwenk, Rudolf 61–2
Scipio Aemilianus, Publius Cornelius 210
Scipio Africanus, Publius Cornelius 49, 89–90, 111, 114, 146, 196, 211, 216
Scotland
    Enlightenment 25, 121
    Highlanders 141–2
Scott, Walter 89–90, 123–4, 142–3
Scribonius Curio, Gaius 207
Scythians 141, 217, 218, 237 n.15
Segrais, Jean Regnault de 89, 91
Selden, John 22
Seneca the Elder
    Controversiae (1 preface 3–5) 178–9, (10 preface 2) 41
    Suasoriae (2.18) 151, (2.22) 239 n.53
Seneca the Younger 158
    Epistles (90.16) 246 n.66, (90.31) 237 n.15
Sepulchral Monuments in Great Britain (Gough) 26
Serres, Michel 175–6, 178
Servius, *Commentary on Virgil, Aeneid* 23, 63, 197, 208, (1.267) 91, (1.182) 64, (3.401–2) 65, (3.411) 232 n.31, (3.703) 72, (6.234–5) 71, (6.359) 72, 233 n.54, (6.900) 72, (10.120) 65
    and Servius Auctus 63
Servius Tullius 168
Seven Sages, the 4–5, 202, 231 n.5
sex 59–60, 89, 146, 153, 181–2, 193; *see also* pederasty
    changes of 107
Shakespeare, William 21, 61, 87–8
shields 59, 142, 190

ships 60, 64, 67, 68, 100, 125, 172, 246 n.67; see also anchors
Sibyl 23, 193, 195, 204
Sicyon 99, 106
Silius Italicus, *Punic War* (13.615–895) 196
Simias 219
similes 60, 69–71, 73, 75, 143, 247 n.32
simplicity
    ancient 139, 140–1, 153, 166
    see also development; *priscus*
Skinner, Quentin 28–9
slaves 13, 64, 88, 114, 137, 148, 159, 212, 217
Solinus, *Collection of Memorable Things* (1.27) 88, (1.35–9) 100, (1.45–7) 101
Solon 1–6, 13, 55, 67, 74, 95, 98–100, 102, 116, 141, 213, 227–9
sophists 4–5, 55, 156, 206, 209, 211
Sophocles 75, 79, 83, 202, 213, 216, 219, 223
    Ajax 190–3, (448–9, 1286–7) 74
    Electra 17, 80–3
    Fellow-Diners 79
    Inachus 238 n.35
    Meleager 238 n.35
    Oedipus the King 61
    Philoctetes 219–20
    Trachinian Women (1–3) 13, 17, 74
    see also Scholia on Sophocles
Sorel, Albert 28
Sosibius (*FGrH* 595) (F3) 113
Sparta 82, 102, 104, 121, 136, 141
Speusippus 110, 114
Statius, *Thebaid* (8.286–93) 69
statues 3, 97, 115, 140, 166, 186, 196; see also Antenor; Apollo Belvedere; Ariadne; Phidias
Stephanus of Byzantium 74
Strabo, *Geography* 74, (4.4.2) 140, (6.1.1) 251 n.38, (7.3.7) 140–1, (7.3.9) 237 n.15, (8.3.5) 238 n.31, (8.6.2) 242 n.45, (9.1.10) 67, (9.3.10) 81, (11.4.3) 246 n.62, (13.1.53) 238 n.29
Stricker, J. A. 61, 83
Strozzi, Giulio 18
Suda (pi 2853) 239 n.46, (phi 180) 214
Suetonius 23, 40
    Augustus (31.2) 101
    On Grammarians (7) 243 n.67
    Terence (1, 4) 114

Sulpicius Blitho (*FRHist* 55) F1 111
survivals, anachronistic 9–10, 26, 101, 119–43, 148, 186, 191, 242 n.48
Swift, Jonathan 252 n.61
swords 121, 175, 191–2
Syncellus, George 97, 243 n.60
synoecism 126, 136

Tacitus
    Annals 216, (3.26) 137, (6.38.1, 12.40.4) 105, (16.5) 246 n.77
    Germania 121, (5.3) 140
    Histories (3.51) 156, (5.3) 21
Taplin, Oliver 61, 70, 77
Tasso, Torquato 89–91
Tatian, *To the Greeks* (31) 113, 116
temporality
    cyclical vs linear 36, 37, 52, 191, 192
    and ethics 79–80
    history of 31, 37, 49–52
    and the moment 181–2
    temporal layers 52, 122
    see also multitemporality
Terence 110, 114
    Brothers (15–21) 114
Terminalia 134
Terpander 110, 113
Tertullian
    Apologeticus (19) 116
    On Idolatry (3) 139
textual criticism
    emendation 23, 113, 237 n.15, 238 n.29
    interpolation 21, 66–7, 218, 237 n.15
Thales 5–6, 203, 227
Themistius (16.205b) 153
Themistocles 115, 191
Theon, *Exercises* (78) 180
Theodorus Meliteniotis 238 n.23
Theopompus (*FGrH* 115) (F154) 237 n.16
Thermopylae, Battle of 85, 151
Theseus 59, 63–4, 67–8, 78, 110–12, 169–72, 185, 218
Thucydides, *History of the Peloponnesian War* 41, 53, 83, 103, 105, 115, 236 n.65, (1.3.3) 66, (1.5–6) 135–6, 141, (1.10.2) 136, (1.12.3) 106, (1.22.4) 152, (1.49.1) 136, (1.70–1) 136, (1.138.3) 191, (2.2.1) 95, 103–4, 109–10, (2.15.6) 126, (2.34) 4,

(2.35–46) 210, (2.65.6) 191, (3.82)
   136, 157, (3.104) 81–2, (4.118.12)
   105, (4.122) 105, 106, (5.19.1) 105,
   (5.20) 104, (6.54.2) 184
Timaeus (*FGrH* 566) (F60) 88, (F127)
   243 n.70
Timanthes (painter) 224, 226
time, *see* temporality
Tiresias 14, 107, 195–6, 214–15, 251 n.49
Tolstoy 124
tragedy 60–2, 64, 73, 83–4, 100, 124, 130,
   140, 166, 190, 213, 220
Traill, H. D. 217
Trojan War 24, 50, 63, 66, 67, 69–71, 75, 79,
   81, 88, 97, 106, 109, 112, 153, 159
trumpets 69–70
Turks 34, 47, 49–50
   Ottoman empire 217
Tylor, E. B. 121–2, 125
Tzetzes, John 68, 115, 243 n.70

Ulpian 207, 210
Underworld 2, 64, 72, 89, 112, 191, 193,
   195–8, 204, 210–11, 212–16, 221
Usener, Hermann 124

Valerius Antias (*FRHist* 25) (F56) 111
Valerius Maximus, *Memorable Doings and*
   Sayings 149, 150, (1.8.11) 186, (2
   preface) 161, (2.7.6) 161, (2.9.4)
   162, (3.2.2) 147, (9.8.ext.1) 232 n.31
Valla, Lorenzo 3, 39–45, 54
Varius Rufus, *On Death* 249 n.8
Varro 24, 39, 64, 66, 107, 114, 139, 155, 164,
   219, 237 n.16, 242 n.29
   On the Countryside (2.1.3–5, 2.1.9) 128,
      (2.11.5) 245 n.44, (2.11.9) 245 n.41,
      (2.11.11) 138
   On the Latin Language (5.42, 43)
      245 n.44, (5.50, 117, 121) 131, (5.54,
      5.89, 105) 128, (5.106, 122, 123, 130)
      245 n.51, (5.166) 245 n.44, (6.2)
      241 n.16, (6.82) 245 n.51
   On Suicide (fr. 407) 214
   Sixty-year Old 251 n.49
   Tomb of Menippus 214
   Ulixes-and-a-half 251 n.49
Vasari, Giorgio 35, 199–201
vase paintings 59, 60, 132–3; *see also*
   Exekias; Oltos

vegetarianism 78–9, 131
Velleius Paterculus, *Roman History*
   (1.3.2–3) 73, (1.7.2–4) 112–13,
   (1.12.6) 88
Veyne, Paul 55–6
Vico, Giambattista 24, 112–13
Virgil 204
   Aeneid 23, 64–5, 84, 124, 204, 252 n.10,
      (1.2–3) 72, (1.5) 189, (1.182) 60,
      (1.169) 60, 76, (1.278–9) 84, (1.448)
      60, (Book 6) 195–8, (6.14–41) 193,
      (6.17) 72, (6.50, 258) 204, (6.366)
      17, 72, (6.900) 72, (7.1–2) 72,
      (7.741) 143, (7.746–9) 142, (8.678)
      142, (9.710–16) 69, (12.706)
      60, (12.945, 950) 189; *see also*
      Servius
   Dido/Aeneas anachronism 18, 87–92,
      93, 201, 217
   Georgics 226
virtus 146–7
Vitruvius, *On Architecture* (2.1.4–5) 138,
   (4.2.2–3) 127, (9 preface 17) 218–19
Voltaire 1, 217
voting 27, 74

Warburg, Aby 11, 119–24, 139
warfare 38, 48, 101, 104, 140, 146–7, 149,
   150, 153, 159, 162; *see also* battles;
   Peloponnesian War; Persian Wars;
   Punic Wars; Trojan War; trumpets;
   weapons
Waugh, Evelyn 27
weapons, *see* battering rams; boomerangs;
   bows and arrows; shields; swords
Wilamowitz-Moellendorf, U. von 221–2.
Wilde, Oscar 9–10
William IV, Duke of Bavaria 45
Winckelmann, Johann Joachim 169–73
writing 24, 53, 62, 132, 237 nn.15–16,
   242 n.48

Xenophon 146, 148, 201, 202, 207, 218
   Anabasis 146
   Education of Cyrus 247 n.13
   On Hunting (5.33) 149–50
   Symposium 206–7
Xerxes 97, 113, 154, 185, 239 n.53

Zoroaster 200, 201, 202

www.ingramcontent.com/pod-product-compliance
Lightning Source LLC
Chambersburg PA
CBHW071808300426
44116CB00009B/1238